Other Books by Ronald Nash

Christianity and the Hellenistic World
Christian Faith and Historical Understanding
The Concept of God
The Word of God and the Mind of Man
Process Theology (editor)
Liberation Theology (editor)
Evangelicals in America
Evangelical Renewal in the Mainline Churches (editor)
Poverty and Wealth
Social Justice and the Christian Church
Freedom, Justice and the State
Ideas of History (editor)
The Light of the Mind: St. Augustine's Theory of Knowledge
The Philosophy of Gordon H. Clark (editor)
The Case for Biblical Christianity (editor)
The New Evangelicalism
Dooyeweerd and the Amsterdam Philosophy
Worldviews in Conflict

Faith & Reason

Searching for a
RATIONAL FAITH

RONALD H. NASH

ZONDERVAN™

GRAND RAPIDS, MICHIGAN 49530

ZONDERVAN™

Faith and Reason
Copyright © 1988 by Ronald H. Nash

Requests for information should be addressed to:

Zondervan, *Grand Rapids, Michigan 49530*

Library of Congress Cataloging-in-Publication Data

Nash, Ronald H.
    Faith and reason : searching for a rational faith / Ronald H. Nash.
        p. cm.
    Bibliography: p.
    Includes index.
    ISBN 0-310-29401-0
    1. Faith and reason.   2. Apologetics—20th century.   3. Evangelicalism.   I. Title.
    BT50.N36 1988
    239—dc19   88-9625

Edited by Dimples B. Kellogg
Designed by Louise Bauer
Cover Design by Mary Cantu

Printed in the United States of America

04 05 06 07 08 /DC/ 18 17 16 15 14 13 12 11

This book is dedicated to
three friends who were part of my search:
Ray Cravens and Richard Troutman
and
to the memory of
Mickey Ashook

CONTENTS

Part 3
SOME ARGUMENTS FOR GOD'S EXISTENCE

Part 4
THE PROBLEM OF EVIL

Part 5
MIRACLES

Part 6
CONCLUSION

PREFACE

Since chapter 1 reports what this book is all about, I will not repeat any of that information here. Instead, I will use this Preface as an opportunity to acknowledge my appreciation to some of the many people who have helped over the years to make this book possible. I have read much over the past thirty years, and some of the material—by way of agreement or disagreement—has contributed to the thinking that helped produce this book. The names of many of those authors appear in the footnotes or the section "For Further Reading."

My students during this same period of thirty years have been a part of most of my books. I have often used them as a sounding board for ideas and arguments that eventually became books; this work is no exception. One of those former students, Dr. Kelly Clark of Gordon College, was kind enough to spend a great deal of time reading the manuscript and offering valuable suggestions and criticisms. His efforts did much to improve the book.

My children, Jeff and Jennifer, were growing up when most of my other books were being written. They took their father's absences of mind or body with uncommon good grace. So too has my wife, Betty Jane. Her contribution to this and other books has been absolutely indispensable.

Four of my other books—all from the same publisher—complement this study. Many things I do not discuss in this book are covered in *The Word of God and the Man of God* (1982), *The Concept of God* (1983), *Christian Faith and Historical Understanding* (1984), and *Christianity and the Hellenistic World* (1984).

Chapter 1

INTRODUCTION

By profession, I am a philosopher. I have been fortunate in being able to spend the last thirty years doing what every philosopher loves to do. This work has included poring through the writings of just about every major figure in the history of ideas. I have had the opportunity to learn from Socrates, Plato, Aristotle, Plotinus, Augustine, Aquinas, Descartes, Locke, Kant, and Hegel, among many others. I have had the chance also to disagree with these giants in the history of human thought. As a philosopher, I've been able to wrestle with the difficult problems that have bothered reflective human beings for millennia.

My profession is one that attracts relatively few people. That's probably for the good since there aren't enough jobs in philosophy to go around now. Actually, the idea of someone's getting paid to do philosophy is relatively new. If one goes back beyond, say, the year 1750, most of the great philosophers thought and wrote about philosophical issues in their spare time. They made their living doing something else.

Although few people are professional philosophers, philosophical thinking is something that every mature, rational person does. It is likely that each reader of this book could report personal beliefs about a large number of philosophical questions. If a person puts enough of these answers together, he has produced something approaching a philosophical system. If the phrase *philosophical system* seems too grandiose, perhaps we could say simply that he has a world-view.

Every reader of this book then holds beliefs about or has opinions about a large number of philosophical subjects. Of course, these sets of beliefs differ in completeness and quality. Many people hold beliefs on various philosophical issues, but they are often unable to say *why* they believe in that way.

Many of the beliefs I've been describing are related in important ways to religion. For example, one inescapable philosophical question is, Does God exist? Once one begins to think about this question, one can very quickly get involved in a bewildering variety of related questions: What is God like? Are there arguments that prove that God exists? Are these arguments sound? Does the existence of evil in the universe constitute evidence against God's existence?

I would like to think that everyone reading this book finds such questions interesting and stimulating at some time in life. All of us have many interests and responsibilities that require our attention: the grass needs mowing, diapers need changing, bills need paying, the car needs gas, there's a football game on television, it's time to fix lunch, I have to drive twenty miles to work and the freeway's already clogged, and so on. Is it possible that there are people, in the United States, let's say, who never wonder if there is life after death, if God exists, if Christianity is true? If such people exist (and I suspect they do), let us hope that they would begin to think about such matters if the right person would only approach them in the right way.

This book has two major purposes. First, it is designed to introduce readers at what I hope is a rather elementary level to the more important questions linking philosophy and religion. I am interested in exploring philosophical questions that have important implications for the truth of or the rationality of religious beliefs that most people in nations like the United States, Great Britain, Canada, and the like should find significant. Second, at the risk of appearing presumptuous, it also offers answers to these questions—at least, to most of them. If some readers find these answers unacceptable, that's fine; this is what philosophy is all about. If my questions and answers lead some readers to different conclusions and also lead them to seek reasons to support their conclusions, I'll feel that I've fulfilled one of my duties as a philosopher.

And so, as I've said, I am a professional philosopher. I am also a Christian. My religious beliefs play a central role in my philosophical system. As a Christian, I am interested in sharing my faith and my reasons for holding those beliefs. I have little use for misguided Christians who regard philosophy or science or any intellectual pursuit as somehow incompatible with Christian faith. I have little respect for uninformed Christians who think that reason and logic are threats to the Christian faith and who describe faith as some kind of irrational leap into a dark abyss. I am a Christian who is interested in showing that the Christian faith has nothing to fear and everything to gain by opening itself up to philosophical examination.

I have written this book for two distinct kinds of reader. First of all, the book is designed to serve as a textbook in college and seminary courses concerned with helping people think about the philosophical questions that a serious study of religion can generate. I am thinking primarily of courses in the philosophy of religion and apologetics.

But I have also written this book for the general reader who wants to know more about these questions. Is Christian belief rational? Is it philosophically respectable? Why do Christians believe the way they do? Are there good answers to the more serious challenges to Christian faith? What is the best way of helping other people see the reasonableness of Christian faith? These issues ought to be of interest to large numbers of people not presently enrolled in an academic program.

Because I wanted the material in this book to be accessible to as many people as possible, I have done my best to make it clear and readable. Given some of the subjects I have to discuss and given my concern to make my presentations philosophically responsible, I have sometimes faced some difficult decisions. I have, with few exceptions, avoided the trap of bombarding the reader with technical terms. Any reader who has had a beginning course in philosophy should be able to whiz right through being already familiar with words like *metaphysics* and *epistemology* (words that are defined when they first appear).

I want this book to serve as an introduction to the subject; but I also want it to introduce the reader to many of the more advanced books and articles on these topics. Nothing will please me more than to learn that this book has led people to study more advanced writings about the theistic arguments, the problem of evil, the problem of miracles, and the rationality of religious belief.

APOLOGETICS AND THE PHILOSOPHY OF RELIGION

Some readers may wonder how the same book might serve as a textbook for courses in the philosophy of religion *and* apologetics. Are these not different courses with different objectives?

It is not as easy to distinguish between apologetics and the philosophy of religion as some like to think. In recent years, philosophy journals have contained numerous articles that quite clearly are essays in the philosophy of religion. But it is equally true that many of these articles are also exercises in apologetics. Additional background information is necessary to clarify what I mean.

The philosophy of religion is the branch of philosophy that studies questions arising out of philosophical reflection about religious claims, beliefs, and practices. A brief sample of the kinds of questions encountered in the philosophy of religion would include the following: What is the nature of religion? What is the nature of God? What does it mean to say that God is omnipotent or omniscient? What is faith, and how is it related to reason? What reasons or arguments, if any, support belief in the existence of God?

Apologetics, on the other hand, is often regarded as a branch of theology. While this claim may seem rather innocuous at first, it contains the uncomplimentary insinuation that, unlike the philosopher of religion, the apologist is a person who has already made up his mind about most of the pivotal issues. The apologist is thought to be someone who begins with his conclusions and tries to set up a chain of reasoning that will make those conclusions appear plausible or convincing. In other words, the apologist already knows what he believes, and any appeal to reasons or arguments is tainted by his prior commitments. But the philosopher of religion, or so the argument goes, is open-minded, personally detached, and willing to follow an argument wherever it leads.

There are so many things wrong with the above analysis that it is hard to know where to start raising objections. For one thing, the great philosophers presented arguments to support positions to which they were already firmly committed. Presenting arguments to defend what one may already happen to believe hardly, by itself, makes such an effort philosophically substandard. Imagine two philosophers, one an atheist and the other a Christian. Suppose further that the atheist publishes an argument attacking some Christian belief while the Christian publishes an essay defending one of his Christian beliefs. Does it make sense to suggest that the Christian writer is doing apologetics while the atheist is writing philosophy of religion?

Most dictionaries use the word *apologist* to mean any person who argues in defense of some position or cause. If we take the word in this broad sense, it is obvious that some people have written as apologists for the Christian faith. But the world also contains apologists for such things as democracy, communism, capitalism, socialism, and aerobics. The world also contains philosophers who act as apologists for atheism. It is important to see that apologetics is not an activity reserved for philosophers who also happen to be religious believers. Much that passes as philosophy of religion is really apologetics as practiced by individuals who reject major tenets of religious belief. I do not say this to be critical of philosophers of religion who may also happen to be atheists. My point is that philosophers who reject the Christian religion do not suddenly become, by virtue of this fact alone, more objective or rational or open-minded than philosophers who are committed Christians or Jews.[1]

Since there is nothing improper about offering arguments in defense or in criticism of some position, I see nothing suspicious or substandard about the activity of doing Christian apologetics. What would be deplorable would be any instance in which any thinker (believer or unbeliever) allows his or her convictions to result in such activities as ignoring evidence or knowingly accepting fallacious arguments.

It seems clear, then, that a great deal of work in the philosophy of religion can also be characterized as apologetics. And this apologetic activity is engaged in by believers and unbelievers alike.

NEGATIVE AND POSITIVE APOLOGETICS

While any position, religious or otherwise, may have its apologists, the term *apologetics* will be used from this point to mean the philosophical defense of the Christian faith. Someone engaged in apologetics intends to show that A (some believer) is within his rights in believing the essential tenets of the Christian faith or that B (some unbeliever) is mistaken in rejecting A's belief.

It is helpful to distinguish between negative and positive apologetics.[2] In negative apologetics, the major objective is producing answers to

---

[1] I also believe it is possible for philosophers to reason about religious issues without having a hidden agenda.

[2] One writer who makes good use of this distinction is George Mavrodes. See his chapter, "Jerusalem and Athens Revisited," in *Faith and Rationality: Reason and Belief in God*, ed. Alvin Plantinga and Nicholas Wolterstorff (Notre Dame, Ind.: University of Notre Dame Press, 1983), pp. 192–218.

challenges to religious faith. The proper task of negative apologetics is removing obstacles to belief. Many people refuse to believe because they think that difficulties like the problem of evil or the alleged impossibility of miracles make the acceptance of some important religious belief untenable. When enough tenets of the Christian faith become unacceptable (for some people, this need involve only one claim such as the Incarnation or the Resurrection), they find unbelief easier than faith.[3] Most of us know people who once gave every appearance of having been believers but came to reject their earlier faith; often this kind of conversion *from* Christianity is explained in terms of their having discovered the same kinds of arguments or objections that keep others from believing in the first place. George Mavrodes places negative apologetics in its proper context:

> Are there really . . . people who would believe in God (or who would continue believing) . . . were it not for something which they take to be a reason *against* holding that belief? A person who thinks that there are people of this sort may well think it to be useful to engage in what we may call "negative" apologetics. That is, he may think it useful to show that apparent reasons against theistic belief (for example, the problem of evil and such) are not as strong as they appear, that they will not stand up under careful scrutiny, and so on. Negative apologetics consists of refuting and rebutting arguments against the faith.[4]

In negative apologetics, the apologist is playing defense. In positive apologetics, the apologist begins to play offense. It is one thing to show (or attempt to show) that assorted arguments against religious faith are weak or unsound; it is a rather different task to offer people reasons why they should believe. The latter is the task of positive apologetics. To quote Mavrodes again: "A person who believes that there are people who would believe if they had reasons which supported the faith might well think it useful to engage in 'positive' apologetics. This would be the attempt to provide such reasons—arguments for the existence of God, for example, or some such thing."[5]

The person engaged in doing positive apologetics is not limited to presenting "proofs" for the existence of God. He may, as Mavrodes explains, find more useful ways to spend his time:

> If we think that someone is resisting or ignoring evidence, then we might try to make that evidence still more insistent, more explicit, and so on. . . . And that, of course, is what the positive apologist tries to do. He tries to find something which the unbeliever already knows and acknowledges, and to show that this acknowledged fact supports, in one way or another, the belief that God exists.[6]

---

[3] My account would be incomplete if I failed to mention that some people refuse to believe for reasons that have more to do with moral and spiritual considerations than with the intellect. When this is the case, philosophical arguments will hardly be successful; the problem lies elsewhere.

[4] Mavrodes, "Jerusalem and Athens Revisited," p. 197.

[5] Ibid.

[6] Ibid., p. 201.

For the rest of this book, then, let us regard any attempt to defeat any challenge to Christian faith as an example of negative apologetics. Efforts to provide reasons or arguments in support of the Christian faith will be instances of positive apologetics.

Recently, in some Christian circles, negative apologetics has had a larger following than positive apologetics. At least if we judge from the literature, many Christian thinkers have not only spent much more time doing negative apologetics, they have seemed to suggest that positive apologetics may not be especially important or useful.[7] In rare cases, some Christian writers have left the impression that positive apologetics may be impossible. Although efforts to downgrade or even dismiss positive apologetics seem extreme, one thing is clear: It is far more difficult to do positive apologetics than negative apologetics. As a prominent Christian philosopher once put it in conversation: "I believe that positive apologetics is important; I'm just not sure I know how to do it."

Negative apologetics is possible, useful, and necessary. That is, it can be done, it should be done, and it needs to be done. Many of the chapters in this book are exercises in negative apologetics. In them, I consider a number of problems that are often thought to weaken or undercut the rationality or plausibility of the Christian faith. While some of these arguments can involve us in some extremely difficult issues, all of them can be shown to be lacking. None of them successfully establishes the falsity or irrationality or implausibility of essential Christian tenets.

But it is important to recognize that the move from negative to positive apologetics involves several major shifts. In professional football, the switch from defense to offense requires a change in personnel. Different skills are required. When someone assumes the mantle of the positive apologist, he is in effect accepting the challenge of proving to some other person that the Christian faith is true or rational or worthy of acceptance or something like this. There is no set formula for doing this sort of thing properly.

LOCATING THE BURDEN OF PROOF

Negative and positive apologetics can also be distinguished with reference to what is called the burden of proof, that is, the responsibility of actually providing the support for some disputed claim. It is difficult for the person doing positive apologetics to avoid the burden of proof. In the case of negative apologetics, however, fairness seems to require that the atheologian carry the burden of proof.[8]

Many atheologians dispute this last claim and insist that the burden of proof must *always* rest on the shoulders of the theist. As Antony Flew maintains, "The debate about the existence of God should properly begin

---

[7] George Mavrodes seems to chide some of his cocontributors to the book *Faith and Rationality* for holding this position. See his chapter, "Jerusalem and Athens Revisited," already cited. Perhaps because they took Mavrodes's criticism to heart, some, including Alvin Plantinga, have since attempted to speak to the issue of positive apologetics. This shift in emphasis should be apparent in Plantinga's forthcoming Gifford Lectures.

[8] An atheologian is anyone who offers arguments *against* religious beliefs.

from the presumption of atheism, that the onus of proof must lie upon the theist."⁹ While the theist *must* defend his belief in God, the atheist, so the argument goes, has no similar obligation with regard to *his* beliefs. According to Flew,

> It is by reference to this inescapable demand for grounds that the presumption of atheism is justified. If it is to be established that there is a God, then we have to have good grounds for believing that this is indeed so. Until or unless some such grounds are produced we have literally no reason at all for believing; and in that situation the only reasonable posture must be that of either the negative atheist or the agnostic.¹⁰

A similar position has been adopted by Australian philosopher Michael Scriven. As Scriven sees it, "We need not have a proof that God does not exist in order to justify atheism. Atheism is obligatory in the absence of any evidence for God's existence. . . . The proper alternative where there is no evidence is not mere suspension of belief. . . . It is *disbelief*."¹¹ For Scriven, "God exists" and "God does not exist" are propositions that reasonable people must treat in different ways. If there is no evidence for the proposition "God exists," it must be denied. But the absence of any evidence for the second proposition, "God does not exist," is no reason for the atheist to feel any discomfort at all.

For those who accept the presumption of atheism, it is always rational to begin by disbelieving that God exists and always irrational to begin by believing that God exists. While it is rational to presume the truth of atheism, it is never rational to presume the truth of theism. While atheism may be presumed innocent until proven guilty, theism should be presumed guilty until proven otherwise. The burden of proof must always rest on the theist.

Though handicaps in such sports as golf make sense, moves like the one atheologians make by presuming atheism are normally what we have in mind when we say that so-and-so has pulled a fast one. Alvin Plantinga has described this kind of thinking as "a piece of merely arbitrary intellectual imperialism."¹² One of the major themes of recent work in this area— especially writings by such Reformed thinkers as Plantinga, Nicholas Wolterstorff, and others—is that it is philosophically irresponsible for theists to allow atheologians to make the rules in this way.¹³

The responsible theist will readily shoulder the burden of proof when he has to. In the case of positive apologetics, the burden of proof would appear to belong to the believer. But one of the more important tasks of

---

⁹Antony Flew, *The Presumption of Atheism* (London: Pemberton, 1976), p. 14.

¹⁰Ibid., p. 22. Of course, many atheologians including Flew are not bashful about presenting their objections to religious faith. But that is another matter. The point at issue here is Flew's claim that Christian belief is irrational or substandard *unless* the believer produces positive reason to support it.

¹¹Michael Scriven, *Primary Philosophy* (New York: McGraw-Hill, 1966), p. 103.

¹²Alvin Plantinga, "Reason and Belief in God," in *Faith and Rationality,* p. 28. I should point out that there are some underlying issues in the atheologian's position that I do not have time to pursue. For readers interested in these other matters, see the discussion immediately following my quote from Plantinga.

¹³The book *Faith and Rationality,* already cited, contains several excellent statements of this position.

negative apologetics is challenging the view that Christian belief is irrational unless it is accompanied by supporting reasons or arguments. The sensible person will reject the claim that theism should be presumed guilty until proven innocent. Later chapters in this book will examine issues like foundationalism, evidentialism, and the proper basicality of belief in God. It may help the reader to realize now that the bottom line to these subsequent discussions concerns the proper placement of the burden of proof.

For Further Exploration—Chapter One

1. Offer examples of several common objections to Christian belief that might stimulate someone to engage in the activity of negative apologetics.
2. Explain the phrase *the burden of proof*. Who has the burden of proof in negative apologetics? in positive apologetics?
3. Explain *the presumption of atheism*. What is your evaluation of it?

Part 1

THE CHRISTIAN
WORLD-VIEW

Chapter 2

WHAT IS A WORLD-VIEW?

A major claim of this book is the importance of approaching the issues it discusses from the perspective of world-views. In this chapter, I explain what a world-view is and identify its major elements. In chapter 3, I discuss some of the significant elements of the Christian world-view. I then introduce the term *Naturalism* as a name for the world-view that is Christianity's major competition in the Western world. In chapter 4, I turn to the question, How do we choose between world-views? I conclude Part 1 by warning that the choice between competing world-views will always result in something less than logical certainty.

THE NOTION OF NOETIC STRUCTURE

Everyone has a noetic structure.[1] Although the term may seem somewhat intimidating at first encounter, it refers to an easily understood notion that will prove to be important for subsequent discussions in this book.[2] Noetic structures have at least four identifiable features.

1. *A person's noetic structure is the sum total of everything that person believes.* Since the objects of beliefs are propositions (statements that are either true or false), a complete inventory of any person's noetic structure would include all the propositions that person believes.[3] A proposition may

---

[1] The word *noetic* comes from the Greek verb *noeo*, which means "to understand" or "to think." The corresponding noun *noesis* means "intelligence" or "understanding."

[2] So far as I can determine, the term *noetic structure* was first used by Alvin Plantinga in the book *Faith and Rationality* (Notre Dame, Ind.: University of Notre Dame Press, 1983). My discussion owes much to Plantinga's treatment of the subject.

[3] For the record noetic structures include true beliefs and false beliefs as well as probably true and probably false beliefs.

be part of my noetic structure even if I am not presently thinking about it, even if it is not at this moment present to my consciousness. In fact, it should be obvious that during any given period of time, we are conscious only of a small fraction of the propositions that make up our noetic structures. While the proposition "eight times twelve equals ninety-six" belongs to the noetic structure of each person reading this book, most of us manage to go for long stretches of time without actually thinking about it.

The beliefs that make up our noetic structures differ greatly in their significance or importance. Most people's noetic structure includes beliefs about such things as the name of Roy Rogers's horse or the year when the first episode of "Leave It To Beaver" appeared on network television. Beliefs like these may come in handy when we play *Trivial Pursuit*, but most people would agree that they rank relatively low in importance when compared to other elements of their noetic structures. It is not surprising, then, that the importance of beliefs is sometimes person-relative. For example, the birthdays of my wife and children are more important to me than they are, say, to the president of the Southern Baptist Convention. Of course, some propositions ought to be important to any educated person who desires to function effectively in a civilized society.

And so everyone has a noetic structure. Just as obviously, the content of each person's noetic structure will be different. People believe different propositions; they also disagree about whether a particular proposition is true or false. The propositions "God exists," "God created the world," and "Jesus Christ is the eternal Son of God" will be part of the noetic structures of traditional Christian believers. The beliefs that such propositions are false will be part of the noetic structures of atheists.

2. *A noetic structure is also characterized by the way its beliefs are related.* Many of our beliefs seem to be totally unrelated. For example, I believe that Villars, Switzerland, is about three miles from the village of Huemoz. I also believe that the Cleveland Indians won the 1948 World Series. If there is any relationship at all between these two beliefs, it escapes me.

While many of my beliefs seem to be totally unrelated, other propositions in my noetic structure are related logically. One such logical relationship is contradiction; two propositions may be logically inconsistent. Consider for example these claims: (a) Ronald Reagan won the 1980 presidential election; and (b) Jimmy Carter won the 1980 presidential election. If I believe (a), then I must regard (b) as false. Two propositions may also be related by the logical relationship of entailment. If I believe that a particular person is a bachelor, then I should also believe that he has never been married.

Quite often, our beliefs are related in ways that have little or nothing to do with logic. The basis of the relationship may be more psychological than logical. Perhaps the fact that I connect two beliefs in some way is rooted in something like training or habit. This may be why I associate East Ninth Street in Cleveland, Ohio, with the world's best Italian restaurant.

Within any noetic structure, it is possible to distinguish between basic and nonbasic beliefs. Most of the things we believe are held on the basis of more fundamental beliefs. It will be helpful to think of them as nonbasic beliefs since they are derived from or inferred from or based upon beliefs that are more basic. A basic belief is one that does not depend upon any other belief. If we compare noetic structures to a building, we can think of basic beliefs as those that constitute the foundation of a person's noetic structure.

3. *Another feature of a noetic structure includes the differing degrees of certainty, firmness, and conviction with which people hold their beliefs.* Every person is more committed to some beliefs than others. All of us feel more confidence or assurance when affirming some beliefs than others. My belief that three times four equals twelve is certainly held with much more firmness and confidence than my belief, say, that the pin oak in my front yard is precisely thirty feet tall. Presumably every theist believes the proposition "God exists" is true. But it should hardly come as news that even theists may believe this proposition with varying degrees of conviction. Perhaps one task of the apologist is to increase the assurance of believers whose faith is wavering.

4. Finally, *the beliefs that constitute any noetic structure will differ with regard to the kind of influence or control they have over the rest of the beliefs in that structure.* Several different analogies may make this point clear.

If we picture a noetic structure as a building, the basic beliefs making up the foundation of the structure are going to count in a way that is not true of nonbasic beliefs that may depend on the foundation. One of my basic, unproven, perhaps unprovable beliefs is that other people have minds.[4] This belief in other minds has a controlling influence on the way I relate to other human beings. For example, I believe that discussions with other people really can involve the exchange of ideas. If I were, for some reason, to abandon my basic belief that other people had minds, it would have a profound (and undoubtedly unsettling) influence on many other elements of my noetic structure.

Some people prefer to picture noetic structures after the analogy of a spider's web. Following this line of thought, we can see how some beliefs seem to lie at the outer limits of our noetic structures. If we should discover tomorrow that we no longer hold that belief, our change of mind would have little or no impact on the rest of our noetic structure. For example, I happen to believe that the lovely village of Castle Combe is about twenty miles from Bath, England. If I should discover that Castle Combe is really thirty miles from Bath, the impact of this new belief would be slight. But suppose I discovered that the village of Castle Combe (which I remember visiting) did not really exist. The consequences of this change of beliefs would be more significant. It might well lead me, for example, to see a doctor.

Unimportant, noncentral, peripheral beliefs can be doubted and even abandoned without producing any dramatic changes in my noetic structure. But changes with regard to central, truly important beliefs will usually have a major effect on my noetic structure.

Obviously, the degree of influence or control that a particular belief has within any given noetic structure will be person-relative. The belief that God exists occupies a central place in some noetic structures, many people reject the proposition entirely, and still others who accept the proposition shove it off to a corner of their noetic structure. In this latter case, if a person whose

---

[4]No one has constructed a good argument that others have minds. This has led some philosophers to say that even though I know that I have a mind, perhaps others are robots.

belief in God functions on the periphery of his noetic structure were to decide someday that he no longer believed in God, the change might well have little impact on the way he continued to think and live. But imagine another person for whom belief in God rests at the center of his noetic structure. In this second case, rejection of or serious doubt about such a pivotal belief would have a rather significant effect on that person's life and thought. Changes regarding pivotal or central beliefs often result in what are called conversions. People can be converted to or from religions like Christianity; they can also become converts to atheism.

THE NOTION OF A WORLD-VIEW

Within the noetic structures of mature, rational people can be found a smaller set of related beliefs that constitute each individual's world-view. A world-view is a conceptual scheme by which we consciously or unconsciously place or fit everything we believe and by which we interpret and judge reality. The philosophical systems of such thinkers as Plato, Aristotle, Spinoza, Kant, and Hegel were world-views. But each reader of this book has his or her own world-view just as surely as Plato did.

Of course, many people have little or no idea what a world-view is, or even that they have one. One of the more important things a philosopher can do for others is to help them realize what a world-view is, assist them in achieving a better understanding of their own world-view, and aid them in improving their world-view. This last task can involve eliminating inconsistencies and providing new information that will help fill in holes in their conceptual system.

> Providing a man with a conceptual framework in which he can see his whole life as being lived in the presence of God is analogous to teaching a man to read a strange script. We can give him a key, a sort of Rosetta stone, by telling him the meaning of one particular inscription. If he believes us he can then understand that inscription. But the test of whether he has really learned how to read the script, and also the confirmation that the translation we gave him was accurate, comes when he encounters all the other inscriptions that are scattered through his world. If he cannot read them, then he has not yet learned that language and he is still subject to the doubt that what we gave him may not have been a translation at all, but rather a message quite unrelated to what was written.[5]

Philosopher W. P. Alston offers another reason why world-views are important:

> It can be argued on the basis of facts concerning the nature of man and the conditions of human life that human beings have a deep-seated need to form some general picture of the total universe in which they live, in order to be able to relate their own fragmentary activities to the universe

---

[5] George Mavrodes, *Belief in God* (New York: Random House, 1970), p. 86. The Rosetta stone is a stone tablet on which an Egyptian decree of 196 B.C. was inscribed in three languages: Greek, Egyptian hieroglyphic, and Demotic. Discovered near the Egyptian town of Rosetta in 1799, this important archaeological find provided the key to deciphering Egyptian hieroglyphics.

as a whole in a way meaningful to them; and that a life in which this is not carried through is a life impoverished in a most significant respect.[6]

The right eyeglasses can put the world into clearer focus. The correct world-view can function in much the same way. When someone looks at the world through the wrong world-view, the world won't make much sense to him, or what he thinks makes sense will, in fact, be wrong in important respects. Donning the right conceptual scheme, that is, viewing the world through the correct world-view, can have important repercussions for the rest of the individual's noetic structure.

Most of us know people who seem incapable of seeing certain points that are obvious to us; perhaps those people view us as equally obdurate. They often seem to have some built-in grid that filters out information and arguments and that leads them to place some peculiar twist on what seems obvious to us. While this may sometimes be the result of something idiosyncratic to them, it is often a function of their world-view. The ability of some people to be open to new beliefs is often a function of the conceptual system in terms of which they approach the world and the claims of others.

Many disagreements between individuals, societies, and nations are often clashes of competing world-views. This is certainly the case between advocates of the prolife and prochoice positions on abortion. It is also true with regard to the growing number of conflicts between secular humanists and religious believers.

It is probably rare when the world-views of two people match in every important detail. It may be helpful to think of different world-views as circles that overlap to a greater or lesser degree.[7] People may disagree over the doctrine of the trinity, but they may share enough beliefs about human personhood to join in opposition to abortion-on-demand. When two people meet whose world-views fail to overlap at all, a major and probably unresolvable clash of views is likely.

VIEWING CHRISTIAN THEISM AS A WORLD-VIEW

Instead of viewing Christianity as a collection of theological bits and pieces to be believed or debated, individuals should approach it as a conceptual system, as a total world- and life-view. Once people understand that both Christianity and its competitors are world-views, they will be in a better position to judge the relative merits of all the systems.

Religious belief should be assessed as a rounded whole rather than taken in stark isolation. Christianity, for example, like other world faiths, is a complex, large-scale system of belief which must be seen as a whole

---

[6] W. P. Alston, "Problems of Philosophy of Religion," in *The Encyclopedia of Philosophy*, reprinted ed. (New York: Macmillan, 1972), 6:286.

[7] While two or more individuals can hold world-views that are generally alike, this situation would not entail that their noetic structures were also identical. One's world-view beliefs are restricted to a relatively small set of significant issues. Two people could share similar views of God, the universe, ethics, and so on. But they could disagree about many other issues of fact (e.g., who is presently leading the American League in batting) or value (e.g., whether they like alfalfa sprouts on their hamburgers).

before it is assessed. To break it up into disconnected parts is to mutilate and distort its true character. We can, of course, distinguish certain elements in the Christian faith, but we must still stand back and see it as a complex interaction of these elements. We need to see it as a metaphysical system, as a world view, that is total in its scope and range.[8]

The case for or against Christian theism should be made and evaluated in terms of total systems. The reason why many people reject Christianity is not due to their problems with one or two isolated issues; it results rather for the simple reason that their anti-Christian conceptual scheme leads them to reject information and arguments that for believers provide support for the Christian world-view. Every world-view has questions it appears to answer unsatisfactorily. The task of negative apologetics is to show that none of the challenges to Christian faith is fatal; none of the problems Christian theism appears to have provides really sufficient reasons why people should reject it. The role of positive apologetics is first to offer support for essential Christian beliefs. But because any proper assessment of the Christian faith requires that it be seen and appraised as a whole, the more important job of positive apologetics is to explain the details of the Christian system and offer reasons why that world-view is superior rationally, morally, and existentially[9] to any alternative system.

Christianity is not simply a religion that tells human beings how they may be forgiven. It is a total world- and life-view. Christians need to recognize that their faith has important things to say about the whole of human life. Once Christians can understand in a systematic way how the options to Christianity are also world-views, they will be in a better position to rationally justify their choice of Christianity.

Because so many elements of a world-view are philosophical in nature, Christians need to become more conscious of the importance of philosophy. Though philosophy and religion often use different language and often arrive at different conclusions, they deal with the same questions, which include questions about what exists (metaphysics), how humans should live (ethics), and how human beings know (epistemology). Philosophy matters. It matters because the Christian world-view has an intrinsic connection to philosophy and the world of ideas. It matters because philosophy is related in a critically important way to life, culture, and religion. And it matters because the systems opposing Christianity use philosophical methods and arguments.

THE IMPORTANT ROLE OF PRESUPPOSITIONS

Our noetic structures contain a number of beliefs that we presuppose or accept without support from other beliefs or arguments or evidence. Such

---

[8] William J. Abraham, *An Introduction to the Philosophy of Religion* (Englewood Cliffs, N.J.: Prentice-Hall, 1985), p. 104.

[9] My use of the word *existentially* here has nothing really to do with any of the forms of existential philosophy. I am referring to the fact, explained shortly, that any world-view must be such that those who accept it intellectually can also live what they profess. Competing world-views need to be tested both in the philosophy classroom and in the laboratory of life.

assumptions are necessary if we are to think at all. In the words of the Christian thinker Augustine (A.D. 354–430), we must believe something before we can know anything. Whenever we think we simply take some things for granted. The consequences of some of these presuppositions for philosophy and religion as well as for thinking in general can be most important.

Often a beginning student of geometry tends to overlook the significance of the axioms at the beginning of her textbook. She rushes over them in order to get into what she thinks is the more important work of solving problems. The axioms, while basic to all the subsequent proofs in the system, are themselves not proven or even provable. However, the advanced student soon realizes that with regard to the ultimate validity of all subsequent argumentation, these basic axioms are more important than the later problems and solutions. After all, the rest of geometry follows only if the axioms are accepted. If they are denied, the propositions deduced from the axioms do not follow since there is nothing for them to follow from; and the validity of the entire system then becomes suspect. In a similar way, human knowledge depends on certain assumptions that are often unexpressed, sometimes unrecognized, and frequently unproven.[10]

As Thomas Morris explains, the most important presuppositions in any person's noetic structure

> are the most basic and most general beliefs about God, man, and the world that anyone can have. They are not usually consciously entertained but rather function as the perspective from which an individual sees and interprets both the events of his own life and the various circumstances of the world around him. These presuppositions in conjunction with one another delimit the boundaries within which all other less foundational beliefs are held.[11]

Even scientists make important epistemological, metaphysical, and ethical assumptions. They assume, for example, that knowledge is possible and that sense experience is reliable (epistemology), that the universe is regular (metaphysics), and that scientists should be honest (ethics). Without these assumptions that scientists cannot justify within the limits of their methodology, scientific inquiry would soon collapse.

Basic assumptions or presuppositions are important because of the way they often determine the method and goal of theoretical thought. They can be compared to a train running on tracks that have no switches. Once a person commits himself to a certain set of presuppositions, his direction and

---

[10] While geometry provides a helpful illustration of the point I make about the importance of presuppositions, the analogy can be pressed too far and thus mislead. Geometric axioms function obviously in a deductive system. I am *not* suggesting that the basic assumptions or presuppositions that underlie a person's noetic structure always or necessarily or even optimally function as axioms from which he then deduces the other elements of his world-view. Presuppositions relate to other elements of a person's noetic structure in a variety of ways. Sometimes the relationship is deductive; often it is not.

[11] Thomas V. Morris, *Francis Schaeffer's Apologetics* (Grand Rapids: Baker, 1987), p. 109. I should make clear that Morris's remarks appear in the course of his exposition of Francis Schaeffer's views.

destination are determined. An acceptance of the presuppositions of the Christian world-view will lead a person to conclusions quite different from those that would follow a commitment, say, to the presuppositions of Naturalism.[12] One's axioms determine one's theorems.[13]

THE NONTHEORETICAL FOUNDATIONS
OF THEORETICAL THOUGHT

A number of Christian writers have attempted to draw attention to the fact that theoretical thought is often strongly affected by nontheoretical considerations. It is hard to ignore the personal dimension to the acceptance and evaluation of world-views, including religious systems like Christianity. It would be foolish to pretend that human beings always handle such matters impersonally and objectively, without reference to considerations rooted in their psychological make-up. Many people demonstrate that they are often incapable of thinking clearly about their world-view. Most of us have met people or read the writings of people who appear so captive to some conceptual scheme that they seem incapable of giving a fair hearing to any argument or piece of evidence that appears to threaten their cherished system. This is true of both theists and nontheists.

Sometimes people have difficulty with competing claims and systems because of philosophical presuppositions. But often, it seems clear, people's theoretical judgments seem inordinately affected by nontheoretical factors. This is the case, for example, when racial prejudice causes people to hold certain untrue beliefs about those who are objects of the prejudice. Sometimes, these nontheoretical factors are idiosyncratic, unique to the particular person, rooted in that person's individual history. Some writers have suggested that another type of nontheoretical influence affects our thinking. According to such writers, human thoughts and actions have religious roots in the sense that they are related to the human heart, the center or religious root of our being.[14] Human beings are never neutral with regard to God. Either we worship God as Creator and Lord, or we turn away from God. Because the heart is directed either toward God or against God, theoretical thinking is never as pure or autonomous as many would like to think. While this line of thinking raises some questions that cannot be

---

[12]This claim assumes that the parties involved think and act consistently. We all know professing Christians whose judgments and conduct conflict with important principles of their faith. Many nontheists, often unconsciously, appear to draw back from positions that their presuppositions seem to entail.

[13]Once again, a qualification may help avoid any misunderstanding. In geometry this sentence is true literally. In a broader discussion of noetic structures and world-views, it is true generally.

[14]I regret the need to resort to metaphors at this point. But we are on difficult terrain. Although the basic point seems true, it is very difficult to sort out all the issues. For an example of one writer who argued for this position, see Herman Dooyeweerd, *In the Twilight of Western Thought* (Philadelphia: Presbyterian and Reformed, 1960). For a nontechnical introduction to Dooyeweerd's work, see Ronald Nash, *Dooyeweerd and the Amsterdam Philosophy* (Grand Rapids: Zondervan, 1962). For a later critique of Dooyeweerd by the same writer see Ronald Nash, *The Word of God and the Mind of Man* (Grand Rapids: Zondervan, 1982).

explored further in this book, it does seem that some people who appear to reject Christianity on rational or theoretical grounds are, in fact, acting under the influence of nonrational factors, that is, more ultimate commitments of their hearts. People should be encouraged to dig below the surface and uncover the basic philosophical and religious presuppositions that often appear to control their thinking.

Though the influence of nontheoretical factors on people's thinking is often extensive, it is never total in the sense that it precludes life-altering changes. Even in the case of Saul of Tarsus—one of early Christianity's greatest enemies—where it might appear that a person was totally dominated by commitments that ruled out any possibility of a change or conversion, things may never be completely hopeless. People do change conceptual systems. Conversions take place all the time. People who used to be humanists or naturalists or atheists or followers of some competing religious faith have found reasons to turn away from their old conceptual systems and embrace Christianity. Conversely, people who used to profess allegiance to Christianity reach a point where they feel they can no longer believe.

This seems an appropriate time to bring up one important matter that should be mentioned in any Christian discussion of this subject. Every wise and informed practitioner of negative and positive apologetics recognizes the essential role that the Holy Spirit of God has to play in all such matters. It is never the ability, skill, or eloquence of the preacher, teacher, or apologist that brings people to faith. Their work, however good it may be, provides at most an occasion that God himself uses to give birth to faith.[15]

Of course, we must also recognize that many changes regarding world-views have little or nothing to do with Christian conversion. Even the noted Christian writer C. S. Lewis admits that he abandoned a naturalistic world-view in favor of an intellectual acceptance of the Christian world-view months before his actual conversion to Christianity.[16] In spite of all the obstacles I have noted, people do occasionally begin to doubt conceptual systems they had accepted for years. And sometimes, as we know, people undergo dramatic changes in their noetic structures.

Is it possible to identify a single set of necessary conditions that will always be present when people change a world-view? I doubt it. After all, many people remain blissfully unaware that they have a world-view, even though the sudden change in their life and thought resulted from their exchanging their old world-view for their new one. What does seem clear is that changes this dramatic usually require time along with a period of doubt about key elements of the world-view. Even when the change may appear to have been sudden, it was in all likelihood preceded by a period of growing uncertainty and doubt. In many cases, the actual change is triggered by an important event, often a crisis of some kind. But I have also heard people recount stories that lay out a different scenario. Suddenly, or so it seemed,

---

[15]Many passages of Scripture merit careful study in this connection. Two that come to mind are Ephesians 2:1–10 and 1 Corinthians, chapters 1 and 2.

[16]Of course, it would be natural for any Christian to see Lewis's intellectual conversion as a God-directed stage in what eventually became his spiritual conversion.

one event or piece of information led these persons to begin thinking along entirely different lines, that is, in terms of a conceptual scheme that was totally different for them or one that they were becoming conscious of for the first time. Quite unexpectedly, these people "saw" things they had overlooked before; or they suddenly "saw" things fit together in a pattern so that there was meaning where none had been discernible before.

People are different; noetic structures are different. It seems quite foolish, therefore, to stipulate that life-transforming changes in those elements of a noetic structure that we have called a world-view must match some pattern. People change their minds on important subjects for a bewildering variety of reasons (or nonreasons).

THE MAJOR ELEMENTS OF A WORLD-VIEW

What kinds of beliefs make up a world-view? A well-rounded world-view includes what a person believes on at least five major topics: God, reality, knowledge, morality, and humankind.

Theology

A world-view will always include either a theology or an atheology. In fact, the most important element of any world-view is what it says or does not say about God. World-views differ greatly over some basic questions. Does God exist? What is the nature of God? Is there but one God? Is God a personal being, that is, is he the kind of being who can know, love, and act? Or is God an impersonal force or power? Because of conflicting views about the nature of God, such systems as Buddhism, Hinduism, Shintoism, and Zoroastrianism are not only different religions; they contain different world-views.[17] Because Christianity, Judaism, and Islam are examples of theism, conservative adherents of these religions hold to world-views that have more in common than they do with dualistic, polytheistic, and pantheistic systems. One essential component, then, of any world-view is its view of God.

Metaphysics

A world-view also includes beliefs about ultimate reality, a subject often discussed under the label of metaphysics. In the philosophical systems of thinkers like Plato, Aristotle, and Hegel, metaphysics often becomes a complex and mysterious subject. A person's world-view need not be complicated to contain metaphysical beliefs. The kinds of views that qualify would include the person's answers to such questions as these: What is the relationship between God and the universe? Is the existence of the universe a brute fact? Is the universe eternal? Did an eternal, personal, and omnipotent God create the world? Are God and the world coeternal and interdependent beings?[18] Is the world best understood in a mechanistic (that is, a

---

[17]There is no need to complicate the discussion by detailing the many divisions that exist within most of the world's major religions.

[18]Advocates of what is known as process theology answer this question in the affirmative. For a detailed analysis of this increasingly influential position, see Ronald Nash, ed., *Process Theology* (Grand Rapids: Baker, 1987).

nonpurposeful) way? Or is there purpose in the universe? What is the ultimate nature of the universe? Is the cosmos ultimately material or spiritual or something else? Is the universe a self-enclosed system in the sense that everything that happens is caused by (and thus explained by) other events within the system? Or can a supernatural reality (a being beyond nature) act causally within nature? Are miracles possible? Though some of these questions never occur to some people, it is likely that anyone reading this book has thought about most of these questions and holds beliefs about some of them.

Epistemology

A third component of any world-view is epistemology, a theory of knowledge. Even people not given to philosophic pursuits hold some epistemological beliefs. The easiest way to see this is simply to ask them if they believe that knowledge about the world is possible. Whether they answer yes or no to this question, their reply will identify one element of their epistemology. Other epistemological questions include the following: Can we trust our senses? What are the proper roles of reason and sense experience in knowledge? Do we apprehend our own states of consciousness in some way other than reason and sense experience? Are our intuitions of our own states of consciousness more dependable than our perceptions of the external world? Is truth relative, or must truth be the same for all rational beings? What is the relationship between religious faith and reason? Is the scientific method the only (or perhaps the best) method of knowledge? Is knowledge about God possible? If so, how? Can God reveal himself to human beings? Can God reveal information to human beings? What is the relationship between the mind of God and the mind of human beings?[19] Even though few human beings think about such questions while watching a baseball game on television (or indeed during any normal daily activities), all that is usually required to elicit an opinion is to ask the question. Most of us hold beliefs on epistemological issues; we simply need to have our attention directed to the questions.

Ethics

Most people are more aware of the ethical component of their world-view than of their metaphysical and epistemological beliefs. We make moral judgments about the conduct of individuals (ourselves and others) and about nations. The kinds of ethical beliefs that are important in this context, however, are more basic than moral judgments about single actions. It is one thing to say that some action of a human being like Adolf Hitler or of a nation like Iran is morally wrong. Ethics is more concerned with the question of *why* that action is wrong. Are there moral laws that govern human conduct? What are they? Are these moral laws the same for all human beings? Is morality totally subjective (like our taste for spinach), or is there an objective dimension to moral laws that means their truth is independent of our preferences and desires? Are the moral laws discovered (in a way more or less similar to the way we discover that "seven times seven equals forty-

---

[19]My answers to many of these questions can be found in my book *The Word of God and the Mind of Man* (Grand Rapids: Zondervan, 1982).

nine"), or are they constructed by human beings (in a way more or less similar to what we call human mores)? Is morality relative to individuals or to cultures or to historical periods? Does it make sense to say that the same action may be right for people in one culture or historical epoch and wrong for others? Or does morality transcend cultural, historical, and individual boundaries?[20]

Anthropology

By anthropology, I do not mean the branch of the social sciences sometimes studied in college courses with this name. My use of the term harks back to the meanings of the two Greek words from which it is derived.[21] Every world-view includes a number of important beliefs about the nature of human beings. Examples of anthropological questions about which most people hold beliefs include the following: Are human beings free, or are they merely pawns of deterministic forces? Are human beings only bodies or material beings? Or were all the religious and philosophical thinkers who talked about the human soul or who distinguished the mind from the body correct? If they were right in some sense, what is the human soul or mind, and how is it related to the body? Does physical death end the existence of the human person? Or is there conscious, personal survival after death? Are there rewards and punishment after death? Are the Christian teachings about heaven and hell correct?

Additional Questions

Are the five points just noted the *only* components of what may properly be called a world-view? While the correct answer to this question is no, consciously held beliefs about other elements of a world-view appear to be less common. I will comment on two.

1. A person's world-view may also include a set of ideals that lays out how he or she thinks things should be. These ideals produce a gap between the way things are and the way they ought to be.[22] Regardless of the actual conditions that may exist in that person's life or society, the individual can have a vision or picture of how things ought to be different. Perhaps there should be less stupidity or corruption among politicians; perhaps I should lose my temper less often; perhaps my eating habits should be different; perhaps there should be more justice or less poverty in the world. These ideals apply to many different aspects of human existence: family, church, school, business, government. Things can always be better than they are.

2. A well-formed world-view may also contain an explanation for the disparity between the way things are and the way they ought to be. Marxists, for example, are prone to blame what they see as problems on the

---

[20] A rather well-known, popularly written set of answers to many of these questions can be found in Part 1 of C. S. Lewis's book, *Mere Christianity* (New York: Macmillan, 1960).

[21] *Logos* can mean "the study of" and *anthropos* is the Greek word meaning "man."

[22] I think it is clear that this set of ideals will be a combined function of those elements of a world-view already noted. Moreover, consciousness of one's major beliefs about God, reality, knowledge, ethics, and humankind would seem to be a necessary condition for an awareness of more developed world-view components.

institutions of capitalism. Christianity attributes the discrepancy between ideal and actual existence to the pervasiveness of sin.

An Important Qualification

Because my purpose thus far has been to make a complicated subject as clear as possible, I've been forced to oversimplify some things. This is a good time to make an important qualification. I do not want to suggest that adherents of the same general world-view will necessarily agree on every issue. Any account of world-views that implied this would be grossly mistaken. Even Christians who share beliefs on all essential issues may disagree on other important points. They may understand the relationship between human freedom and the sovereignty of God in different ways. They may disagree over how some revealed law of God applies to a twentieth-century situation. They may squabble publicly over complex issues like national defense, capital punishment, and the welfare state, to say nothing about the issues that divide Christendom into different denominations.

Do these manifold and important disagreements undercut the case I've been making about the nature of the Christian world-view? Not at all. A careful study of these disagreements will reveal that they are differences within a broader family of beliefs. When two or more Christians argue over some issue, one of the steps they take to justify their position and to persuade the other is to show that their view is more consistent with basic tenets of the Christian world-view.[23]

However, it is also important to recognize that disagreement on some issues should result in the disputant's being regarded as someone who has left that family of beliefs, however much he or she desires to continue to use the label. For example, many religious liberals in the West continue to use the Christian label for views that are clearly inconsistent with the beliefs of historic Christianity. Whether they deny the trinity or the personality of God or the doctrine of creation or the fact of human depravity or the doctrine of salvation by grace, they make clear that the religious system they espouse is totally different from what has traditionally been meant by *Christianity*. A religion without the incarnate, crucified, and risen Son of God may be a plausible faith, but it certainly is not the *Christian* religion. Much confusion could undoubtedly be eliminated if some way could be found to get people to use important labels like Christianity in a way that is faithful to their historic meaning.[24] Since this is not going to happen, people will have to live with the confusion or find other ways of making careful distinctions.

CONCLUSION

Whether we know it or not—whether we like it or not—each of us has a world-view. These world-views function as interpretive conceptual schemes to explain why we "see" the world as we do, why we often think

---

[23]For some examples of this, see Ronald Nash, *Poverty and Wealth* (Westchester, Ill.: Crossway, 1986), and Ronald Nash, *Social Justice and the Christian Church* (Grand Rapids: Baker, 1983).

[24]I should point out that contemporary Marxism has the same problem. See the discussion in Nash, *Poverty and Wealth*, pp. 89–102.

and act as we do. Competing world-views often come into conflict. These clashes may be as innocuous as a simple argument between people or as serious as a war between two nations. It is important, therefore, that we understand the extent to which significant disagreements reflect clashes between competing world-views.

World-views are double-edged swords. An inadequate conceptual scheme can, like improper eyeglasses, hinder our efforts to understand God, the world, and ourselves. The right conceptual scheme can suddenly bring everything into proper focus. But the choice among competing world-views involves a number of difficult questions. For one thing, we must always contend with the ever-present possibility of nontheoretical factors having an adverse effect on our theoretical judgments. For another, it is difficult to be sure which criteria or tests should be used in selecting among world-views.

For Further Exploration—Chapter Two

1. Discuss the importance of world-views.
2. Identify several instances in your own life when nontheoretical considerations like love, fear, or prejudice affected your thinking about nonreligious matters. Do the same with regard to your thinking about religious questions.
3. Identify the five major elements of a world-view.
4. What are the most important elements of your world-view?

Chapter 3

THE CHRISTIAN WORLD-VIEW

Since I have already stated that Christian theism should be seen as a world-view, it will be helpful if I provide a brief outline of its content.

THEOLOGY

The Christian world-view is theistic in the sense that it believes in the existence of one supremely powerful and personal God. Theism differs from polytheism in its affirmation that there is only one God (Deut. 6:4). It parts company with the various forms of panentheism by insisting that God is personal and must not be confused with the world that is his creation. Theism must also be distinguished from pantheism, the position that regards the world as an eternal being that God needs in much the same way a human soul needs a body. Theists also reject panentheistic attempts to limit God's power and knowledge, which have the effect of making the God of panentheism a finite being.[1] Other important attributes of God, such as his holiness, justice, and love, are described in Scripture.

Historic Christian theism is also trinitarian. The doctrine of the trinity reflects the Christian conviction that the Father, the Son, and the Holy Spirit are three distinct centers of consciousness sharing fully in the one divine nature and in the activities of the other persons of the trinity. An important corollary of the doctrine is the Christian conviction that Jesus Christ is both fully God and fully man. Christians use the word *incarnation* to express their

---

[1] For a fuller discussion, see Ronald Nash, ed., *Process Theology* (Grand Rapids: Baker, 1987).

belief that the birth of Jesus Christ marked the entrance of the eternal and divine Son of God into the human race.

METAPHYSICS

An important metaphysical tenet of the Christian world-view is the claim that God created the world *ex nihilo* (from nothing). The Bible begins with the claim, "In the beginning God created the heavens and the earth." Many early Christian thinkers found it important to draw out certain implications of the biblical view of God and stipulate that God created the world *ex nihilo*. This was necessary, they believed, to show the contrast between the Christian understanding of creation and an account of the world's origin found in Plato's philosophy, a view held by a number of intellectuals in the early centuries of the Christian church.[2] Plato had suggested that a Godlike being, the Craftsman, had brought the world into being by fashioning an eternal stuff or matter after the pattern of eternal ideas that existed independently of the Craftsman. This creative activity took place moreover in a space-time receptacle or box that also existed independently of the Craftsman. Such early Christian thinkers as Augustine wanted the world to know that the Christian God and the Christian view of creation differed totally from this Platonic picture. Plato's god (if indeed that is an appropriate word for his Craftsman) was not the infinite, all-powerful, and sovereign God of the Christian Scriptures. Plato's god was finite and limited. In the Christian account of creation, nothing existed prior to creation except God. There was no time or space; there was no preexisting matter. Everything else that exists besides God depends totally upon God for its existence. If God did not exist, the world would not exist. The cosmos is not eternal, self-sufficient, or self-explanatory. It was freely created by God.

The existence of the world, therefore, is not a brute fact; nor is the world a purposeless machine. The world exists as the result of a free decision to create by a God who is eternal, transcendent, spiritual (that is, nonmaterial), omnipotent, omniscient, omnibenevolent, loving, and personal. Because there is a God-ordained order to the creation, human beings can discover that order. It is this order that makes science possible; it is this order that scientists attempt to capture in their laws.

The Christian world-view should be distinguished from any version of deism. This theory dares to suggest that although God created the world, he absents himself from the creation and allows it to run on its own. This view and several twentieth-century varieties seem to present the picture of a God (or god) who is incapable of acting causally within nature.[3] While no informed Christian will argue with the assured results of such sciences as

---

[2] For more on this, see Ronald Nash, *Christianity and the Hellenistic World* (Grand Rapids: Zondervan, 1984).

[3] This certainly appears to have been the view of such twentieth-century theologians as Paul Tillich and Rudolf Bultmann. While the term *Naturalism* will be explained later in this chapter, there is some justification for describing thinkers like Tillich and Bultmann as religious naturalists. They may have believed in God, but their God was effectively precluded from any providential or miraculous activity within nature. For more, see chapter 18.

physics, biology, and geology, the Christian world-view insists that such divine activities as miracles, revelation, and providence remain possible.

EPISTEMOLOGY

The study of epistemology can quickly involve one in some fairly sticky problems. In fact, one should admit that on many epistemological issues (for example, the dispute between rationalists and empiricists), a wide variety of options seem to be consistent with other aspects of the Christian world-view. But there do seem to be limits to this tolerance. For example, the Christian world-view is clearly incompatible with universal skepticism, the self-defeating claim that no knowledge about anything is attainable. The fact that this kind of skepticism self-destructs becomes clear whenever one asks such a skeptic if he knows that knowledge is unattainable.

It also seems obvious that a well-formed Christian world-view will exclude views suggesting that humans cannot attain knowledge about God. Christianity clearly proclaims that God has revealed information about himself.[4] Nor will an informed Christian deny the importance of the senses in supplying information about the world. As St. Augustine observed, the Christian "believes also the evidence of the senses which the mind uses by aid of the body; for if one who trusts his senses is sometimes deceived, he is more wretchedly deceived who fancies he should never trust them."[5] In his own epistemology, Augustine was a rationalist in the sense that he gave priority to reason over sense experience. Augustine probably had a very good theological reason for defending the general reliability of sense experience. He undoubtedly realized that many claims made in the Bible depended upon eyewitness testimony. If the senses are completely unreliable, we cannot trust the reports of witnesses who say that they heard Jesus teach or saw him die or saw him alive three days after the crucifixion. If the experiences of those who saw and heard a risen Christ were necessarily deceptive and unreliable, an important truth of the Christian faith may be compromised.

In recent Christian writing about epistemology philosophers apparently operating on different tracks have found agreement on an important point. In the case of my own track (a kind of Christian rationalism that received its first formulation in the writings of St. Augustine), it is a mistake to accept an extreme form of empiricism that claims that *all* human knowledge arises from sense experience. Older advocates of this empiricism used to illustrate their basic claim by arguing that the human mind at birth is like a *tabula rasa*, a blank tablet. At birth, the human mind is like a totally clean blackboard; absolutely nothing is written on it. In other words, human beings are born with no innate ideas or knowledge. As the human being grows and develops, the senses supply the mind with an ever-increasing stock of information. All human knowledge results, on this model, from what the

---

[4]I defend this claim in *The Word of God and the Mind of Man* (Grand Rapids: Zondervan, 1982).

[5]Augustine, *City of God;* trans. Marcus Dods (New York: Modern Library, 1950), 19.18.

mind does with ideas supplied through the senses—the basic building blocks of knowledge.

My alternative to this extreme kind of empiricism can be summarized in the claim that *some* human knowledge does not arise from sense experience.[6] As many philosophers have noted, human knowledge of the sensible world is possible because human beings bring certain ideas, categories, and dispositions to their experience of the world. The impotence of empiricism is especially evident in the case of human knowledge of universal and necessary truth. Many things in the world could have been otherwise. The typewriter I am using at this moment happens to be brown; but it could have been red. Whether it is brown or not is a purely contingent feature of reality. Whatever color the typewriter happens to be, it could have been colored differently. But it is *necessarily* the case that my typewriter could not have been brown all over and red (or any other color) all over at the same time and in the same sense. The necessary truth that my typewriter is brown all over and not at the same time red all over cannot be a function of sense experience. Sense experience may be able to report what is the case at a particular time. But sense experience is incapable of grasping what *must* be the case *at all times*. The notions of necessity and universality can never be derived from our experience. Rather, they are notions (among others) that we bring to sense experience and use in making judgments about reality.

How do we account for the human possession of these *a priori* (that is, independent of sense experience) categories of thought or innate ideas or dispositions that play such an indispensable role in human knowledge? According to a long and honored philosophical tradition that includes Augustine, Descartes, and Leibniz, human beings have these innate ideas, dispositions, and categories by virtue of their creation by God. In fact, this may well be part of what is meant by the phrase *the image of God*.[7] After all (Christians believe), God created the world. It is reasonable to assume that he created humans such that they are capable of attaining knowledge of his creation. To go even further, it is reasonable to believe that he endowed the human mind with the ability to attain knowledge of himself.

Recently, a number of philosophers approached a very similar position from a different direction, namely, the epistemology of the eighteenth-century Scottish philosopher Thomas Reid. Nicholas Wolterstorff explains:

> At the very foundation of Reid's approach is his claim that at any point in our lives we have a variety of dispositions, inclinations, propensities, to believe things—*belief dispositions* we may call them. What accounts for our beliefs, in the vast majority of cases anyway, is the triggering of one and another such disposition. For example, we are all so constituted that upon having memory experiences in certain situations, we are disposed to have certain beliefs about the past. We are all disposed, upon having certain

---

[6] I consciously reject an extreme type of rationalism that claims that *no* human knowledge arises from sense experience. Plato apparently held this latter view. But, as explained earlier, St. Augustine did not; nor do I.

[7] I have explored the roots of this theory in the writings of St. Augustine in my book *The Light of the Mind: St. Augustine's Theory of Knowledge* (Lexington: University Press of Kentucky, 1969). This work is then brought up to date in *The Word of God and the Mind of Man*.

sensations in certain situations, to have certain beliefs about the external physical world. Upon having certain other sensations in certain situations, we are all disposed to have certain beliefs about other persons.[8]

Continuing to follow Reid's trail, Wolterstorff goes on to note that Reid was also interested in how humans came to have these belief-producing dispositions or mechanisms. It was Reid's conviction, Wolterstorff explains,

> that somewhere in the history of each of us are to be found certain belief dispositions with which we were simply "endowed by our Creator." They belong to our human nature. We come with them. They are innate in us. Their existence in us is not the result of conditioning. It must not be supposed, however, that all such nonconditioned dispositions are present in us at birth. Some, possibly most, emerge as we mature. We have the disposition to acquire them upon reaching one and another level of maturation.[9]

Alvin Plantinga draws attention to an important similarity between what Thomas Reid said concerning the belief-forming mechanisms that make knowledge of the world possible and what Reformed thinkers like John Calvin said about belief in God.

> Reformed theologians such as Calvin . . . have held that God has implanted in us a tendency or nisus to accept belief in God under certain conditions. Calvin speaks, in this connection, of a "sense of deity inscribed in the hearts of all". Just as we have a natural tendency to form perceptual beliefs under certain conditions, so says Calvin, we have a natural tendency to form such beliefs as *God is speaking to me* and *God has created all this* or *God disapproves of what I've done* under certain widely realized conditions.[10]

Plantinga shows no reluctance in describing the idea of God as "innate." In fact, in a later chapter, we will see how this view enables contemporary Reformed thinkers to give what many see as a new twist to some old arguments for God's existence.

Even though I must close this discussion and move on to the next topic, the issues raised in this section will appear prominently in later chapters. The Christian world-view is no ally of skepticism. Human beings can know God's creation; they are also capable of attaining knowledge about God. Nor should this surprise anyone. It is exactly what we should have expected.

---

[8] Nicholas Wolterstorff, "Can Belief in God Be Rational?" in *Faith and Rationality,* ed. Alvin Plantinga and Nicholas Wolterstorff (Notre Dame, Ind.: University of Notre Dame Press, 1983), p. 149.

[9] Ibid., p. 150. It is also open to such classic rationalists as Augustine (or myself) to concur with what Wolterstorff describes in this paragraph. Classic rationalists always distinguished between a person's having certain ideas innately (at birth) and becoming conscious of those ideas as he reaches some level of maturation. Another important comment: Wolterstorff goes on to note that Reid also acknowledged the existence of belief dispositions that are "acquired by way of conditioning" (Ibid.). This is a perfectly sensible point to make.

[10] Alvin Plantinga, "Self-Profile," in *Alvin Plantinga,* ed. James E. Tomberlin and Peter van Inwagen (Boston: D. Reidel, 1985), pp. 63, 64. Plantinga's quote comes from Calvin's *Institutes of the Christian Religion,* bk. 1, chap. 3, pp. 43–44.

ETHICS

The fact that all human beings carry the image of God (itself one of Christianity's *anthropological* claims) explains why human beings are creatures capable of reasoning, love, and God-consciousness; it also explains why we are moral creatures. Of course, sin (another of Christianity's anthropological presuppositions) has distorted the image of God and explains why humans turn away from God and the moral law; why we sometimes go wrong with regard to our emotions, conduct, and thinking.

But because of the image of God, we should expect to find that the ethical recommendations of the Christian world-view reflect what all of us at the deepest levels of our moral being know to be true. As C. S. Lewis pointed out,

> Christ did not come to preach any brand new morality. . . . Really great moral teachers never do introduce new moralities: it is quacks and cranks who do that. . . . The real job of every moral teacher is to keep on bringing us back, time after time, to the old simple principles which we are all so anxious not to see.[11]

When one examines the moralities of different cultures and religions, certain differences do stand out. But Lewis was more impressed by the basic, underlying similarities.

> Think of a country where people were admired for running away in battle, or where a man felt proud of doublecrossing all the people who had been kindest to him. You might just as well try to imagine a country where two and two made five. Men have differed as regards what people you ought to be unselfish to—whether it was only your own family, or your fellow countrymen, or everyone. But they have always agreed that you ought not to put yourself first. Selfishness has never been admired.[12]

According to the Christian world-view, God is the ground of the laws that govern the physical universe and that make possible the order of the cosmos. God is also the ground of the moral laws that ought to govern human behavior and that make possible order (or peace)[13] between humans and within humans.[14]

Christian theism must insist that there are universal moral laws. In other words, the laws must apply to all humans, regardless of when or

---

[11] C. S. Lewis, *Mere Christianity* (New York: Macmillan, 1960), p. 78.

[12] Ibid., p. 19.

[13] *Peace* was St. Augustine's term. His treatment of the subject in Book 19 of *The City of God* ought to be regarded as required reading for anyone who fancies himself an educated person.

[14] Each of the areas of theology, metaphysics, epistemology, ethics, and anthropology includes its share of important but different questions that cannot be pursued in this study. One such problem in ethics is the precise relationship between God and morality. For some technical discussions of the topic, see Philip L. Quinn, *Divine Commands and Moral Requirements* (Oxford: Clarendon Press, 1978), and Robert Merrihew Adams, "A Modified Divine Command Theory of Ethical Wrongness," in *Religion and Morality* ed. Gene Outka and John P. Reeder, Jr. (Garden City, N.Y.: Anchor Press, Doubleday, 1973).

where they have lived. They must also be objective in the sense that their truth is independent of human preference and desire.

Much confusion surrounding Christian ethics results from a failure to observe the important distinction between principles and rules. Let us define moral principles as more *general* moral prescriptions, general in the sense that they are intended to cover a large number of instances. Moral rules, on the other hand, will be regarded as more *specific* moral prescriptions that are, in fact, applications of principles to more concrete situations.

The difference between principles and rules contains advantages and disadvantages. One advantage of moral principles is that they are less subject to change. Because of the larger number of instances they apply to, they possess a greater degree of universality. One disadvantage of any moral principle is its vagueness. Because principles cover so many situations, it is often difficult to know exactly when a particular principle applies. Rules, however, have the advantage of being much more specific. Their problem concerns their changeability. Because they are so closely tied to specific situations, changes in the situation usually require changes in the appropriate rule. For example, St. Paul warned the Christian women of Corinth not to worship with their heads uncovered. Some Christians have mistakenly regarded Paul's advice as a moral principle that should be observed by Christian women in every culture at all times. But a study of the conditions of ancient Corinth reveals that the city's prostitutes identified themselves to their prospective customers by keeping their heads uncovered. In the light of this, it seems likely that Paul's advice was not a moral principle intended to apply to Christians of all generations but a rule that applied only to the specific situation of the Christian women of Corinth and to women in similar situations.[15]

I recognize that the distinction I am drawing here suffers from some degree of impreciseness. This is due in part to the fact that the difference between principles and rules is sometimes relative. That is, Scripture actually presents a hierarchy of moral prescriptions beginning at the most general level with the duty to love. This duty to love is then further broken down into the duties to love God and love man (Matt. 22:37–40) and then still further into the more specific duties of the Decalogue (Rom. 13:9–10). And, of course, the still more specific duties spelled out in the New Testament, such as the prohibition against the lustful look and hatred, are further specifications of the Ten Commandments (Matt. 5:21–32). The distinction between principles and rules suggests that whenever you have two scriptural injunctions, where a more specific command is derived from one more general, you can regard the more specific injunction as the rule and the other as the principle. It is possible to read 1 Corinthians 13 in this way. First, Paul proposes love as a moral duty binding on all men. Then he proceeds to provide more specific rules about how a loving person will behave; for example, he will be kind and patient.

Based on our distinction between principles and rules plus a careful

---

[15]Even if my particular interpretation of 1 Corinthians 11 is challenged, my point can be made in terms of other New Testament passages. See, for example, Paul's remarks in Romans 14 concerning Christians' eating meat that had been offered to pagan gods.

study of the New Testament, several conclusions can be drawn. (1) The New Testament gave first-century Christians plenty of rules. But, of course, the rules cover situations that may no longer confront twentieth-century Christians, such as Paul's injunction against eating meat offered to idols. (2) The New Testament does not provide twentieth-century Christians with any large number of rules regarding our specific situations. The reason for this should be obvious. The rules were given to cover first-century situations. A first-century book that attempted to give moral rules to cover specific twentieth-century situations would have been unintelligible or irrelevant to readers in the intervening nineteen hundred years. What moral help could the first-century Christians in Rome or Ephesus have derived from such moral rules as "Thou shalt not make a first strike with nuclear weapons" or "It is wrong to use cocaine"? (3) At the same time, some of the New Testament rules apply to situations that have existed throughout time. Passages dealing with acts of hating, stealing, lying, and the like continue to be relevant because the acts are similar. (4) But often what many people miss is the importance of searching out the moral *principles* behind the New Testament rules. These principles are equally binding on humans of all generations. A careful consideration of the Bible's first-century rules can enable us to infer the more general principles behind them, principles that apply to us today. It may be unimportant today whether Christian women keep their heads covered, but it is important that they avoid provocative dress and behavior. Though few Christians in our generation are bothered by pagan butchers who have offered their wares as a sacrifice to a false god, we can profit from the principle that we should do nothing that causes a weaker person to stumble.[16]

While a properly formed Christian world-view allows a great deal of leeway regarding the positions sincere Christians may take on many of the really tough problems that can arise in the formulation of an ethical theory, informed Christians will have to reject some views. One such view is the position called situation ethics, which asserts that Christian ethics imposes no duty other than the duty to love. In determining what he should do, the situationist declares, the Christian should face the moral situation and ask himself what is the loving thing to do in this particular case. There are no rules or principles that prescribe how love will act. Indeed, each loving individual is free to act in any way he thinks is consistent with love as he understands it. The point to situation ethics is, then, that Christian ethics provides absolutely no universal principles or rules. Nothing is intrinsically good except love; nothing intrinsically bad except nonlove. One can never prescribe in advance what a Christian should do. Depending on the situation, love may find it necessary to lie, to steal, even presumably to fornicate, to blaspheme, and to worship false gods. The only absolute is love.

A proper response to situation ethics will begin by pointing out that love is insufficient in itself to provide moral guidance for each and every

---

[16]Another qualification may help some readers. I am not suggesting that Scripture presents us with a casuistic system of morality in which specific moral duties can always be deduced from more general moral statements. Casuistry always leads to a type of legalism that is condemned by Scripture. But I do think a recognition of a biblical hierarchy of rules and principles can help us determine our duty.

moral action. Love requires the further specification of principles or rules that suggest the proper ways in which love should be manifested. Because human beings are fallen creatures whose judgments on important moral matters may be affected by moral weakness, love needs guidance from divinely revealed moral truth. Fortunately, Christians believe, this content is provided in the moral principles revealed in Scripture.

In spite of all this, life often confronts us with ambiguous moral situations in which even the most sincere among us can agonize over what to do. There are times when we just do not know enough about ourselves, the situation, or the moral principle that applies to be sure we are doing the right thing. As many of us also know, weakness of will can also hinder moral decision-making.

In the unambiguous situations of life, Scripture teaches, God judges us in terms of our obedience to his revealed moral law. But how does God judge us in more ambiguous situations where the precise nature of our duty is unclear? God looks upon the heart, Scripture advises. We are judged if we break God's commandments—this is certain. But in those cases where we may not know which commandment applies or where we may have incomplete knowledge of the situation, God's judgment will take into account not merely the rightness of our act's consequences (something that we ourselves are often unable to determine in such ambiguous situations) but the goodness of our intentions.

ANTHROPOLOGY

William J. Abraham provides some remarks that can serve as an introduction to the complex subject of what the Christian world-view teaches about human beings.

> Human beings are made in the image of God, and their fate depends on their relationship with God. They are free to respond to or reject God and they will be judged in accordance with how they respond to him. This judgment begins now but finally takes place beyond death in a life to come. Christians furthermore offer a diagnosis of what is wrong with the world. Fundamentally, they say, our problems are spiritual: we need to be made anew by God. Human beings have misused their freedom; they are in a state of rebellion against God; they are sinners. These conclusions lead to a set of solutions to this ill. As one might expect, the fundamental solution is again spiritual. . . . in Jesus of Nazareth God has intervened to save and remake mankind. Each individual needs to respond to this and become part of Christ's body, the church, where they are to grow in grace and become more like Christ. This in turn generates a certain vision of the future. In the coming of Jesus, God has inaugurated his kingdom, but it will be consummated at some unspecified time in the future when Christ returns.[17]

What a paradox humankind is! The only bearers of the image of God on planet earth are also capable of the most heinous acts. As Pascal put it, "What a freak, what a monster, what a chaos, what a subject of contradic-

---

[17]William J. Abraham, *An Introduction to the Philosophy of Religion* (Englewood Cliffs, N.J.: Prentice-Hall, 1985), pp. 104, 105.

tion, what a marvel! Judge of all things, and imbecile earthworm; possessor
of the truth, and sink of uncertainty and error; glory and rubbish of the
universe."[18] In another passage, Pascal wrote,

> Man is but a reed, the weakest in nature, but he is a thinking reed. The
> whole universe need not arm itself to crush him; a vapor, a drop of water
> is enough to kill him. But even though the universe should crush him,
> man would still be nobler than what kills him since he knows that he dies,
> and the advantage that the universe has over him; the universe knows
> nothing of it.[19]

The essential paradox here—the greatness and the misery—of humankind flows out of two important truths. God created humans as the apex of
his creation; our chief end, in the words of the Westminster Catechism, is to
glorify God and enjoy him forever. But each human being is fallen, is in
rebellion against the God who created him and loves him.

Christianity simply will not make sense to people who fail to
understand and appreciate the Christian doctrine of sin. Every human being
lives in a condition of sin and alienation from his or her Creator. Each has
sinned and fallen short of God's standard (Rom. 3:23). As John Stott
counsels, sin "is not a convenient invention of parsons to keep them in their
job; it is a fact of human experience."[20] The sin that separates us from God
and enslaves us

> is more than an unfortunate outward act of habit; it is a deep-seated
> inward corruption. In fact, the sins we commit are merely outward and
> visible manifestations of this inward and invisible malady, the symptoms
> of a moral disease. . . . Because sin is an inward corruption of human
> nature we are in bondage. It is not so much certain acts or habits which
> enslave us, but rather the evil infection from which these spring.[21]

In the writings of the nineteenth-century Christian writer Søren
Kierkegaard, human alienation from God often rises to the surface in the
form of moods like despair. As Kierkegaard described it in his rather
technical way, two aspects of human existence (the finite/temporal and the
infinite/eternal) compete for dominance in the life of every human being.
Unless a person succeeds in getting these two dimensions into proper
relation and manages somehow to unify them, he or she will never really be
a self. Apart from God, each human being is a divided self.

Clearly, each of us is finite in many respects. We are limited and
restricted by our bodies, by our circumstances, by our surroundings, by our
weakness of will. A constant and unavoidable reminder of the limitations of
our existence is provided by death—the actual death of others and the
realization of the inevitability of our own death. But there is also another side
to our existence, a side that takes on dimensions of infinity or eternity. For
one thing, our desires seem to transcend the finite limitations of our bodies.
We always desire more than we have; we always want more than we can

[18]Blaise Pascal, *Selections from The Thoughts*, trans. Arthur H. Beattie (New York: Appleton-Century-Crofts, 1965), p. 68.
[19]Ibid., p. 30.
[20]John Stott, *Basic Christianity* (Grand Rapids: Eerdmans, 1967), p. 61.
[21]Ibid., pp. 75, 76.

possibly achieve. No matter what we have accomplished or attained in the way of fame, fortune, pleasure, or happiness, we want more. In a very real sense, our appetites are never satisfied. This is not to ignore times when thoroughly satiated individuals pause, momentarily content with the most recent satisfaction of their desires. But the contentment soon disappears, and they are back on the trail, searching for more.

The frustration resulting from the human inability to ultimately satisfy all desires is just one manifestation of the tension between the finite and infinite poles of our being. Another example is the tendency of many individuals to seek escape from reality through flights of fantasy. Rather than confront the truth about the closed frontiers of their existence, many people prefer to live in a world of dreams and illusions. In spite of their physical age, such people suffer from lifelong immaturity. They never really grow up.

Because most people never succeed in pulling the finite and infinite sides of their being together, they go through life suffering the spiritual and emotional consequences of being divided selves. Despair is one result of the failure to put the various parts of one's life together. Despair is essentially enthusiasm that has gone astray, that has lost its bearings; it is a zeal for things that either disappear when they are most wanted or fail to deliver all that they seem to promise. If, in a person's unconscious, he or she begins to feel that all the deepest yearnings of the soul will eventually end up unsatisfied, the onset of despair makes a kind of perverse sense. It is perfectly understandable how one's unconscious, under these conditions, might react by repressing enthusiasm, thus producing the mood of despair.

The victim of moods like despair is frequently unaware of the problem. Kierkegaard clearly thought that despair is often unconscious. The individual senses dimly that something is wrong, without ever being able to put a finger on it. The great extent to which despair functions in human lives below the level of consciousness may be one more result of the refusal of many people to face the truth about themselves and their world. The truly unhappy person who mistakenly believes himself or herself happy tends to regard everyone who threatens that illusion as an enemy.

Moods like despair are also indications that the major source of human trouble lies within, not in external circumstances. Consider the contrast in the writings of St. Paul between *sins*, the overt acts, and *sin*, the depraved nature within. Human beings are not self-sufficient; we cannot cure ourselves. We can become selves, we can grow up and develop into complete human beings only through a proper relationship with God. The finite and infinite must be joined from without, by God himself. Despair is only one symptom of estrangement from God and consequently from the self. Divided selves can achieve the unity of selfhood only in a faith-relationship with God.

One final aspect of Kierkegaard's analysis deserves attention. Moods like despair indicate

> that people are not wholly or ultimately made for this world. There is "something eternal" in us. We are to find the fulfillment of our passion for meaning and security, which is expressed in a distorted way by our typical immersion in these worldly projects, in a realm which is not subject to disappearance. A human being is not an absurdity, a futile passion, doomed either to repression or the most poignant unhappiness.

He is, rather, a wayward child of God, whose restlessness and anxiety and despair can and should drive him into the arms of his Father. His despair is indeed a sickness, but it is curable when he finds his true home.[22]

The eternal factor that God has implanted within leaves all of us ultimately frustrated, unhappy, and restless until we finally enter into his rest. As Augustine put it, God has made us for himself, and our hearts are restless until they rest in him. Human beings are driven to seek an eternal peace, in which everything will finally be in its proper place, in which perfect order both in the world and in the soul will be attained. Despair may be one way God informs us that we are to look beyond ourselves for our ultimate peace. It is one of several moods and affective states that ought to remind alert people that we should know better than to think that our highest good can be found in this life.

The Christian world-view recognizes the human need for forgiveness and redemption and stresses that the blessings of salvation are possible because of Jesus' death and resurrection. Christ's redemptive work is the basis of human salvation. But human beings are required to repent (be sorry) of sins and believe. Accepting Christ as one's Lord and Savior brings about a new birth, a new heart, a new relationship with God, and a new power to live.[23] Christian conversion does not suddenly make the new Christian perfect. But the Christian has God's nature and Spirit within and is called to live a particular kind of life in obedience to God's will. Finally, the Christian world-view teaches, physical death is not the end of personal existence.

CHRISTIANITY'S "TOUCHSTONE PROPOSITION"

Even my short outline of the Christian world-view may seem involved to some readers. Is it possible to boil everything down to one proposition? In this connection, William Halverson makes an interesting comment:

> At the center of every world-view is what might be called the "touchstone proposition" of that world-view, a proposition that is held to be *the* fundamental truth about reality and serves as a criterion to determine which other propositions may or may not count as candidates for belief. If a given proposition P is seen to be inconsistent with the touchstone proposition or one's world-view, then so long as one holds that world-view, proposition P must be regarded as false.[24]

There is value in seeing how Halverson's suggestion applies to what has already been said about the Christian world-view. Is there one touchstone proposition or control-belief or ultimate presupposition that is the fundamental truth of this particular world-view and that also serves as the test that any belief must pass before it can be included as part of the world-view?

---

[22]Robert C. Roberts, "The Transparency of Faith," *The Reformed Journal* (June 1979), p. 11.

[23]See John 3:3–21; Galatians 2:20; Hebrews 8:10–12; and 1 John 3:1–2.

[24]William H. Halverson, *A Concise Introduction to Philosophy*, 3d. ed. (New York: Random House, 1976), p. 384.

One proposition that certainly seems to fill the bill is the following: "Human beings and the universe in which they reside are the creation of the God who has revealed himself in Scripture."[25] The basic presupposition of the Christian world-view is the existence of the God revealed in Scripture.

This linkage between God and the Scriptures is quite proper. It is true, naturally, that this particular touchstone proposition allows the Christian ready access to all that Scripture says about God, the world, and humankind. While that is certainly an advantage, it is hardly an unfair advantage. What would be both unwise and unfair would be any attempt to separate the Christian God from his self-disclosure. As Carl F. H. Henry points out, God is not "a nameless spirit awaiting post-mortem examination in some theological morgue. He is a very particular and specific divinity, known from the beginning solely on the basis of his works and self-declaration as the one living God."[26]

Any final decision regarding the existence of the Christian God and the truth of the Christian world-view will necessarily involve decisions about a number of issues related to the Christian Scriptures. Since the details of that world-view flow from the Christian's ultimate authority, any negative reaction to one will likely produce a negative reaction to the other. Of course, to turn the coin over, a positive evaluation of one side of this equation should bear positively on the other. The Christian cannot pretend that his world-view was formulated in a revelational vacuum.

A COMPETING WORLD-VIEW

The major competition to the Christian world-view in the part of the world normally thought of as Christendom is a system that often goes by the name of Naturalism.[27] The touchstone proposition or basic presupposition of Naturalism states: "Nothing exists outside the material, mechanical (that is, nonpurposeful), natural order." William Halverson unpacks some of the details of this system:

> Naturalism asserts, first of all, that the primary constituents of reality are material entities. By this I do not mean that only material entities exist; I am not denying the reality—the real existence—of such things as hopes, plans, behavior, language, logical inferences, and so on. What I am asserting, however, is that anything that is real is, in the last analysis, explicable as a material entity or as a form or function or action of a material entity.[28]

What about God and the notion of creation? Halverson explains:

[25]By Scripture, I mean of course the canonical books of the Old and New Testaments.

[26]Carl F. H. Henry, *God, Revelation and Authority*, vol. 2: *God Who Speaks and Shows* (Waco, Tex.: Word, 1976), p. 7.

[27]In the discussion that follows, my primary objective is to provide a brief, simple overview of Naturalism. If a more detailed analysis were possible, I would point out that Naturalism may, in fact, appear in different packages that may use different language and emphasize different points. For more on this subject, see chapter 18.

[28]Halverson, *Concise Introduction to Philosophy*, p. 394.

Theism says, "In the beginning, God"; naturalism says, "In the beginning, matter." If the theoretical goal of science—an absolutely exhaustive
knowledge of the natural world—were to be achieved, there would
remain no reality of any other kind about which we might still be
ignorant. The "ultimate realities," according to naturalism, are not the
alleged objects of the inquiries of theologians; they are the entities that are
the objects of investigations by chemists, physicists, and other scientists.
To put the matter very simply: materialism is true.[29]

The second major implication of Naturalism's touchstone proposition is
that the universe is a closed system. As Halverson puts it,

Naturalism asserts, second, that what happens in the world is theoretically explicable without residue in terms of the internal structures and the
external relations of these material entities. The world is, to use a very
inadequate metaphor, like a gigantic machine whose parts are so
numerous and whose processes are so complex that we have thus far
been able to achieve only a very partial and fragmentary understanding of
how it works. In principle, however, everything that occurs is ultimately
explicable in terms of the properties and relations of the particles of which
matter is composed. Once again the point may be stated simply:
determinism is true.[30]

The universe is a closed system in the sense that everything that
happens "within the universe" is caused by or explained by other natural
events "within the system."[31] Hence, there is never need to seek the
explanation of anything that exists in some alleged reality that lies "outside"
the natural order. Nature then can be viewed as a type of closed box.
Nothing that occurs within the box (nature) requires a cause or explanation
of anything that lies "outside" the box.[32] A consistent naturalist will view
human beings as part of this great deterministic machine.

Given these presuppositions, it is small wonder that people influenced
by Naturalism object to major elements of the Christian world-view. Any
naturalist is precluded from believing in God, spirit, soul, angels, miracles,
prayer, providence, immortality, heaven, sin, and salvation as Christians
normally understand these notions for one simple reason: such beliefs are
logically incompatible with the naturalist's world-view.

It is difficult to see any common ground between these two competing
systems. It is small wonder, then, that committed and consistent advocates of
these two antithetic systems have difficulty carrying on a dialogue in any
meaningful way. Fortunately, it is possible for there to be common ground
between individual persons. While the basic presuppositions of these two
systems clash at every point, the adherents of these competing world-views

---

[29] Ibid.

[30] Ibid.

[31] "Within the system" is one of several possibly misleading expressions that often
have to be used in such accounts. Actually, naturalists believe there is nothing that
exists "outside" nature. The word nature includes everything that exists. "If you cannot
locate something in space and time, or if you cannot understand it as a form or
function of some entity or entities located in space and time, then you simply cannot
say anything intelligible about it. To be is to be some place, some time" (Halverson,
Concise Introduction to Philosophy, p. 394).

[32] Once again, since the box is all that exists, there is nothing "outside" the box.

may share enough in common to leave open at least the possibility of discussion, dialogue, and perhaps even a little persuasion. Unless such common ground at the level of individual persons (not systems) does exist, there is no point in advocates of competing systems trying to reason with each other. Perhaps representatives of different world-views will find common ground in the laws of logic; possibly they may agree about the moral correctness of some action or cause; perhaps they can touch base with regard to something like a parent's love for her child.

The apologist for the Christian world-view will attempt to show the naturalist how beliefs or values that are important to the naturalist cannot easily be assimilated into his world-view. Of course, the apologist for Naturalism will try to do the same sort of thing to the Christian. As William Halverson explains, it is impossible to predict how people will respond to challenges to their world-view:

> Suppose, now that the holder of a certain world-view encounters some fact that he cannot incorporate into it, and suppose further that he is unable to think of any way in which he can modify his world-view to accommodate the new fact. What are his options? He may retain his world-view and acknowledge that he has an unresolved problem on his hands, or he may abandon his world-view altogether in favor of another that appears to him to be more adequate to the facts as he perceives them.[33]

Halverson is correct in noting how people respond to such challenges, but his account oversimplifies things by ignoring the extent to which humans can be influenced by nontheoretical considerations. In many cases, there is more going on than a simple exchange of information followed by totally objective, detached reasoning to some conclusion. One of the imponderables in all such exchanges concerns the personal, nontheoretical, and nonrational influences in the other person's life. It should hardly be surprising, then, that all arguing in such matters will have an unavoidable personal dimension. The very same argument or approach or line of reasoning that is so fruitful with one person may fail with another.[34]

The Christian world-view's major competitor in the West is Naturalism.[35] It helps to remember two things about Naturalism. (1) It can assume different forms or use different language; sometimes it can require a little effort to unmask the naturalistic presuppositions underlying a particular system. (2) Assorted naturalists can be inconsistent, just like everyone else.

---

[33]Halverson, *Concise Introduction to Philosophy*, p. 385.

[34]The person-relative character of arguments and proofs will be examined in more detail in a later chapter.

[35]This claim is, of course, a generalization. Christian theism's competition assumes both religious and nonreligious forms. Its religious competitors include variations of the major world religions, many of which are increasingly influential in the nations of the West. For a discussion of a different kind of religious challenge, see Douglas R. Groothuis, *Unmasking the New Age* (Downers Grove, Ill.: InterVarsity Press, 1986), and Norman L. Geisler and J. Yutaka Amano, *The Reincarnation Sensation* (Wheaton, Ill.: Tyndale, 1986). The movements described in these books often exhibit the influence of Eastern religions. Needless to say, even disputes between Christianity and such religious competitors will have to be dealt with on the level of world-views.

Therefore, it is possible that particular naturalists may cling to beliefs (especially beliefs about normative matters) that are logically incompatible with, or cannot be justified in terms of, their touchstone proposition.

If we grant that there is merit in calling the world-view described in the previous section Naturalism, there may be equal merit in describing the Christian world-view as a form of Supernaturalism. To be sure, the term *Supernaturalism* does have its disadvantages, due largely to its frequent association with the fantastic novels and movies of such authors as Stephen King. But if we can free the word from all such associations, it can be useful in pointing to the fact that the naturalist's picture of reality is incomplete. Reality is not a closed box or system; the universe is not forever closed to reordering from a level of reality more ultimate than nature. There is a reality that transcends the natural and that reorders the natural from "outside." The word *supernatural* is a perfectly good term to describe such a reality.

CONCLUSION

While all mature thinking persons have a world-view, many of them are unaware of the fact. People often evidence great difficulty attaining consciousness of key elements of their world-view. Most of us know individuals who seldom think deeply enough to ask the right questions about God, metaphysics, epistemology, ethics, and anthropology. One of the important tasks for philosophers, theologians, and apologists (and the like) is first to get people to realize that they do have a conceptual system. The second step is to help people get a clearer fix on the content of their world-view. What do they believe about the existence and nature of God, about humankind, morality, knowledge, and ultimate reality? The third step is to help people evaluate their world-view and either improve it (by removing inconsistencies and filling in gaps) or replace it with a better world-view. In the next chapter, I will examine recommendations regarding the best or most promising way to go about making a choice among competing world-views.

For Further Exploration—Chapter Three
1. Explain the differences between theism and polytheism, pantheism and panentheism.
2. Explain creation *ex nihilo*. Discuss its significance for both theology and philosophy.
3. Why should an apologist avoid discrediting sense experience?
4. Explain what some philosophers call our human belief-forming mechanisms. What did Thomas Reid teach about these dispositions?
5. Explain the distinction between moral principles and rules; identify a few examples of this distinction in the Bible.
6. Explain and evaluate situation ethics.
7. Present your reaction to what the Christian world-view teaches about human sin.
8. Explain the touchstone proposition of the Christian world-view.
9. Explain and evaluate Naturalism.

Chapter 4

HOW TO CHOOSE
A WORLD-VIEW

Christian theism is only one of a number of competing conceptual systems. On what grounds can people make a reasoned choice among world-views? Which world-view is most likely to be true? What is the best or most promising way to approach this kind of question?

When faced with a choice among competing touchstone propositions of different world-views, we should choose the one that, when applied to the whole of reality, gives us the most coherent picture of the world. After all, Gordon Clark explains, "If one system can provide plausible solutions to many problems while another leaves too many questions unanswered, if one system tends less to skepticism and gives more meaning to life, if one world-view is consistent while others are self-contradictory, who can deny us, since we must choose, the right to choose the more promising first principle?"[1] The purpose of this chapter is to pursue this general line of thought and fill in some of the necessary details.

TESTING A WORLD-VIEW

From one perspective, there are six criteria by which we should test world-views. Because there is merit in seeing the relationships among these criteria, they can also be treated as three groups of two, namely, (1) the tests of reason and exerience, (2) the tests of the outer world and the inner world, and (3) the tests of theory and practice. It is possible to reduce the number of tests still further because they obviously overlap. For example, the tests

---

[1] Gordon C. Clark, *A Christian View of Men and Things* (Grand Rapids: Eerdmans, 1952), p. 34.

grouped under (1) and (2) can be viewed as extensions of the theoretical test of category (3) while the tests of the outer and inner worlds are extensions of experience. If a diagram is any help in this matter, the tests I'll be discussing are related as follows:

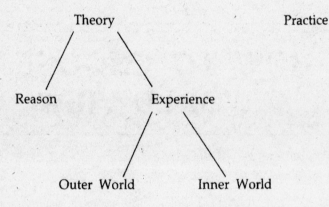

It is also possible to regard all six criteria as elaborations of one basic test, coherence. The term *coherence* points to the fact that the various elements of the world-view should hang together internally and should fit all that we know about reality.

THE TESTS OF REASON AND EXPERIENCE

Reason

What I mean by the test of reason is logic or the law of noncontradiction. Since contradiction is always a sign of error, we have a right to expect a conceptual system to be logically consistent, both in its parts (its individual propositions) and in the whole. A conceptual system is in obvious trouble if it fails to hang together logically.

Logical incoherence can be more or less fatal depending on whether the contradiction exists among less central beliefs or whether it lies at the very heart of the system. It is because of this second, more serious, kind of failing that such systems as skepticism and solipsism self-destruct.[2] While truly committed skeptics and solipsists are fortunately few and far between, the history of philosophy contains other examples of internally inconsistent positions or systems that found rather wide acceptance, at least for a time.

---

[2] The self-defeating nature of skepticism can be seen as follows. If the skeptic states that no one can know anything, one need merely ask the skeptic if *he* knows that no one can know anything. On the other hand, if the skeptic affirms the proposition that "No propositions are true," one need only ask him if *his* proposition is true. Either the skeptic will contradict himself by claiming his view as the one exception to what obtains for everyone else, or he will slink away in silence after admitting that his own touchstone proposition is false or unknowable.

A solipsist is a person who claims that he alone exists. To whom, one may ask, does he make this claim?

One example of such a system is the Logical Positivism that was so popular in Western Europe, Great Britain, and the United State during the 1930s and 1940s.[3]

The touchstone proposition of Logical Positivism was something called the verification principle. Logical positivists thought they had discovered a criterion of meaningfulness that would exclude all kinds of claims that gave them trouble, for example, statements like "God exists." Only two kinds of propositions can have meaning, the positivists argued: those that are true because of the meaning of their constituent terms (called analytic statements)[4] and those that are verifiable by sense experience (called synthetic statements). Positivists delighted in showing, or so they thought, that theological, metaphysical, and ethical statements failed to meet either criterion of meaningfulness. And so, because such statements were neither analytic (true or false by virtue of the meanings of their words) nor synthetic (true or false because they were verifiable by experience), they were discarded as meaningless. This meant that statements like "God exists" were neither true nor false; they were meaningless!

The positivists used their verification principle like a sledgehammer, smashing a great many of the traditional positions in philosophy including beliefs about God, the soul, and morality. At least they did so until people began to ask about the cognitive status of the positivists' hallowed principle. What kind of statement is *it*? As things turned out, the positivists' criterion of meaning showed itself to be meaningless, since it could be classified as neither an analytic nor a synthetic statement. Efforts to rescue the verification principle failed.[5] And so today, it is quite difficult to find any philosopher who is willing to claim publicly the label of Logical Positivism. The movement is dead and quite properly so.

Many philosophers have argued that determinism, an essential element of Naturalism, is self-refuting. According to J. R. Lucas, if what the determinist says is true,

> he says it merely as the result of his heredity and environment, and of nothing else. He does not hold his determinist views because they are true, but because he has such-and-such stimuli; that is, not because the *structure* of the universe is such-and-such but only because the configuration of only part of the universe, together with the structure of the determinist's brain, is such as to produce that result. . . . Determinism, therefore, cannot be true, because if it was, we should not take the determinists' arguments as being really arguments, but as being only conditioned reflexes. Their statements should not be regarded as really

---

[3] The book that came to be regarded as the most influential statement of Logical Positivism was A. J. Ayer's *Language, Truth and Logic* (London: Gollancz, 1936).

[4] Examples of analytic statements include tautologies like "Some spinsters are unmarried ladies" (which are necessarily true) and contradictions like "Some spinsters are married ladies" (which are necessarily false). An example of a synthetic statement would be "some spinsters drive American-made cars."

[5] One could spend years reading nothing but criticisms of Logical Positivism. Two critiques of the verification principle from different perspectives are Alvin Plantinga, *God and Other Minds* (Ithaca: Cornell University Press, 1967), and Brand Blanshard, *Reason and Analysis* (La Salle, Ill.: Open Court, 1962).

claiming to be true, but only as seeking to cause us to respond in some way desired by them.[6]

H. P. Owen agrees that

determinism is self-stultifying. If my mental processes are totally determined, I am totally determined either to accept or to reject determinism. But if the sole reason for my believing or not believing X is that I am causally determined to believe it I have no ground for holding that my judgment is true or false.[7]

J. P. Moreland is one of many philosophers who claim that physicalism, another corollary of Naturalism, is also self-refuting. Physicalism is the position that "the only thing which exists is matter (where matter is defined by an ideal, completed form of physics)."[8] According to a physicalist view of man, Moreland observes, "a human being is just a physical system. There is no mind or soul, just a brain and central nervous system."[9] Now, Moreland continues, "if one claims to know that physicalism is true, or to embrace it for good reasons, if one claims that [physicalism] is a rational position, which should be chosen on the basis of evidence, then this claim is self-refuting."[10] Moreland's reason for saying this is that physicalism implies that rationality is impossible. Moreland's summary of his argument is impressive for both its brevity and its power:

In sum, it is self-refuting to *argue* that one *ought* to *choose* physicalism *because* he should *see* that the *evidence* is good for physicalism. Physicalism cannot be offered as a rational theory because physicalism does away with the necessary preconditions for there to be such a thing as rationality. Physicalism usually denies intentionality [the capacity to have thoughts *about* other things] by reducing it to a physical relation of input/output, thereby denying that the mind is genuinely capable of having thoughts *about* the world. Physicalism denies the existence of propositions and nonphysical laws of logic and evidence which can be in minds and influence thinking. Physicalism denies the existence of a faculty capable of rational insight into these nonphysical laws and propositions, and it denies the existence of an enduring "I" which is present through the process of reflection. Finally, it denies the existence of a genuine agent who deliberates and chooses positions because they are rational, an act possible only if physical factors are not sufficient for determining future behavior.[11]

---

[6] J. R. Lucas, *Freedom of the Will* (Oxford: Clarendon Press, 1970), pp. 114–15.

[7] H. P. Owen, *Christian Theism* (Edinburgh: T and T Clark, 1984), p. 118.

[8] J. P. Moreland, *Scaling the Secular City* (Grand Rapids: Baker, 1987), p. 78.

[9] Ibid.

[10] Ibid., p. 92.

[11] Ibid., p. 96. Moreland astutely notes that his argument against physicalism does not commit what is sometimes called the genetic fallacy. According to this fallacy, it is a mistake to infer the falseness of a belief because of problems connected with the origin of the belief. Moreland's argument against physicalism, as he explains, "is not an example of the genetic fallacy, for in order for there to even be such a fallacy, one must be able to distinguish the process of the origin of a belief (including the psychology of discovery) from the rational justification of that belief. But if *all* the factors which cause our beliefs are physical, then such a distinction is itself

World-views, then, should be submitted to the appropriate rational test, the law of noncontradiction. Inconsistency is always a sign of error. As noted, some philosophical positions or systems seem to self-destruct in the sense that they are internally self-defeating. The charge has been leveled against at least two major tenets of the naturalistic world-view, namely, determinism and physicalism. Clearly, the charge of inconsistency should be taken seriously.[12] Unless proponents of a world-view can successfully rebut the charge, they ought to regard their system as being terminally ill.

For all its importance, however, the test of logical consistency can never be the only criterion by which we evaluate world-views. At most, logic can be only a negative test. While the presence of a contradiction will alert us to the presence of error, the absence of contradiction does not guarantee the presence of truth. For that, we need other criteria.

Experience

What I have to say about this subject can be stated briefly. Just as a conceptual system must pass the test of reason, it must also satisfy the test of experience. We have a right to expect world-views to touch base with human experience. World-views should throw light on our experiences of the world. They should explain our experiences easily and naturally. They should be relevant to what we know about the world and ourselves.

A number of world-view beliefs fall short of this test, in my opinion. They include the following:

1. God created the world six thousand years ago.
2. Pain and death are illusions.
3. All of reality is an illusion.
4. All human beings are innately good.
5. Miracles are impossible.[13]

I do not want my position on this subject misunderstood. I do not believe that the exclusive test of truth-claims is their conformity with human observation.[14] I am not an empiricist; that is, I do not believe that all human knowledge begins with sense experience.[15] Nor do I assume that humans are always capable of approaching sense-information in an impersonal and detached way. And I certainly do not believe that proponents of competing world-views will always interpret the same sense-information in the same way. But I do insist on taking the common sense view that no world-view deserves respect if it ignores or is inconsistent with human experience. I also insist, however, that the human expeience we consider when evaluating

---

impossible, for there would be no rational factors or rational agents which could be affected by them" (Ibid., p. 229).

[12] Later in this book, I will examine attempts to uncover a contradiction at the heart of Christian theism. This charge, made in connection with the problem of evil, can be answered.

[13] My assessment of such matters persuades me that there is sufficient evidence in some cases to substantiate that miracles have occurred.

[14] That should be clear because of what I say about reason as a test.

[15] See *The Word of God and the Mind of Man* (Grand Rapids: Zondervan, 1982), especially chap. 7.

world-views be broad enough to include experience of the outer and inner worlds.

THE TESTS OF THE OUTER AND INNER WORLDS

My language in this section should not be understood in a way that suggests I view the human being as some kind of "ghost in a machine." Phrases like *outer world, inner world,* and *the world outside us* are simply metaphors that come naturally to all of us who do not, at the moment, happen to be reading a paper to a philosophy seminar. My language is not intended to imply any particular metaphysical theory (for example, an opinion with regard to the mind-body problem) or epistemological view (such as a representative theory of sense-perception). To use a rather fancy term, my language is *phenomenological language,* that is, it describes the way different things appear to us. My experience of my typewriter at this moment is *of* an object that appears to exist outside of and independent of my consciousness or awareness of the typewriter. My consciousness of my own mental states (expressible in propositions like "I am hungry") is *of* something that most people can describe quite comfortably as belonging to their inner world. As long as the language is understood in a nonliteral way, there is no problem.

The Outer World

The test of the outer world can be handled quickly since my major objective in this section is to point out that there is more to human experience than our experience of the outer world. It is quite proper for a scientist to object when some world-view conflicts with what he knows is an empirically verified statement about the world. This is one reason why none of the readers of this book, I trust, believe the world is flat. It does appear, however, that many people who make strong public pronouncements about the importance of testing the claims of Christianity (and other world-views) against the reports of our senses (the outer world) fail to give proper credit to a large set of experiential claims that provide information about people's conscious states (the inner world).

The Inner World

World-views should fit what we know about the external world. But they also need to fit what we know about ourselves. Examples of this second kind of information include the following: I am a being who thinks, hopes, experiences pleasure and pain, believes, desires. I am also a being who is often conscious of right and wrong and who feels guilty and sinful for having failed to do what was right. I am a being who remembers the past, is conscious of the present, and anticipates the future. I can think about things that do not exist. I can plan and then execute my plans. I am able to act intentionally; instead of merely responding to stimuli, I can will to do something and then actually do it. I am a person who loves other human beings. I can empathize with others and share their sorrow and joy. I know that someday I will die; and I have faith that I will survive the death of my body. And as I explained in an earlier chapter, I seem often to be overcome by moods and emotions that suggest that the ultimate satisfaction I seek is unattainable in this life.

One example of how the test of the inner world can be put to good use is C. S. Lewis's book, *Mere Christianity*.[16] Lewis began his book by getting his readers to reflect on their own moral consciousness. Each human being makes distinctions between right and wrong. Even people who profess to be ethical relativists act contrary to their profession when they themselves have been wronged. When someone wrongs us, our protests make it clear that we believe the other person is aware of the same moral law. What interests Lewis about the remarks people make when they quarrel is this:

> the man who makes them is not merely saying that the other man's behaviour does not happen to please him. He is appealing to some kind of standard of behaviour which he expects the other man to know about. And the other man very seldom replies: "To hell with your standard." Nearly always he tries to make out that what he has been doing does not really go against the standard, or that if it does there is some special excuse. He pretends there is some special reason in this particular case why the person who took the seat first should not keep it, or that things were quite different when he was given the bit of orange, or that something has turned up which lets him off keeping his promise. It looks, in fact, very much as if both parties had in mind some kind of Law or Rule of fair play or decent behaviour or morality or whatever you like to call it, about which they really agreed. And they have. If they had not, they might, of course, fight like animals, but they could not *quarrel* in the human sense of the word. Quarrelling means trying to show that the other man is in the wrong. And there would be no sense in trying to do that unless you and he had some sort of agreement as to what Right and Wrong are; just as there would be no sense in saying that a footballer had committed a foul unless there was some agreement about the rules of football.[17]

What conditions best explain the fact of human moral consciousness? What world-view best accounts for this information about our inner world? Lewis goes on to test several competing world-views in terms of their adequacy as an explanation for this phenomenon. He dismisses materialistic views of the universe because they cannot account for moral consciousness. He rejects pantheism because a pantheistic God is beyond good and evil; no real moral distinctions are possible in a pantheistic universe. He rejects dualism (the belief in two coequal and coeternal deities, one good and the other evil) because it cannot explain how we know which of the two ultimate principles is good.[18]

One reason why many tend to concentrate on the outer world as the major empirical test of world-views may be the difficulties that accompany efforts to look "inward."

> When formulating a philosophy of life, I contend that the least accessible fact, and thus the most baffling to isolate and classify, is the complex

---

[16] C. S. Lewis, *Mere Christianity* (New York: Macmillan, 1960), especially Book 1.
[17] Ibid., pp. 17–18.
[18] Ibid., Book 2, chap. 1. Of course, there cannot be two ultimate principles. Such a claim contradicts the meaning of *ultimate*.

moral and spiritual environment of the philosopher himself. Most efforts at abstraction fail to impress the common man because sages seldom take time to interpret life from within the center of their own perspective as individuals. . . . A world view remains truncated to the degree that a thinker fails to deal with data gained by a humble participation in the moral and spiritual environment. . . . What it means to be held in a moral and spiritual environment can only be learned as one acquaints himself with the realities that already hold him from existence itself. This pilgrimmage into inwardness is a painfully personal responsibility, for only the individual himself has access to the secrets of his moral and spiritual life.[19]

But no matter how hard it may be to look honestly at our inner self, we are right in being suspicious of those whose defense of a world-view ignores or rejects the inner world.

THE TESTS OF THEORY AND PRACTICE

Theory

Once again, I can be brief. What I mean by this test includes everything already said about the tests of reason, experience, the outer world, and the inner world. But while there is an indisputable theoretical aspect to our testing of world-views, there is also more.

Practice

World-views should be tested not only in the philosophy classroom but also in the laboratory of life. It is one thing for a world-view to pass certain theoretical tests; it is another for that world-view also to pass an important practical test, namely, can the people who profess that world-view in theory also practice what they believe in their daily lives? Can a person *consistently* live the system he professes? Or do we find that he is forced to live according to beliefs borrowed from a competing system? Such a discovery, I suggest, should produce more than embarrassment.

This practical test played an important role in the work of the Christian thinker Francis Schaeffer. As Thomas Morris explains Schaeffer's position:

> No non-Christian can be consistent in the correspondence of at least some of their daily thoughts and actions with the relevant conclusions which would logically follow from their basic sets of presuppositions. The orientation of [Schaeffer's] position was that non-Christians would have a difficult time of consistently working out their presuppositions as they lived in the context of their own [inner world] and the external world.[20]

---

[19] Edward John Carnell, *The Case for Biblical Christianity*, ed. R. Nash (Grand Rapids: Eerdmans, 1969), p. 58.

[20] Thomas Morris, *Francis Schaeffer's Apologetics* (Grand Rapids: Baker, 1987), pp. 21–22. Schaeffer's work has been misunderstood, ironically enough, by a number of evangelical thinkers. For one attempt to set the record straight, see Ronald Nash, "The Life of the Mind and the Way of Life," in *Francis Schaeffer: Portraits of the Man and His Work*, ed. Lane T. Dennis (Westchester, Ill.: Crossway, 1986), chap. 3. Also worth consulting, in the same book, is the chapter by Lane Dennis titled "Schaeffer and His Critics."

Schaeffer's practical or existential test helped lay the foundation for his punch line:

> Only the presuppositions of historic Christianity both adequately explain and correspond with the two environments in which every man must live: the external world with its form and complexity; and the internal world of the man's own characteristics as a human being. This "inner world" includes such human qualities "as a desire for significance, love, and meaning, and fear of nonbeing, among others."[21]

One thing should be clear: any reader who comes to believe that Schaeffer's comments are true will have a powerful reason to accept the Christian world-view. We should keep his words in mind as we continue our journey.

A QUESTION ABOUT METHOD

In the first part of this chapter, I examined several different tests that can be used to support judgments about the adequacy of competing world-views. I now want to carry the matter of testing world-views a bit further by throwing light on the kind of method or procedure I am recommending. One thing in particular I want to make clear is that my method is *not* deductive.

History's most famous syllogism[22] begins with the general statement that "All men are mortal," provides a minor premise that is more specific ("Socrates is a man"), and ends with a conclusion ("Socrates is mortal"), the truth of which is already implicit in the premises. The validity of a deductive argument is a function of its form, not its content. That is, *any* argument that has the same logical form/23? as our famous model is valid, regardless of the particular words that may be substituted. The conclusion of a valid deductive argument never contains information that is not already present in the premises. The major advantage of any valid deductive argument is that it provides *logical certainty*. In the case of any valid argument, if the premises are true, then the conclusion *must* be true.[24]

Inductive reasoning also assumes a number of different forms. It may involve reasoning from a few specific cases to a generalization about the many. Or it may involve what is called analogical reasoning: because two

---

[21]Ibid., p. 21. In this paragraph, Morris is both paraphrasing and quoting Schaeffer.

[22]Deductive reasoning need not take the form of my famous example. Deductive reasoning may be hypothetical (If p, then q; p; therefore, q) or disjunctive in form (either p or q; not q; therefore, p). Obviously, this paragraph is not supposed to replace an entire textbook on logic.

[23]The logical form of our syllogism can be made clear by substituting letters for the terms of the original argument: All A is B; All B is C; therefore All A is C. Any argument having this form is valid. Other valid and invalid forms of the categorical syllogism are identified in standard logic texts.

[24]Every beginning logic student also learns that validity and truth should be distinguished. Truth (or falsity) is a property of the particular propositions that make up an argument. Validity (or invalidity) is a property of arguments. If the premises of a valid argument are true, then the conclusion must be true. But if one or more of an argument's premises are false, nothing may be inferred about the truth or falsity of the conclusion.

things are thought to be alike or analogous in one respect, one infers that
they are alike in another way. The key respect in which inductive reasoning
differs from deductive is the absence of logical certainty in inductive
thinking. The most that any inductive argument can provide is probability.

Since the method recommended in this chapter is not deductive, its
conclusions lack logical certainty; probability in this kind of reasoning is
unavoidable. Some people find this hard to understand and to accept. They
act as though recommending a procedure that provides "only" probability is
not simply suspicious; it is downright subversive. Since such judgments
manifest a clear misunderstanding of what is or is not possible in such
reasoning, it requires some comment. But before I make these comments, I
want to distinguish my approach from a few who have sought to provide
"certainty" by adopting a deductive approach.

Deductive Presuppositionalism

Gordon H. Clark (1902–85) was one of this century's more original,
influential, and important evangelical thinkers.[25] In addition to writings in
which he articulated and defended pivotal issues in philosophy and
theology, Clark developed a unique approach to apologetics that could be
called deductive presuppositionalism. It was presuppositional because, he
maintained, the Christian should not attempt to reason his way to God or to
prove God's existence; he should begin by presupposing the existence of the
God who has revealed himself in the Scriptures. Clark's presuppositionalism
was *deductive* in the sense that he treated his basic presupposition much like
a geometrical axiom. He then insisted on *deducing* everything else he knew
(and everything else he claimed that *anyone* could know) from Scripture.
Arthur Holmes describes Clark's method perfectly when he writes:

> Thus, from the information contained in the Scriptures we should be able
> to deduce an epistemology and a theory of language, and indeed the
> essential ingredients of an entire philosophic system. This is precisely
> what Clark tries to do in his writings, whether on education, epistemol-
> ogy and religious language, on political theory, or whatever. The
> Scriptures provide sufficient axioms for a complete deductive system.[26]

---

[25] Some of Clark's more important books are *A Christian View of Men and Things*
(Grand Rapids: Eerdmans, 1952); *Thales to Dewey* (Boston: Houghton, Mifflin Co.,
1956); and *Religion, Reason and Revelation* (Philadelphia: Presbyterian and Reformed,
1961). A complete Clark bibliography through 1968 can be found at the end of *The
Philosophy of Gordon H. Clark*, ed. Ronald Nash (Philadelphia: Presbyterian and
Reformed, 1968). The Trinity Foundation plans eventually to republish as many of
Clark's more than thirty books as possible. Their progress in this worthy project may
be traced by checking *Books in Print*. Though I part company with Clark on the issues
discussed in this chapter, his influence on my thought can be detected in a number of
my books including *The New Evangelicalism* (Grand Rapids: Zondervan, 1963); *Ideas of
History*, 2 vols. (New York: Dutton, 1969); *The Light of the Mind: St. Augustine's Theory
of Knowledge* (Lexington: University Press of Kentucky, 1969); and *The Word of God and
the Mind of Man* (Grand Rapids: Zondervan, 1982).

[26] Arthur Holmes, "The Philosophical Methodology of Gordon Clark," in *The
Philosophy of Gordon H. Clark*, ed. Nash, p. 219.

As I see it, Clark went too far on two key issues. First, he erred by viewing the Christian world-view as a deductive or axiomatic system like geometry. Second, he believed that human knowledge is limited to the propositions contained in the Bible or to propositions deduced from those in Scripture. According to Clark's deductive presuppositionalism, if some proposition is not actually revealed in Scripture or deducible from other propositions so revealed, it is unknowable by human beings. One major difficulty with Clark's theory is its obvious incompatibility with all kinds of human knowledge not attainable in the way he describes. I know, for example, that my wife exists; but I see no way of deducing the true proposition that reports her existence from anything in the Bible. I also know that in 1948, Lou Boudreau led his American League team in batting with an average of .355. Surely anyone who would deny that humans can know such propositions is using the word *knowledge* in a very idiosyncratic way.

Arthur Holmes sketches a proper response to Clark's extreme position:

> Philosophy as a part of life and an expression of faith is no purely logical science, abstracted from life, that proceeds unimpassionately. Philosophy done from any perspective is more like adducing meanings than deducing conclusions, more like expanding a world-hypothesis than working out a theorem, more like the elaboration of a vision or the etching in of a coherent picture than the operation of a computer. Other variables are at work than a specified set of presuppositions, variables which axiomatization cannot fully overcome but which are ingredient to the philosopher's historico-cultural situation, his individual existence, even to his particular heritage of faith and thought within the spectrum of Biblical Christianity.[27]

As this book explains, it is possible to describe Christianity as a logically coherent view without surrendering to the false model of deductive presuppositionalism. Some rather extreme followers of Clark (and the somewhat similar approaches of thinkers like Cornelius Van Til and Rousas Rushdoony) have gone so far as to suggest the need of deducing disciplines like mathematics and economics from the Bible. While such efforts, I think, constitute a *reductio ad absurdum* of deductive presuppositionalism, they should not detract from the value of other elements of Clark's splendid work.

Inductive Presuppositionalism

One way to clarify the difference between the deductive approach of Clark and myself is to describe my view as a kind of inductive presuppositionalism. Because inductive reasoning can proceed in so many different ways and because no single model or example totally captures what I want to say, I'm going to examine several types of reasoning that illustrate the approach I have in mind. I should add that I am hardly the first person to see value in these illustrations.

British philosopher Basil Mitchell has compared the testing of world-views to the way in which one seeks the correct interpretation of a written text.[28] Every student of the Bible and other great literature knows how

---

[27] Ibid.
[28] See Basil Mitchell, *The Justification of Religious Belief* (New York: Seabury, 1973), pp. 40ff.

difficult it can be sometimes to grasp the author's meaning in a particular phrase, sentence, or paragraph. The best interpretation is the one that gives the best account of the message of the entire text within its historical and literary context. Before a final interpretation is suggested, one should study carefully the vocabulary, the textual context, and the historical setting in which the text was written. The most likely interpretation is the one that fits best all the relevant information. No matter how carefully the interpreter does her work, no interpretation can ever achieve logical certainty. Competing interpretations will be more or less probable, depending on how well they fit.

The interpretation of historical events is another example of the kind of reasoning used in evaluating world-views. When Elizabeth I became queen of England in 1558, her official title read: "Elizabeth, by the Grace of God, Queen of England, France, and Spain, Defender of the Faith, etc."[29] This raises an interesting question. What is that "etc." doing in the queen's title? Here is something that seems to cry out for explanation. Ernest Nagel summarizes one historian's attempt to make sense of that "etc.":

> The legal historian F. W. Maitland proposed the following explanation. He first showed that the ["etc."] in the proclamation was not there by inadvertence but had been introduced deliberately. He also pointed out that Elizabeth was confronted with the alternatives either of acknowledging [with her sister, the late Queen Mary] the ecclesiastical supremacy of the Pope or of voiding the Marian statutes and breaking with Rome as her father had done—a decision for either alternative being fraught with grave perils, because the alignment of political and military forces both at home and abroad which favored each alternative was unsettled. Maitland therefore argued that in order to avoid committing herself to either alternative for the moment, Elizabeth employed an ambiguous formulation in the proclamation of her title—a formulation which could be made compatible with any decision she might eventually make. In consequence, according to his own succinct summary statement of the explanation, 'So we might expand the symbol thus: ["etc."]—and (if future events shall so decide, but no further or otherwise) of the Church of England and also of Ireland upon earth the Supreme Head.'[30]

The historian approaches his material much as the interpreter approaches his text. Both are confronted with the challenge to understand and to explain something. Both gather as much relevant information as they can. Both advance a theory or hypothesis; perhaps other interpreters and historians offer competing hypotheses. Maitland's hypothesis was that the appearance of the "etc." in Queen Elizabeth's title was not an accident or a sign of laziness on someone's part; it was there for a reason. And the reason is to be found in the perilous historical circumstances that obtained when Elizabeth ascended to the throne. To have laid claim explicitly to headship of the Church of England in 1558 would certainly have led to war with Spain and possible insurrection within England. To renounce any further claim to

---

[29] I have taken the liberty of changing spelling and punctuation to make the title easier to read.

[30] Ernest Nagel, *The Structure of Science* (New York: Harcourt, Brace & World, 1961), p. 552. Nagel's quote from Maitland comes from F. W. Maitland, "Elizabethan Gleanings," in *Collected Papers* (London, 1911), 3:157–65.

such authority over the English Church at that time seemed unwise. And so, Maitland theorized, Elizabeth decided to stall for time by including that apparently innocuous "etc." in her official title. Later, when future events made her options clearer and a final decision safer, she could announce all that the "etc." included. Is Maitland's interpretation correct? Any final decision depends on whether it fits all that we know about the times and about the make-up of Elizabeth's mind better than any rival interpretation. Once again, the most that any interpretation can hope to achieve is a high degree of probability.

A third analogy can be found in the processes by which fictional detectives like Sherlock Holmes and Hercule Poirot and aspiring amateur detectives like the House-Senate committee investigating the Iran-Contra affair go about solving mysteries. Most people who read the novels of Sir Arthur Conan Doyle and Agatha Christie attempt to "solve" the mystery before the correct answer is finally revealed. Consciously or unconsciously, the reader advances and withdraws various hypotheses (proposed solutions) as the plot unwinds. The disclosure of new information may disconfirm one theory and give greater plausibility to another. The correct answer is the one that fits best all the clues.

Thus far, one property characterizes the best textual interpretations, historical explanations, and solutions to mystery novels, namely, *coherence*. The best theory is the one that coheres best with everything else we know; the best interpretation, explanation, or answer is the one that fits best all the data.

Another example of my recommended procedure for evaluating world-views can be found in the way scientists seek an explanation for some phenomenon. When a scientist encounters a situation that requires explanation, he asks, What conditions make sense of this situation? He usually finds it necessary to consider a number of different possibilities. The various alternatives he examines become hypotheses, which are then confirmed or disconfirmed by how well they explain his phenomenon. This is similar to the way a literary scholar settles on the meaning of a text, to the way a historian reaches a decision about the explanation of a historical event, and to the way Sherlock Holmes solved a crime. Which explanation, which hypothesis, best makes sense of this situation? This procedure is similar to what goes on when we evaluate world-views. Honest inquirers say to themselves, *Here is what I know about the inner and outer worlds. Now which touchstone proposition, which world-view, does the best job of making sense out of all this?*

Literary scholars, historians, detectives, scientists, and world-view examiners who are good at their job don't stop with the first piece of information that confirms their theory; they keep looking. As the amount of confirmatory information increases, so too does the probability of the hypothesis increase. Taking a large number of observations together provides a cumulative case that enhances the likelihood that the hypothesis is true. Thomas Morris provides a helpful illustration:

> Suppose we are in a windowless room and we are considering two rival hypotheses: It is raining outside and It is sunny outside. There are many events that would be expected to occur if the rain hypothesis were true,

but not if the sun hypothesis were true, such as: water beating on the roof, a friend coming in soaked, water running in the street, etc. Suppose we hear the sound of water beating on the roof (an observation of one of the above events). This observation confirms and raises the probability of the rain hypothesis. Do we then *know* that the rain hypothesis is true, that it is raining outside?[31]

The answer, of course, is no. Even though we happen to hear water beating on the roof, it might be due to someone's using a hose to spray water on the roof. It is still possible, even though we hear water running off the roof, that the sun is shining outside. Morris continues,

Likewise, suppose that we see a friend enter the room soaking wet. This observation also confirms and raises the probability of the rain hypothesis, but neither does it prove conclusively that it is true. The man with the water hose could have drenched him. Finally, suppose that we hear the sound of passing cars on wet pavement. This would also be a confirming observation, but again not alone decisive, since it may be that the city street sweeper has just washed the street, and the weather itself is beautifully sunny. Although no one of the above observations would conclusively prove that it is raining outside, their cumulative effect would raise the probability of the rain hypothesis so high that we would be fully justified in believing that it is raining outside. This belief can be said to be a justified subjective response to and result of the cumulative probability given to the rain hypothesis by the three confirming observations.[32]

Morris is quick to admit that in our daily lives, we do not operate in terms of such a formal procedure. We do not consciously advance and then sort through competing hypotheses simply to reach a decision about whether the sun is shining outside. But, he concludes,

we do naturally react to the individual and cumulative effects of sights and sounds (etc.) in determining what is and what is not going on around us in our environment (broadly speaking). This is how we live daily. *There is a human capacity to naturally respond to evidences, confirmation, and probability without necessarily ever being consciously aware that this is what is going on.* Such a response is basic to every act of responsible decision making, whether decisions of physical action or of belief.[33]

If one hypothesis or explanation fits better with our observations of the inner and outer worlds, if one hypothesis makes better sense theoretically and existentially, would we not be foolish to reject it in favor of a hypothesis that fared less well?[34]

---

[31] Morris, *Schaeffer's Apologetics*, p. 96.

[32] Ibid., pp. 96–97.

[33] Ibid., p. 97.

[34] I don't want to press the analogy of a scientific hypothesis too far. For one thing, it would be a serious error to regard a faith-commitment to Jesus Christ as analogous to the way we sometimes put forward tentative hypotheses. But at the same time, faith in Jesus Christ and our belief in the truth of the Christian world-view *are* related to information and experiences that serve to confirm or disconfirm such belief. Jesus did not ask his followers to believe against all reason or in the absence of reason. On the contrary, he gave them reasons *to* believe. I discuss some aspects of the

The Problem of Certainty

But what about certainty? Individuals might ask, is there not something sacrilegious about a purported justification of religious belief that leaves us with nothing more than probability? Is there not some alternative approach that would allow us to believe with certainty? And if so, would not such an alternative have more to commend it than, say, a system that promises nothing more than probability?

What such questions reveal, I fear, is a serious misunderstanding on the part of the questioners. They need instruction on the difference between the kind of certainty found in mathematics and logic (call it logical certainty) and that available in other areas (call it psychological or moral certainty).

Logical certainty is found exclusively in such areas as formal logic, geometry, and mathematics. Examples of propositions that can be known with logical certainty include these:

1. Seven plus five equals twelve.
2. No object can be round and square at the same time in the same sense.
3. Either Richard Nixon was the thirty-sixth president of the United States or he was not the thirty-sixth president of the United States.

Logical certainty is limited to this kind of thinking. Number 1 is true, of course, because of the laws of mathematics. Number 2 is true because of the law of noncontradiction. Number 3 is true because of the law of the excluded middle. In order for any proposition to be certain in this logical sense, it must be necessarily true or false.

But propositions such as "Jesus Christ rose bodily from the grave," "God created the world," and "The Bible contains sixty-six books" cannot attain logical certainty; nor can informative propositions about history, geography, physics, astronomy, or home economics; nor can *any* world-view. Once one leaves the arena of purely formal reasoning for the world of blood, sweat, and tears, one is required to abandon logical certainty for probability. Informative judgments about particular things and events (or collections of things and events) can never rise above probability. But this is hardly cause for regret. As Edward John Carnell once observed:

> This admission that Christianity's proof for the resurrection of Christ cannot rise above probability is not a form of weakness; it is rather an indication that the Christian is in possession of a world-view which is making a sincere effort to come to grips with actual history. Christianity is not a deductively necessary system of thought which has been spun out of a philosopher's head, wholly indifferent to the march of human history below it.[35]

But even though no world-view can rise above logical probability, it may still be believed with moral certainty. A single proposition or system of

---

relationship between faith and reason in *Christian Faith and Historical Understanding* (Grand Rapids: Zondervan, 1984), chap. 8.

[35] Edward John Carnell, *An Introduction to Christian Apologetics* (Grand Rapids: Eerdmans, 1948), pp. 114–15.

propositions that is only probable in the logical sense may still generate certainty in the psychological or moral sense.

> Rational probability and complete or perfect moral assurance are by no means incompatible. We are morally assured that there was a man named George Washington, though the rational evidence for his existence is only probable. All the mind need be convinced of is coherence to be morally assured. . . . The arguments for Christianity—though but probable in rational strength—move the Christian to act upon the supposition of the truth of the Christian faith.[36]

Before acting—often in matters that could have a significant impact on our lives and happiness—we seldom stop and engage in a process of making formal inferences. Before entering an elevator, for example, few normal people enter information about the elevator into a portable computer to check the probabilities of reaching their destination safely. We often act in life with far greater assurance (moral certainty) than the evidence warrants. We do not really *know* many of the things we assume for practical purposes. We act on probabilities so strong that for practical purposes they become indistinguishable from certainties.

To demand logical certainty in the matters under consideration in this book is bizarre. My admission that we must deal in terms of probabilities (in the logical sense) is not a defect; it is a clue that we are dealing responsibly with an inescapable feature of the real world.

For Further Exploration—Chapter Four

1. What is meant by saying that logical consistency is a *negative* test?
2. Select Logical Positivism, determinism, or physicalism, and discuss the claim that it self-destructs.
3. Discuss the importance of the practical test for world-views.
4. Discuss the features common to testing scientific hypotheses, historical explanations, and world-views.
5. Explain why logical certainty is not attainable in such investigations. Do you find this troubling? Why or why not?

---

[36]Ibid., p. 118.

Part 2

THE RATIONALITY OF RELIGIOUS BELIEF

Chapter 5

THE EVIDENTIALIST CHALLENGE TO RELIGIOUS BELIEF

English publications in the philosophy of religion recently have tended to focus on five major issues: (1) arguments for the existence of God; (2) analyses of the nature of God; (3) the problem of evil; (4) miracles; and (5) the rationality of belief in God. Part 3 of this book will examine some of the issues raised in the contemporary debate over the theistic arguments. The problem of evil and the question of miracles will be treated in Parts 4 and 5 respectively. Since I have already devoted a separate book to the contemporary philosophical discussion of God's nature, I will not repeat that material here.[1] That leaves us, then, with the general topic for this part of the book: the rationality of belief in God.

Older students of the philosophy of religion and apologetics—that is, people who may have looked at the literature as recently as twenty years ago—would have some familiarity with topics (1), (3), and (4).[2] Topic (5), the rationality of religious belief, has become a hot issue only in the past decade. The attention it has begun to receive in philosophy journals and books is due largely to the work of a small team of philosophers, most notably Alvin Plantinga (University of Notre Dame), William Alston (Syracuse University), George Mavrodes (University of Michigan), and Nicholas Wolterstorff (Calvin College).[3]

---

[1] See Ronald Nash, *The Concept of God* (Grand Rapids: Zondervan, 1983).

[2] I should add, however, that the recent literature has added a lot of new wrinkles to these issues.

[3] Perhaps the best place to begin one's study of the work of these gentlemen is *Faith and Rationality: Reason and Belief in God*, ed. A. Plantinga and N. Wolterstorff (Notre Dame, Ind.: University of Notre Dame Press, 1983). Perhaps the seminal works by this group of writers were Alvin Plantinga's *God and Other Minds* (Ithaca, N.Y.:

We all have some initial idea of what it means for people to be rational or irrational. We believe it's good when people's beliefs are rational; we begin to get concerned when beliefs appear irrational. Every Christian theist would like to think that he's acting rationally when he affirms his belief in God. Every naturalist would like to persuade the theist that he is not.

There are degrees of irrationality. Consider the following examples of what I judge to be irrational beliefs. As one moves down the list, I think, the beliefs become increasingly irrational and hence cause for increasing concern for the person holding the belief.[4]

1. Jones believes that Cleveland, Ohio, is America's premier city.
2. Jones believes that he is Napoleon.
3. Jones seriously doubts that other people in the world have minds.
4. Jones believes that tomorrow the sun will rise in the West.
5. Jones believes that Ronald Nash is America's best golfer.
6. Jones believes that God told him to shoot his philosophy teacher.
7. Jones believes that he is God.[5]

Sometimes, what we think of as irrational behavior and beliefs overlap with what we regard as madness. When critics suggest that the religious beliefs of Christians are irrational, they mean something short of madness. But it is clear that they don't regard the charge of irrationality as a compliment. Christians have a stake in trying to show that Christian believing is a rational enterprise.

But if the discussion of the rationality of religious belief is important, it can also get fairly complicated. We will find ourselves examining issues that will be new to many readers. Some of these questions and the language used to discuss them may seem difficult to some at first. Portions of these next few chapters may have to be read several times before some readers catch on. The importance of the topic, however, requires that it be discussed.[6]

This chapter and the following one will examine two forms the modern challenge to the rationality of religious belief has taken: evidentialism and foundationalism. Since the labels of *evidentialism* and *foundationalism* identify overlapping positions, these chapters will cover much of the same ground in different language. I regard this as a plus. Every teacher recognizes times

---

Cornell University Press, 1967), and George Mavrodes's *Belief in God* (New York: Random House, 1970). Mavrodes's book is now published by University Press of America.

[4]This generalization is open, I suppose, to minor disagreement about this or that belief. But certainly the beliefs near the bottom of the list exhibit more serious signs of irrationality than those near the top of the list.

[5]It is worth noting that Jesus believed he was God and Christians think he was correct in this belief. See my discussion of this issue in chapter 19.

[6]A word to those readers who regard themselves as novices when it comes to philosophy; if the book is being read outside an academic setting, no great harm will occur if the reader skips to Part 3 and then returns to Part 2 after finishing the rest of the book. But for those students using this as a textbook, there are good reasons for placing this topic in Part 2. For one thing, it lays a foundation for the particular approach Part 3 makes to the theistic arguments.

when important but difficult material can be taught more effectively by presenting it in several different ways, by approaching it from several different directions. But even though evidentialism and foundationalism may be different ways of saying essentially the same thing, our examination of each position will help us see somewhat different points.

EVIDENTIALISM

Perhaps the most poignant and influential statement of the evidentialist thesis is to be found in a little essay titled "The Ethics of Belief" written by a nineteenth-century mathematician named W. K. Clifford. The one sentence in which Clifford sums up his essay captures the essence of evidentialism: "It is wrong always, everywhere, and for anyone, to believe anything upon insufficient evidence."[7] As Clifford saw it, people have duties and responsibilities with respect to their epistemological activities, one of which is that it is immoral to believe anything without proof or evidence. This is especially so, Clifford thought, in the case of religious beliefs. According to Clifford, there is never sufficient evidence or proof to support religious belief. Therefore, anyone who accepts a religious belief (such as the belief that God exists) is guilty of acting immorally, irresponsibly, and irrationally.

One ironic feature of evidentialism is that it has been adopted by thinkers on opposite sides of the theistic fence. While some use evidentialism to attack theism, others use it to defend theism. In the hands of an antitheistic evidentialist, the argument might go something like this:

1. It is irrational to accept theistic belief in the absence of sufficient evidence.
2. There is insufficient evidence to support belief in God.
3. Therefore, belief in God is irrational.

But there are also a great many theistic evidentialists around whose general line of argument goes like this:[8]

1. It is irrational to accept theistic belief in the absence of sufficient evidence.
2. There is sufficient evidence to support belief in God.
3. Therefore, belief in God is rational.

In other words, theistic evidentialists and their antitheistic counterparts start from the same presupposition, namely, that the rationality of religious belief depends upon the discovery of evidence or arguments to support the belief. Theistic and antitheistic evidentialists part company over the question

---

[7] W. K. Clifford, "The Ethics of Belief," in *Readings in the Philosophy of Religion*, ed. Baruch A. Brody (Englewood Cliffs, N.J.: Prentice-Hall, 1974), p. 246. Clifford's essay was published in his *Lectures and Essays* (London: Macmillan, 1879) and has been reprinted in countless anthologies.

[8] For one apparent example of an evidentialist approach to apologetics, see R. C. Sproul, John H. Gerstner, and Arthur W. Lindsley, *Classical Apologetics: A Rational Defense of the Christian Faith and a Critique of Presuppositional Apologetics* (Grand Rapids: Zondervan, 1973 [rev. 1982]).

of whether such evidence actually exists; but both agree that evidence is necessary!

Somewhere along the way, Clifford's original thesis that *all* beliefs are guilty until proven innocent underwent a major transmutation. However it happened, evidentialism became linked with the presumption of atheism that I described in chapter 1. In the view of contemporary antitheistic evidentialists like Antony Flew and Michael Scriven, the burden of proof always rests on the theist; religious beliefs should be presumed guilty until shown to be otherwise. It is always the believer's responsibility to produce reasons or evidence to support his belief, and if he fails, the proper conclusion to draw is that the belief is irrational. Without supporting evidence, the believer's persistence in believing is an irrational and morally defective act.

PLANTINGA'S REJECTION OF EVIDENTIALISM

Many theists agree to play the game according to the evidentialist's rules—which obliges them to produce evidence that will satisfy the evidentialist's sense of epistemological propriety—but Alvin Plantinga recommends a totally different course. Plantinga wonders why anyone should accept the major claim of the evidentialist.[9] Stephen Wykstra explains:

> Many charge that belief in God is irrational because there is insufficient evidence for it. Theists often respond with arguments for theism, but Plantinga's way is different: he challenges the underlying supposition— "evidentialism"—that theism *needs* evidence. Against all evidentialists— theists and nontheists alike—he urges that theistic belief "can be entirely right, rational, reasonable, and proper without any evidence or argument whatever."[10]

As Plantinga asks, "Why should we think a theist must have evidence, or reason to think there *is* evidence, if he is not to be irrational? Why not suppose, instead, that he is entirely within his epistemic rights in believing in God's existence even if he has no argument or evidence at all?"[11] It will help if I contrast Plantinga's position with that of the theistic evidentialist, noted earlier. The theistic evidentialist, we recall, held the following:

1. It is irrational to accept theistic belief in the absence of sufficient evidence.
2. There is sufficient evidence to support belief in God.
3. Therefore, belief in God is rational.

Plantinga agrees with 3; indeed, much of his philosophizing is intended to defend the rationality of belief in God. Plantinga also happens to agree with 2, a point that is often overlooked. In other words, he believes there may be reasons that support belief in God. But—and here comes the catch—

---

[9]The major premise of the evidentialist is proposition (1), noted earlier: "It is irrational to accept theistic belief in the absence of sufficient evidence."

[10]Stephen Wykstra, review of *Faith and Rationality* in *Faith and Philosophy* 3 (1986): 206.

[11]Alvin Plantinga, "Reason and Belief in God," in *Faith and Rationality*, p. 30.

even though there may be reasons that support belief in God, those reasons (or that evidence) are not necessary to make such a belief rational. Plantinga, therefore, rejects 1, the evidentialist thesis. The rationality of religious belief does not depend on the discovery of supporting arguments or evidence.

EVIDENTIALISM'S FATAL FLAWS

This is an appropriate occasion to unveil evidentialism's two fatal flaws. Let us remind ourselves of W. K. Clifford's misguided claim: "It is wrong always, everywhere, and for anyone, to believe anything upon insufficient evidence" (taking the word *evidence* to mean argument or proof).

1. Numerous critics of Clifford have pointed out how his view, if accepted, would undercut all epistemic activity. There are countless things that we believe (and believe properly, justifiably, and rationally) without proof or evidence. We believe in the existence of other minds; we believe that the world continues to exist even when we are not perceiving it. There are countless things that we not only believe but have a *right* to believe even though we lack proof or evidence. If we followed Clifford and eliminated from our noetic structure all beliefs for which no proof or evidence is supplied, we would lose our right to affirm a large number of important claims that only a fool would question. And so it is clear that we have a right to believe *some* things without evidence or proof. Since belief in God turns out to belong to the same family of beliefs, we also have a right to believe in God without supporting evidence or arguments.

2. Clifford's thesis is self-defeating. For Clifford, it is immoral to believe *anything* without proof. But where is the proof for Clifford's claim? What evidence does Clifford provide for his belief that it is immoral to believe anything in the absence of evidence? First, Clifford warns his reader against acting immorally with respect to his epistemic activities. But then he turns around and acts "immorally" by advancing a thesis for which he provides no proof or evidence. Clifford is confronted by a dilemma of his own making. Either evidentialism is false, or it fails the evidentialist's own test of rationality. If it is false, then believing it is an irrational and immoral act. If it fails the evidentialist's tests, then (on his own grounds) believing it is an irrational and immoral act. Either way, evidentialism is in big trouble.

SOME QUESTIONS

Why Is Plantinga's Challenge to Evidentialism Important?

Given the fact that Plantinga believes there may be arguments or evidence to support belief in God, is his rejection of the evidentialist thesis really that important? What difference does it make?

Plantinga's challenge to evidentialism is important for a number of reasons. First, an acceptance of the evidentialist thesis is unwarranted for reasons noted in the previous section. Since it places the theist in an unfair situation—he has to do something that the atheist doesn't—why accept this burden? Just because most theists, including Plantinga, are aware of reasons and evidence that support belief in God, it doesn't follow that those arguments are equally persuasive to nontheists or that *all* theists need the arguments in order to be rational. And when nontheists reject the reasons offered by theists, that fact accompanied by their earlier acceptance of the evidentialist thesis leaves theists' recommended beliefs in big trouble. It is difficult enough to persuade an opponent of the reasonableness of any philosophical position without also accepting an additional handicap. Plantinga's advice to the theist is: don't do it. Don't allow the atheologian to set the rules.

Evidentialism is also worth challenging because it places belief in God in the wrong family of beliefs. Some human beliefs—most notably scientific beliefs—are evidence-essential. That is, if our belief (for example, that the earth orbits around the sun) lacked relevant evidence, we'd be justified in regarding the belief as in serious trouble. But many important human beliefs are not evidence-essential in the sense that their rationality requires supporting evidence. An example of this second kind of belief—the second family of beliefs—is my belief in other minds. Plantinga doubts that any argument yet offered constitutes proof or evidence that other people have minds.[12] But even the failure of such arguments is less important than the simple fact that we believe that other people have minds without even seeking such proof. Our beliefs that other selves exist, that they are persons and not androids, and that they have intrinsic value and should be treated in certain ways are seldom proportioned to proofs or arguments. Belief in God and belief in other minds are in the same epistemological boat. Since belief in other minds is rational without supporting evidence, so too is belief in God.

The problem with evidentialism, as Plantinga sees it, is not so much that evidentialism is false as it is irrelevant to belief in God. Efforts to use evidentialism with regard to belief in God are like trying to use a hammer in cases where the proper tool is a screwdriver. Evidentialism is inappropriate both to beliefs in persons and to belief in God.

What Does *Evidence* Mean?

No doubt, it has occurred to some readers that the word *evidence* is a rather slippery term. Can Plantinga sharpen the focus of the term? As a matter of fact, Plantinga's earlier discussions of evidentialism did leave some of his readers confused for precisely this reason. Plantinga now distinguishes two kinds of evidence: (1) propositional evidence and (2) the evidence provided by direct experience. By propositional evidence, Plantinga means an argument. Propositional evidence is inferential in the sense that one draws, derives, or infers one proposition (the conclusion) from one or more other propositions (the premises). The inferential process may be either deductive or inductive.

It is important to see that Plantinga understands the evidence from direct experience to be nonpropositional and noninferential. For example, my belief that I had Wheaties for breakfast this morning is based on certain experiences that produce the belief immediately, that is, without my inferring the belief from premises. While such experiences may serve as a ground for memory-beliefs (like "I had Wheaties for breakfast") or beliefs about present perceptions (like "I see a book on the shelf"), these

---

[12]Plantinga analyzes the most popular arguments offered in support of this belief in his *God and Other Minds*.

experiences typically do not function as part of any reasoning process in which I infer "It's a hot and muggy day" from other propositions. My belief that it's a hot and muggy day is produced or triggered immediately and noninferentially from certain experiences.

To summarize, sometimes we use the word *evidence* to mean evidence from direct experience; sometimes we use it to mean arguments or proofs. When Plantinga objects to evidentialism by stating that belief in God can be rational in the total absence of evidence, what he means is evidence in the propositional sense (i.e., arguments). In other words, the rationality of belief in God does not depend on the believer's ability to supply proofs or arguments. But Plantinga does think that belief in God (like a great many nonreligious beliefs) may be related in noninferential ways to certain experiences. These issues will be examined again in the next chapter.

What Does *Rationality* Mean?

Sooner or later, any discussion of the rationality of belief in God is going to have to get around to an explanation of the word *rationality*. Some people are surprised (and disappointed) to discover the frequency with which philosophers have difficulty coming up with a totally satisfactory analysis of fundamental concepts. Even Socrates found it easier to criticize other people's faulty notions of such ideas as justice, virtue, and knowledge than to provide adequate analyses of his own. One can read a great many contemporary philosophic attempts to elucidate the notion of rationality and conclude that all of them fall short in one way or another. Often, in such cases, some philosophers simply appeal to the idea of rationality as what they call a "primitive notion." What they mean by this move is that most people operate with a primitive understanding of rationality. Even if they (or their philosophy instructor) may be unable to produce a totally satisfactory definition of the term, we at least (as in the case of pornography) know irrationality when we see it. This primitive understanding of the notion is enough to enable us to pass over the difficult job of defining the term and engage in the practical business of evaluating the rationality of different beliefs.

Even though the world is still awaiting a definitive analysis of rationality, it is helpful to see the progress that has been made in this matter. It seems clear that rationality should *not* be equated with two things. First, as we have already seen, it is false to say that a belief is rational only if supported by proofs or arguments (i.e., propositional evidence). A belief may be rational even though I may be unable to produce any supporting argument.[13] Second, it is false to say that a belief is rational only if that belief is true. While this claim may surprise some readers, a little reflection should show that it is correct. People have in the past behaved quite rationally with regard to beliefs that we now know to be false. An example would be the medieval astronomers who calculated the movements of the planets on the basis of the Ptolemaic model of the solar system. Those astronomers were acting rationally even though their model of the solar system was false. It is also possible for a person to believe only true propositions and not be rational. A person might come to believe a true proposition by accident, or

---

[13]This is so, for example, in the case of my belief in other minds.

he might come to hold what is a true belief for really irrational reasons, for example, by studying the entrails of a dead cat.

This difference between truth and rationality accounts for a distinction that William Rowe makes between friendly and unfriendly atheism. Rowe has described himself as a friendly atheist. Because he is an atheist, he thinks the key propositions of theists are false. But even though he does not accept the proposition "God exists" as true, he is willing to admit that people who do accept it can be rational in their belief.[14] There do seem to be good reasons, then, not to tie the concepts of rationality and truth too closely together.

But surely it is not enough to say what rationality is not. Can any steps be taken that will help us understand (even partially) what rationality is? For one thing, rationality is a property of some beliefs (and other cognitive acts).[15] Words like *justification, warrant, reasonability,* and *positive epistemic status*[16] are synonyms for this property.

The word *rationality* can also describe a certain attitude that we should have toward our cognitive activities. As we know, human beings have certain moral duties; but we also have epistemic duties, that is, obligations with respect to cognitive activities like believing. As Alvin Plantinga explains, being rational means doing "the right thing with respect to [what one believes]. It is to violate no epistemic duties. From this point of view, a rational person is one whose believings meet the appropriate standards."[17] Being rational is believing in an epistemically responsible way; it is believing in ways that obey our epistemic duties or at least do not violate any of them.

I once found myself in a rather minor disagreement with a professional historian about some matter pertaining to the New Testament. When the argument finally had to be terminated, I explained to the historian that all he had to do to reveal the extent of his misunderstanding of the subject was to do some elementary research in one or two of the basic authorities on the subject. The historian muttered something to the effect that he had better things to do with his time, that he knew he was right, and walked away. This strikes me as a fairly good example of someone acting in an epistemically irresponsible way. If the truth about some issue can be determined simply by "getting the facts," to ignore those "facts" is to act irrationally, that is, to violate certain fundamental epistemic duties. A belief may be described as rational if a person has a *right* to that belief. One of the things that determines whether such a right exists is if that person has treated that belief in an epistemically responsible way.

---

[14]See William L. Rowe, *Philosophy of Religion* (Encino, Calif.: Dickenson, 1978), p. 94. In case it needs saying, an unfriendly atheist would be someone who believes that "God exists" is false and who also judges that no one accepting that proposition can possibly be rational.

[15]A cognitive act is an act like believing, thinking, remembering, and so on.

[16]*Positive epistemic status* is a technical phrase that sometimes appears in recent discussions of rationality. It refers to the fact that when we evaluate or appraise beliefs or other epistemic acts, we may regard them in a positive or negative light. Jones's belief that Nash is America's premier golfer has very little warrant; it has *negative* epistemic status.

[17]Plantinga, "Reason and Belief in God," p. 52.

More recently, Alvin Plantinga has extended his analysis of rationality even further.[18] Plantinga takes issue with several accounts of rationality already known to philosophers. For example, he disagrees with the view that rationality should be identified *exclusively* with fulfilling our epistemic duties. As we have seen, he does think that rationality involves the fulfillment of such duties. But rationality must be more than this.[19] Some philosophers have sought to explain rationality in terms of coherence. They have suggested that the rationality of a belief is proportionate to the degree to which it coheres with a set of relevant beliefs. Though such coherence, Plantinga says, is a necessary condition of rationality,[20] it fails as a sufficient condition. That is to say, a radical incoherence within a person's noetic structure is a sign that something is wrong; but coherence by itself does not necessarily guarantee that everything is all right.[21] Still other philosophers have said that beliefs are rational if they are formed in a reliable manner, that is, by some reliable belief-producing mechanism. The catch here is that the process by which some belief is produced may be reliable (the belief it produces happens to be correct) even though the process itself is defective. For example, as one result of taking a certain drug a person might be led to believe that God exists. While we might not wish to fault the belief, we'd hardly be right if we pronounced a belief produced in such a way to be rational.

Plantinga thinks a better, more adequate account of rationality is available. He suggests that a belief is rational if its formation results from a person's "cognitive faculties working properly in an environment for which they are suited."[22] He makes two separate but equally important points in this statement. First of all, in order for a person to be rational, his or her cognitive equipment must be functioning properly. In other words, the faculties by which beliefs are formed and sustained must be free of any malfunction, must be working the way they're supposed to work. Some examples will make this clearer. My cognitive faculties are *not* working properly when they are impaired by a brain tumor, by mental illness, or by drugs and alcohol. If someone who has been diagnosed as paranoid believes that some other person intends to hurt him, then—to the extent that the belief results from the paranoia—we're justified in questioning the rationality of the belief. If some person comes to hold a belief solely as the result of some strong emotion such as hatred or avarice overriding his reasoning faculties, the belief ought to be judged as lacking in positive epistemic status;

---

[18] At the time I write these words, Plantinga has not yet published these views. They appear in several unpublished papers he has read at various meetings. My quotations come from those papers.

[19] As Plantinga explains, I may act quite earnestly and conscientiously in my effort to fulfill my cognitive duties and fail because something (like a brain tumor perhaps) causes my cognitive faculties to work improperly.

[20] Clearly, any person who recognizes the presence of contradictions in his noetic structure and ignores them is acting irrationally.

[21] Nothing in this paragraph undercuts my appeal to *coherence* in Part 1. I used the word in a broader sense.

[22] Unless identified otherwise, quotes from Plantinga in this section come from the unpublished papers, noted earlier.

it is unwarranted, unjustified, and irrational. So when we believe rationally, our cognitive equipment is working the way it is supposed to work.

But there is more to rationality than the proper functioning of our cognitive equipment. Plantinga states that our cognitive faculties must be working properly in an appropriate environment. Suppose my eyes (and the rest of my cognitive equipment) are functioning properly but certain conditions in the environment frustrate my efforts to see something. There might be dense fog or insufficient light. If I'm driving a car through thick fog, I might form the belief that the two lights that seem to be coming closer are the reflection of my headlights in the fog. If it turns out, however, that those two lights are the headlamps of a fifty-ton truck heading straight for my front bumper, I (or at least my family and friends) might have reason to regret the irrationality of my belief. In such a case, there is nothing wrong with my cognitive equipment. The problem lies in an environment to which my cognitive faculties are not properly attuned. When my cognitive equipment is functioning properly in an environment to which my cognitive powers are suited, Plantinga says, then a belief is rational to the extent that I do, in fact, accept that belief on those grounds.[23]

CONCLUSION

The wise apologist will refuse to be backed into the evidentialist's trap. He will not assume that his beliefs are substandard in some way unless he can first prove something. Such an apologist puts himself and his faith at a disadvantage. A person may be rational in holding certain beliefs, even if he cannot provide others with proofs that will satisfy them. A person may be within his epistemic rights in believing that God exists, even in the absence of supporting proofs and arguments.

Of course, none of this implies that the nonevidentialist thinks reason, evidence, and arguments are either irrelevant or unimportant. Nor does it mean that the nonevidentialist believes that theism lacks supporting reasons. The nonevidentialist may well believe that plenty of arguments confirm his beliefs. He simply denies that his producing of such arguments is a necessary condition for his act of holding that belief to be rational.

For Further Exploration—Chapter Five

1. Explain what evidentialism is and show that you understand how it can be used by both theists and antitheists.
2. Which claim made by the evidentialist is challenged by Alvin Plantinga?

---

[23]Plantinga's account of rationality raises an interesting side issue. He writes: "The easiest and most natural way to think of proper functioning . . . is in terms of design: a machine or an organism is working properly when it is working in the way it was designed to work by the being that designed it. And clearly the best candidate for being the being who has designed our cognitive faculties would be God." My own statement of a position like Plantinga's can be found in my book *The Word of God and the Mind of Man* (Grand Rapids: Zondervan, 1982), chaps. 6, 7, 8, and 11. Also see Nash, "Gordon Clark's Theory of Knowledge," in *The Philosophy of Gordon H. Clark* (Philadelphia: Presbyterian and Reformed, 1968), pp. 141–47.

3. How is W. K. Clifford's evidentialist thesis self-defeating?
4. Give at least two reasons why it is important to challenge evidentialism.
5. Does a rejection of evidentialism oblige one to regard all evidence as unimportant or irrelevant to belief in God? Why or why not?

Chapter 6

FOUNDATIONALISM AND THE RATIONALITY OF RELIGIOUS BELIEF

I have already warned that this chapter will cover much of the same territory as the last chapter. One justification for this procedure is pedagogical: sometimes teachers can improve students' understanding of a subject by approaching the same material from different angles. But this chapter will do more than cover the subject of the last chapter in different language. Our study of foundationalism, the subject of this chapter, will acquaint the reader with an extremely helpful picture of human knowledge. Reflection about this picture—along with what we should or should not learn from it—can clarify a number of points that might otherwise be more difficult to grasp.

WHAT IS FOUNDATIONALISM?

Foundationalism is a particular model or picture of human knowledge. It is one of several ways of looking at such related topics as belief, rationality, and justification. The key analogy in the foundationalist picture of knowledge is a structure such as a building where various upper levels or stories are supported by lower stories. The entire structure is supported by a set of beliefs that serves as the foundation for the entire superstructure. As Alvin Plantinga explains, foundationalism is the view

> that some of our beliefs are based upon others. According to the foundationalist a rational noetic structure will *have a foundation*—a set of beliefs not accepted on the basis of others; in a rational noetic structure some beliefs will be basic. Nonbasic beliefs, of course, will be accepted on the basis of other beliefs, which may be accepted on the basis of still other beliefs, and so on until the foundations are reached. In a rational noetic

structure, therefore, every nonbasic belief is ultimately accepted on the basis of basic beliefs.[1]

According to foundationalism, then, noetic structures should be thought of as hierarchies in which every belief is either basic or derivative (nonbasic). Derivative beliefs are those that are grounded on or dependent in some way on more basic beliefs. Basic beliefs are those not derived from or dependent on other beliefs. In order for a belief to be rational, it must either be a basic belief or be justified by its relation to a basic belief. Every noetic structure contains such basic beliefs that are not derived from or dependent on other beliefs. These basic beliefs can be said to make up the *foundation* of that particular noetic structure.

The foundationalist picture of human knowledge has dominated Western philosophy for centuries. Thinking of epistemological activities in terms of the picture provides answers to some important questions. For example, *When should a belief be eliminated from a noetic structure?* Answer: When that belief is neither properly basic[2] nor properly grounded on a properly basic belief. *How should we judge the strength of a nonbasic belief?* Answer: In terms of the degree of support it receives from basic beliefs. *When does argument end?* Answer: When it arrives at properly basic beliefs.

TWO KINDS OF FOUNDATIONALISM

Two quite different forms of foundationalism can be found in today's intellectual marketplace. *Narrow foundationalism* insists that only beliefs that satisfy two or three specific criteria are properly basic, that is, belong properly in the foundation of a rational noetic structure. *Broad foundationalism* agrees with the distinction between basic and nonbasic beliefs and with the claim that the rationality of nonbasic beliefs depends on the extent to which they are supported by properly basic beliefs. But broad foundationalism breaks with narrow foundationalism over the latter's attempt to limit properly basic beliefs to those that satisfy two or three criteria. A broad foundationalist is willing to allow many different kinds of beliefs to qualify as properly basic—to belong properly in the foundation of a rational noetic structure—even though they do not meet the strict criteria of the narrow foundationalist.

Narrow Foundationalism

What I call narrow foundationalism is characterized by two theses:

1. Within any noetic structure, some beliefs are properly basic (do not require justification in terms of any more fundamental beliefs); basic beliefs serve to justify, ground, or otherwise support other (nonbasic) beliefs.
2. Only beliefs that are evident to the senses, self-evident, or incorrigible may be properly basic.

---

[1] Alvin Plantinga, "Reason and Belief in God," in *Faith and Rationality* (Notre Dame, Ind.: University of Notre Dame Press, 1983), p. 52.

[2] A *properly* basic belief is a belief that rightly belongs in the foundation of a rational noetic structure.

Thesis (1) is held by anyone who is a foundationalist. What differenti-ates a narrow from a broad foundationalist is thesis (2), the narrow foundationalist's insistence that in order to be properly basic, a belief must be evident to the senses, self-evident, or incorrigible. The obvious question then becomes: What do the terms *evident to the senses, self-evident,* and *incorrigible* mean?

Claims that are *evident to the senses* are statements whose truth or falsity depends upon human experience. If I am crossing a street in Manhattan, I would be wise to treat a claim like "I see a fast-moving yellow taxicab driving straight toward me" as basic.[3] It is basic because in all our normal experiences, we don't stop and ask *why* we think we see a taxicab or a tree or a mountain—if what we see is a taxi, a tree, or a mountain. We don't wonder what grounds support our belief at that moment. We simply see the taxi and believe that we see the taxi. And so, many foundationalists thought that any belief evident to the senses qualified as a properly basic belief.

In the past century or so, narrow foundationalists have tended to drop beliefs that are evident to the senses from the class of properly basic beliefs. The reasons for this are grounded in some fairly technical philosophical debates; since those debates are not particularly relevant to this book, I have chosen to ignore them. But there is one important reason why I have decided to include beliefs that are evident to the senses in my discussion. Shortly I will distinguish between those thinkers who use narrow foundationalism in an attempt to attack the rationality of religious belief and those who use it to defend claims such as "God exists." Because beliefs that are evident to the senses are indispensable to theists who are also narrow foundationalists, it is important to keep this class of properly basic beliefs in the ball park.[4]

Self-evident propositions are statements that people see are true or false simply by understanding them. Consider any mathematical truth like "three plus three equals six." Once one understands the proposition, its truth is seen immediately. Of course, propositions may also be self-evidently false as in the case of "The square root of nine is two." Self-evident propositions are necessarily true or necessarily false. The following are self-evident proposi-tions:

The sum of the angles of any triangle is 180 degrees.

Everything blue is colored.

All bachelors are unmarried men.

---

[3] This assumes, of course, that I really do see such a vehicle.

[4] In other words, if I were simply going to discuss contemporary narrow foundationalists of an antitheistic bent, I could safely ignore beliefs that are evident to the senses from the class of properly basic beliefs. But the world also contains narrow foundationalists who are theists and who attempt to argue for the rationality of theism in ways that presuppose the two theses of narrow foundationalism already described. If you happen to be such a theist and believe that the rationality of belief in God depends on your discovering some proof or argument that satisfies the narrow foundationalist's criteria, you are going to have to argue for the existence of God on the basis of some claims that are evident to the senses or attempt to defend a variation of the ontological argument. If this still isn't clear, study the arguments for God's existence in Part 3 of this book and notice how dependent they are on human observation and experience.

Clearly, self-evident propositions are properly basic; they belong properly in the foundation of any noetic structure. They are propositions that people have a right to believe without basing them on any more basic belief.

Incorrigible propositions are statements that cannot be doubted, even though they fall short of logical necessity. Imagine that you look to the left and see a table with a red book lying on it. Now consider two statements you might use to report what you see:

1. There is a red book on that table.
2. I seem to see a table with a red book on it.

These two statements are different in ways that help us understand what an incorrigible proposition is. Notice that 1, "There is a red book on that table," makes a report about what you take to be a state of affairs existing independently of your consciousness. You are making a claim about something in the external world, the world outside your consciousness. Notice also that 1 may be mistaken for a number of possible reasons. Perhaps you are color-blind, and even though there is a book on the table, the book is actually green. Or suppose it's not a book at all but only something that looks like a book under the conditions. Or perhaps you're dreaming or someone has hypnotized you. Whenever we make reports about what is or is not the case outside our minds, we might be mistaken. Propositions like 1 are *not* incorrigible.

But now consider proposition 2, "I seem to see a table with a red book on it." Here, no claim is being made about the external world. Instead, the claim is exclusively about what is present immediately to my consciousness. As long as I limit my propositions to reports about the way things appear to me or seem to me, I can never be mistaken. How could I? I might be mistaken about there actually being a red book on the table. But if I look and seem to see a red book—if I am appeared to in the way we always are when we "see" things—the proposition "I seem to see a table with a red book on it" is incorrigible, above reproach and properly basic. Incorrigible propositions, then, are statements in which we report truthfully whatever is present in our consciousness. The way to turn any dubitable proposition about the world (such as "I am now in Monument Valley") into an indubitable proposition is simply to preface the proposition with "It seems to me." It may be untrue that I am now in Monument Valley; perhaps I've seen too many John Wayne movies lately. But whether I'm awake or asleep, rational or not, if my report that "It seems to me that I'm in Monument Valley" faithfully describes what is present to my consciousness, it is an incorrigible proposition. And as an incorrigible proposition, it is properly basic for me; I have a right to believe it without support from any other belief.

To review, a foundationalist is someone who pictures noetic structures hierarchically. Every noetic structure is composed of two kinds of belief: (1) nonbasic beliefs that are believed, justified, and made rational by virtue of their relationship to other, more basic beliefs; and (2) basic beliefs, which do not require support from other beliefs. Basic beliefs make up the foundation of a person's noetic structure. Every foundationalist agrees that self-evident and incorrigible propositions point to beliefs that are properly basic; as we've seen, some foundationalists think that beliefs evident to the senses are also properly basic. When a person utters a proposition that passes one of these tests, it makes no sense for someone to say, "Prove it!" Anyone demanding a proof for a self-evident or an incorrigible proposition would reveal only that he has problems. Anyone crossing a street hearing the warning, "Look out for the taxi!" (a proposition evident to the senses) who demanded proof before acting might well encounter problems of a different kind.

What we have called a *narrow foundationalist* insists that self-evident and incorrigible propositions along possibly with beliefs evident to the senses are the *only* properly basic beliefs. This is a very serious claim. Unless the nonbasic beliefs in some person's noetic structure can eventually be traced back to some supporting basic belief that is evident to the senses, self-evident, or incorrigible, those nonbasic beliefs must be judged to be unwarranted, unjustified, and irrational. In order for a belief to be rational for a narrow foundationalist, it must either be a basic belief or be derived from a basic belief.

How does the narrow foundationalism discussed in this chapter relate to the evidentialism examined in the last chapter? If *A* (some basic belief) provides a reason, warrant, or justification for believing *B* (some nonbasic belief), we can see that *A* is evidence for *B*. In other words, narrow foundationalism is simply another way of stating the evidentialist view of rationality. In the language of the last chapter, a belief is irrational unless it is supported by evidence, that is, an argument or a proof that tracks back eventually to some truth that cannot be doubted. In the words of the narrow foundationalist, nonbasic beliefs are irrational unless supported by a chain of reasoning that eventually shows their dependence on beliefs that are self-evident or incorrigible or evident to the senses.

How is all this relevant to Christian theism? Narrow foundationalism is assumed in the writings of people attempting to show that the Christian faith is irrational. For example, an atheologian might say: "Unless you theists prove that God exists, I don't have to take your position seriously. You claim that God exists; now prove it."

Now when Christians have accepted the burden of proof implied by such a challenge, they find that what many atheologians mean by a proof is an argument that sooner or later is shown to depend upon propositions that are evident to the senses, self-evident, or incorrigible. In other words, narrow foundationalism plays a crucial role in a two-stage attack on the rationality of belief in God. Step one: Christians are put on the defensive by being told that they have the burden of proof. Nothing more can happen until and unless they prove that their God exists. Step two: the atheologian will reject any proof that does not terminate finally in the limited kinds of belief that he considers properly basic. So Christians are not only obliged to prove God's existence, they must also tie their belief in God somehow to propositions that the narrow foundationalist regards as properly basic.

Surprisingly, many Christian apologists in the past have agreed to play the atheologian's game, and they have played it according to the atheologian's rules. Apparently without much thought about what they were doing, many apologists have agreed that the only proper way to begin the task of apologetics is to accept the challenge and prove that God exists. As though this were not enough, these same apologists then sought to prove the existence of God through arguments that rested sooner or later on propositions evident to the senses, self-evident, or incorrigible.[5]

In the last chapter, we noted how theists and atheists have used evidentialism to support their respective causes. We also noted how both sides in this dispute were wrong, not simply in the particulars of this or that argument, but in their fundamental approach. In this chapter, we will argue that the use of narrow foundationalism by both friends and enemies of theism is equally mistaken.

Broad Foundationalism

There is nothing especially wrong with approaching human knowledge via a foundationalist model or picture. The problem comes when, as we have seen, foundationalists restrict properly basic beliefs to two or three categories. In the rest of this chapter, we will see what happens when a foundationalist recognizes the limitations and problems of narrow foundationalism and opens up the foundation of his noetic structure to other kinds of properly basic beliefs. In particular, we will see what happens when a broad foundationalist (someone who believes that the foundations of a noetic structure may properly include basic beliefs that are not evident to the senses, self-evident, or incorrigible) decides that belief in God is a properly basic belief.

OBJECTIONS TO NARROW FOUNDATIONALISM

In this section, I will examine the two major objections that have been raised to narrow foundationalism. In none of this, however, do I dispute the claim that beliefs that are evident to the senses, self-evident, or incorrigible are properly basic. What I and other critics of narrow foundationalism maintain is that these are not the *only* kinds of properly basic beliefs.

Objection One

Narrow foundationalism is incompatible with a great deal of what everyone knows. As Alvin Plantinga argues, if narrow foundationalism is true,

> then enormous quantities of what we all in fact believe are irrational. . . . [R]elative to propositions that are self-evident and incorrigible, most of the beliefs that form the stock in trade of ordinary everyday life are not probable. . . . Consider all those propositions that entail, say, that there are enduring physical objects, or that there are persons distinct from myself, or that the world has existed for more than five minutes; none of these propositions, I think, is more probable than not with respect to what is self-evident or incorrigible for me.[6]

---

[5] One of the best examples of a Christian thinker who adopted this approach was the French philosopher Descartes (1596–1650).

[6] Plantinga, "Reason and Belief in God," pp. 59, 60. In all his writings on the subject, Plantinga focuses his attention on those contemporary narrow foundationalists who limit properly basic beliefs to those that are either self-evident or incorrigible. His second objection takes care of those other narrow foundationalists willing to include beliefs that are evident to the senses.

Hence, narrow foundationalism is much too restrictive; it results in many of our most important beliefs being irrational. As Plantinga goes on to say, many propositions that fail the narrow foundationalist's tests

> are properly basic for me. I believe, for example, that I had lunch this noon. I do not believe this proposition on the basis of other propositions; I take it as basic; it is in the foundations of my noetic structure. Furthermore, I am entirely rational in so taking it, even though this proposition is neither self-evident nor evident to the senses nor incorrigible for me.[7]

According to narrow foundationalism, true memories fail the test of rationality since they are themselves neither basic beliefs nor based on properly basic beliefs. But surely, any theory that casts doubt on the rationality of not only memory-beliefs but also all kinds of other beliefs, such as our belief in the external world or other minds, is deficient. Our knowledge of true memories or other persons or the continuing existence of the external world is not inferential, that is, based on more basic beliefs. But it most assuredly *is* knowledge. As Plantinga sees it, this means we have to admit such beliefs into the foundation of our noetic structure; even though such beliefs do not pass the restrictive tests of the narrow foundationalist, they too must be properly basic. One problem with narrow foundationalism, then, is its greatly restricted view of what qualifies as a properly basic belief.

Objection Two

Narrow foundationalism fails its own test of rationality; it is self-referentially absurd. As we all remember (if we forget narrow foundationalism for a moment and trust our memories), narrow foundationalism advances the thesis that *properly basic beliefs must be evident to the senses, self-evident, or incorrigible*. It is interesting to observe what happens when one asks the narrow foundationalist whether this thesis is evident to the senses, self-evident, or incorrigible or based on propositions that are. A little reflection will show that none of these conditions obtain. From this fact, several interesting consequences follow.

It is clear that the narrow foundationalist himself accepts a belief (i.e., his theory) as properly basic even though it fails to satisfy his own criteria of proper basicality. Since the narrow foundationalist fails to provide any arguments, reasons, or evidence for his thesis and since it fails his own tests for proper basicality, it follows that his acceptance of his thesis violates his own epistemic duties. Since being rational means fulfilling one's epistemic duties, it follows that the narrow foundationalist is behaving irrationally when he advances his thesis.

It is also clear that the narrow foundationalist accepts at least one proposition (again, his thesis) as properly basic that is an exception to his thesis. His own practice shows that there are other ways in which a belief may become part of the foundation of a noetic structure. Even the narrow foundationalist is forced to admit (in practice, at least) that a belief that is not evident to the senses, self-evident, or incorrigible may be properly basic.[8]

---

[7] Ibid., p. 60.
[8] Earlier, I pointed out that one mark of an adequate theory is its proponents' ability

And so, we can thank the narrow foundationalist for opening this door. We can follow his lead and begin to consider the possibility that other propositions may be properly basic.

PLANTINGA'S ALTERNATIVE TO NARROW FOUNDATIONALISM

Alvin Plantinga has provided a valuable service in drawing attention to the often unnoticed way that one particular model of human knowledge (narrow foundationalism) has influenced discussions of the rationality (or irrationality) of religious belief. He has also provided a clear account of the nature of foundationalism along with powerful criticisms of narrow foundationalism. What is wrong with narrow foundationalism is not its recognition that every noetic structure contains basic beliefs that provide justification for (and thus serve as the foundation for) that noetic structure's nonbasic beliefs. What is wrong is the exclusivism of the narrow foundationalist who claims that only a few types of belief are properly basic, a claim that is used both to eliminate belief in God from the foundation and to undermine the rationality of belief in God.

Plantinga's challenge to narrow foundationalism includes two key moves. The first is the claim that narrow foundationalism is too restrictive with regard to the kinds of belief it recognizes as properly basic. While it is certainly true that self-evident and incorrigible beliefs (and possibly beliefs evident to the senses) belong properly in the foundation of a person's noetic structure, it is also the case that many other kinds of propositions may be properly basic. Narrow foundationalism is unable to do justice to the privileged status we accord to a great many beliefs that are not evident to the senses, self-evident, or incorrigible. Examples of beliefs that should be treated as properly basic include our belief in the existence of the external world, our belief in the existence of other selves, and our memory-beliefs.

Plantinga's second key move against those narrow foundationalists who would seek to use their position to undermine the rationality of belief in God is to refute that position and then declare that "belief in God is properly basic." Belief in God belongs properly in the foundation of a person's noetic structure. Plantinga's move at this point is so bold that it requires time for the significance of his claim to sink in. In Plantinga's words, "Under widely realized conditions it is perfectly rational, reasonable, intellectually respectable and acceptable to believe that there is such a person as God without believing it on the basis of propositional evidence."[9] It is perfectly reasonable to believe that God exists *without* arguments, reasons, or (propositional) evidence. A Christian may be entirely within his epistemic rights to believe in God, even though he may not be able to prove God's existence to someone else; indeed, even though he may not be able to think up any argument for himself. Belief in God, like any foundational belief, does not need support from any other belief; it is basic!

---

to live that theory without cheating and borrowing from some competing theory. The narrow foundationalist cannot live consistently within the constraints of his system.

[9] This quotation comes from recent public lectures, as yet unpublished (but expected to appear as part of his Gifford Lectures). Propositional evidence is evidence in the form of an argument.

In one of its many facets, Plantinga's position is reminiscent of the view of faith and reason set forth by St. Augustine, a position that would centuries later reappear in the work of such Protestant Reformers as John Calvin. Augustine saw that in order for any person to know anything, he must begin by believing something. *Credo ut intelligam;* I believe in order that I may understand. Augustine saw that this meant that faith is not simply a religious activity; nor is it optional. Faith is operative in every person's life. If it weren't, we could not know anything.[10]

One perfectly legitimate way for faith to operate is for us to accept propositions as true on the testimony of some reliable authority. After all, this is how we come to learn about history; it is also the way in which most people are introduced to religious truth. Plantinga uses the example of a teenager who comes to believe that God exists without basing his belief on any propositional evidence:

> What about the 14-year old theist brought up to believe in God in a community where everyone believes? This 14-year old theist, we may suppose, does not believe in God on the basis of [propositional] evidence. He has never heard of the cosmological, teleological, or ontological arguments; in fact no one has ever presented him with any evidence at all. And although he has often been told about God, he does not take that testimony as evidence; he does not reason thus: everyone around here says God loves us and cares for us; most of what everyone around here says is true; so probably *that* is true. Instead, he simply believes what he is taught.[11]

In Plantinga's example, testimony functions as a ground or triggering-condition of the teenager's faith apart from his consciously drawing any inferences from or about that testimony. The teenager believes that God exists; but this belief did not come about as a result of any evidence or argument. The teenager's belief is basic in the sense that it is not derived from nor based upon any more basic belief.

One important claim made in chapter 5 of this book is that belief in God is similar to our belief in other minds. There is no argument (or so Plantinga has argued) or evidence that can prove that other people have minds. But, Plantinga insists, we have a perfect right to hold this belief, even in the total absence of proof or evidence. Belief in other minds is a properly basic belief. So too is belief in God. In both cases, we have a right to hold the belief, even if we cannot come up with an argument that will prove the belief to ourselves or to someone else.

SOME CLARIFICATIONS OF PLANTINGA'S POSITION

Plantinga takes pains to eliminate several possible grounds for misunderstanding his position. For one thing, he argues that his claim that belief in God is properly basic does not entail that belief in God is arbitrary. In other

---

[10]For more on Augustine's view of faith and reason, see Ronald Nash, *The Light of the Mind: St. Augustine's Theory of Knowledge* (Lexington: University Press of Kentucky, 1969), chap. 3. Augustine's position is much more complex than my brief remarks can indicate.

[11]Plantinga, "Reason and Belief in God," p. 35.

words, Plantinga's position does not preclude anyone's making intelligent choices among competing basic beliefs.

Just because Plantinga regards belief in God as properly basic, it doesn't follow that he has to regard *any* belief as properly basic, including especially absurd beliefs. Plantinga claims that some properly basic beliefs do not satisfy the criteria accepted by the narrow foundationalist. In other words, he rejects narrow foundationalism and asserts that belief in God, like belief in other minds, may under widely realized conditions be properly basic. But this hardly obliges Plantinga to accept *any* belief as properly basic.[12]

Nor does it follow from Plantinga's identification of belief in God as a properly basic belief that he denies the possibility of there being adequate grounds or justifying conditions for such a belief. All he does is deny that such grounds are a necessary condition for such a belief's being rational or properly basic. In Plantinga's view, it is possible for a basic belief to have grounds, to be justified. What marks a belief as properly basic is the fact that in certain circumstances we do not typically look beyond that belief for any justifying conditions; we simply take it as basic, as in the case of the yellow taxicab noted earlier.

But sometimes circumstances may push us into an attitude where we seek grounds for the belief. Just because we *can* look for grounds and may in fact find some, it doesn't follow that the belief is no longer properly basic. All that is required for a belief to be properly basic is that a person be rational or justified in accepting it without necessarily basing it on other beliefs. But if the need arises, it may still be possible to provide grounds for a belief that is otherwise basic. If a belief is properly basic, anyone holding it has a license to accept it with or without additional grounds. The fact that other grounds may be available does not weaken or compromise the privileged status of a properly basic belief. Many people hold properly basic beliefs (for example, that the world exists independent of their awareness of it) without recognizing them as such. Many fail to take advantage of the opportunities afforded by properly basic beliefs and thus spend a lot of time and effort trying to prove what does not require proof.

In short, then, a belief may be properly basic and still be justifiable. Supplying justification or grounds for a belief does not compromise the proper basicality of that belief. A belief is properly basic, not because there never are any justifying grounds, but because the belief is rational even though such grounds are not known or offered.[13]

THE BOTTOM LINE

What is Plantinga driving at? Why do Reformed epistemologists like him spend so much time and effort countering evidentialism and narrow foundationalism? What is the bottom line to all this discussion?

Plantinga's defense of the proper basicality of belief in God is an

---

[12] A lot more needs to be said about all this and Plantinga has said it. See his discussion in "Reason and Belief in God," pp. 74ff.

[13] Once again, this raises issues best discussed in a different kind of book. Fortunately, Plantinga has already discussed them in his "Reason and Belief in God," pp. 78ff.

exercise—and a major exercise at that—in *negative* apologetics. He is defending the rationality of the theist's belief in God against a serious challenge. According to that challenge, belief in God must be deemed irrational and worthy of rejection unless and until the theist supports that belief with arguments or proofs. History is full of people who stopped short of belief in God for the simple reason that they assumed the evidentialist view of things. And when they failed to find an argument that satisfied them, they concluded that belief in God was noetically substandard. Plantinga's intent is to challenge such an attitude. Belief in God may be perfectly rational, even in the absence of any proof or argument.

At this point, someone may raise an objection. Suppose we grant, he might say, that Plantinga's attack on evidentialism and narrow foundationalism does leave the believer with the right to take belief in God as properly basic. How does Plantinga's position *on this point* convince an agnostic or atheist that he should take belief in God as properly basic? How does Plantinga's view *on this matter* show the non-Christian that his basic beliefs are incorrect? The answer is simple: Plantinga's views *on this subject* were never intended to do *that! That* is the business of *positive* apologetics, not negative apologetics.[14] Plantinga is being criticized here because his defense of the proper basicality of belief in God is such an apparently weak tool in positive apologetics, yet he has not been doing positive apologetics at all! The confusion might be compared to someone who has just watched Dwight Gooden of the New York Mets strike out the opposing team in the top half of the first inning and then complain that the Mets had failed to score during that time. There are times when playing defense is important. But scoring runs must wait until your team leaves the field and comes up to bat.

Suppose we grant, then, that Plantinga has been engaged in the legitimate task of playing defense. It would be natural to wonder how he does the business of positive apologetics. At present, we will have to wait awhile for an answer. He works very carefully on those problems that interest him at the time. For good and sufficient reasons, he has seen fit to limit his work thus far to some important exercises in negative apologetics.[15]

In Part 1 of this book, I sketched the method by which I believe positive apologetics is done best. According to that procedure, there are tests by which we can judge among world-views and the basic beliefs underlying those world-views. My world-view includes belief in God as one of its basic beliefs. A naturalist may well regard the nonexistence of God as one of his basic beliefs. This might be a good time to go back and reread chapters 2, 3 and 4 and see how one might proceed to reach a decision as to which touchstone proposition, which basic belief, which world-view, comes out ahead.

Plantinga's recent work provides some hints that he himself looks favorably on approaching the work of positive apologetics in terms of world-views. In a recent paper, he makes an important statement to the effect that the kind of epistemological activity we've been examining in Part 2 is rooted in the world-view of the investigator:

---

[14] It might be even more correct to say that it is *God's* business.

[15] In Part 4 of this book, we will have occasion to view his work in a different area of negative apologetics, the problem of evil.

Here we see the ontological and ultimately religious roots of the epistemological question as to the warrant or lack thereof for belief in God. What you properly take to be rational, at least in the sense in question, depends upon what sort of metaphysical and religious stance you adopt; it depends upon what kind of beings you think human beings are, and what sorts of beliefs their noetic faculties will produce when they are functioning properly. Your view as to what sort of creature a human being is will determine, or at any rate heavily influence, your views as to what it is rational or irrational for human beings to believe. And so the dispute as to whether theistic belief is rational can't be settled just by attending to epistemological considerations; it is at bottom not merely an epistemological dispute, but an ontological or theological dispute. You may think humankind is created by God in the image of God—and created both with a natural tendency to see God's hand in the world about us, and with a natural tendency to recognize that he has indeed been created and is beholden to his creator, owing him worship and allegiance. Then of course you will not think of belief in God, as in the typical case, a manifestation of wishful thinking or any other kind of intellectual defect. (It is then more like a deliverance of sense perception or memory—or perhaps the faculty responsible for *a priori* knowledge.) On the other hand, you may think we human beings are the product of blind evolutionary forces; you may think there is no God, and that we are part of a Godless universe. Then perhaps you will be inclined to accept the sort of view according to which belief in God is an illusion of some sort, properly traced to a sort of disease or dysfunction on the part of the individual or society.[16]

In other words, the disagreement over whether belief in God is basic or not, is rational or not, may well turn out to be a reflection of a more basic clash between two competing world-views, theism and Naturalism.

CONCLUSION

It is unfair to complain that Plantinga's work, as described in this chapter, seems to offer so little for the task of positive apologetics. It wasn't intended to do this. It is an exercise in negative apologetics; as such, it defends the rationality of belief in God against an unworthy opponent (narrow foundationalism) that has had far more influence than it deserves.

Chapter 7 will serve as a bridge between Parts 2 and 3 of this book. First, it will serve as a conclusion to Part 2 by filling in additional details of Plantinga's position. Second, it will serve as an introduction to Part 3 by sketching how a Reformed epistemologist like Plantinga approaches natural theology.

For Further Exploration—Chapter Six

1. What is foundationalism?
2. Explain the difference between basic and nonbasic beliefs.
3. Explain the difference between narrow and broad foundationalism.
4. What is a self-evident proposition? What is an incorrigible proposition?

---

[16]For the record, this quotation comes from an as-yet unpublished paper by Plantinga.

5. Compare the first objection to foundationalism in this chapter to chapter 5's first objection to evidentialism.
6. Compare this chapter's second objection to foundationalism to chapter 5's second objection to evidentialism.
7. Explain what it means to say that belief in God is properly basic. What is the significance of this claim?
8. Relate what Plantinga says about belief in God to our belief in other minds. Give examples of other properly basic beliefs that do not meet the tests of narrow foundationalism.
9. Explain why Plantinga's defense of the proper basicality of belief in God is an example of negative apologetics.

Chapter 7

WHAT ABOUT NATURAL THEOLOGY?

Because of its transitional role, this chapter could serve as either the last chapter of Part 2 or the first chapter of Part 3. In relation to Part 2 of the book, this chapter will tie together several loose ends arising from our rejection of the evidentialist-foundationalist approach to belief in God. Eventually, we will get around to the question, What attitude should someone who rejects evidentialism and narrow foundationalism take toward the traditional and well-known efforts to "prove" the existence of the God of Christian theism? In Part 3, we will examine several representative attempts to offer arguments in support of God's existence. We will see that such arguments play significantly different roles in evidentialist-foundationalist systems and in the kind of approach taken in this book.

NATURAL THEOLOGY

What Is Natural Theology?

Natural theology is an attempt to discover arguments that will prove or otherwise provide warrant for belief in God without appealing to special revelation, e.g., the Bible. One major assumption of natural theology is that belief in God is *not* properly basic. When natural theologians set out to prove or otherwise establish God's existence, they usually sought to base God's existence on more basic beliefs. They tried to show that belief in God rests upon properly basic beliefs, that is, beliefs that any reasonable person can and will accept. The basic beliefs that natural theologians appealed to as providing a foundation for belief in God included beliefs. that were self-evident, incorrigible, or evident to the senses. Whether done intentionally or not, natural theology has usually involved a major concession to the.

evidentialist-foundationalist model of rationality. If Christian theism is to be rational on this view, it *must* be supported with arguments or proofs; and those arguments must eventually be linked to beliefs that narrow foundationalists regard as properly basic.

Is Natural Theology Necessary?

Certainly many leading Christian thinkers down through the centuries have acted as though natural theology was a necessary first step in establishing the credibility of theism. One twentieth-century writer who seems to represent this position is E. L. Mascall who writes: "The arguments for the existence of God are not fallacious, and to anyone who understands what they are about and is capable of following them they can carry complete conviction. Nor are they unnecessary, for without them . . . our belief will not be explicitly rational."[1]

In this paragraph, Mascall certainly seems to claim that valid arguments for God's existence are available and are necessary if the Christian's faith is to be rational. Natural theology is necessary, not optional. Not only are valid arguments for God's existence necessary and available, these arguments are—for anyone who understands and follows them—coercive in the sense that they compel people to accept the conclusion that God exists. When natural theology is done properly it will succeed in its task of bringing people to faith.

A number of things are wrong with this approach. For one thing, as the two previous chapters have noted, this approach is positively wrong-headed in its capitulation to the evidentialist-foundationalist model of rationality.[2] The kind of natural theology in view here misconstrues the proper relationship between argument and rational justification. As Alvin Plantinga explains:

> Argument is not needed for *rational justification;* the believer is entirely within his epistemic rights in believing, for example, that God has created the world, even if he has no argument at all for that conclusion. The believer does not need natural theology in order to achieve rationality or epistemic propriety in believing; his belief in God can be perfectly rational even if he knows of no cogent argument, deductive or inductive, for the existence of God—indeed, even if there is no such argument.[3]

And so, natural theology is not necessary for *epistemological reasons.* The kind of narrow foundationalism that has led so many theists and nontheists to believe that such proofs or arguments are necessary is fatally flawed.[4] Belief in God is properly basic and is thus rational even when unsupported by arguments.

---

[1] E. L. Mascall, *He Who Is: A Study in Traditional Theism* (London: Darton, Longman & Todd, 1966), p. 80. For the record, Mascall seems to have softened his position in later writings. See his *Existence and Analogy* (London: Darton, Longman & Todd, 1966), pp. 89–90, and his *Words and Images* (London: Darton, Longman & Todd, 1968), pp. 84–85.

[2] To clarify, the foundationalism in view here is *narrow* foundationalism.

[3] Alvin Plantinga, "Reason and Belief in God," in *Faith and Rationality* (Notre Dame, Ind.: University of Notre Dame Press, 1983), p. 65.

[4] Once again, see the arguments that support this contention in chapters 5 and 6.

But natural theology is also unnecessary for *experiential* reasons. Most people have come to believe that God exists without arguments or proofs. Plantinga is only pointing to what most of us already know when he writes that "arguments or proofs are not, in general, the source of the believer's confidence in God. Typically the believer does not believe in God on the basis of arguments; nor does he believe such truths as that God has created the world on the basis of arguments."[5]

Further doubts about making natural theology a first step in theology, philosophy of religion, and apologetics arise when one recognizes the serious problems affecting the arguments to which natural theologians appeal. The natural theologian acts as though he is presenting a valid argument based on indisputable premises to open-minded people. But as we have seen, the people to whom these arguments are directed are seldom neutral observers. Moreover, the truth of key premises and the validity of key inferences are often questionable.[6] Wise and responsible theists will not attempt to bring people to faith through the use of unsound arguments.

Even if sound arguments[7] for the existence of God were available, it doesn't make much sense to suppose that arguments would be the only way God would choose to make his existence known to people. As C. Stephen Evans points out:

> People differ greatly in their intelligence, reasoning ability, education and so on. If the knowledge of God could *only* be obtained through a process of logical reasoning, then more intelligent people would have an advantage over less intelligent people in coming to know God. But this seems unfair; nor is it consistent with what most religions have maintained about the knowledge of God: intellectual ability doesn't necessarily lead to a better knowledge of God. Much more important are moral qualities like love, courage and honesty. It seems reasonable to think that God might use some methods besides reason to make his presence known (though of course he might use reason too).[8]

Evans's point is made even more important by recent developments in the theistic arguments. A number of competent, contemporary philosophers have presented what they take to be sound arguments for the existence of God. Most of these attempts, however, lead to an ironic situation: the more plausible these contemporary theistic arguments are thought to be, the less intelligible they are to nonspecialists in philosophy. So even if some of these arguments should prove to be sound, they result in a situation where any increase in plausibility is accompanied by a massive decrease in the numbers of people who can understand them. Such efforts hardly support the contention that natural theology is an indispensible enterprise.

---

[5] Plantinga, "Reason and Belief in God," pp. 64–65.

[6] Examples of some of these problems will be presented in Part 3.

[7] Once again, a sound argument must satisfy two conditions: (1) every statement in the argument must be true; and (2) the form of the argument must satisfy the principles of logic. Formally, the argument must be valid; and its content (the statements that serve as its premises and conclusion) must be true.

[8] C. Stephen Evans, *The Quest for Faith* (Downers Grove, Ill.: InterVarsity Press, 1986), p. 21.

Claims that natural theology is necessary must deal with a serious theological objection. According to the Bible, we should start with God, not something more basic about God. In Plantinga's words, "There is nothing by way of proofs or arguments for God's existence in the Bible; that is simply presupposed. The same should be true of the Christian believer then; he should *start* from belief in God rather than from the premises of some argument whose conclusion is that God exists."[9] The importance of starting with God—of treating belief in God as basic—is a prominent theme of such Protestant Reformers as John Calvin.[10] Contemporary Reformed thinkers such as Carl F. H. Henry echo this concern:

> One must begin with God not only to get to God, but to get to anything. . . . From a certain vantage point, the concept of God is determinative for all other concepts; it is the Archimedean lever with which one can fashion an entire world view. . . . The modern attempts logically to prove the existence of the Christian God betray almost invariably a failure adequately to appreciate this revelatory principle. The Hebrew-Christian writers nowhere argue to God with Aristotle or any other philosopher as a stepping stone. And this not because of philosophic inability as much as an awareness of the significance of revelation. . . . Where God has spoken, revealed truth becomes the starting point of consistent knowledge; revelation is the test of truth, furnishes the framework and corrective for natural reason, introduces consistency into fragmentary human knowledge.[11]

It is only on revelational ground that one can have a correct concept of God as the personal, sovereign, self-sufficient, omnipotent Creator and Judge of the universe. Once this truth is recognized, theists will be wary of theories suggesting that God and his personal self-disclosure in Scripture must be reasoned *to* on the basis of any claims thought to be more basic.

Is Natural Theology Useless?

Thus far, it seems, there are several good reasons to think that natural theology is *not* necessary. But it is possible that language about the necessity of natural theology is ambiguous enough for us to take all this just a bit more slowly. I have argued that natural theology is not necessary in the sense that Christian theists have to present sound arguments in support of their position before it can be considered rational. Natural theology is not necessary if by this we mean that without coercive proofs for the existence of God, Christian theism should be dismissed as irrational.

But what if we understand natural theology in a less ambitious way? Suppose, for example, that we regard it as an inquiry into whether the Christian world-view fits what we know about the outer and inner worlds. Suppose, in other words, that instead of seeking coercive proofs for

---

[9]Plantinga, "Reason and Belief in God," p. 65.

[10]With respect to Calvin, Plantinga writes: "What the Reformers held was that a believer is entirely rational, entirely within his epistemic rights, in *starting with* belief in God, in accepting it as basic, and in taking it as a premise for argument to other conclusions" (Ibid., p. 72).

[11]Carl F. H. Henry, *Remaking the Modern Mind* (Grand Rapids: Eerdmans, 1946), pp. 232, 171, 196, 227.

conclusions that all right-minded and open-minded persons would accept, we view our task as the more modest one of seeing if the Christian world-view does what we should expect any world-view to do.

And what if we understand the word *necessary* in some other sense? I have argued that the presentation of sound, coercive arguments is not a necessary condition for Christianity's being rational. Christians do not *have* to engage in the activity of doing natural theology, nor do they have to do it successfully. But surely nothing said earlier in this book implies that natural theology in the weaker sense noted above is useless. If Christian theism is true, we should expect to find all kinds of evidence, reasons, arguments, and other considerations that support it in some way. It is one thing to insist that the discovery of arguments or proofs is necessary if Christian theism is to be rational. It is quite another thing to acknowledge that this kind of activity can be useful in other ways.

Even though theistic belief does not require arguments, it would be wrong to assume that good arguments cannot be found. Even though belief in God is properly basic, good arguments are available if someone should want them. It is one thing to *need* an argument; it is something else to *have* an argument to bolster or confirm a belief. As C. Stephen Evans points out, "Though faith does not have to be based on reasons, honest, critical reflection on one's faith can have great value, both for religious believers and for those whose ultimate faith is in something other than God."[12]

Earlier, I explained that Alvin Plantinga's defense of the claim "belief in God is properly basic" is an important move in negative apologetics. It releases the Christian from the *obligation* of "proving" that God exists before that belief can properly be considered rational. But as the rest of this book will show, there is plenty of room left for arguments on any number of subjects. To quote Evans again: "For someone who is troubled by doubt, rational reflection is inescapable. It simply is not possible to will all doubts away. To hide from problems is a sign that faith is in trouble."[13] Moreover, there are large numbers of people for whom belief in God is not basic and who would give honest and sincere consideration to the claims of the Christian faith if presented with reasons that make sense to them. The search for reasons and arguments is not inconsistent with the earlier claim that belief in God is properly basic; it is to engage in a different kind of activity from the one that concerned us in earlier chapters of the book. It is to begin the task of *positive* apologetics.

AN IMPORTANT RECAPITULATION

This is a good place to pause, catch our breath, and see how many points made earlier in the book tie together. This brief recapitulation will then make it easier when we begin considering the problems still ahead of us.

A long time ago (or so it may seem), we distinguished two senses of the word *evidence*. First, there is what can be called propositional evidence. This is evidence we look for when seeking the reasons why our noetic structure

---

[12]Evans, *Quest for Faith*, p. 23.
[13]Ibid., p. 22.

includes a particular nonbasic belief. With regard to any nonbasic belief I hold, I can ask *why* I hold that belief. My support for any nonbasic belief will take the form of providing some more basic propositions to which the nonbasic belief is related inferentially. For example, my noetic structure includes the nonbasic belief "John F. Kennedy is mortal." When I or someone else asks why I believe this, I can support it in terms of some inferential or reasoning process in which I base "John F. Kennedy is mortal" on one or more beliefs that are more basic; perhaps I can even trace it back to some properly basic belief. This process could be deductive[14] or inductive.[15] Propositional evidence is always relevant with regard to nonbasic beliefs. Nonbasic beliefs are related inferentially to other beliefs; and these other beliefs function as propositional evidence for the beliefs that they support.

But a second kind of evidence is provided by direct experience. This nonpropositional, noninferential kind of evidence is relevant to *basic* beliefs. Basic beliefs come into being or are sustained by processes that have no *necessary*[16] inferential component. Basic beliefs result from a natural, noninferential process related to our nature, the way we're made.[17]

In an earlier chapter, I explained how certain human dispositions predispose us to believe certain things when we find ourselves in certain situations. When I am appeared to in the way I normally am when it seems that I'm sitting down to a breakfast of eggs and bacon, I am naturally disposed to believe that there really are eggs and bacon on the plate before me.

I also discussed how a number of philosophers including Thomas Reid have explained all this: the dispositions that noninferentially produce beliefs like these results from God's having constituted the human mind in a certain way. As Arthur Holmes explains,

> According to Thomas Reid, God so constituted the mind that we believe without proof that external objects exist, we believe that memory tells of a past, we believe the causal principle[18] and the axioms of geometry, we believe there is a distinction between right and wrong, and that God exists. These beliefs which we know so surely to be true are, according to Reid, spontaneous interpretations of experience rather than logical inferences. The appearance of a sign is followed by belief in the thing signified; a sensation by belief in its present existence; a remembrance by

---

[14]For example, I'd be in good company if I accepted as premises the claims "All men are mortal" and "John F. Kennedy is a man." My belief that "John F. Kennedy is mortal" would then be inferred deductively from my premises.

[15]In this second case, I would gather all that I know about what happened in Dealy Plaza in Dallas, Texas, on November 22, 1963, and infer inductively that "John F. Kennedy is mortal."

[16]The word *necessary* is very important here. Reasoning and the drawing of inferences *may* play some role in the case of some basic beliefs. The important point is that nonbasic beliefs have a *necessary* inferential component while basic beliefs do not.

[17]Or if some object to the metaphysical presupposition they think I've smuggled in at this point, we could say that basic beliefs result from a natural, noninferential process related simply to the way we are.

[18]The "causal principle" Holmes refers to concerns the readiness with which, under the conditions so familiar to us, we believe that one event is the cause of another.

belief in its past existence; and imagination is not accompanied by belief at all. This is all due to the human constitution, a matter of common sense, not reason, and it is common to all men. Our very nature evokes universal beliefs and bears witness to their truth.[19]

In chapter 6, we noted Plantinga's answer to the objection that his view that belief in God is properly basic makes belief in God groundless. Plantinga counters that claim by explaining how basic beliefs like "I see a tree" can have grounds or justifying circumstances. In fact, if we were not in circumstances of a certain kind, we probably wouldn't be disposed to believe that we see a tree. Various circumstances (such as experiences of a certain kind) may trigger or serve as justifying grounds for a basic belief (like "I had toast and coffee for breakfast") without being part of a formal argument with premises and a conclusion. Certain conditions then may, in conjunction with certain God-given dispositions, trigger beliefs that are properly basic. As Plantinga puts it,

> Our cognitive faculties [are] designed to enable us to achieve true beliefs with respect to a wide variety of propositions—about our immediate environment, about our own interior life, about the thoughts and experiences of other persons, about the past, about our universe at large, about right and wrong . . . and about God. These faculties work in such a way that under the appropriate circumstances we form the appropriate belief. More exactly, the appropriate belief is *formed in us;* in the typical case we do not *decide* to hold or form the belief in question, but simply find ourselves with it. . . . upon being appeared to in the familiar way, I find myself holding the belief that there is a large tree before me; upon being asked what I had for breakfast, I reflect for a moment and then find myself with the belief that what I had was eggs on toast. In these and other cases I do not *decide* what to believe; I don't total up the evidence . . . and make a decision as to what seems best supported; I simply believe.[20]

The history of philosophy is full of failed attempts to justify basic beliefs such as our belief in the external world and our belief in other minds. It also tells the story of misguided efforts to certify the reliability of belief-forming mechanisms such as the senses and memory. But as Stephen Wykstra notes, "Our creaturely epistemic condition is that we must *trust* the basic belief-forming mechanisms with which we are endowed, presuming their reliability until we have reasons for revising them."[21]

So, we see that for contemporary Reformed epistemologists like Plantinga and Wolterstorff as for Thomas Reid before them, God has created humans in such a way that when we have experiences of a certain kind (such

---

[19] The quote comes from an unpublished paper by Arthur Holmes, "The Justification of World View Beliefs."

[20] This long quotation comes from one of several as-yet unpublished papers by Plantinga. There is good reason to think this paper will serve as the basis for Plantinga's forthcoming Gifford Lectures.

[21] This remark by Wykstra appears in his review of the Plantinga-Wolterstorff book *Faith and Rationality*. The review is in the journal *Faith and Philosophy* 3 (1986): 207. It is not entirely clear whether, in this and in other Wykstra comments quoted later, he is simply describing the views of Reformed epistemologists like Plantinga and Wolterstorff or whether he also shares their position.

as seeming to see a red rose in the garden), there is a natural tendency for us to believe (immediately and noninferentially) that there *is* a red rose in the garden. While Reid himself refused to take this additional step, other thinkers taught that God has also created us with a similar tendency or disposition (the *sensus divinitatis*) to believe in God. Plantinga relates this position to views he thinks can be found in the work of John Calvin:

> According to Calvin everyone, whether in the faith or not, has a tendency or *nisus*, in certain situations, to apprehend God's existence and to grasp something of his nature and actions. This natural knowledge can be and is suppressed by sin, but the fact remains that a capacity to apprehend God's existence is as much part of our natural noetic equipment as is the capacity to apprehend perceptual truths, truths about the past, and truths about other minds. Belief in the existence of God is in the same boat as belief in other minds, the past, and perceptual objects; in each case God has so constructed us that in the right circumstances we form the belief in question.[22]

The views being discussed in this section are part of what is being called a Reformed alternative to the evidentialist-foundationalist approach to belief in God. In this Reformed view, "theism is properly produced by non-inferential 'dispositions' implanted in us by God. On this view, rational God-beliefs are triggered by a variety of circumstances; looking at an intricate flower, we are disposed to believe that 'God is to be praised for this.'"[23] Even though such experiences or circumstances may be regarded as *evidence* for some person's belief in God, it is evidence that is noninferential, nonargumentative, and nonpropositional. As Wykstra explains, "Such experiences are not 'evidence' from which theism is *inferred;* rather, they 'actuate' an appropriate noninferential disposition, as hearing someone cry triggers belief that she feels pain. Such basic beliefs self-evidentially entail that God exists, so if they are proper, so is theism."[24]

Reformed Epistemology and Natural Theology

This Reformed account of human knowledge provides us with a new way[25] of viewing the arguments so beloved by natural theologians. Appeals to the sorts of evidence utilized in the cosmological and teleological arguments for God's existence carry so much weight with so many people because God has implanted in each human being a natural tendency to see his hand in the world. Edward John Carnell once approached this view in some comments about the apostle Paul's words in Romans 1:20: "Paul truly taught that God is known through sense perception but that does not involve us in empiricism [or natural theology]. May it not equally be that, *knowing* God (by innate knowledge, which Paul teaches) we are *reminded* of Him in

---

[22]Plantinga, "Reason and Belief in God," pp. 89–90.
[23]Wykstra, review in *Faith and Philosophy*, p. 207.
[24]Ibid. The point in this paragraph should not be confused with the *evidence of the senses,* one of narrow foundationalism's criteria of proper basicality, which is propositional and inferential.
[25]Obviously, it is a new way only for those unfamiliar with the long history of this approach.

His works?"[26] Carnell went on to conclude that "rather than building up a knowledge of God through a patient examination of the content of sense experience, we proceed to such experience *equipped* with an awareness of God."[27] Whether we say with Plantinga that humans are born with a disposition to believe in God or say with Carnell that God has given us an innate knowledge of himself, this God-endowed disposition or knowledge makes it possible for humans to recognize God in the creation.[28]

But all this brings us to a possible problem. If every human being is born with a disposition to believe in God, then why doesn't every human being come to recognize God's existence? If we knew a person who did not come to hold a particular belief (such as the belief that he is seeing a tree) while being appeared to in the typical and familiar way, we would conclude that his cognitive equipment was malfunctioning somehow. The Christian world-view teaches that something has happened to the human race that affects not only our actions and dispositions but also our noetic structure. As Plantinga puts it,

> God has created us in such a way that we have a strong tendency or inclination toward belief in God. This tendency has been in part overlaid or suppressed by sin. Were it not for the existence of sin in the world, human beings would believe in God to the same degree and with the same natural spontaneity that we believe in the existence of other persons, an external world, or the past. This is the natural human condition; it is because of our presently unnatural sinful condition that many of us find belief in God difficult or absurd. The fact is, Calvin thinks, one who does not believe in God is in an epistemically substandard position—rather like a man who does not believe that his wife exists, or thinks she is like a cleverly constructed robot and has no thoughts, feelings, or consciousness.[29]

The introduction of sin and the Fall at this point is not some arbitrary or ad hoc measure. Everyone familiar with Christianity knows that the Fall plays a central role in the Christian view of man and the world. It would be strange to write a book about the Christian world-view and act as though sin—or the set of Christian beliefs about sin—did not exist. We are fallen creatures. The Fall affects not only what we do but how we think. There is a noetic dimension to sin. Sin has clouded the human mind so that often we cannot see the truth.

The position set forth in this chapter holds several important implications for the so-called theistic arguments. Even if we should discover that some—or even all—theistic arguments fail as *proofs* for God's existence, they

---

[26] Edward John Carnell, *An Introduction to Christian Apologetics* (Grand Rapids: Eerdmans, 1948), p. 149n.

[27] Ibid., p. 151n.

[28] I am less confident than other philosophers that there is a hard and fast distinction between innate dispositions and innate ideas. But that is a subject best left for another book. For a brief discussion, see my *The Word of God and the Mind of Man* (Grand Rapids: Zondervan, 1982), chap. 7.

[29] Plantinga, "Reason and Belief in God," p. 66. A number of thinkers like Karl Marx and Sigmund Freud argued that the reason some people believe in God is because their cognitive equipment is malfunctioning. If Plantinga is right, it is the cognitive equipment of atheists like Marx and Freud that is malfunctioning.

may still be useful insofar as they function as evidence or grounds for belief. An argument may provide reasons that support belief, even though it falls short of being a proof.[30] Even if various arguments for God's existence are not sound, they may still draw attention to things like order and purpose that can complement and support the believer's conviction that God exists. In other words, even if an argument fails as a proof, it may still function as evidence or a justifying ground that can help trigger belief. Since humans have the *sensus divinitatis*, consideration of a theistic argument may present them with information or lead them to experiences that, in conjunction with God-implanted dispositions, will help trigger belief in God in ways similar to how nonreligious experiences or other justifying conditions trigger such beliefs as "I am now seeing a tree."

Part 3 of this book will consider several familiar attempts to "prove" the existence of God. It is a mistake to approach such arguments with a do-or-die attitude. The rationality of belief in God does not depend on the discovery of some irrefutable argument, whatever such an argument might look like. But even though the discovery of one or more sound arguments for God's existence is not necessary in order for Christian theism to be rational, such activity may be useful and helpful in other ways.

For Further Exploration—Chapter Seven

1. What is natural theology?
2. Discuss the relation between natural theology and foundationalism.
3. Give your answer to the following: Is natural theology necessary? Is it useless? Why or why not?
4. Discuss the differences between propositional and nonpropositional evidence.
5. Explain Thomas Reid's view about the role that God-implanted dispositions play in human knowledge.
6. Many philosophers have tried and failed to come up with arguments to justify belief in other minds and in the existence of the external world. What are your thoughts about these failures?
7. What is the *sensus divinitatis*? Do you see any connection between it and the kinds of claims one encounters in the standard arguments for God's existence?

---

[30]The word *proof* is a slippery and often misunderstood term. I offer an analysis of the notion in chapter 8.

Part 3

SOME ARGUMENTS FOR GOD'S EXISTENCE

Chapter 8

ON PROVING THAT
GOD EXISTS

Let's see where we are as we approach midpoint of our search for a rational faith. In Part 1, I explained the importance of viewing Christian theism and its competitors as world-views or conceptual systems. I discussed some of the more significant ways in which the Christian world-view differs from its major Western competitor, Naturalism. I drew attention to the important distinction between negative and positive apologetics and also described my approach to evaluating the Christian world-view vis-à-vis any competing system.

Part 2 dealt primarily with a question in negative apologetics. All too often, Christian theists have allowed themselves to be placed in the unfair position of having to "prove" certain claims before their position will be admitted to the bar of rationality. Many refuse to give serious consideration to the claims of Christian theism simply because they begin by assuming the evidentialist challenge to religious faith and then fail to find satisfactory arguments or proofs that in their judgment establish Christianity's rationality. Others who may once have been theists have been led to abandon their former convictions because, once again, they assumed that the rationality of theism depended upon the discovery of arguments or proofs; when those arguments were not forthcoming, it was natural that such people—given their presumption of evidentialism—would turn away from beliefs now regarded as irrational. Meeting the evidentialist challenge, then, is an important first step in negative apologetics. Belief in God is properly basic; so far as the rationality of the Christian's personal faith is concerned, the discovery of proofs or arguments is not necessary. When it comes to challenging the rationality of Christian faith, the burden of proof rests with the atheologian.

But the discussion of evidentialism and narrow foundationalism in Part 2 also led us in directions that afford us a perspective on natural theology that differs from what we find in the writings of philosophers of religion and apologists who accept the evidentialist approach. For thinkers like this, the discovery of arguments that "prove" the existence of God (along with other essential Christian concerns) is regarded as necessary if their enterprise is to have intellectual integrity, if it is to be rational. Moreover, the search for arguments that will do the desired job proceeds on the basis of several questionable assumptions, namely, that the presentation of the right "facts" or the right "proof" is sufficient to persuade any open-minded person. Part 2 noted a number of problems with this approach.

But then I pointed out that even though arguments for God's existence are not necessary, it hardly follows that they are useless. For one thing, many people, including a large number of theists, do not believe that belief in God is properly basic. Providing help for such people may well make it necessary to search for reasons, evidence, arguments, and the like. But to embark on this kind of activity is to switch from negative to positive apologetics. The purpose of this chapter is to examine more fully what it means to "prove" something. We will find that the notion of proof is far more complex than many realize. I will then explore what it might mean to "prove" the existence of God. I will argue that many people approach the task with an ideal or standard of proof that is inappropriate for the subject. Because their standard for a proof is much too high, they are often disappointed with the results or frequently think there is something wrong with their conclusion (i.e., that God exists) when, in fact, the problem rests with their idea of what qualifies as a "proof."

WHAT IS A PROOF?

What Constitutes a Good Argument?

A proof is an argument. An argument is a set of at least two propositions, one of which is affirmed on the basis of the other(s). The proposition[1] that is asserted on the basis of the other(s) is called the conclusion. The proposition(s) that serves as the ground for the conclusion is the premise (or premises). In order to qualify as a proof, an argument should satisfy two conditions.

1. The form or logical structure of the argument must be *valid*. Over the centuries, students of logic have studied the major forms of deductive reasoning and identified the valid (correct) argument forms. One frequently encountered kind of reasoning is the mixed hypothetical syllogism. In this argument form, the first premise is a hypothetical statement like "If Nash plays eighteen holes of golf today, then he will shoot a score higher than eighteen." The second premise is a categorical statement[2] like "Nash plays eighteen holes of golf today." And the conclusion is also a categorical

---

[1] By proposition, I mean simply a sentence that is either true or false.

[2] A categorical statement or proposition is a simple declarative sentence. Categorical propositions should be contrasted with hypothetical statements that have the form, "If p, then q," with disjunctive statements (either p or q), and with conjunctive statements (p and q).

statement; in this case, "therefore, Nash will shoot a score higher than eighteen."

Mixed hypothetical syllogisms may take four possible forms, two of them valid and two of them invalid. The two valid forms have been given names and look like this:

A. *Modus Ponens*   B. *Modus Tollens*
   If p, then q If p, then q
   p not q
   Therefore, q Therefore, not p

Any argument that has the form of either *modus ponens* or *modus tollens* is *valid*, which is simply to say that if the argument's premises are true, then its conclusion *must* also be true. If an argument has one of these two forms, it is impossible for that argument's premises to be true and also for its conclusion to be false.

Consider the following as examples of *modus ponens* and *modus tollens*:

A. If Nash plays eighteen holes, his score will be higher than eighteen.
   Nash plays eighteen holes.
   Therefore, Nash's score will be higher than eighteen.
B. If Nash plays eighteen holes, his score will be higher than eighteen.
   Nash's score is less than eighteen.[3]
   Therefore, Nash did not play eighteen holes.

The two invalid forms of the mixed hypothetical syllogism have also been given names and look like this:

C. *The Fallacy of*   D. *The Fallacy of*
   Affirming the   *Denying the*
   Consequent[4]   *Antecedent*
   If p, then q If p, then q
   q not p
   Therefore, p Therefore, not q

The problem of reasoning in these fallacious ways becomes apparent as soon as one considers examples like the following:

C. If Nash plays eighteen holes, his score will be higher than eighteen.
   Nash's score is higher than eighteen.
   Therefore, Nash played eighteen holes.[5]
D. If Nash plays eighteen holes, his score will be higher than eighteen.
   It is false that Nash plays eighteen holes.
   Therefore, it is false that Nash's score is higher then eighteen.

---

[3] There are several alternate ways of making the same claim, e.g., "It is false that Nash's score is higher than eighteen"; "It is not the case that Nash's score is higher than eighteen." Likewise, the conclusion could be worded "It is false that Nash played eighteen holes."

[4] In a hypothetical statement, the first clause is the antecedent and the second clause is the consequent.

[5] Obviously, I could take more than eighteen shots without necessarily playing a full eighteen holes. I've been known to do this well on one hole.

The mixed hypothetical syllogism is worth special attention here because other argument forms can be reduced to it. Take our old stand-by argument about Socrates: "All men are mortal"; "Socrates is a man"; "Therefore, Socrates is mortal." This argument is what we call a categorical syllogism[6] and has the following form:

> All *A* is *B*.
> All *C* is *A*.
> Therefore, All *C* is *B*.

Another way of putting this argument-form is saying that *if* the two premises are true, then the conclusion must be true. If we lump the two premises together and call them *p*, we're really saying that if *p* is true, then *q* (the conclusion) is true. In other words, the inference in any argument from the premises to the conclusion takes the form of a hypothetical statement in which the antecedent clause (if *p*) sums up all the premises and the consequent clause (then *q*) stands for the conclusion. One thing meant by validity, then, is this: *if* the premises of an argument are true, then the conclusion must be true.

2. But of course every student of logic knows that an argument may be formally valid and still contain one or more false statements. Consider the following:

> All dogs are reptiles.
> All reptiles lay eggs.
> Therefore, all dogs lay eggs.

Even though this argument is formally valid,[7] the conclusion and at least one of the premises is false. Because truth and validity are different properties,[8] students of logic talk about a second test that any good argument must satisfy: it must be *sound*. In order for an argument to be sound, the argument must be valid, and the propositions that make up the argument must all be true. Theists who set out to prove the existence of God should be careful to see that their arguments are not merely valid; their arguments should be sound.

What Constitutes a Good Proof?

The criteria of a good (that is, a sound) argument are beyond dispute. The argument's propositions must be true, and its inferences must be valid. Note that these characteristics are really independent of psychological or personal factors such as whether an individual's personal history predisposes him to view the argument favorably or unfavorably. Does the mere fact that a collection of claims and inferences constitutes a good argument automatically make that argument a good *proof*?

The answer to this important question is complicated by the fact that

---

[6] In a categorical syllogism, all the premises and the conclusion are categorical statements.

[7] Our new argument has the familiar form: All *A* is *B*; All *B* is *C*; Therefore, All *A* is *C*.

[8] Truth is a property of the propositions (the premises and conclusion) that make up an argument. Validity is a property of arguments.

the phrase *good proof* can be used in two different ways. On the one hand, we could say that a good proof is a good (sound) argument that any reasonable person should accept. We might call this the objective notion of proof. While in many contexts, this is a perfectly legitimate notion of proof, it fails to capture the essence of what we take to be proving something in other contexts. Most of us, I imagine, have been in situations where we offered perfectly good arguments (or so we thought) that perfectly reasonable people failed to accept. Was there anything wrong with the people who were unconvinced by our argument? It would be hard to justify such a conclusion in *all* such cases. Or was there something wrong with our argument? Not if it really was sound.

Fortunately, there is another way of understanding the notion of a good proof. In this second sense, we can say that a good proof is a good (sound) argument that actually leads another person to accept its conclusion. In other words, in order to be a good proof (in this second sense), an argument must not only satisfy certain logical criteria, it must also meet an important *psychological* test; it must actually succeed in persuading someone to accept the conclusion. Consider the strangeness of a situation where a person responds to an argument by saying, "Although you have offered a good proof for your position, I remain unpersuaded." In this subjective sense of *proof*, any argument (even a good one) that fails to persuade its targeted audience falls short of being a good proof. A good proof is an argument that works.

Note several other points about this subjective notion of proof. For one thing, *proofs are person-relative*. This claim actually says two things. (1) *Proofs are relative*, which is simply to admit the obvious, namely, that the same argument may function as a proof for one person and result in little more than contempt from someone else. (2) *Proofs are relative to individual persons*. Even when an argument is directed to some large audience, the people in that audience must always respond as individuals. And their response will reflect varying features in their past and present personal history. In fact, we could take this point even further and state that proofs are relative to individual persons in particular circumstances. Had someone presented one of the more complicated arguments for God's existence to me when I was too young or too unprepared to appreciate it, the argument would undoubtedly have failed as a proof. Before an argument can function as a proof, any number of conditions must be satisfied. The person must understand what is being said; he must "see" that the key claims in the argument are true; he must believe that the argument is sound; and he must not have a strong emotional aversion to claims made in or implied by the conclusion.

All of this is to say that proofs must pass tests that are both logical and psychological. No argument can become a proof *for some person* until it persuades that person. In the real world, unfortunately, the logical and psychological requirements we have noted often get separated. While many perfectly good arguments fail to persuade large numbers of people, many perfectly bad arguments persuade people by the millions. Examples of the latter are readily available in television commercials and the speeches of politicians. As experience so clearly shows, any argument may function as a proof with some person or other. So let us agree that no proof (that is, an argument that has persuaded someone) can be a *good* proof unless it is also a good argument. But our analysis also forces us to admit that no good argument can also be a good proof unless it also persuades someone to accept its conclusion.

Given the person-relative nature of proofs, then, it seems highly unlikely that there is any such thing as a proof for God's existence that will convince everyone. Perhaps we should approach cautiously the efforts of theologians and philosophers who seem to be seeking arguments that will prove the existence of God to *everyone*.

George Mavrodes suggests that we view proofs in the same way we look at tools.[9] Some people become so personally attached to their proofs that they feel threatened when those proofs fail to gain universal acceptance. But, Mavrodes observes, this is not how we react when we find that a particular tool (a hammer, let us say) cannot do a job as well as some other tool. What we do is temporarily discard the first tool and look for another more suited to the job at hand. Mavrodes suggests we adopt the same attitude toward our proof. If a proof works, that's fine. But if it doesn't, discard it and look for another. People shouldn't lose confidence in their arguments simply because some other person fails to find them convincing. We shouldn't become so personally attached to our arguments that we cannot set them aside for the sake of something better. Some people evidence stress when some pet argument is rejected by others. Some even come to doubt the beliefs their arguments were thought to support. But why would anyone in his right mind allow the simple fact that someone else rejects one of his arguments to produce doubt in his own mind? Why allow the noetic problems of other people to act as constraints on one's own intellectual life? Even should I fail to discover an argument that proves God's existence (or the truth of some other essential Christian belief) to some person, it is doubtful that anything of philosophical significance would follow.

WHY DO PROOFS FAIL?

All of us know arguments that function as proofs *for us* but leave many others unmoved. Of all the reasons why proofs fail with particular people, three seem worthy of special notice.

The Problem of the Doubted Premise

Under this heading, I want to draw attention to something more than the fact that some attempted proofs are rejected because one of the premises in the argument is either false or believed to be false. Often, the cogency[10] of a particular argument for some person depends upon that person's "seeing" something. While this is a difficult notion to make clear, a close analogy can be found in the case of a person's seeing the point to a joke. Most of us have

---

[9] See George Mavrodes, *Belief in God* (New York: Random House, 1970), chap. 2.
[10] In order for some argument to be cogent for some person such as Jones, two conditions must be met: (1) the argument must be sound; and (2) Jones must know that the argument is sound. If some argument is sound and Jones fails to recognize its soundness, the argument will not be cogent *for Jones*. Obviously, the same argument may be cogent for one person and not cogent for another.

been in situations where the same joke that produced almost uncontrollable laughter on the part of some seemed totally unfunny to others in the same audience.[11] What happens when one person "sees" the point to a joke and someone else does not? Well, that is hard to say. We sometimes use metaphors to describe what we think happens. We can say, for example, that a particular joke *registered* with one person, but not another. But this is not especially helpful. One individual's personal history may have made him better prepared than the other; the hard-to-define quality that we call a sense of humor differs greatly from person to person.

Likewise, the degree to which various people find some philosophical or theological or apologetic argument cogent will depend on the extent to which they "see" something in a premise. For example, the cogency of some arguments for God's existence depends on some person's seeing the impossibility or absurdity of an infinitely long series. Another type of argument depends on someone's seeing the point to what is called the principle of sufficient reason or to a question like "Why is there something rather than nothing?" People who see the points to such matters are usually persons who find the arguments that appeal to such things persuasive. If one's argument for God's existence depends upon such a point's being seen when it is not, there are few options. One can attempt in various ways to help the person acquire the necessary insight or one can try a different argument (which may require that the person *see* something else) or one can decide that perhaps no apparent argument or approach will do the job.

To summarize, some arguments use premises that are clearly false or that particular individuals may believe are false. But often the acceptability of one or more premises in an argument is less a function of their truth than it is of someone's seeing something such as "There really are lots of impressive signs of design and purpose in the world." Many philosophical and theological arguments are rejected, then, not because the person knows or believes that a particular premise is false, but simply because he fails to see something that others regard as obvious. Every argument for God's existence that I know about contains at least one premise that will appear problematic to large numbers of people. This is one more reason why such arguments are person-relative.

The Problem of the Questioned Inference

But even if all the persons to whom we are presenting an argument find the premises acceptable, we may still be a long way from gaining their acceptance of our argument. Just as the premises in some proffered argument may be clearly false, so the inference (or inferences) in an argument may be clearly invalid. But there are other times when we question key inferences even though we cannot recognize precisely what is wrong— even though we cannot identify the precise fallacy that we believe is involved. Every inference can be reduced to the familiar hypothetical form, "If *p*, then *q*." Many arguments are rejected because people cannot *see* (here's that notion again) the connection between one proposition and another. Consider an example used earlier: "If Nash plays eighteen holes of golf, then Nash will take more than eighteen shots." It is possible to imagine all kinds

---

[11]I guess we could say, then, that jokes are also person-relative.

of people who might have difficulty seeing the connection between the antecedent and the consequent.[12] They may have never walked around a golf course, for example, or they may have an unusually high estimate of Nash's golfing ability (such as supposing it possible that Nash score a hole in one every time he hits a golf ball). But once any rational person sees the relevant points contained in the hypothetical statement, he will accept the connection between its parts.

Many philosophers and theologians believe that all familiar versions of the theistic arguments suffer from logical problems in the sense that one or more key inferences are clearly invalid. Whether such thinkers are right or not, a more modest claim *is* true: every familiar version of the theistic arguments contains key inferences that large numbers of people question either because they believe the inference is invalid or because they fail to see in some way the logical connection between two claims. When an argument is rejected because of the presumed invalidity of a key inference, one can deal with this by attempting to show that the inference really is valid. But how does one deal with a case where an inference is questioned simply because a person fails to see something, that is, the logical connection between two propositions? Obviously, no single answer will apply in every case. And so we have still another reason why proofs are person-relative.

The Problem of the Rejected Conclusion

Some philosophers refer to what they call the *G. E. Moore Shift*. This rather cute title is given to a move often encountered in philosophical arguments. It is named in honor of George Edward Moore (1873–1958), a British philosopher whose writings earlier in this century drew considerable attention to the matter. Moore noticed that arguments often fail to bring about an acceptance of their conclusion even when people agree that the key inference is valid and even though they initially find nothing objectionable about the premises. In other words, it is possible to have a situation in which two people express no initial objection to some proposition (call it *p*) and then agree that if *p* were true, then *q* would be true. That is, they agree about some inference that takes the familiar form,

If *p*, then *q*
p
Therefore, *q*

But suppose that *q* in this case stands for the proposition "God exists." Whatever *p* may be (that is, whatever proposition may be thought, if true, to entail the existence of God), some people are more committed to the denial of *q* than to the acceptance of *p*. That is, they might be prepared to agree that *if* the antecedent were true, *then* the consequent ("God exists") would be true. But they are more convinced that the consequent is false than that the antecedent is true. This allows such people to rebut the theist's argument in the following way:

If *p*, then *q*

---

[12]Once again, the antecedent of a hypothetical statement is the "if" clause and the consequent is the "then" clause.

Not q
Therefore, not p

Suppose we substitute for p and q and end up with the following (admittedly oversimplified) argument:

If the world had a beginning, then God exists.
The world had a beginning.
Therefore, God exists.

As we know, the world contains some individuals who are more strongly committed to the falsity of the conclusion than they are to the truth of the antecedent. In such cases, it is not enough that these individuals accept the logical connection between the antecedent and the consequent. Their rejection of the conclusion will lead them also to reject the antecedent:

If the world had a beginning, then God exists.
But God does not exist.
Therefore, it is false that the world had a beginning.

And so, arguments may fail as proofs because people doubt one or more premises, question key inferences, or simply reject the conclusion. And in any of these cases, the rejection of the argument may hang in some way on considerations that have more to do with the individual's psychological make-up than with matters of truth or validity.

HOW HIGH SHOULD OUR STANDARDS BE?

What standards must an argument satisfy before it qualifies as a proof? We must be careful not to set the standards of proof too high.[13] If our standards of proof are too rigorous for the material we're dealing with, we can make our search for the truth much more difficult than it has to be. We are all familiar with the standards of proof in a deductive system like geometry. In geometry, such things as probability, personal judgment, the weighing of evidence, and noncoercive arguments[14] are inappropriate. The standards of proof in geometry are as high as they can possibly be. There are times when anything short of logical certainty is enough to disqualify a proposed proof.

While few people would place a world-view like Christianity in the same category with a geometric system, many people nonetheless act as though any adequate proof for a proposition like "God exists" must meet equally high standards. In fact, they might say, how can we be satisfied with anything less, given all that is at stake in our reflection about God? It is important to remember, however, that reasonable people do recognize how different kinds of inquiry can proceed quite properly with different but appropriate standards of proof. Philosopher Rem B. Edwards offers some helpful comments on this point:

---

[13] Obviously, we should also avoid setting the standard of proof too low.
[14] A coercive proof is one that rational people seem compelled to accept. A noncoercive proof is one that may still be disputed by reasonable people.

It is sometimes maintained that unless a very strict proof or set of related proofs is offered, nothing is proved at all. For example, it is sometimes held that unless all the premises of an argument are absolutely certain and the pattern of reasoning indubitably valid, the proof is utterly worthless. If one adheres strictly to this rigid deductive ideal, however, one is forced to conclude that there are *no* worthwhile proofs anywhere except possibly in mathematics, and even here the tendency is to regard axioms as system-relative and not absolutely indubitable in all possible contexts. Certainly there are no such proofs to be found either in natural science or in philosophy.[15]

While some philosophers have made the mistake of thinking that their proofs met such high standards, Edwards wisely counsels that "in the final analysis we must settle for a more modest understanding of what constitutes a rationally justified philosophical belief.[16] He then applies his comments to arguments designed to prove the existence of God.

Occasionally, perhaps, even some of the traditional proofs for the existence of God have been interpreted as providing conclusive evidence for their theistic conclusions. From the outset, however, we must recognize that it is a mistake so to regard them, not because we know before we even begin that they do not prove anything, but rather because we know that there are *no* philosophical beliefs anywhere that are supported by conclusive evidence. To expect indubitable premises and rigorous deductive validity from the traditional proofs [for God's existence] is to expect too much. No philosophical proofs of anything rest on indubitable premises. Philosophical proof simply cannot meet such exacting requirements, but this is not to make lame excuses for sloppy thinking.[17]

Edward's good advice should be taken to heart as we examine several theistic arguments in the next few chapters.

As Edwards has explained, not even philosophical arguments can meet the high standards of some people. But perhaps the analogy of a different arena of argument and proof can make our point clearer. Consider the standards applied in many courts of law. In criminal cases where the seriousness of the matter could result in imprisonment or execution, the law is correct in requiring proof beyond any reasonable doubt. But there are many other kinds of cases tried in law courts where less proof may be acceptable. C. Stephen Evans explains:

In a civil damage suit over an airplane crash, it is not necessary to prove beyond any reasonable doubt that the crash was due to the airline's negligence, but only that it seems highly likely or probable that was so "in the judgment of a prudent person." The task in this sort of case is to make a judgment which is in accordance with "the preponderance of the evidence." A "clear and convincing proof" in this context is defined in terms of "a high probability." This seems to me to be the kind of "reasonable case" we ought to strive for in religious matters as well. We ought to strive to make a judgment which is in accordance with "the

[15]Rem B. Edwards, *Reason and Religion* (New York: Harcourt Brace Jovanovich, 1972), p. 222.
[16]Ibid.
[17]Ibid.

preponderance of evidence" and which seems highly probable or plausible.[18]

If we accept the relevance of Evans' analogy between proofs in the kinds of court cases he describes and proofs for such religious claims as "God exists," several important points follow. For one thing, as Evans notes, "good evidence for religious faith will not be some kind of absolute proof that some philosophers seem to seek. Rather, it will be evidence which is sufficient to satisfy a reasonable person."[19] Though such proofs are perfectly appropriate for their subject matter, they will seldom result in universal acceptance. "Must an argument be universally accepted to be a proof? Accepted by all sane people who consider it? Frequently something like this standard seems to be presupposed in these discussions. . . . Such a concept of proof seems impossibly high. It also seems unfair, since this is not the standard of proof we require for nonreligious areas."[20] Juries in court cases are not required to seek proof beyond all *possible* doubt, only beyond a *reasonable* doubt.

Furthermore, Evans notes, "the case for religious faith will not be based on a single argument functioning as a proof, but upon the total evidence available from every region of human experience."[21] Rem B. Edwards makes a similar claim when he writes,

> Giving philosophical proof is very similar to what a lawyer does in a courtroom. The philosopher "builds up a case." He explains as best he can why he believes what he does and why he rejects the chief alternatives to his position, and he is always willing to examine and re-examine the elements out of which his case is built. Many lines of converging evidence must be put together into a coherent case. . . . Many complex elements enter into the case for belief in God. Often the diverse "proofs" are compared, quite correctly, to strands or fibers in a rope, none of which does the work of the whole rope, yet some of which must do some work if the rope is to have any strength at all.[22]

The case for God's existence should be cumulative. There is nothing wrong with reaching a decision based on a cumulative argument. After all, Evans states "one bit of evidence against a criminal may not be enough to convict him. The same may be said of a second or third bit, or any number of bits, when taken in isolation. If each bit does have some force, however, then all of the bits taken together may be more than enough to convict the accused and send him off to prison."[23] Our judgment in such matters, then, is seldom the result of one argument or piece of evidence.

It should also be obvious from everything said above that the most we should expect from such arguments is probability. We will have to deal with probability when considering the truth of the premises or when assessing the connection between the argument's premises and conclusion, or both. But

---

[18]C. Stephen Evans, *The Quest for Faith* (Downers Grove, Ill.: InterVarsity Press, 1986), pp. 28–29.

[19]Ibid., p. 29.

[20]Ibid., p. 26.

[21]Ibid., p. 29.

[22]Edwards, *Reason and Religion*, p. 223.

[23]Evans, *Quest for Faith*, pp. 25–26.

probabilistic arguments can bolster and confirm a belief; often they are strong enough to produce moral or psychological certainty.[24]

Another point derivable from our analogy meshes with an important claim made earlier. To quote Evans again, "Religious faith is not guilty until proven innocent. No special burden of proof rests on the religious believer, since opponents of religious belief are committed to world views which are equally risky."[25] We are justified in regarding belief in God as innocent until proven guilty.

Finally, the weighing of evidence in all such matters is something that must be done by human beings, not computers. As Edwards explains this point:

> Assessing the strength of [the case of God's existence], like giving a judgment in a courtroom, is not like running a mathematical proof through a computer. Many complex elements enter into the case for belief in God. . . . As in a courtroom verdict, the verdict for or against the existence of God cannot be rendered in some purely automatic fashion. Finally, when all is said and done, someone must simply pass judgment.[26]

Each of us must interpret and weigh the arguments; each of us is ultimately responsible for our own final decision.

DEDUCTION OR INDUCTION?

A large number of people approach the theistic arguments with the conviction that only *deductive* arguments should be deemed appropriate. Many atheologians treat nondeductive approaches to God's existence with scorn before proceeding to attack the soundness of the deductive arguments that are presented. Many theists agree with their nontheistic counterparts that there is something suspicious about any inductive argument purporting to support the conclusion that God exists.

This deductive-or-nothing attitude fails to appreciate that inductive or probabilistic arguments are perfectly appropriate in some contexts. In truth, inductive reasoning is all that's available for some subject matters. Suppose one finds himself part of that large company of theists who recognize difficulties with the familiar deductive arguments for God's existence. Is there any harm—initially at least—in seeing what value or plausibility various inductive arguments may have? One thinker who has taken this approach is the British philosopher Richard Swinburne. While Swinburne admits there are "valid deductive arguments to the existence of God," he points out that "they start from premises which are far from generally accepted."[27] But one condition must be met by any good argument; it must begin with premises that everyone knows or accepts and then proceed by steps that are logically correct and seen to be logically correct.

According to thinkers like Swinburne, the proper way to argue for

---

[24]To repeat a point made earlier, moral certainty must always be distinguished from logical certainty.

[25]Evans, *Quest for Faith,* p. 29.

[26]Edwards, *Reason and Religion,* p. 223.

[27]Richard Swinburne, *The Existence of God* (Oxford: Clarendon Press, 1979), p. 14.

God's existence is to utilize inductive arguments. As Swinburne explains, an inductive argument is "an argument from premises to a conclusion in which the premises count in favour of, provide evidence for, the conclusion, without entailing it."[28] In other words, the truth of the premises does not necessarily imply the truth of the conclusion; they may only imply that the conclusion is probably true. Agreeing with Swinburne and others, Richard Purtill suggests an approach to God's existence in which "the underlying pattern of all arguments for the existence of God is that of inference to God as the best explanation of certain very general features of our experience: change, causal order, contingency order and understandability, [and] the objectivity of morality."[29] Purtill explains how this inductive approach works in connection with the teleological argument:

> A number of philosophers now regard this [teleological] argument as an inductive argument based on the principle that we should accept the hypothesis which gives the highest probability to the observed facts. It is argued that the hypothesis of design by God gives the highest probability to the apparent order and understandability of the universe, and that therefore the hypothesis of design should be preferred to nontheistic explanations.[30]

According to this approach—which will be adopted in this book—the theistic arguments should not be viewed as deductive arguments that drive us inescapably to the conclusion that God exists. They should be approached rather as efforts to direct our attention to certain features of reality (the inner and outer worlds). The noted features of reality are exactly what we should expect to find if the theistic world-view is true. The case for theism is made even stronger when we find things in the world that we would not expect to find if Naturalism were true or if theism were false.

Atheologian Antony Flew criticizes philosophers who admit that certain arguments fail as deductive proofs and who then attempt to utilize them as inductive proofs. He writes:

> It is occasionally suggested that some candidate proof, although admittedly failing as a proof, may sometimes do useful service as a pointer. This is a false exercise of the generosity so characteristic of examiners. A failed proof cannot serve as a pointer to anything, save perhaps to the weaknesses of those who have accepted it. Nor, for the same reason, can it be put to work along with other throw outs as part of the accumulation of evidences. If one leaky bucket will not hold water that is no reason to think that ten can.[31]

But Richard Swinburne answers Flew by pointing out that arguments that may be deductively weak can be inductively strong:

> But of course arguments which are not deductively valid are often inductively strong; and if you put three weak arguments together you may often get a strong one, perhaps even a deductively valid one. The

[28] Ibid., p. 45.
[29] Richard L. Purtill, "The Current State of Arguments for the Existence of God," *Review and Expositor* 82 (1985): 532.
[30] Ibid., p. 522.
[31] Antony Flew, *God and Philosophy* (New York: Dell, 1966), pp. 62–63.

analogy in Flew's last sentence is a particularly unhappy one for his purpose. For clearly if you jam ten leaky buckets together in such a way that holes in the bottom of each bucket are squashed close to solid parts of the bottoms of neighbouring buckets, you will get a container that holds water.[32]

Swinburne thinks it is clear that a number of inductive theistic arguments that may be weak when considered alone may, when taken together, make up a quite strong cumulative case. Sometimes, he admits, "philosophers consider the arguments for the existence of God in isolation from each other, reasoning as follows: the cosmological argument does not prove the conclusion, the teleological argument does not prove the conclusion, etc., etc., therefore the arguments do not prove the conclusion."[33] But treating these same arguments as parts of a cumulative case can lead to a quite different conclusion:

An argument from p to r may be invalid; another argument from q to r may be invalid. But if you run the arguments together, you could well get a valid deductive argument: the argument from p and q to r may be valid. The argument from "all students have long hair" to "Smith has long hair" is invalid, and so is the argument from "Smith is a student" to "Smith has long hair"; but the argument from "all students have long hair and Smith is a student" to "Smith has long hair" is valid.[34]

The fact that arguments that may be weak when considered separately may support each other becomes even more clear when we consider inductive arguments:

That Smith has blood on his hands hardly makes it probable that Smith murdered Mrs. Jones, nor (by itself) does the fact that Smith stood to gain from Mrs. Jones's death, nor (by itself) does the fact that Smith was near the scene of the murder at the time of its being committed, but all these phenomena taken together (perhaps with other phenomena as well) may indeed make the conclusion probable.[35]

Although none of the theistic arguments by themselves prove that God exists or even that God's existence is probable, Louis Pojman argues,

Together they constitute a cumulative case for theism. There is something crying for an explanation: Why does this grand universe exist? Together the arguments for God's existence provide a plausible explanation of the existence of the universe, of why we are here, of why there is anything at all and not just nothing.[36]

The explanatory power of theism is based not on single, isolated arguments but on the cumulative case one gets by reflecting on the existence of the universe, the order of the universe, and the facts of human rationality, moral consciousness, and religious experience.

---

[32]Swinburne, *Existence of God*, p. 14.

[33]Ibid., p. 13.

[34]Ibid.

[35]Ibid.

[36]Louis J. Pojman, *Philosophy of Religion: An Anthology* (Belmont, Calif.: Wadsworth, 1987), p. 28.

SCIENTIFIC EXPLANATIONS VERSUS PERSONAL EXPLANATIONS

Richard Swinburne has one final contribution to make at this point. He suggests that we view the theistic arguments as explanations. He then sets up a contrast between two antithetic types of explanation: scientific explanations and personal explanations. In a scientific explanation, the effect is inferred from accompanying causes, conditions, and the relevant laws. The paradigm of a scientific explanation is the way various phenomena are explained in physics.[37] A personal explanation, in contrast, is one where the phenomena are explained in terms of some rational agent's intentional action. One good place to see personal explanations in action is in history.[38] Understanding and explaining a historical action require attention to the agent's reasons for acting within the context of the full set of circumstances, real and imagined, that surrounded his action.

In a typical theistic argument, the theist draws attention to certain phenomena (of either the outer world or the inner world) that need explanation. Now suppose we find that a scientific (that is, a nonpersonal) explanation fails to do justice to the phenomena. *If* we have only two choices—if an explanation must be either scientific or personal—and if we discover that phenomena like human rationality cannot adequately be explained in terms of impersonal causes and conditions, it is natural to conclude that we must then seek for an explanation in terms of the intentional action of some rational agent. Swinburne provides an example:

> When a detective argues from various bloodstains on the woodwork, fingerprints on the metal, Smith's corpse on the floor, money missing from the safe, Jones's having much extra money to—Jones's having intentionally killed Smith and stolen his money, he is arguing to an explanation of the various phenomena in terms of the intentional action of a rational agent. Since persons are paradigm cases of rational agents, I will term explanation in terms of the intentional action of a rational agent personal explanation.[39]

Given the kind of phenomena Swinburne describes in this paragraph, only an explanation in terms of some person's intentional action can possibly do justice to the evidence. Likewise, Swinburne continues,

> when the theist argues from phenomena such as the existence of the world or some feature of the world to the existence of God, he is arguing . . . to an explanation of the phenomena in terms of the intentional action of a person [i.e., God]. . . . A theistic explanation is a personal explanation. It explains phenomena in terms of the action of a person.[40]

---

[37]See Carl G. Hempel, "Explanation in Science and History," in *Ideas of History*, ed. Ronald Nash (New York: Dutton, 1969), 2: 79–106. Hempel's rather famous position failed to do justice to personal explanations. The shortcomings of his position are pointed out in later essays in this same volume.

[38]See William Dray, "The Historical Explanation of Actions Reconsidered," in *Ideas of History*, pp. 106–24. For a summary of Dray's position, see Ronald Nash, *Christian Faith and Historical Understanding* (Grand Rapids: Zondervan, 1984), chap. 3.

[39]Swinburne, *Existence of God*, p. 20.

[40]Ibid., pp. 22, 93.

Swinburne's category of personal explanation is an important contribution to the debate over God's existence. When major features of the inner and outer worlds cannot be given an adequate scientific explanation, we will have to give added weight to any personal explanation that does explain them. Should we ever become convinced that important features of reality require explanation in terms of the intentional actions of a rational Being, we'll have discovered significant support for belief in the existence of God.

For Further Exploration—Chapter Eight

1. Explain how someone who regards belief in God as properly basic could consistently seek and use "proofs" for God's existence.
2. Provide several reasons why proofs are person-relative.
3. Note some of the more important things that follow if proofs for God's existence are person-relative.
4. Using the example of a court of law, explain how it is possible to set the standards of proof too high.
5. Explain how arguments that are deductively weak may be inductively strong.
6. What is your present evaluation of what the book calls a cumulative argument for God's existence?
7. Explain the difference between scientific and personal explanations. Show the relevance of the latter for some arguments for God's existence.

Chapter 9

COSMOLOGICAL ARGUMENTS FOR GOD'S EXISTENCE

The mere existence of the world is a fact that requires explanation. Providing this explanation is the task of what is called the cosmological argument.[1] Actually, there are quite a few cosmological arguments around, and they differ greatly in comprehensibility and plausibility. Since it would be quite impractical to consider anything approaching a full range of forms taken by this approach, I have decided to concentrate on what I take to be the two versions most worthy of our attention.[2]

But before we begin, it will be helpful to remember several points made earlier. Even should we find a version of the cosmological argument that appears valid, it will still contain premises that are doubtful or unacceptable to large numbers of people. In every instance where this is the case, the argument—even though it may be formally valid—will still fail to qualify as a *good* argument *for those people*. We should be neither surprised nor disappointed if we discover that the cosmological arguments we examine fail as deductive proofs. We should look beyond the argument's value (or lack of value) as a deductive proof and examine what contribution it makes to providing warrant or support for the existence of God. And we should study

---

[1] The term *cosmological* comes from two Greek words. *Logos* is a Greek word that has many meanings, one of them being "reason." *Kosmos* is the Greek word meaning "world," but it also includes the idea of orderliness. When the Greeks used *kosmos*, they meant a world that exhibits order and not chaos. Hence, the word referred to something more than mere existence.

[2] To say that the specific arguments I discuss are "worthy of attention" does not necessarily mean that they are especially strong arguments. The first version I consider merits attention not because of its strength as an argument but because it happens to be an especially popular form of the argument.

how the argument does this not simply by itself, but also in conjunction with the kinds of considerations that are made evident by other kinds of theistic arguments.

GOD AS THE TEMPORAL FIRST CAUSE

Cosmological arguments reason back from the existence of the world to a principle or being that explains the world. This being or principle is called in various versions of the argument by such names as the First Cause, the Prime Mover,[3] the Necessary Being, or the Sufficient Reason. In this section of the chapter, we'll be concerned with a form of the cosmological argument that attempts to show that God is the First Cause of the universe.

The first thing we need to note about our argument is the ambiguity of the phrase *First Cause*. Some being or principle may be said to be the First Cause in a temporal or a logical sense.[4] If something is the First Cause in the temporal sense, it exists at the beginning of a series of causes and effects. In this temporal sense, God would be the First Cause if he initiated the long series of causes and effects that have brought the world to its present state.

Many of us have seen people construct extremely long and complex series of adjacent dominoes. Setting up thousands of these dominoes can take days. Then at some appropriate moment, someone tips over the first domino and sets up a chain reaction in which all the dominoes are eventually toppled. After we have watched thousands of dominoes fall in this way, it is natural to ask for the First Cause of the entire event. In this context, the quest for the First Cause ends when we discover the event or action or cause that tipped the first domino and started the chain reaction.

To take another example, suppose the car we are driving is forced to stop at a railroad crossing. We watch as the first railroad car rolls by. If we happen to be in a reflective mood, we might wonder about what causes its motion since there is no locomotive pulling the train. We quickly see that the first car is moving because it is being pushed by the car behind it. Our attention then turns to why the second car is moving. The answer, not surprisingly, is that it is being pushed by a third car, and so on.

Of course, whenever any of us had this experience, we found that sooner or later the series of cars ended and that the entire series of cars was being pushed by its First Cause, the locomotive. But suppose there had been no First Cause, which in the case of our example was the locomotive that imparted motion to the car immediately in front of it and then, through that car, imparted motion to all the other cars in the train. Can we really conceive of a series of moving railroad cars apart from some First Cause that got the series started? But of course our series of dominoes and railroad cars are *finite*

---

[3] The term *Prime Mover* is an especially outdated term with links to certain strains in medieval philosophy and, prior to that, to the Greek philosopher Aristotle. Philosophers and theologians who attempted to reason to a Prime Mover of the world used the word *motion* as a synonym for *change*. I will ignore such versions of the cosmological argument since the reasoning involved and the problems they raise are similar to those I'll be examining in this first part of the chapter.

[4] We'll examine what it means to say God is the First Cause in the second or logical sense in the next section of this chapter.

series. Since each such series has a definite starting point, it is easy to imagine that none of the subsequent effects could have occurred without help from that First Cause back at the beginning.

But what happens when we try to conceive of a series of falling dominoes or moving railroad cars that is *infinitely* long? If we had the power somehow to go back to the "beginning," we would find that, in truth, there was no beginning! There was no first domino; there is rather an infinitely long series of dominoes that have been falling *forever*. There is no first railroad car or locomotive; there is simply an infinitely long series of railroad cars, each one being pushed by the one behind it.

Some people think that all such talk about infinitely long series of causes and effects is nonsensical in some way. Regardless of how long such a series may be, they believe, one simple truth applies in all cases: if there were no First Cause, there would have been no first effect and no second effect and so on. Take away the First Cause and none of the other events in the series would have occurred. Anyone who thinks this way or "sees" this point is a good candidate for this first version of the cosmological argument. When we change the example from falling dominoes and moving railroad cars to the much more complicated series of causes and effects that have brought the universe to its present state, the same kind of reasoning suggests the necessity of a First Cause of the world. Whatever the first effect was that marked the beginning of the universe, unless it was a *first* effect (which means there was a *First* Cause), none of the other events in that long, complex series would have come about.

If our minds resist the possibility of an infinitely long series of moving railroad cars or falling dominoes (a moving series that had no First Cause imparting motion or change to all subsequent members of the series), it is easy to see why many people find it difficult to conceive of an infinite series of causes and effects in the world. Surely, such people believe, there must have been a First Cause that started the series of changes that eventually resulted in what we presently see going on in reality. Since an infinite series like this is impossible (so the argument goes), there must have been a First Cause in the temporal sense, and that First Cause is God.

There are several well-known reasons why this first version of the cosmological argument fails as a deductive proof, i.e., fails to imply necessarily that God exists. For one thing, the argument is consistent with a situation in which the possible First Cause that initiated the causal series no longer exists. We can see this by imagining a *very* long series of falling dominoes that might take fifty years to complete. Imagine someone who comes on the scene near the end, watches the last domino fall, and then wonders about the First Cause of this series. While such a person might be justified in believing that the causal series in question had a First Cause, it might well be the case—given the long period of time involved—that the being whose action caused the first domino to fall no longer existed. Causes can initiate causal series and cease to exist at some later time. If we adopt exclusively the stance of natural theology and reject all input from special revelation, how can we be sure that the First Cause of the universe still exists? If we insist on calling *that* First Cause God, perhaps God got the world started—created the world—and then for some reason stopped existing. An alleged proof that led us to a First Cause that might no longer exist is hardly something theists should rejoice over. In other words, even if we believe our argument has demonstrated that the world had a First Cause, how do we know that the First Cause is eternal?

Moreover, how do we know that the First Cause is perfect? Christians believe in a very specific kind of God. One word that seems to capture the most important characteristics of this God is *perfect*. The medieval philosopher and theologian St. Anselm explained all this by saying that *God is that being than which a greater being cannot be conceived*. God's knowledge is perfect in the sense that it is inconceivable that any being's knowledge could be more complete. God's moral character is perfect in the sense that it is inconceivable that any being could surpass God morally. And God's power is perfect in a similar way. Does the cosmological argument we've been examining bring us, in its conclusion, to a First Cause that is perfect? If it does not and if the argument really does prove the existence of a god, we may have to face the possibility that the argument has proved the existence of some god other than the Christian God. This problem results from the fact that the world (the effect for which we're seeking a cause) is finite. There are all kinds of limits (spatial, temporal, and otherwise) to the universe. If we adopt only the stance of natural theology and admit no privileged information from any other source such as divine revelation, how can we possibly know that the creator of this finite world is itself more than finite? The answer, of course, is that we cannot. At most, it seems, all that this argument could demonstrate is the existence of a *finite* First Cause, a most unsatisfactory discovery.

Finally, how can we be sure that the world had just *one* First Cause? After all, the world is an extremely complex entity. Perhaps the world as it presently exists is the result of several different cause-effect series, each started by a different First Cause, coming together at various points.

It is clear, I trust, that I am not claiming the world was created by a being that no longer exists or by a finite being or by many gods. I am simply pointing out, as many others have before me,[5] that if we reject special revelation and attempt to reason our way from what we know about the world to the existence of a supposed First Cause, the most that reason can establish still leaves us a long way from the one, eternal, infinite, loving, holy, and personal God of the Bible.

GOD AS THE LOGICAL FIRST CAUSE

When the term *First Cause* is used in its temporal sense, the search for a First Cause hopes to end with the discovery of a being or principle that lies at the beginning of a temporal series of causes and effects. As we have seen, the approach at best leaves one far short of a being with the essential characteristics of the God of the Christian Scriptures.

Some have found a second version of the cosmological argument more

---

[5]The major classical source for these objections to the first form of the cosmological argument is David Hume's *Dialogues Concerning Natural Religion*, first published in 1779, three years after Hume's death. One of the better available editions of the work is *Dialogues Concerning Natural Religion*, ed. Nelson Pike (Indianapolis: Bobbs-Merrill, 1970).

promising. In this second approach, the argument is seen as an attempt to prove the existence of a being that is a First Cause in the logical sense of the word *first*. If a being is first in some temporal order, he exists at the beginning of that order. If something is first in the order of being, then it is the ultimate or most important being. When the president's wife is described as the first lady, no reference to her age is intended. The word *first* refers to the preeminence of her position; it refers to her importance. Consequently, to describe God as the logical First Cause is to view him as the ultimate cause or condition of everything that exists.

At this point, we need an example to help us get started. Let us recall our example of the falling dominoes. When we first considered this case, we were looking for the event or action that served as the temporal first cause of the entire network of causes and effects; we were looking for the efficient cause at the beginning of the sequence that produced the first effect and so on. But there is another kind of cause or condition without which our long series of toppling dominoes could not exist *as a series*. I am not referring simply to the mere existence of the dominoes. Dominoes as such can exist in many different environments. We can dump millions of them out of an airplane and watch them fall to earth. We can empty huge boxes of them on quicksand or in an ocean. But if we're to have any number of dominoes standing on end such that the falling of each domino to the left causes the domino on the right to fall, our dominoes must rest on a certain kind of surface. Air or water or quicksand will not do in this case. We need something firm enough to support the dominoes without itself causing them to move.

Now this floor or table (or whatever else it might be) functions as a necessary condition for the series of falling dominoes every bit as much as the finger (or whatever) that pushes the first domino. If that finger is the first temporal cause, the floor or table can be viewed as the First Cause in the logical sense. It is the underlying ground or support without which the series could not exist *as a series*.

How is all this relevant to God's being the *logical* First Cause of the universe? The Judeo-Christian notion of creation includes more than the idea that the world had a beginning in time. It *also* includes the notion that the *continued* existence of the world is ontologically dependent on God. This idea has been captured nicely in the following equations:

God minus the world equals God.
The world minus God equals nothing.

God's creative activity did bring the world into existence out of nothing; but it also involves God's continually sustaining the world in its existence. God is the necessary condition of the world in two senses: (1) Had God not created the world in the first place, it would never have come into existence; and (2) should God ever will to withdraw his sustaining power, the world would cease to exist. To describe God as First Cause is to say more than that he was the efficient cause that started the causal series we know as the world. It is also to recognize that God is the ultimate ground without which the world would not and could not exist. God *is* the temporal First Cause of the world, whether or not this proposition is entailed by a sound deductive argument. But God is also the logical First Cause of the world. It is this second point that our second form of the cosmological argument seeks to establish.

This second type of cosmological argument avoids at least two problems that appeared to undercut attempts to prove the existence of a First Cause in the temporal sense. For one thing, the search for a temporal First Cause requires one to prove that an infinite series of causes and effects is impossible. Even the great Thomas Aquinas decided that this was something that no philosopher could prove.[6] Our second version of the cosmological argument makes this matter irrelevant; we are not concerned with how long the causal series is or even with what caused the series to start. Even if the series were infinitely long (in the past) and hence even if the series had *no* First Cause in the temporal sense, the causal series would still require a First Cause in the *logical* sense. The existence of the series would still be ontologically dependent upon some ultimate ground.[7] But the argument we're considering has a second advantage over the first. One of the difficulties with the first version concerned how we know that the First (temporal) Cause still exists. This would not be a problem with our second argument since the ultimate ground of the world would necessarily have to exist when the world began *and* during all the time that the world has existed. Had there ever been even a single instant when the First (logical) Cause of the world ceased to exist, the world would have ended.

The particular version of the cosmological argument now before us can be set up in several different ways. I am going to follow one of the better-known paths and build the argument around three key notions: the principle of sufficient reason, the notion of a contingent being, and the idea of a necessary being.

The Principle of Sufficient Reason

As explained by philosopher Richard Taylor, the principle of sufficient reason (PSR for short) is the belief "that there is some explanation for the existence of anything whatever, some reason why it should exist rather than not."[8] For anything that exists or is the case, the PSR states that there must be a reason or an explanation.

Suppose that nothing existed. Nothingness does not require a reason or an explanation. But the existence of something—of anything—does legiti-mate the question, Why? We would need no reason to explain the

---

[6] Obviously, my comment about Aquinas does not assume necessarily that Aquinas was correct. But when a philosopher is as good as Aquinas and when that philosopher is perhaps the leading champion of cosmological reasoning as Aquinas was, his view should be accorded some weight. Frederick Copleston provides a helpful discussion of Aquinas's position regarding creation from eternity in his *History of Philosophy*, vol. 2 (Westminster, Md.: Newman Press, 1950), chap. 36.

[7] Another clarification may be necessary. I am arguing hypothetically. I am saying that the questions of God's being the temporal First Cause and the logical First Cause can be separated; they are distinct issues. For the record, I believe in the doctrine of creation *ex nihilo*. Any self-professed Christian thinker who does not is either uninformed or toying with heresy.

[8] Richard Taylor, *Metaphysics*, 2d ed. (Englewood Cliffs, N.J.: Prentice-Hall, 1974), p. 104.

nonexistence of the world. But given the fact that the world exists, we are driven to wonder *why* it exists. Some philosophers have sought to capture the wonder we feel in the presence of being by asking us to reflect on the question, Why is there *something* rather than *nothing*? Of course, the PSR has lots of other applications. It drives us to ask such things as why our car won't start this morning, why I have a headache, why an airplane crashed, why some proposition is true, and why the Cleveland Indians lost another ball game last night.

Some thinkers have tried to challenge the PSR. How, they ask, can we be so sure that everything must have a sufficient reason? Well admittedly, we are at one of those continental divides in philosophical thinking. We're back to one of those points that some see clearly while others see nothing at all.[9] As Richard Taylor sees it, belief in the PSR "seems to be almost a part of reason itself."[10] There is something about the human mind that leaves us restless in the presence of something that we're told is simply unexplainable. Something pushes us to seek an explanation, even when we're told that there is none. Let us agree that the argument we're considering will get nowhere with anyone who denies the principle of sufficient reason. But the rest of us may be justified in believing that people who make such a claim are bound to be inconsistent in the sense that they will repeatedly evidence the principle they deny.

The Notion of Contingent Being

Contingent beings have their explanation or sufficient reason in something other than themselves. A contingent being is anything that depends on something else for its existence. It is also a being whose nonexistence is possible. If the existence of some being (call it A) depends on some other being (B), the nonexistence of B would entail the nonexistence of A. The nonexistence of a contingent being is logically possible. A contingent being, then, lacks self-sufficiency; it is not the cause or ground of its own existence. Unless one or a number of other beings existed and conditions obtained, A would not exist.

Obviously, contingent beings exist. In fact, no one has yet discovered anything but contingent beings in our cosmos. The Ohio River is a contingent being; it did not always exist and its nonexistence in the future is possible. All the automobiles I've owned have proven to be contingent beings. Mount Saint Helens did not always exist, and as recent experience shows, it is within the realm of possibility that it might cease to exist. Even the nonexistence of planet earth is possible, which, of course, implies the contingency of everything that exists on planet earth.

Human beings are contingent. We would not have come into existence had it not been for other human beings; we could not continue to exist without favorable conditions in our environment such as food, water, oxygen, the proper temperature, the absence of blood clots in our arteries, and so on.

---

[9]Of course, even critics of the PSR ought to be curious enough to want to know why some people believe in the PSR. Such curiosity would simply be another manifestation of the PSR's operation in their own noetic structure.

[10]Taylor, *Metaphysics*, p. 104.

The Idea of Necessary Being

Is everything that exists (and has existed) a contingent being? Some people think not and have introduced the notion of a noncontingent or necessary being. A necessary being, if it exists, is the complement of a contingent being. Since a contingent being is one whose nonexistence is possible, a necessary being is one whose nonexistence is impossible. In other words, contingent beings may or may not exist, but a necessary being *must* exist. Of course, we don't know yet whether there is such a thing as a necessary being, but if there is, it exists necessarily. Moreover, a necessary being does not depend on any other being for its existence. It is self-caused. To draw on a term from the Middle Ages, a necessary being exists *a se* (in itself); hence the term *aseity*. As Richard Taylor puts all this,

> To say that something is self-caused . . . means only that it exists, not contingently or in dependence upon something else, but by its own nature, which is only to say that it is a being which is such that it can neither come into being nor perish. . . . If it makes sense to speak of anything as an *impossible* being, or something that by its very nature does not exist, then it is hard to see why the idea of a necessary being, or something that in its very nature exists, should not be just as comprehensible.[11]

A necessary being would be an eternal being. There *could never* have been a time when it didn't exist, and there *could never* be a time when it could cease to exist.

A Statement of the Argument

British philosopher J. L. Mackie, one of this century's more eminent atheologians, has provided a clear summary of the argument we are considering. He wrote:

> Nothing occurs without a sufficient reason why it is so and not otherwise. There must, then, be a sufficient reason for the world as a whole; a reason why something exists rather than nothing. Each thing in the world is contingent, being causally determined by other things: it would not occur if other things were otherwise. The world as a whole, being a collection of such things, is therefore itself contingent. The series of things and events, with their causes, with causes of those causes, and so on, may stretch back infinitely in time; but, if so, then however far back we go, or if we consider the series as a whole, what we have is still contingent and therefore requires a sufficient reason outside this series. That is, there must be a sufficient reason *for* the world which is *other than* the world. This will have to be a necessary being, which contains its own sufficient reason for existence. Briefly, things must have a sufficient reason for their existence, and this must be found ultimately in a necessary being. There must be something free from the disease of contingency, a disease which affects everything in the world and the world as a whole, even if it is infinite in past time.[12]

It may help if I use a picture to explain what's going on. Imagine a circle big enough to encompass the entire universe, that is, the sum total of

---

[11]Ibid., p. 111.
[12]J. L. Mackie, *The Miracle of Theism* (Oxford: Clarendon Press, 1982), p. 82.

contingent beings. Every individual thing that exists within the circle—within the world—is a contingent being; there is no contingent being that exists outside the circle. All of this is quite proper, given the fact that the world or universe or cosmos is the sum total of all contingent beings.

With respect to any individual thing existing within the circle, it is proper to ask what its sufficient reason is.[13] We would hardly be surprised if we discovered that the sufficient reason for everything existing within the circle was something else inside the circle. This is simply another way of saying that the sufficient reason for every contingent being is some other contingent being or beings. With regard to any contingent being, it is appropriate to ask why it exists, and the answer to that question will always drive us to some being other than itself.

We have agreed that every individual thing within the circle is contingent. But what shall we say about the world itself? Is it (the world, the sum total of all contingent beings) contingent? The point here goes beyond the claim that all parts of the world are contingent. We have reached the point where many people think it makes sense to believe that the whole cosmos is contingent. After all, if every part of the world (past, present, and future) is contingent, it certainly makes sense to regard the entire world as contingent.

Suppose we allow this last step for the sake of argument, just to see where it takes us. If the world (the sum total of all contingent beings) is contingent, then it is proper to ask for the sufficient reason for the world. Notice that we are not asking why this or that part of the world exists; now we are asking why the whole thing exists. Notice also that we are not asking what first brought the world into existence. We are looking for the sufficient reason, the ultimate ground, the logical First Cause, without which the world would not exist. Why does the world exist? What is the sufficient reason for the entire total of contingent beings?

Only two answers to this question are possible. First, we might try to find the explanation for the existence of the world in some contingent being or set of contingent beings. But this won't work because we have already agreed that the world—what we are trying to explain—is the sum total of *all* contingent beings. And it is true by definition that a contingent being depends on something else for its existence. We are seeking a sufficient reason for everything within our circle, and by definition again, there are no contingent beings *outside* the circle. We cannot explain the sum total of contingent beings by simply postulating another contingent being and acting as though this new contingent being were somehow outside the circle and thus a possible explanation for the world. If any being is a contingent being, it is inside the circle and thus part of what we are trying to explain.

There seems, then, to be only one other possibility. The world (the sum total of all contingent beings) exists because it (like all contingent beings) depends upon a being other than itself. But in this case, the existence of the world must depend on the existence of a being that is *not* contingent. And if the only possible explanation for the existence of the world is a noncontin-

---

[13] After all, a contingent being is one that has its sufficient reason or explanation in some other being.

gent being, this explanation must be a *necessary* being. Once again, Richard Taylor provides some illuminating remarks:

> From the principle of sufficient reason it follows, of course, that there must be a reason, not only for the existence of everything in the world but for the world itself, meaning by "the world" simply everything that ever does exist, except God, in case there is a God. . . . it would certainly be odd to maintain that everything in the world owes its existence to something, that nothing in the world is either purely accidental, or such that it just bestows its own being upon itself, and then to deny this of the world itself. One can indeed *say* that the world is in some sense a pure accident, that there simply is no reason at all why this or any world should exist, and one can equally say that the world exists by its very nature, or is an inherently necessary being. But it is at least very odd and arbitrary to deny of this existing world the need for any sufficient reason, whether independent of itself or not, while presupposing that there is a reason for every other thing that ever exists.[14]

Can we not continue to push our search for sufficient reasons further and ask what is the sufficient reason for our necessary being?[15] As my earlier remarks made clear, the sufficient reason for any necessary being is *itself*, not something else. By definition, a necessary being is *self-caused*; it is a being that *must* exist because its nonexistence is impossible. If all this were not the case, the being in question would not be necessary.[16] Should anyone begin looking for the sufficient reason of a necessary being, he would reveal one important bit of information about himself: he does not know the meaning of the term *necessary being*.

Some have thought that this argument could be countered by regarding the world as the necessary being. Of course, in a free country, anyone who wishes may think that the world is a necessary being. Whether such a claim is plausible, however, is another matter. To heed the comments of Richard Taylor one more time:

> For we find nothing whatever about the world, any more than in its parts, to suggest that it exists by its own nature. Concerning anything in the world, we have not the slightest difficulty in supposing that it should perish, or even that it should never have existed in the first place. We have almost as little difficulty in supposing this of the world itself. . . . It would seem, then, that the world . . . is contingent and thus dependent upon something other than itself for its existence, if it depends upon anything at all. And it must depend upon something, for otherwise there could be no reason why it exists in the first place.[17]

---

[14]Taylor, *Metaphysics*, p. 105.
[15]This is the sort of thing young children do when they ask why God exists.
[16]There has been a rather confused debate over whether God is a logically necessary being or is necessary in some nonlogical sense. A number of philosophers and theologians have shied away from the notion of a logically necessary being. Their reasons for doing this, however, have been less than impressive. I have examined this question elsewhere; see Ronald Nash, *The Concept of God* (Grand Rapids: Zondervan, 1983), chap. 9.
[17]Taylor, *Metaphysics*, p. 110.

This book refers to numerous instances when theists appear—or so their opponents think—to see things that are not there. But now, it seems, the sock is on the other foot. If some atheologian believes his best strategy for countering our second cosmological argument requires him to regard the sum total of contingent beings as a necessary being, I'll not discourage him. I can think of few moves that would enhance the plausibility of theism more than this.[18]

An Objection

Wise critics of the second form of the cosmological argument will avoid claims that the world is a necessary being and look elsewhere for an objection. The argument most often cited goes like this. The second form of the cosmological argument commits the so-called fallacy of composition. This fallacy is committed when someone argues that because something is true of the parts of some whole, it must also be true of the whole; if every part of some whole has a certain property, the whole entity also has that property. That such reasoning is fallacious can be seen in the following example:

Each individual drink on the table is tasty.
Therefore, a drink composed of all the other drinks on the table will be tasty.

It is possible to have a basketball team made up of five individually excellent players. But as many coaches and fans can testify, the fact that each member of the team has a certain property (excellence) does not guarantee that the team will be excellent. Clearly, there are many times when what is true of the parts of a whole is *not* true of the whole.

Opponents of the second form of the cosmological argument then apply this truth to the kind of reasoning we have been examining. Suppose we find ten apples on a table and want to know the sufficient reason for each apple's being there. Suppose also that after a little investigation we learn that each apple was placed on the table by the same person. At this point, we have our sufficient reason for each apple. Does it make sense in this case to seek a further explanation for the entire group of apples? Does it make sense to say that even though we admittedly have a sufficient reason why each individual apple is on the table, we won't rest until we find the sufficient reason why the collection of ten apples is there? In this example once we have explained how each apple got on the table, we have also explained how the entire group of apples got there.

There are two ways, critics say, in which the proponent of our present cosmological argument may commit the fallacy of composition. As we have seen, he argues that since each part of the whole (the world) is contingent, therefore the whole is contingent. This cosmological argument can get absolutely nowhere without the crucial claim that the world (the whole class

---

[18]I readily admit I have not offered a proof that shows the world is *not* a necessary being. The discovery of such a proof would be a significant philosophical achievement, which may explain why no one has done it. Once again, we are at a point where people part company on the basis of whether or not they "see" (or think they "see") something. The burden of showing that the world is a necessary being rests squarely on the shoulders of the atheologian. This is a burden he's welcome to carry.

of contingent beings) is itself contingent and thus requires a sufficient reason for *its* existence. Moreover, the proponent of our cosmological argument argues that since there must be a sufficient reason for each part of the whole, there must also be a sufficient reason for the whole. Does our example of the basketball team not show that what is true of the parts need not be true of the whole? Does our example of the apples not show that once one has found a sufficient reason for each part of some whole, it makes no sense to seek an additional sufficient reason for the whole?

An Answer

Though many objections look good at first glance, second and third glances have a way of showing that what may have appeared as a solid structure is really a house of cards. The fallacy of composition is what philosophers call an informal fallacy. In the case of informal fallacies, one must pay attention to more than the *form* of the argument (in this case, reasoning from the parts to the whole); one must also consider the *content* of the argument.

Sometimes one cannot reason from the parts to the whole; but sometimes one *can*. It all depends on the case. Consider a new example. Suppose it is true that every individual brick in a wall has the property of being red. Given this fact, one would be correct in inferring that the wall is then red. Here is a situation where a property of each part turns out also to be a property of the whole. What this shows is that reasoning from the parts to the whole is not always mistaken. Anyone who claims that *all* reasoning from the parts to the whole is fallacious is committing a different fallacy known as hasty generalization.

CONCLUSION

So where are we? Well, we should be able to see that the most frequently cited objection to the second cosmological argument is inconclusive. All it does is point out that *sometimes* reasoning from the parts to the whole may be mistaken. But the critic fails to show that *this* is one of those times. In fact, if the critic were to attempt to show that this is one of those times, he'd have to smuggle in somehow the assumption that the world is a necessary being. One thing seems clear: efforts to dismiss our present cosmological argument as an instance of the fallacy of composition beg the question.

But it is also time to admit that our second cosmological argument is something less than coercive. As we have seen, the plausibility of the major objection to the argument requires that someone "see" something—that our argument's inference from the parts to the whole is like examples of the fallacy of composition. Frankly, I find this point extremely hard to see. But the plausibility of the cosmological argument also depends on someone's seeing something such as the propriety of the principle of sufficient reason or the correctness of viewing the sum total of contingent beings as a contingent being.

Given the impotence of the atheologian's limited weapons against this argument, no theist need be ashamed of it. As I have said repeatedly, the purpose of such arguments is not to demonstrate the rationality of belief in

God. Belief in God is properly basic; it is rational as it stands. The theist is looking for some tools he can use in the task of positive apologetics. Proofs are person-relative; therefore, *this* proof is person-relative. If someone sees what needs to be seen in this case, the theist will have found a tool that can be used with that person. If not, it will be necessary to discard this tool and try another.

For Further Exploration—Chapter Nine

1. Explain why the kind of theistic argument covered in this chapter is called the *cosmological* argument.
2. Explain the difference between a temporal First Cause and a logical First Cause.
3. Summarize the three problems noted in connection with the first version of the cosmological argument. Does the second version manage to avoid these problems?
4. Define the terms *principle of sufficient reason,* *contingent being,* and *necessary being.* Then using these terms, explain the second version of the cosmological argument.
5. Explain and evaluate the claim that the second form of the cosmological argument commits the fallacy of composition.

Chapter 10

THE TELEOLOGICAL ARGUMENT

While cosmological arguments for God's existence deal primarily with the existence of the world, teleological arguments focus on certain features of the existing world, notably its apparent order and design. The eighteenth-century version of the argument is outlined well by David Hume (1711–76), perhaps its most famous philosophical critic. Hume wrote:

> Look round the world: contemplate the whole and every part of it: You will find it to be nothing but one great machine, subdivided into an infinite number of lesser machines, which again admit of subdivisions to a degree beyond what human senses and faculties can trace and explain. All these various machines, and even their most minute parts, are adjusted to each other with an accuracy which ravishes into admiration all men who have ever contemplated them. The curious adapting of means to ends, throughout all nature, resembles exactly, though it much exceeds, the productions of human contrivance—of human design, thought, wisdom, and intelligence. Since therefore the effects resemble each other, we are led to infer, by all the rules of analogy, that the causes also resemble, and that the Author of Nature is somewhat similar to the mind of man, though possessed of much larger faculties, proportioned to the grandeur of the work which he has executed. By this argument *a posteriori*, and by this argument alone, do we prove at once the existence of a Deity and his similarity to human mind and intelligence.[1]

Another well-known critic of the argument, the German philosopher Immanuel Kant (1724–1804), testifies to the powerful effect this kind of

---

[1] David Hume, *Dialogues Concerning Natural Religion*, ed. Nelson Pike (Indianapolis: Bobbs-Merrill, 1970), p. 222. A warning: Hume sets up the argument in a form that is easy to rebut.

reasoning can have, even on individuals who eventually reject it. As Kant explains, the teleological argument

> always deserves to be mentioned with respect. It is the oldest, the clearest, and the most accordant with the common reason of mankind. It enlivens the study of nature, just as it itself derives its existence and gains ever new vigor from that source. This ever-increasing evidence which, though empirical, is yet so powerful, cannot be so depressed through doubts suggested by subtle and abstruse speculation, that it is not at once aroused from the indecision of all melancholy reflection, as from a dream, by one glance at the wonders of nature and the majesty of the universe— ascending from height to height up to the all-highest.[2]

Suppose the first American astronauts to walk on the moon had brought back, along with moon rocks, an oblong black box that appeared from the outside to have been crafted by machines. Suppose further that, when opened, the box contained the workings of a camera: it had parts that functioned like the lens, shutter, and other components of a camera. Obviously, such an object would excite enormous and justifiable curiosity about how it came to be. It is hard to imagine any skeptic's gaining respect by maintaining that the principle of sufficient reason did not apply to such an object. Equally absurd would be efforts to explain the box in terms of chance, natural forces. The very nature of the object pointed to its having been made by an intelligent being. The human mind properly balks at the suggestion that a cameralike object was produced by chance, natural forces. But then how much more should we reject claims that something far more intricate, such as the human eye, resulted from anything less than an intelligent being. According to William Paley (1743–1805), author of *Natural Theology*, the most famous statement of the argument:

> There cannot be a design without a designer; contrivance without a contriver; order without choice; arrangement without anything capable of arranging; subserviency and relation to a purpose without that which could intend a purpose; means suitable to an end, and executing their office in accomplishing that end, without the end ever having been contemplated or the means accommodated to it. Arrangement, disposition of parts, subserviency of means to an end, relation of instruments to a use imply the presence of intelligence and mind.[3]

It would be foolish to ignore or deny the powerful psychological effect that signs of apparent purpose and design in the world can have on many people. But we should not allow these psychological considerations to blind us to various logical problems that critics of teleological reasoning refer to in their rejection of the teleological argument. Perhaps these objections can be answered or possibly they will force proponents of the teleological argument to formulate the argument in ways that avoid the objection or perhaps

---

[2] Immanuel Kant, *Critique of Pure Reason*, trans. Norman Kemp Smith (New York: St. Martin's, 1965), p. 520.

[3] William Paley, *Natural Theology*, ed. Frederick Ferré (Indianapolis: Bobbs-Merrill, 1963), pp. 8–9. My comment that Paley's book is the most *famous* statement of the teleological argument does not imply that it is the best formulation of the argument. In fact, Paley's argument seems surprisingly susceptible to David Hume's objections, published posthumously in his *Dialogues Concerning Natural Religion* (1779).

teleological reasoning will have to be abandoned as a lost cause. Whatever decision we make in this regard, it seems clear that the next step must be an examination of the major objections that have been raised to the teleological argument. Three objections will be noted.

THREE OBJECTIONS TO THE TELEOLOGICAL ARGUMENT

The Reliance Upon Analogy

Many critics have noted that the teleological argument is an example of reasoning on the basis of analogy. This kind of argument is used whenever one reasons to a conclusion on the basis of some similarity or analogy between two or more things. Because A and B are believed to be alike with respect to C, the argument goes, they must also be alike with respect to D. Now, proponents of the teleological argument contend, the universe and such human creations as houses and machines are analogous in the sense that they exhibit (in Hume's words) a "curious adapting of means to ends"; that is, they exhibit purpose and design. Since the universe and machines are analogous in this regard, it is natural to conclude that they are analogous in another way. Houses and machines are products of intelligence. Therefore, the universe must also be the product of an intelligent mind.

Several points must be noted here. For one thing, no argument from analogy can ever provide conclusive proof. Even though two things may be alike in some respects, it does not necessarily follow that they are alike in other respects. Consider a series of cases in which the analogy on which I base a conclusion gets increasingly stronger. Suppose I am planning to buy a new car and conclude that because a friend was extremely satisfied with his purchase of a similar car, I will be satisfied with my purchase. But consider several different ways in which the two cars can be similar. (1) Suppose the only respect in which the two cars are similar is their color. While there is certainly an analogy of sorts in this case, it seems totally irrelevant to what leads most people to be satisfied with a car, namely, its performance. (2) Suppose the two cars are both manufactured in the United States. Even though there is a point of similarity here, millions of people who have purchased American-made cars will testify that this fact alone says nothing about the buyer's ultimate satisfaction with his purchase. This point of analogy is too weak to support the conclusion. (3) Suppose the two cars are manufactured by the same company, General Motors for example. Or imagine that they are even made by the same division of General Motors, Chevrolet. While the analogy is getting stronger, the experiences of many car buyers make it clear that even this similarity hardly supports the conclusion that if my friend was satisfied with his car, I'll be satisfied with mine. (4) Even if we stipulate the closest possible analogy—say that the two cars are identical models made in the same factory on the same day—no knowledgeable person would think his conclusion followed with anything even approaching certainty.

The logic of arguments from analogy, therefore, is less than clear. In fact, it seems, it might be wise to avoid reasoning based on analogies when alternative kinds of argument are available.

Not only are arguments based on analogy weak in the respect just noted, they are also subject to another problem: the conclusion follows only if someone is willing to accept the analogy. If someone believes the world is analogous to something humans construct, then it is likely that he or she will conclude that the world has been constructed by an intelligent being. As we have seen, it can often be quite difficult to get people to "see" the truth of a premise in a deductive argument; it can be even more difficult to get them to "see" the point to an alleged analogy.

Still another problem can be summarized in a paraphrase of an old adage: he who lives by analogy, dies by analogy. According to David Hume, it is possible to explain the features of the universe that so impress teleologists in terms of other analogies that do not lead us to God. What if we abandon the analogy of a house or machine and think of the world in terms of a different analogy that does not entail an intelligent creator? Suppose, Hume suggested, we stop thinking of the world after the analogy of a house or watch and think of it, instead, after the analogy of a living organism.

Hume did not actually think the world was a living being. He was simply pointing out that once we begin arguing for a conclusion on the basis of a supposed analogy, we should consider other possible analogies that have equal or greater explanatory power. Hume thought it was possible to explain everything about the world that impresses the teleologist by thinking of the world as a living organism. We know that organisms like plants and the human body are living things that develop in ways often suggesting order and design; plants and other living organisms exhibit an apparent adaptation of means to ends without also leading anyone to seek an earthly craftsman or builder. Hume's point is that the teleologist is a victim of his own analogy. It is always possible to provide a different analogy that will explain apparently purposeful adaptations of means to ends in a nonpurposive way. Since Hume rejects the teleologist's analogy, he also rejects the teleologist's conclusion.

An Alternative Explanation

Taken by themselves, none of the considerations noted above disprove the existence of God. But they do illustrate some of the grounds on which people have dismissed teleological reasoning as inconclusive. While teleological reasoning does provide a hypothesis that explains certain features of the world, there are alternative hypotheses that may account for the same features equally well and, in the process, weaken or even undercut the teleological hypothesis. Since Charles Darwin in the midnineteenth century, it has become fashionable in some circles to view the theory of evolution as a competing hypothesis that explains the apparent design in nature without appeal to an intelligent creator. As William Rowe declares:

> Since the development of the theory of evolution, the Teleological Argument has lost some of its persuasive force, for we now possess a fairly well-developed naturalistic hypothesis that makes no mention of intelligent design. Briefly put, the Darwinian theory of natural selection purports to explain why nature contains so many organisms whose various parts are so well-fitted to their survival. According to this theory, animals and plants undergo variations or changes that are inherited by their descendants. Some variations provide organisms with an advantage over the rest of the population in the constant struggle for life. Since

plants and animals produce more offspring than the environment will support, those in which favorable variations occur tend to survive in greater numbers than those in which unfavorable variations occur. Thus, it happens that over great periods of time there slowly emerge large populations of highly developed organisms whose parts are so peculiarly fitted to their survival.[4]

Some enemies of theism get carried away with what they think the evolutionary hypothesis entitles them to believe. Blind to the many gaps in their theory that, thus far at least, can be filled only by a leap of faith, they cloak their commitment to evolution with a religious fervor that would put any fundamentalist to shame. With regard to the relation between evolution and theism two points deserve mention. First, evolution and theism are not logically incompatible; even if the most comprehensive theory of evolution were true, it would not follow that theism is false. Second, evolution is not even logically incompatible with an expanded version of the teleological argument. In one of the more interesting and ironic developments in the history of ideas, a number of twentieth-century thinkers have viewed evolution as part of a total package for which a naturalistic, nontheistic explanation is inadequate.

One example of such an attempt to include evolution within a broader teleological argument can be found in the work of F. R. Tennant (1866–1957).[5] While older versions of the argument concentrated on particular examples of apparent design (such as the human eye), newer versions concentrate on the general order of nature. Tennant did not look simply at physical nature. The universe for which he sought an explanation included the human mind with its capacity for abstract thinking, moral consciousness, and self-consciousness. As Linwood Urban explains such thinking,

In summary, the argument maintains that the natural order not only makes possible human survival but also supports and fosters the moral and spiritual values of intelligent beings, and that this is the kind of universe one would expect a wise, benevolent, and powerful deity to have designed. Since the focus of the argument is not on the small-scale phenomena cited by Paley but on the large-scale phenomenon of the evolutionary process itself, it has become known as the Wider Teleological Argument.[6]

Even if, for the sake of argument, we assume the truth of a universal evolutionary hypothesis, the fact that this process produced creatures with intelligence, creativity, moral awareness, self-consciousness, and God-consciousness demands an explanation that Naturalism seems powerless to provide.

Some have objected to the Wider Teleological Argument by pointing out that no human being can have knowledge of the whole universe, a claim that by itself seems rather obvious. Suppose, the argument continues, we

---

[4] William L. Rowe, *Philosophy of Religion: An Introduction* (Encino, Calif.: Dickenson, 1978), p. 54.

[5] See F. R. Tennant, *Philosophical Theology*, 2 vols. (New York: Cambridge University Press, 1928).

[6] Linwood Urban, *A Short History of Christian Thought* (New York: Oxford University Press, 1986), p. 176.

grant that the small part of the universe of which we have knowledge does exhibit apparent design. What about the far greater part of the universe about which we have no knowledge? Perhaps total chaos dominates the greater part of the universe. The teleologist takes the apparent purpose he finds in this small part of the universe and imputes order to the entire universe. Clearly, he is reaching too far. There is no justification for reasoning that since the small part of the universe we know exhibits design, therefore the entire universe is a harmony of purpose and order.

It is hard to see anything very impressive about this argument. It is actually a dressed-up version of an old fallacy known as the appeal to ignorance. On reflection, I rather doubt that many atheologians would feel comfortable introducing this fallacy into the debate about theism. After all, if it were permitted, some friends of theism could wield it to much greater effect I suspect than most atheologians.

Human ignorance about the cosmos as a whole would be a problem in cases where one were setting forth a deductive version of the teleological argument. Deductive arguments are invalid in any case when the conclusion states more than the premises. Given the demonstrable lack of total human knowledge about the universe, any deductive argument that concluded with a claim about the order of the entire universe would have to be invalid. But we are not dealing with a deductive argument; we are dealing with probability. In the absence of any evidence that chaos reigns in the greater universe, the most reasonable position holds that the kinds of order that characterize the known world also characterize the unknown.

A Final Objection

Spatial limitations will allow consideration of only one additional objection to teleological reasoning. But many find it a persuasive argument. The basic point to the argument is that the kind of reasoning used by the teleologist can also work against his theistic conclusion. As we have seen, the teleologist believes the world exhibits order and design, and these signs provide warrant or support for the conviction that the world has an intelligent being as its cause. But, this objection goes, the world exhibits other traits besides order and design; it also exhibits many signs of disorder and disharmony. Suppose we are inspecting a painting. If various features of a painting entitle us to conclude that the painter was a genius, would not the discovery of imperfections in the painting justify doubts about the artist's ability? Teleologists argue that the world was created because of the good things they claim to see in the world. But what about all the "bad" things? Don't they count against the supposed designer? At the very least, the argument goes, a fair appraisal of the total picture—both good and bad— seems to undercut any confidence that the universe was created by an infinite, all-powerful, all-wise, omnibenevolent God.

This line of argument, of course, plunges us into the complexities of the problem of evil. Since we will devote several chapters to this central issue later in the book, there is little point in pursuing this matter further at this point. Perhaps the reader should pause a bit and reflect on how he or she would respond to this challenge.

A NEW TWIST

In a book first published in 1963, American philosopher Richard Taylor presented a significant new variety of the teleological argument. He introduced his argument with an interesting example that bid his reader to imagine herself in a coach on a British train. Looking out the window, the passenger sees a large number of white stones on a hillside lying in a pattern that spells out the letters: THE BRITISH RAILWAYS WELCOMES YOU TO WALES. Should such a passenger be in a reflective mood on such an occasion, she might well begin to contemplate how those stones happened to be in that particular arrangement. It is possible that, without any intelligent being having anything to do with it, the stones simply rolled down the hillside over a period of many years and just happened to end up in an arrangement that resembled the letters noted above. However implausible we find the hypothesis that the arrangement of the stones was a purely accidental happening, we must admit that such a thing is logically possible. Of course, Taylor admits, the most natural reaction to seeing the stones would be a conviction that the arrangement of stones was brought about by one or more humans who intended that it communicate a message. And so, Taylor admits that there are at least two explanations for the arrangement of the stones: a natural, nonpurposive explanation and an explanation in terms of the intentions of at least one intelligent being.

Taylor's next step in the development of his argument is critical. Suppose, he suggests, that the passenger decides, solely on the basis of stones she sees on the hillside, that she is in fact entering Wales. Taylor is not insisting that the purposive account of the stones is in fact the true one. His argument is purely hypothetical. *If* the passenger infers that the stones communicate a true message (and that she is thereby really entering Wales), it would be quite inconsistent for her also to assume that the positioning of the stones was an accident. Once you conclude that the stones really do convey an intelligible message, Taylor continues,

> you would, in fact, be presupposing that they were arranged that way by an intelligent and purposeful being or beings for the purpose of conveying a certain message having nothing to do with the stones themselves. Another way of expressing the same point is that it would be *irrational* for you to regard the arrangement of the stones as evidence that you were entering Wales, and at the same time to suppose that they might have come to have that arrangement accidentally, that is, as the result of the ordinary interactions of natural or physical forces. If, for instance, they came to be so arranged over the course of time, simply by rolling down the hill, one by one, and finally just happening to end up that way, or if they were strewn upon the ground that way by the forces of any earthquake or storm or what-not, then their arrangement would in no sense constitute evidence that you were entering Wales, or for anything whatever unconnected with themselves.[7]

Taylor's analysis thus far seems correct. If I were the passenger and if I thought the arrangement of the stones were a result of chance, natural

---

[7] Richard Taylor, *Metaphysics*, 2d ed. (Englewood Cliffs, N.J.: Prentice-Hall, 1974), p. 115.

forces, there would be something quite bizzare about my also believing, solely on the evidence provided by the stones, that I was indeed entering Wales. But if I concluded, solely on the evidence provided by the stones, that I was entering Wales, consistency would seem to require that I also believe the arrangement of the stones was not an accident.

But what does all this have to do with the existence of God? Taylor invites us to consider similar reasoning about our sense organs:

> Just as it is possible for a collection of stones to present a novel and interesting arrangement on the side of a hill . . . so also it is possible for such things as our own organs of sense to be the accidental and unintended results, over ages of time, of perfectly impersonal, nonpurposeful forces. In fact, ever so many biologists believe that this is precisely what has happened, that our organs of sense are in no real sense purposeful things, but only appear so because of our failure to consider how they might have arisen through the normal workings of nature.[8]

In the case of the stones, the simple fact that they exhibited a particular shape or pattern did not constitute proof that there was purpose or intention behind the arrangement. Likewise, Taylor observes, "the mere complexity, refinement, and seemingly purposeful arrangement of our sense organs do not, accordingly, constitute any conclusive reason for supposing that they are the outcome of any purposeful activity. A natural, nonpurposeful explanation of them is possible, and has been attempted—successfully, in the opinion of many."[9] But then Taylor finds the opening he has been seeking. Even those individuals who view their sense organs as the product of chance, natural, and nonpurposeful forces depend on them to deliver information about the world that they regard as true. "We suppose, without even thinking about it, that they [our sense organs] reveal to us things that have nothing to do with themselves, their structures, or their origins."[10] Such people, Taylor thinks, are just as inconsistent as the person who derives a true message from a nonpurposeful arrangement of stones.

> It would be irrational for one to say *both* that his sensory and cognitive faculties had a natural, nonpurposeful origin and *also* that they reveal some truth with respect to something other than themselves, something that is not merely inferred from them. *If* their origin can be entirely accounted for in terms of chance variations, natural selection, and so on, without supposing that they somehow embody and express the purposes of some creative being, then the most we can say of them is that they exist, that they are complex and wondrous in their construction, and are perhaps in other respects interesting and remarkable. We cannot say that they are, entirely by themselves, reliable guides to any truth whatever, save only what can be inferred from their own structure and arrangement. If, on the other hand, we do assume that they are guides to some truths having nothing to do with themselves, then it is difficult to see how we can, consistently with that supposition, believe them to have arisen by accident, or by the ordinary workings of purposeless forces, even over ages of time.[11]

[8]Ibid., pp. 116–17.
[9]Ibid., p. 117.
[10]Ibid., pp. 117–18.
[11]Ibid., pp. 118–19.

While Taylor is clearly on to something, careful readers will realize that his argument does not prove that God exists. Taylor himself points out that his argument implies "almost nothing with respect to any divine attributes, such as benevolence."[12] But even though Taylor has not provided a sound deductive argument that entails the existence of the God described in Scripture, he has pointed out one more piece of evidence that can help people for whom belief in God is not basic reach a decision about the existence of God. Everything we find in nature that points to harmony, design, purpose, and intelligence is consistent with the Christian presupposition that God exists and provides supporting evidence for it. If I believe in the God described in Scripture, I should expect to find that the world is lawlike and exhibits signs of purpose and design; I should expect to discover that my sensory organs give me reliable information about the world; I should expect to find that my rational faculties enable me to draw sound inferences and discover truth.

CONCLUSION

For centuries, religious thinkers have appealed to the presence of apparent design and purpose in the universe as some kind of positive proof that God exists. It is important to realize that the many alleged examples of design and the reasoning that accompanied the examples accomplished far less than these teleological enthusiasts often recognized. As an argument that somehow proves conclusively the existence of the God of the Bible, the teleological argument comes up short.

But this hardly means that religious believers should ignore all these signs of apparent design and purpose. The question is, What should we make of them? When dealing with any puzzle or mystery, rational people look for clues. They also try to see how *all* the clues tend to confirm or disconfirm competing attempts to resolve the mystery. The innumerable signs of purpose in the universe are clues that should not be ignored or explained away. Theists are correct when they recognize the important warrant their belief in God receives from such evidence.

For Further Exploration—Chapter Ten

1. Show that you understand how the version of the teleological argument discussed in the first half of the chapter is based on reasoning from analogy. How have some critics used this fact to challenge the argument?
2. How has evolution been thought to weaken the teleological argument? How do versions of the Wider Teleological Argument answer those who appeal to evolution? What are your thoughts on this whole matter?
3. Explain the major point to Richard Taylor's formulation of the teleological argument.
4. Even if the teleological argument fails as a deductive argument, discuss what you take to be its value as an inductive argument.

---

[12]Ibid., p. 119.

Chapter 11

RELIGIOUS EXPERIENCE

Based on my observations spanning a period of more than thirty-five years, far more people are religious believers because of religious experiences they've had than because of arguments they've heard. Even the few Christians I've met who appear sometimes to disdain the religious experiences (or at least the more extreme religious experiences) of others and claim that their faith is grounded not on experience but on God's revelation in Scripture overlook an important point. The revealed texts that function properly as an authority for their beliefs and conduct are products of the religious *experiences* of the inspired human authors who penned them. And whether we wish to count it as a *religious* experience or not, the *only* way we can learn about the content of that special revelation is through some experience such as hearing the Word or reading the Word. While Christian believers should beware of those who exalt their private religious experiences above the normative Scriptures or who get carried away by excessive emotionalism, Christians have to acknowledge the importance of religious experience and be prepared to defend it.

Religious experience plays a vital role in initiating Christian belief and practice. New Testament faith never originates in a cognitive vacuum. Human beings have to know all sorts of things about themselves (notably their sin and their need of a Savior), about God (including God's holiness, love, and provision of a Savior), and about the eternal, divine Son of God whose death and resurrection make their salvation possible. Another experiential factor that plays a necessary role in the initiation of faith is the work of the Holy Spirit who convicts "the world of guilt in regard to sin and righteousness and judgment" (John 16:8). People must know certain basic truths about God and themselves, they must recognize that those truths pertain to them, and they must assent to those truths and trust in the sovereign, personal God who loves them (John 3:16).

Religious experience plays an indispensable role in initiating Christian belief, and it performs a similar function in sustaining and supporting that faith. As philosopher William Alston puts it, "Somehow what goes on in the experience of leading the Christian life provides some ground for Christian belief, makes some contribution to the rationality of Christian belief."[1] Alston goes on to say:

> We sometimes feel the presence of God; we get glimpses, at least, of God's will for us; we feel the Holy Spirit at work in our lives, guiding us, strengthening us, enabling us to love other people in a new way; we hear God speaking to us in the Bible, in preaching, or in the words and actions of our fellow Christians. Because of all this we are more justified in our Christian beliefs than we would have been otherwise.[2]

Experiences like these provide important support for our faith. "If I could not find any confirmation of the Christian message in my own experience," Alston adds,

> I would be less justified in accepting that message than I am in fact. To generalize the point, suppose that no one had ever experienced communion with God, had ever heard God speaking to him or her, had ever felt the strengthening influence of the Holy Spirit in a difficult situation. In that case Christian belief would be a less rational stance than it is in fact.[3]

Religious experiences vary widely as to the kinds of events that produce them:

> Religious experiences can be generated by perceptions of individual objects (a grain of sand, a bird), by a train of events, by actions—for instance, the memorable account of Jesus setting his face to go to Jerusalem to his Passion. Even a passage of philosophical reasoning may do this, as when someone contemplates the incompleteness of all explanation, the intellectual opacity of space and time, and feels compelled—with a sense of mystery—to posit a divine completeness and unity.[4]

Religious experiences that exhibit a strong moral component may include

> experiences of divine discontent, interpreted as intimations of God's existence and call to moral endeavor, the conviction of sin correlative to a sense of God's own holiness, the sense of divine aid in the rectifying of one's moral life, and, in Christian evangelical terms, a sense that one has been redeemed or saved by God's action on man's behalf.[5]

---

[1] William P. Alston, "Christian Experience and Christian Belief," in *Faith and Rationality*, ed. A. Plantinga and N. Wolterstorff (Notre Dame, Ind.: University of Notre Dame Press, 1983), p. 103.

[2] Ibid.

[3] Ibid.

[4] Ronald W. Hepburn, "Religious Experience," in *The Encyclopedia of Philosophy*, ed. Paul Edwards (New York: Macmillan, 1967), 7:165.

[5] Ibid.

Richard Swinburne has helpfully distinguished five kinds of religious experiences.[6] First, people sometimes have an experience of God while perceiving some common or public object. I may hear bells tolling in the New Year and suddenly sense the presence of an eternal God. I may view the heavens at night and be overcome by a sense of my own finiteness and contingency. In this kind of religious experience, some common or public phenomenon is perceived in a religious way.

Second, people also have religious experiences as a result of their perceiving phenomena that are quite uncommon. An example would be the experiences the disciples had of the resurrected Jesus. With regard to such uncommon phenomena, Swinburne says, "A skeptic might have had the same visual sensations . . . and yet not have the religious experience."[7]

Third, people have private sensations that they can describe in their normal vocabulary. For example, I might have a dream or vision or hear a voice that I describe in language adequate to enable some other person to understand my experience. No one else in my immediate area may have seen what I saw or heard what I heard; but what I experienced, while private, is still effable in the sense that I can describe it in words.

Fourth, people also have private experiences that are ineffable; they are not describable in normal vocabulary. Most mystical experiences seem to fit in this category.[8]

Fifth, Swinburne says that people "have religious experiences which the subject does not have by having sensations. It seems to the subject, perhaps very strongly, that he is aware of God or of a timeless reality or some such thing, and yet not because he is having certain sensations; it just seems so to him, but not through his having sensations."[9] Without seeing or hearing anything, someone in a dark room may become aware of another person's presence. Likewise, people testify that they have become aware of God's presence or something like this, even though they had no specific sensation.

THE ARGUMENT FOR GOD'S EXISTENCE
FROM RELIGIOUS EXPERIENCE

A number of philosophers and theologians have maintained that there is an argument for God's existence based on religious experience. According to such thinkers, humans do not necessarily have to reason our way to God.

---

[6] See Richard Swinburne, *The Existence of God* (Oxford: Clarendon Press, 1979), pp. 250–51.

[7] Ibid., p. 250.

[8] Many philosophy of religion texts that contain a discussion of religious experience limit their treatment exclusively or primarily to the experiences of mystics. I have always found this surprising and a bit disappointing. While I have had many experiences that I would classify as religious, I have never had a mystical experience nor have I ever met a mystic. I believe that I'm rather typical in this regard. Largely for this reason, my discussion of religious experience will ignore the rare and atypical kinds of mystical experiences and deal instead with the much more common kinds of religious experiences described in Swinburne's first, second, third, and fifth categories.

[9] Swinburne, *Existence of God*, p. 251.

Our knowledge that God exists can rest on our experience of God. One of the better known accounts of this argument appears in the work of the British theologian John Baillie.[10]

Baillie argued that people can know that God exists on the basis of their having a direct experience of God. It is possible to know that God exists in much the same way I know that the black telephone on my desk exists. To put Baillie's argument in a more formal way, he claimed:

If I have a direct experience of *x*, then *x* exists.
I have a direct experience of God.
Therefore, God exists.

If I have a direct experience of the telephone on my desk, then the telephone exists. Likewise, a direct experience of God is sufficient (for the person having the experience) to establish that God exists. As William Alston expresses this point, human experience or perception of God "plays an epistemic role with respect to beliefs about God importantly analogous to that played by sense perception with respect to beliefs about the physical world."[11]

A stronger and more detailed version of the argument from religious experience has been provided by William Rowe. Though Rowe's formulation turns out to be a preliminary step in what he believes is a strong objection to the argument from religious experience, it helps us understand the major steps of the argument. According to Rowe, the argument has five steps:[12]

1. When subjects have an experience they take to be of *x*, it is rational to conclude that they really do experience *x* unless we have positive reasons to think their experience delusive.
2. Experiences occur which seem to their subjects to be of God.
3. There are no good reasons for thinking that all or most experiences which seem to their subjects to be of God are delusive.
4. It is rational to believe that at least some experiences which seem to their subjects to be of God really are experiences of God.
5. Therefore, it is rational to believe that God exists.

Rowe allows step 2 of the outlined argument to stand. No informed person can deny that some people have experiences that seem to them to have God as their object. Rowe is also unaware of any evidence that disqualifies step 3. Rowe reminds us that we do not allow an occasional misleading experience to lead us to doubt all our other nonreligious experiences. And so, he thinks, even if many religious experiences appear

---

[10]See John Baillie, *Our Knowledge of God*, 2d ed. (New York: Scribner, 1959).

[11]William P. Alston, "Perceiving God," *The Journal of Philosophy* 83 (1986): 655. Alston's article is worth studying since he offers answers to many of the objections usually raised against the view we're considering.

[12]See William Rowe, "Religious Experience and the Principle of Credulity," *International Journal for Philosophy of Religion* 13 (1982): 85–92. Rowe's formulation appears on p. 87. I use Rowe's words for every line of the argument except for step (3) where I omit some technical qualifications.

questionable, it hardly follows that *all* of them are delusive. Rowe knows of no argument that could prove that every supposed religious experience is delusive. As Baillie's argument implies, if just one person has one genuine experience of God, it follows that God exists. Since steps 4 and 5 of the argument are inferences from the steps above them, Rowe admits that his only hope of offering a cogent criticism of the argument requires that he challenge step 1.

A closer look at step 1 reveals that others besides Rowe have noticed its crucial role in the argument from religious experience. As a matter of fact, something like step 1 plays an important role in any supposed knowledge from sensory experience. The claim stated in step 1 is so important that it has even been given a name—*the principle of credulity*. As British philosopher C. D. Broad explains this principle,

> The practical postulate which we go upon everywhere else is to treat cognitive claims as veridical unless there be some positive reason to think them delusive. This, after all, is our only guarantee for believing that ordinary sense-perception is veridical.[13] We cannot *prove* that what people agree in perceiving really exists independently of them; but we do always assume that ordinary waking sense-perception is veridical unless we can produce some positive ground for thinking that it is delusive in any given case. I think it would be inconsistent to treat the experiences of religious mystics on different principles. So far as they agree they should be provisionally accepted as veridical unless there be some positive ground for thinking that they are not.[14]

Broad is correct in drawing attention to the important role that the principle of credulity plays in our ordinary, nonreligious experiences. We treat such experiences as veridical unless we have reason to think otherwise. To ignore the principle and regard our experiences as delusive until they are proven veridical would entrap us in a skepticism from which no escape seems likely. The sensible person, then, will always take his experiences as veridical unless he has good reasons to do otherwise. Of course, Broad also points out the importance of extending the same courtesy to religious experiences. The principle of credulity says that experiences are innocent until proven guilty. The burden of proof rests on the person who thinks that any experience—religious or nonreligious—is delusive.

THE CASE AGAINST THE ARGUMENT

Let's review where we are. We are considering a particular formulation of the argument from religious experience that looks pretty impressive. The argument notices that many people have had experiences that seemed to be of God. Regardless of the fact that many such experiences are possibly

---

[13]I will explain what it means for an experience to be veridical shortly. For now, it is enough to say that a veridical experience is one that reports truthfully what is the case. If I have an experience of some object and the experience is not delusive, the experience is veridical.

[14]C. D. Broad, *Religion, Philosophy and Psychical Research* (New York: Harcourt, Brace and Co., 1953), p. 197. Richard Swinburne makes important use of the principle of credulity in his book *The Existence of God*, pp. 244–76.

delusive, there is no good reason to believe that all of them are. Given the principle of credulity—step 1—it is rational to believe that some of these religious experiences are veridical. Therefore, it is rational to believe that God exists. As William Rowe has pointed out, anyone wanting to counter this argument will have to find a suitable challenge to step 1.

William Rowe advises us against discarding the principle of credulity. If we reject the principle for all experiences (nonreligious and religious), we would be saying that *all* experiences should be judged guilty until proven innocent, a move that would entail skepticism with regard to a great deal of what we think we know about the world. On the other hand, Rowe admits, if we retain the principle of credulity with regard to nonreligious experience and reject it only with respect to religious experience, our move will appear arbitrary. So anyone like Rowe who wishes to counter the use of the principle of credulity in our argument for God's existence must tread carefully so as to avoid skepticism on the one hand and the appearance of a bigoted arbitrariness on the other.

Rowe decides to argue that the particular formulation of the principle of credulity in step 1 is inadequate. Once again, step 1 stated: "When subjects have an experience they take to be of x, it is rational to conclude that they really do experience x unless we have positive reasons to think their experience delusive." Rowe thinks that step 1 must be qualified so that it reads as follows: "When subjects have an experience they take to be of x, and we know how to discover positive reasons for thinking their experiences delusive, if such reasons do exist, then it is rational to conclude that they really do experience x unless we have some positive reasons to think their experiences are delusive."[15] While Rowe believes we can continue to use his modified version of the principle of credulity for both religious and nonreligious experiences, the added clause spells trouble, he thinks, for alleged experiences of God since such experiences cannot meet the additional test. Therefore, even if we accept the revised principle of credulity with regard to all experience, supposed religious experiences will fail to satisfy the principle—or so Rowe claims.

We should remember that Rowe admits that the argument from religious experience utilizing the original formulation of the principle of credulity in step 1 is a strong argument for God's existence. Should Rowe's challenge to step 1 end up being less than impressive, we would appear to be justified in thinking that Rowe's effort to weaken one particular argument for God's existence ends up doing just the opposite. Given the powerful argument Rowe has constructed, the failure to produce a convincing objection to step 1 might justifiably bolster the confidence of many that God does exist.

What is the key difference between our original step 1 and Rowe's reformulation? The original wording of the principle stated that any outer-directed experience should be treated as innocent until proven guilty. Until someone can show that my experience of x is not veridical, I am justified in thinking that it is veridical; and of course, if I have warrant for thinking that my experience of x is veridical, then it follows that I have warrant for thinking that x exists. What step 1 does is place the burden of proof on the

---

[15]Rowe, "Religious Experience and the Principle of Credulity," p. 89.

person who rejects my claim that I have had an experience of God, that my experience is veridical, and that therefore God exists.

Rowe obviously thinks that his revised statement of the principle of credulity justifies different treatment for religious experiences. He believes this different treatment is justified because people who have had religious experiences do not know how to discover positive reasons for thinking their experiences delusive. But it is not at all clear that Rowe is correct on this point. While I certainly don't advise theists to make this move, anyone who has had a religious experience can satisfy a literal interpretation of Rowe's demand by appeal to what some have called eschatological verification.[16] A believer might admit the difficulty of producing reasons that could show the veridicality or nonveridicality of his religious experiences *in this life*. But, the believer could claim, the veridicality of these earthly religious experiences will be confirmed by what will or will not occur *after death*. Of course, in one sense, this kind of move is much too easy—which is why I won't use it. But in another sense, the appeal to possible experiences after death does meet the demands of Rowe's revised principle, *as he stated it*.

I suspect that Rowe is even more anxious to exclude claims about possible religious experiences after death than he is to eliminate talk about supposed religious experiences in this life. Hence, I am confident that he would quickly find a way to revise his revised principle in a way to eliminate eschatological verification. I raise the issue, not because I think it's a line of argument that has much apologetic value, but because it does draw attention to a problem in Rowe's reformulation of the principle of credulity. To be quite frank, Rowe knows in advance what experiences he wants to protect and what experiences he wants to disqualify. Rowe may be engaged in an act of philosophical gerrymandering. Just as politicians sometimes attempt to draw the boundaries of a voting district in a way that will give unfair advantage to candidates of their party, so Rowe may be trying to draw the boundaries of what will count as an innocent experience in a way that will preclude religious experiences from any rightful place within the lines. At least, some of us may think this claim is justified.

Surprisingly, Rowe has difficulty showing just where these lines are supposed to be. What does it mean to *know how to discover positive reasons for thinking some experience delusive*? In at least one case (that of eschatological verification), we have found a way of doing this that meets the literal demands of Rowe's test that we know he'll reject. I will shortly suggest some other ways in which theists can distinguish between veridical and nonveridical religious experiences; and I suspect that Rowe will be equally unhappy with them. One thing we should consider is the possibility that perhaps no attempt by a religious believer to meet the test of Rowe's revised principle will satisfy him.

As I see it, the big problem here is figuring out what Rowe is trying to say in his revision of the principle of credulity. As nearly as I can tell, Rowe's position is similar to an argument against religious experience that appeared

---

[16]British philosopher and theologian John Hick developed the notion of eschatological verification to counter a now outdated challenge to religious belief from a system known as Logical Positivism. See John Hick, *Faith and Knowledge* (Glasgow: Fontana, 1974), pp. 177–78.

in a 1959 book by Charles B. Martin.[17] C. B. Martin did not deny that people have what they take to be religious experiences; he did not dispute that people *seem* to have experiences of God. But Martin did challenge the veridicality of such experiences.

Most of us have had nonveridical experiences, that is, experiences where things were not what they seemed to be. Well-known examples of nonveridical experiences include the parallel railroad tracks that appear to meet at the horizon or the oar immersed in water that appears to be bent. Alcoholics who see pink rats are having a nonveridical experience. When Scrooge perceived Marley's ghost in Dickens' *Christmas Carol*, his first reaction was skepticism. How do I know, Scrooge asked, that you're not a blot of mustard or a bit of undigested beef? Had Scrooge been a philosopher, he might have asked, "How do I know that my present experience is veridical?"

In order for an experience to be veridical, an experience of some object must satisfy the following conditions: the object exists, the person's experience is such that he is conscious of the object, and the object is part of the cause of the person's experience. At this moment, I am experiencing a tan IBM electric typewriter. My experience of the typewriter is veridical if the typewriter exists, if I am conscious of it, and if my awareness of the typewriter is—at least in part—caused by the typewriter. This last condition means that if the typewriter did *not* exist, I would not be perceiving it.

Suppose, however, that I am actually at home in bed and simply dreaming about a typewriter. After a while, writing books can do this sort of thing to a person. In my case, my experience of the typewriter would be nonveridical. Or suppose that my senses are deceiving me and that my typewriter is actually red or made in Albania. Even though, in this second kind of case, my typewriter exists, my experience would be nonveridical in certain respects.

What Charles B. Martin tried to show is the impossibility of knowing that experiences of God are veridical. Once again, the argument from religious experience goes like this:

1. Nonreligious experiences provide warrant for the existence of their objects.

2. Therefore, experiences of God provide warrant for the existence of God.

Martin challenged this reasoning by claiming that there are important differences between human experiences of things like typewriters and alleged "experiences" of God. Religious experiences are different enough from our "normal" experiences to suggest that they should not be taken at face value. For one thing, we can always test the veridicality of ordinary, nonreligious experiences by means of what Martin called "checking procedures." Suppose I perceive a piece of blue paper on the table. Suppose also that I am interested in discovering if my experience of the blue paper is veridical. It is important to note here that, for Martin, the actual existence of the blue paper "is not to be read off from my experience" of what seems to

---

[17]Charles B. Martin, *Religious Belief* (Ithaca, N.Y.: Cornell University Press, 1959).

be blue paper.[18] Just because I perceive a piece of blue paper, it does not follow from my experience alone that the blue paper really exists. My confidence about the existence of the blue paper is bolstered by the availability of various checking procedures. Perhaps I have a Polaroid camera, take a picture of the blue paper, and check to see if the blue paper appears in the right spot in the picture. Perhaps I can pick up the paper. Or possibly other people are in the room and I can ask if they perceive the blue paper on the table. According to Martin, "It is only when I admit the relevance of such checking procedures that I can lay claim to apprehending the paper, and, indeed, the admission of the relevance of such procedures is what gives meaning to the assertion that I am apprehending the paper. *What I apprehend is the sort of thing that can be photographed, touched, and seen by others.*"[19]

C. D. Broad had the same point in mind when he wrote:

> Now, in the case of sense-perception there are several tests which we can use to tell whether a perception is delusive or not. We can check one sense by another, e.g., sight by touch. We can appeal to the testimony of others and find out whether they see anything that corresponds to what we see. Finally, we can make inferences from what we think we perceive, and find whether they are verified. We can say: "If there are really rats running about my bed my dog will be excited, bread and cheese will disappear, and so on." And then we can see whether anything of the kind happens.[20]

Such tests seem relevant enough. The obvious problem, it seems, is the difficulty of applying such tests to the kinds of experiences people have when they believe they are perceiving God. And so we find Martin asking, *What checking procedures are available when someone claims to have had an experience of God?* Photographs are out of the question. Since the religious experiences we're considering are subjective, independent support from other persons seems impossible.

Martin did not deny the subjective component of alleged religious experiences, any more than a doctor would deny the subjective experience of the alcoholic who "perceives" pink rats running around his bed. What is at stake is the veridicality of such experiences. How can anyone else check my claim that I had an experience of God? How can the person who had the experience check it? In Martin's view "It is quite obvious . . . that the religious statement 'I have a direct experience of God' has a different status from the physical object statement 'I see a star' and shows a distressing similarity to the low-claim assertion 'I seem to see a star.'"[21]

Charles B. Martin and William Rowe appear to be running on the same (or at least on closely parallel) tracks. Both Martin and Rowe believe that religious experiences must be treated differently from other experiences. Their major reason for this seems to be that religious experiences, unlike ordinary, nonreligious experiences, cannot be checked. Since religious experiences cannot be checked (Martin's language) or since we do not know

---

[18]Ibid., p. 87.
[19]Ibid., pp. 87–88.
[20].Broad, *Religion, Philosophy and Psychical Research*, p. 168.
[21]Martin, *Religious Belief*, p. 75.

how to discover reasons for thinking some religious experiences are delusive (Rowe's language), they should not be treated as veridical. For both Martin and Rowe, religious experiences should be regarded as guilty until proven innocent. Even if the principle of credulity is relevant to nonreligious experiences, the different status of religious experiences, obliges us to treat them differently. For both Martin and Rowe, the burden of proof rests with the person who dares to claim that some supposed religious experience is veridical. And for both of them, it is hard to see how any attempt at such a proof will satisfy them.

THE VINDICATION OF THE ARGUMENT FROM RELIGIOUS EXPERIENCE

Any attempt to rescue the argument from religious experience will have to deal with the kinds of claims made by Martin and Rowe to the effect that religious experiences deserve different treatment from nonreligious experiences because they lack something (for example, checking procedures) available for nonreligious experiences.

One good place to begin seeking a reply to the Martin-Rowe argument against religious experience is George Mavrodes's 1970 book, *Belief in God*.[22] Mavrodes begins his reply by picking up on Martin's use of a photograph as an example of a checking procedure. Martin, we recall, claimed that our experience of the blue paper could be checked by using a photo of the paper to confirm our original experience. But, Mavrodes points out, we took the photo because we didn't trust our direct experience of the blue paper. Is Martin telling us that we can now trust our direct experience of the photograph? If we couldn't trust our direct experience of the blue paper, how are we suddenly justified in trusting our direct experience of the *picture* of the blue paper? If direct experience is an unreliable guide to the existence of the paper, it is also an unreliable guide to the existence of the photograph. In Mavrodes's words,

> In some particular circumstance I may have doubt about some putative experience, perhaps my apparent seeing of a piece of blue paper. In that case I might resort to photography or to the testimony of friends to resolve my uncertainty. This procedure does not enable me, however, to substitute a "checked" experience for the unchecked variety. It enables me, rather, to substitute one unchecked experience for another. If I do not rely upon my vision of the paper, I do rely upon my vision of the photo, or upon my sense of touch, or upon the accuracy of my hearing when I listen to my friends' report. I can, perhaps, seek a check for any of these that I wish but to look for a check for all of them is self-stultifying. If I cannot rely upon some unchecked experience of my own, I just cannot get anything out of experience and I must give up the empirical route to knowledge.[23]

The same reasoning that might lead us to doubt the existence of the blue paper should lead us to question the existence of anything that might

---

[22]George Mavrodes, *Belief in God* (New York: Random House, 1970). Mavrodes's book is now published by University Press of America.

[23]Ibid., p. 76.

serve as a checking procedure. How do I know my experience of the blue paper is veridical? Is it because I have an experience of a picture of the blue paper? Then how do I know my experience of the picture is veridical? Is it because I experience other people in the room and that experience includes my hearing them say that they too see the paper (or the picture)? How do I know that my experience of these other people is veridical?

Suppose I have an experience of something (call it *A*) and want to know if my experience of *A* is veridical. Suppose I come up with a checking procedure for *A* (call it *B*). Do I not need a checking procedure for *B* (namely, *C*)? And another checking procedure for *C* (namely, *D*)? And so to infinity? Either the Rowe-Martin demand traps us in an infinite regress (which is absurd), or we are forced to recognize that sooner or later, we must rest on the conviction that one of our experiences *is* veridical. Since we all have to make this move somewhere, why not make it at the beginning—with our direct experience of the paper?

Of course, the proper use of the principle of credulity really makes all of this unnecessary. Typically, we tend to regard our experiences as veridical unless we have good reason to think otherwise. At least one of our two authors (Rowe) believes the principle of credulity (when properly formulated) should lead us to treat nonreligious experiences as veridical unless we have reason to think otherwise.[24] If this is so, then why get involved in all this talk about checking procedures? The answer lies in the claim that the availability of checking procedures marks an important difference between nonreligious and religious experiences. Mavrodes's analysis of these alleged checking procedures shows the serious problem that is simply ignored by those who attribute importance to such checks. The problem is this: anyone who begins the process of seeking checking procedures will not continue the process to infinity—of this I am sure. The demand for checking procedures will end, probably at the first or second check. The person may terminate his search for checks with his photo of the blue paper or with the testimony of independent eyewitnesses or something similar. But the obvious question is, What is the person's reason for ending his search for checks at *that* point? As we have seen, there is no more reason to take the word of that final checking procedure than there was to trust the original experience as veridical.

Philosopher Peter Losin invites us to reflect on the procedure by which we actually do identify sensory experiences as nonveridical. He writes,

> In most cases, I think, we do so by appealing to *other* sensory experiences, the assumed veridicality of which, together with other things we know about the object(s) of those experiences and/or the conditions under which the experiences occur, entails or renders likely the nonveridicality of the particular sensory experience(s) in question. These other sensory experiences can be my own or those of other perceivers.[25]

In other words, when I identify some sensory experience *A* as nonveridical, I do so by appealing to some other experience (*B*), and so on.

---

[24]Of course, as we've seen, Rowe thinks he has reasons to believe that religious experiences don't quite fill the bill on this matter.

[25]Peter Losin, "Experience of God and the Principle of Credulity: A Reply to Rowe," *Faith and Philosophy* 4 (1987): 63–64.

Somewhere along this line, I simply have to *assume* that one of these other experiences is veridical.[26] Now, Losin argues, there is absolutely no reason why the theist cannot follow a similar procedure while investigating the possible nonveridicality of his religious experiences.

> I am suggesting it is open to the theist to claim that the kind of reasoning we typically engage in in checking particular sensory experiences can perform a similar function in cases of experience of God. We can assume, if only provisionally, "for the sake of argument," that some experience of God or other is probably veridical; on this basis other experiences of God can be identified and dismissed as non-veridical.[27]

After all, the person who decides that one of his experiences is nonveridical will do so because he assumes that some other experience (his own or someone else's perhaps) *is* veridical. Why can't the religious believer follow precisely the same procedure when considering the possible nonveridicality of some religious experience? George Mavrodes describes a few of the ways this sort of thing might be done:

> If in some experience a person really does apprehend God then he can of course claim that God *can* be apprehended by others in a similar sort of experience. He may also claim that God *could* reveal Himself in other sorts of experiences. And he may claim that God *could* do other things that would result in clues to the existence and presence of God. . . . With respect to corroborating experience of other sorts, by other people, the status of religious experience is fundamentally similar to, not different from, that of other types of experience.[28]

Groups of believers in the same religious community could, for example, get together and compare notes on their religious experiences.

Suppose we grant that our act of checking some experience brings us sooner or later to some other experience that we simply assume is veridical, even if only for the sake of argument. The adoption of this procedure by the Christian theist would seem to allow him—at least provisionally—to assume the veridicality of the religious experiences that were the ground of the biblical revelation. May we not assume "for the sake of argument" (as Losin says) that the experiences of those who were recipients of special revelation that led to the production of an inspired and authoritative Scripture were veridical? And if so, would that not allow us to use, for the sake of argument, the product of those earlier experiences as one test of our own religious experiences? Hence, if someone has a putative experience of God today that contradicts the clear teaching of Scripture about the character of God, let us say, we could claim to have a good reason for questioning the veridicality of the contemporary experience.[29] But isn't this precisely the kind of test that

---

[26]Of course, as Losin points out, other things I know about the objects are relevant. If I perceive a log burning in the fireplace just before going to bed, I expect to perceive cold ashes in the morning. But if instead I perceive the unburnt log, I have at least *prima facie* reason to question the veridicality of my experience the night before.

[27]Losin, "Experience of God," p. 65.

[28]Mavrodes, *Belief in God*, p. 77.

[29]Of course, none of this implies that Scripture is the only test of contemporary religious experiences.

Rowe required in his revised principle of credulity? And doesn't this give us one more reason to doubt the significance of Rowe's challenge to the integrity of religious experience?

To this point, we've been comparing a person's direct experience of God to the direct experience of an inert object like a piece of paper. As Mavrodes states, "The world contains many things and not all of them are as inert as a piece of paper. To demand that the corroboration of every experience should be equally as easy as substantiating the existence of the paper is simply to exhibit a foolish disregard for the relevant facts."[30] Experiencing a living being like God is bound to be more complex than simply perceiving an inert physical object.

> Since we do not know just what conditions are sufficient even for seeing a piece of paper, it would not be surprising if we also did not know what is involved in some person's failure to meet God. Beyond this, however, it seems clear that if Christian theologians are correct then God will be experienced only when He chooses to reveal Himself. . . . The failure, then, of one person to apprehend God has very little significance against someone else's positive claim. For it is quite possible that the failure stems from the fact that the man is in some way yet unready for that experience, or from the fact that God—for reasons which we may or may not guess— has not yet chosen to reveal Himself to him.[31]

Losin concludes his evaluation of Rowe's treatment of religious experience by writing:

> In the end it strikes me that Rowe has simply assumed that reasons drawn from experiences of God cannot themselves be "reasons for thinking that particular experiences of God are delusive," that experiences of God cannot themselves provide a . . . [provisional] means for the critique of other such experiences. I see no reason to think that this assumption is true, and good reason to think that, when suitably amended and applied to sensory experience, it is false. Nor do I see the slightest reason why we cannot use knowledge or beliefs about God not gleaned from experience of God to identify and dismiss particular experiences of God as non-veridical. We proceed in something like this way when sensory experiences are at issue; it is [Richard] Swinburne's suggestion that we proceed in similar ways with experience of God. There are epistemically interesting differences between sensory experience and experience of God, but they do not lie in the presence or absence, or even in the character, of criteria for identifying and dismissing instances of each as non-veridical.[32]

CONCLUSION

We began by noting that William Rowe has provided what appears to be an especially strong argument for God's existence based on religious experience. According to Rowe, the only way to evade the argument is to find a way of showing that the principle of credulity (properly formulated) does not give the person who has a putative religious experience the same

---

[30] Mavrodes, *Belief in God*, p. 79.
[31] Ibid.
[32] Ibid., p. 69.

rights that he has with regard to ordinary, nonreligious experiences. The reason for this lies in the Rowe-Martin allegation that religious experiences are different somehow; and those differences to be found supposedly in the noncheckability of religious experiences mean that religious experiences should not be considered veridical until shown otherwise. In the case of religious experiences, we should begin by assuming that they are not subject to the protection of the principle of credulity. Religious experiences are guilty until proven innocent. And if so, of course, the supposed argument from religious experience collapses.

However, we have noted that attempts to set religious experiences apart from ordinary, nonreligious experiences are beset by arbitrariness, philosophical gerrymandering, and assorted other acts of philosophical malfeasance. Since Rowe's attempt to defeat the argument he presented so well has failed, it appears that until a stronger objection makes an appearance, we are justified in treating the argument from religious experience with respect.[33]

For Further Exploration—Chapter Eleven

1. Discuss the importance of religious experience.
2. Summarize Baillie's argument from religious experience.
3. Explain *the principle of credulity*. Discuss its role in an argument from religious experience. Why does Rowe advise against rejecting the principle for *all* experience?
4. How did C. B. Martin challenge the veridicality of supposed religious experiences?
5. Summarize Mavrodes's reply to Martin.
6. What are your present thoughts about the plausibility of God's existence with respect to religious experience?

---

[33]The organization of the argument in this chapter requires that a separate problem be considered only in this footnote. Some may wonder about times when people in competing religious traditions report what appear to be similar religious experiences. Does this fact not undercut the argument we have been considering? William Alston replies: "What is (should be) claimed is only *prima facie* justification [from religious experience]. When a person believes that God is experientially present to him, that belief is justified *unless* the subject has sufficient reasons to suppose it to be false or to suppose that the experience is not, in these circumstances, sufficiently indicative of the truth of the belief" (Alston, "Perceiving God," p. 657). In nonreligious cases, two people often experience the same object and then interpret their experience differently. Clearly, this occurs in the case of religious experiences. It is possible to maintain that religious experiences in competing religions point to the existence of the object (God) without requiring us to believe that the competing conceptual systems within which the experiences occur are equally true or false. The similar religious experiences of people in conflicting religious traditions may be a sign that humans can tap into a reality beyond the human or that this reality can break into human consciousness.

Chapter 12

A POTPOURRI OF OTHER ARGUMENTS

There are lots of other interesting arguments for God's existence. In this, the final chapter of Part 3, I will note several that in my judgment have potential.

The reader should realize that in order to set up these arguments properly and then deal adequately with objections, much more space is needed than I can possibly allot to this chapter. Quite honestly, the need to bring Part 3 to a close and get on with the important matters still ahead clashes with my conviction that I ought to draw attention to a few more theistic arguments. But the need to be brief places me in a catch-22 situation. Should I introduce several arguments and then leave the reader feeling unsatisfied because I have failed to establish all the premises or answer all the objections? Or should I say nothing and perhaps leave some readers with the false impression that the three previous chapters contain all that's worth saying on the subject of God's existence? Neither course of action is satisfactory. I have decided to take the former path and err on the side of saying too little about too much. This seems better than saying nothing at all.

The arguments I'll be considering in this chapter, like those covered in earlier chapters, are not coercive. That is, I do not regard them as arguments people must accept if they are to be rational. Lots of reasonable people look at such arguments and find them unconvincing. In all likelihood, many of them will find their minds unchanged by anything I say in this chapter. But, it is clear, many other people find the premises of some of these arguments quite acceptable.

Quite often, people do not have to be persuaded of the truth of claims that function as premises in these arguments. Typically, people much like you and me simply find ourselves holding these beliefs. Whenever this is the case, it is possible that we can use these beliefs as premises in what will turn out to be an effective argument for that person. Given the person-relativity of proofs, what more should we expect? It is helpful to remember that arguments can be good arguments even when they are not coercive, even when their premises fall short of being the sorts of claims that every reasonable man or woman accepts.

Each of these arguments draws attention to some phenomenon such as the moral law or truth that requires explanation. It then asks what condition or set of conditions best explains this feature of the inner or outer world? How might a naturalist account for this phenomenon? Is a naturalistic explanation adequate? Does theism provide a better explanation?[1]

Another way of looking at these arguments is to see them as attempts to place people in situations where they "see" something and where the *sensus divinitatis* can take over in a way that produces conviction.[2] When someone uses the teleological argument in this way, he does not view the argument as a sound deductive argument in which the proposition "God exists" follows necessarily from claims about order and design in the world. Instead, he attempts to direct the attention of others to some of the impressive signs of this order and design. He then asks if such design and order make sense in a nontheistic universe and allows the *sensus divinitatis* to take over. As we know, such attempts often fail to produce the desired results.[3] With these qualifications and warnings duly noted, I turn to these other arguments.

THE MORAL ARGUMENT

Many human experiences seem to point to the existence of moral laws or standards of behavior. Our failure to do something that we believe we ought to do may lead us to feel guilt. The failure of others to perform certain duties toward us may produce feelings of resentment or anger or sorrow. Whenever we dare to suggest to someone else that his conduct is wrong, we are doing more than appealing to our own moral standard. Moral criticism like this would make no sense unless we also believed that the other person knew about the same moral standard. It is interesting to note that the person whose moral conduct is being criticized seldom denies the existence of the moral standard. That is, such people seldom try to argue that there is nothing wrong with cheating or stealing or lying. Such people attempt rather to find some way of showing that what they did doesn't violate the principle or at least is a justifiable exception to the moral standard.

C. Stephen Evans points out that

> this standard, this "law" if you will, is therefore not simply a description about how people behave. It is a prescription about how people should behave, though one they are constantly violating. So morality is not

---

[1] For any readers with short memories, this might be a good time to review chapter 4.

[2] See chapter 7.

[3] For a review of some of the reasons why such arguments fail, see chapter 8.

simply a law of nature like the law of gravity. It doesn't describe how things in nature go on, but how human behavior ought to go on.[4]

An important feature of this moral law is what we take to be its *objectivity*. By comparison, the laws of mathematics are objective (not subjective) in the sense that their truth is totally independent of human feelings and desires. When we deal with objective truth, it does not matter whether we like it; it is simply true—and that's all there is to it! In a similar way, the moral law is independent of our feelings and desires. As C. S. Lewis explains, "There is nothing indulgent about the Moral Law. It is as hard as nails. It tells you to do the straight thing and it does not seem to care how painful, or dangerous, or difficult it is to do."[5] The Moral Law doesn't care whether we like it, whether we want to obey it, or whether we're disposed to do it. It informs us that this is our duty, now do it!

Not surprisingly, this view of morality is unsettling to lots of people— not the least because of its possible implications for God's existence. And so one can discover many different attempts to undermine the claim that there is an objective moral law that is the same for all human beings. Theists should be encouraged by the weakness of these countermoves. For example, some attempt to argue that human moral consciousness results from learning or conditioning, which, if true, would undermine the presumed objectivity of the moral law. Ed Miller notes one serious weakness in this line of thinking. He writes that the fact

> that something is learned is hardly evidence against its objective truth and validity. We learn that two plus two equals four, and that war is bad, and we learn all kinds of things which we believe to be nonetheless true. Is there, in fact, anything that we claim to know that we have not learned in one way or another? And though people may disagree about their interpretation of "good," it does not follow from this that there *is* no objective good. We may just as easily conclude from the fact that people often disagree in their interpretations of the world that the world does not exist, or from the fact that some people cannot see that two plus two equals four that perhaps it doesn't.[6]

So far as objective truth is concerned, absolutely nothing follows from the fact that two individuals or two cultures disagree over the morality of a particular action any more than that their disagreement over some nonethical issue might be thought to imply the absence of any objective truth in this nonethical case. When person *A* says the world is flat and person *B* claims the world is round, it hardly follows that there is no objective truth about this issue. Similarly, when person *A* says that abortion on demand is morally acceptable and person *B* says it is wrong, it does not follow that the morality of the practice is purely a matter of taste. In both cases, we are dealing with beliefs: *A* believes the world is flat while *B* believes otherwise. As we know, there is an objective truth on this issue; therefore, one person's belief is correct and the other's is not. Likewise, ethical disputes involve conflicting

[4]C. Stephen Evans, *The Quest for Faith* (Downers Grove, Ill.: InterVarsity Press, 1986), p. 45.

[5]C. S. Lewis, *Mere Christianity* (New York: Macmillan, 1960), p. 37.

[6]Ed L. Miller, *God and Reason* (New York: Macmillan, 1972), p. 87.

beliefs. Even in especially difficult cases where we may have trouble knowing which belief is correct,[7] it is difficult to see what would justify the conclusion that in ethical disputes *no* beliefs are objectively and universally true.

Equally implausible are attempts to explain moral beliefs in terms of the supposed evolution of instincts or social feelings. According to C. Stephen Evans,

> The moral order does not seem to consist of any such things [i.e., instincts and feelings]. It is not an instinct, because it is itself the standard by which we judge our instincts to be good and bad. And it is not merely a social impulse or feeling. People who have dulled their consciences often are in fact obligated to do things, yet have no such feelings of obligation whatsoever. On the other hand, people with tender consciences often *feel* obligated to do things which no reasonable person would claim they really ought to do. Feelings and real obligations can't be identical.[8]

I do not want to leave the impression that the case for the objectivity of moral laws rests solely on the weakness of arguments against such objectivity. "If we did not believe," Ed Miller writes,

> that there is an objective and unchanging foundation of moral values and ideals, then we would never bother to make such judgments, at least not seriously. On the contrary, that we continue to exercise moral judgment, not only in reference to ourselves but also to others, is clear evidence that we do, in fact, take such judgments as counting for something and as being ultimately and objectively significant. In this way, it may be argued, it is self-contradictory (practically speaking) to make judgments of moral value and to deny at the same time that there is any objective basis of morality. What can be more comical than someone who spends the day fanatically and passionately crusading for the eradication of certain evils, while in the evening he delivers cool lectures on the relativity of all ideals?[9]

The belief in the existence of an objective and universal moral law certainly qualifies as a rational belief. For anyone who recognizes this fact, the next natural step is to ask, What is the source and ground of the moral law? British philosopher Hastings Rashdall does a nice job of summarizing the answer to this question that constitutes the moral argument for God's existence:

> We say that the Moral Law has a real existence, that there is such a thing as an absolute [i.e. objective] Morality, that there is something absolutely [i.e., objectively] true or false in ethical judgements, whether we or any number of human beings at any given time actually think so or not. . . . We must therefore face the question *where* such an ideal exists, and what

---

[7] Of course, there are times when neither of two competing beliefs might be true because there is a third alternative. But so long as the law of noncontradiction obtains, there can never be a time when both competing beliefs are true.

[8] Evans, *Quest for Faith*, p. 47. An excellent account of the relation between the objective truth of moral judgments and the subjective feelings that often accompany such judgments can be found in Mortimer J. Adler, *Six Great Ideas* (New York: Macmillan, 1981), chaps. 9–14.

[9] Miller, *God and Reason*, p. 90. Note Miller's use of the Existential Test.

manner of existence we are to attribute to it. Certainly it is to be found, wholly and completely, in no individual human consciousness. . . . Only if we believe in the existence of a Mind for which the true moral ideal is already in some sense real, a Mind which is the source of whatever is true in our own moral judgments, can we rationally think of the moral ideal as no less real than the world itself. Only so can we believe in an absolute standard of right and wrong, which is as independent of this or that man's actual ideas and actual desires as the facts of material nature. The belief in God . . . is the logical presupposition of an "objective" or absolute Morality. A moral ideal can exist nowhere and nohow but in a Mind; an absolute moral ideal can exist only in a Mind from which all Reality is derived. Our moral ideal can only claim objective validity in so far as it can rationally be regarded as the revelation of a moral ideal eternally existing in the mind of God.[10]

In earlier chapters, we asked which world-view best explains the existence of a contingent universe, of a cosmos exhibiting many remarkable signs of order and design, and the existence of religious experiences of God, some of which certainly have the right to be considered veridical. The question now is this: Which world-view best explains our consciousness of an objective moral order? The answer of Christian theism to all these questions is both plausible and respectable. It is an answer for which no one need apologize. And perhaps one of the more important things we can learn from apologetics is that we don't have to apologize for our beliefs.

THE ARGUMENT FROM TRUTH

Theists have more resources at their disposal than they often realize. One oft-neglected argument for God's existence invites us to reflect about the ground of truth. So far as I know, this argument makes its first appearance in Book 2 of Augustine's *On the Freedom of the Will*, written in A.D. 395. There is at least one clue that Thomas Aquinas thought the line of reasoning sound.[11] Its two major modern proponents appear to be Gordon H. Clark and Alvin Plantinga. Since Clark and Plantinga present different versions of the argument that address audiences with somewhat different philosophical interests, I am going to look at the argument from both contemporary perspectives. This makes sense because it is sometimes easier to understand a difficult argument when approaching it from two different directions. While Clark's presentation is simpler, it may puzzle readers who are unaccustomed to talking about truth apart from propositions, the carriers of truth. Plantinga's version of the argument is more in tune with the contemporary way in which philosophers typically think of truth.

Clark's Version of the Argument

Gordon Clark's account of the argument from truth utilizes six steps:[12]

---

[10]Hastings Rashdall, *The Theory of Good and Evil* (Oxford: Clarendon Press, 1907), 2:211–12.
[11]See Aquinas's *De Veritate* Question I, Article 2, Reply.
[12]For Clark's argument, see Gordon H. Clark, *A Christian View of Men and Things* (Grand Rapids: Eerdmans, 1952), pp. 318ff.

1. Truth exists.
2. Truth is immutable.
3. Truth is eternal.
4. Truth is mental.
5. Truth is superior to the human mind.
6. Truth is God.

1. "Truth exists." Clark establishes this point by reminding us of the self-defeating nature of any attempt to deny the existence of truth.[13] Since skepticism is false, there must be knowledge; and if there is knowledge, there must exist the object of knowledge, namely, truth.

2. "Truth is immutable." It is impossible for truth to change. As Clark says, "Truth must be unchangeable. What is true today always has been and always will be true."[14] For Clark, all true propositions are eternal and immutable truths. He has no use for pragmatic views of truth that imply that what is true today may be false tomorrow. If truth changes, then pragmatism will be false tomorrow—if, indeed, it could ever be true. Truth itself is unaffected by the fact that sentences like "I am now typing" are sometimes true and usually false. Since I'll present a rather long argument in defense of this claim later in this chapter, I'll assume that this possible problem can be answered and move on to Clark's next point.

3. "Truth is eternal." It would be self-contradictory to deny the eternity of truth. If the world will never cease to exist, *it is true* that the world will never cease to exist. If the world will someday perish, then *that* is true. But truth itself will abide even though every created thing should perish. But suppose someone asks, "What if truth itself should perish?" Then it would still be true that truth had perished. Any denial of the eternity of truth turns out to be an affirmation of its eternity.

4. "Truth is mental." The existence of truth presupposes the existence of minds. "Without a mind, truth could not exist. The object of knowledge is a proposition, a meaning, a significance; it is a thought."[15]

For Clark, the existence of truth is incompatible with any materialistic view of man. If the materialist admits the existence of consciousness at all, he regards it as an effect and not a cause. For a materialist, thoughts are always the result of bodily changes. This materialism implies that all thinking, including logical reasoning, is merely the result of mechanical necessity. But bodily changes can be neither true nor false. One set of physical motions cannot be truer than another. Therefore, if there is no mind, there can be no truth; and if there is no truth, materialism cannot be true. Likewise, if there is no mind, there can be no such thing as logical reasoning from which it follows that no materialist can possibly provide a valid argument for his position. No reason can possibly be given to justify an acceptance of materialism. Hence, for Clark, any denial of the mental nature of truth is self-stultifying. In Clark's words,

---

[13] In case some readers have forgotten, the claim "Truth does not exist" can be countered by asking whether the claim itself is true or false. If it is false, then truth exists; and if the claim is true, then truth exists.

[14] Clark, *Christian View*, p. 319.

[15] Ibid.

If a truth, a proposition, or a thought were some physical motion in the brain, no two persons could have the same thought. A physical motion is a fleeting event numerically distinct from every other. Two persons cannot have the same motion, nor can one person have it twice. If this is what thought were, memory and communication would be impossible. . . . It is a peculiarity of mind and not of body that the past can be made present. Accordingly, if one may think the same thought twice, truth must be mental or spiritual. Not only does [truth] defy time; it defies space as well, for if communication is to be possible, the identical truth must be in two minds at once. If, in opposition, anyone wished to deny that an immaterial idea can exist in two minds at once, his denial must be conceived to exist in his own mind only; and since it has not registered in any other mind, it does not occur to us to refute it.[16]

To summarize Clark's argument thus far, truth exists and is both eternal and immutable. Furthermore, truth can exist only in some mind.

5. "Truth is superior to the human mind." By this, Clark means that by its very nature, truth cannot be subjective and individualistic. Humans know certain truths that are not only necessary but universal. While these truths are immutable, the human mind is changeable. Even though beliefs vary from one person to another, truth itself cannot change. Moreover, the human mind does not stand in judgment of truth; rather truth judges our reason.[17] While we often judge other human minds (as when we say, for example, that someone's mind is not as keen as it should be), we do not judge truth. If truth and the human mind were equal, truth could not be eternal and immutable since the human mind is finite, mutable, and subject to error. Therefore, truth must transcend human reason; truth must be superior to any individual human mind as well as to the sum total of human minds. From this it follows that there must be a mind higher than the human mind in which truth resides.

6. "Truth is God." There must be an ontological ground for truth. But the ground of truth cannot be anything perishable or contingent. Since truth is eternal and immutable, it must exist in an eternal Mind. And since only God possesses these attributes, God must be truth.

Is all this any more than the assertion that there is an eternal, immutable Mind, a Supreme Reason, a personal, living God? The truths or propositions that may be known are the thoughts of God, the eternal thoughts of God. And insofar as man knows anything he is in contact with God's mind. Since further, God's mind is God, we may . . . say, we have a vision of God.[18]

---

[16]Ibid., pp. 319–20.

[17]For the source of this view, see Augustine's *On The Teacher* as well as his *On True Religion*. For an exposition of the extremely important but tricky argument of Augustine's *On The Teacher*, see Ronald Nash, *The Light of the Mind: St. Augustine's Theory of Knowledge* (Lexington: University Press of Kentucky, 1969), chap. 6.

[18]Clark, *Christian View*, p. 321. Clark's comments late in this paragraph raise another complicated problem that sometimes passes under the label of Ontologism. For more on this, see Nash, *The Light of the Mind*, chap. 8. Relevant to all this is the importance of repudiating the oft-made claim that human knowledge of God's nature can never be univocal; it can only be analogical. The serious weaknesses in the analogical approach to God are spelled out in Edward John Carnell's *An Introduction to*

Therefore, when human beings know truth, we also know something of God's nature. There is a sense in which all knowledge is a knowledge of God.

Clark's position in all this is essentially correct. Since Clark's time, however, philosophers in the English-speaking world tend to think they've achieved levels of sophistication that make Clark's way of stating things appear outdated. It is worth seeing, then, if a certain fuzziness in Clark's presentation can be rubbed off. One way to do this is to see how Alvin Plantinga expresses what amounts to the same argument.

Plantinga's Version of the Argument

Contemporary philosophers like Plantinga who see merit in the Augustinian argument that provides the foundation for Gordon Clark's remarks are actually interested in more than just the notion of truth. Many philosophers affirm the existence of a whole host of abstract objects that supposedly exist eternally and necessarily; these abstract, eternal entities include properties, relations,[19] states of affairs,[20] numbers, and propositions. As some readers may have guessed, I regard myself as part of this tradition. Everyone in this tradition who is also a theist faces the challenge of explaining the relationship between such eternal objects and the sovereign God. The Augustinian answer to this problem is that eternal objects like properties and numbers "subsist" eternally in the mind of God. This is an interesting way of stating both that such entities exist eternally and that they depend upon God for their existence. If God did not exist, they would not exist. But perhaps we should not get ahead of our argument. Suppose we simply find ourselves part of that fairly impressive group of philosophers who recognize that things like properties and propositions exist eternally. What then?

Well, suppose that in order to simplify things a bit, we focus only on propositions. The first question, obviously, is, What is a proposition? Many

---

Christian Apologetics (Grand Rapids: Eerdmans, 1948), chaps. 8–9, and in Ronald Nash, ed., *The Philosophy of Gordon H. Clark* (Philadelphia: Presbyterian and Reformed, 1968), pp. 149–51.

[19] Plato taught that for every class concept (universal) there exists something (some particular) that corresponds to that concept. Consider, for example, any sentence of the form "*S* is *P*" (where *S* is any subject and *P* is any property) and substitute for *P* any one of a countless number of predicates like red, true, tall, square, and so on. Because such predicates can be applied to a large number of particular things, they came to be known as universal terms. The predicate *red* is a universal inasmuch as the word can denote innumerable particular instances of the color. The class of universals includes properties like redness and relations like similarity and betweenness. Philosophers who hold that universals, like properties, exist in some way apart from the particular things that exemplify them came to be known as realists. Thinkers who disagreed came to be called nominalists because, for the most part, they suggested that universals were nothing more than words (Latin: *nomina*). For any bona fide nominalist, properties do not exist; only particular things exist.

[20] It is easier to provide examples of states of affairs than a definition. The basic idea here is that a state of affairs exists for and corresponds to every proposition. If the proposition in view is, let us say, "Ted Kennedy ran for the presidency in 1980," the corresponding state of affairs would be "Ted Kennedy's running for the presidency in 1980."

philosophers distinguish between sentences and propositions. A sentence is some combination of words in a particular language. If a sentence has meaning, its meaning is said to be the proposition expressed by the sentence. Consider, for example, the following sentences: (1) "John is the husband of Mary," and (2) "Mary is the wife of John." It is clear that (1) and (2) are different sentences that nonetheless refer to the same state of affairs. Both sentences have the same meaning and thus express the same proposition.

Most philosophers who accept the distinction between sentences and propositions regard propositions (and their corresponding states of affairs) as eternal entities. The truth-value of these eternal propositions never changes. If p is a proposition, then p has always existed and has always been either true or false. Like many philosophical doctrines, this view no doubt seems odd to anyone hearing it for the first time. It is a tribute to the philosophical art that so many apparently weird theories are not only accepted but become the objects of fierce devotion. Since any defense of this theory of propositions is beyond the scope of this book, let me simply assume it is true and see what follows for those who recognize its truth.

The claim that propositions (as distinct from sentences) are eternally true or false entities seems contradicted by propositions that contain a reference to time or place. Consider the sentence "Nash is now typing." At the moment, the statement is true. But it obviously ceases to be true the instant I lift my fingers from the keys and turn off the machine. Since the statement under consideration is sometimes true and usually false, how can one seriously maintain that propositions are eternally true? The answer lies in the fact that the example ("Nash is now typing") is too poorly framed to serve as the real proposition in question. The doctrine that propositions are eternally true requires any statement that is in effect "open" because of some reference to time or place to be "closed." This can be done by eliminating tensed verbs and making explicit any relevant information that may only have been implied in the original.

My original statement ("Nash is now typing") is what I have called an "open statement." It contains a temporal reference (the word *now*). In order to approximate the proposition we need, it is necessary to remove any reference to time in the verb and then close the statement by making explicit a reference to the precise time. And so we get something like "Nash is (tenselessly) typing at 3:03 P.M. on September 2, 1987." The proposition expressed by this sentence corresponds to a particular state of affairs, namely, Nash's typing at 3:03 P.M. on September 2, 1987. This state of affairs (i.e., Nash's typing . . .) can be expressed in a wide variety of sentences just as our earlier state of affairs (John's being married to Mary) can be stated in different sentences. Some of these sentences can be correctly uttered by some people, but not by others. For example, I am the only one who can correctly refer to the state of affairs, Nash's typing, by writing, "*I* am typing at 3:03 P.M. on September 2, 1987." No one else can correctly refer to this state of affairs by using the singular first-person pronoun. And, of course, the same state of affairs must be expressed in different sentences at different times. Someone who knows my plans for the day could say at 8:00 A.M. on September 2, "Nash will be typing at 3:03 today." Or at 3:03, he could see me working and truthfully say, "Nash is now typing." Or on September 3, he could say, "Nash was typing yesterday at 3:03 P.M." I see no problem in allowing that all these different utterances refer to the same piece of information, describe the same state of affairs. The changing truth-value of different statements does not mean that the truth-value of the corresponding propositions undergoes change. When a proposition is formulated properly, the truth-value of that proposition never changes. The proposition "Nash is typing at 3:03 P.M. on September 2, 1987" was not only true at that time; the proposition is still true today and will continue to be true. It is eternally true!

What I've done is provide a more contemporary elaboration of Gordon Clark's claims that truth exists and that truth is eternal and unchanging. It is now time to see how Alvin Plantinga expresses his version of the argument from truth. First of all, Plantinga sides with those philosophers who "have thought it incredible that propositions should exist apart from the activity of minds. How could [propositions] just *be* there, if never thought of?" It is tempting, Plantinga continues, "to think of propositions as ontologically dependent upon mental or intellectual activity in such a way that either they just are thoughts, or else at any rate, couldn't exist if not thought."[21] It seems then, that "truth cannot be independent of noetic activity on the part of persons."[22] In other words, the existence of some mind is a necessary condition for the existence of any proposition. Since truth is a property of propositions, truth also requires some mind as a necessary condition. All of this is simply another way of stating the point Clark makes—that is, that truth is mental.

But now Plantinga, like others before him, sees a problem. Even though true propositions require the existence of minds, we seem driven to seek a ground for true propositions other than individual human minds or the totality of human minds. For one thing, if the only minds that exist are human minds, there are clearly far too many propositions to go around. While "truth cannot be independent of noetic activity on the part of persons," it must also be the case that truth "must be independent of *our* [i.e., human] noetic activity."[23] Since truth is unchanging and eternal, it requires as its ontological ground a mind quite different from human minds. Plantinga quotes with approval the words of Thomas Aquinas: "Even if there were no human intellects, things could be said to be true because of their relation to the divine intellect. But if, by an impossible supposition, intellect did not exist and things did continue to exist, then the essentials of truth would in no way remain."[24] In other words, should every human mind cease to exist, truth would continue to exist because of its relation to the mind of God. But if (impossible though it may be) no mind including God's mind existed, truth would cease to exist.

Plantinga sums this up by writing:

---

[21] This and a few other quotations from Plantinga have their source in papers as yet unpublished.

[22] Alvin Plantinga, "How to be an Anti-Realist," *Proceedings and Addresses of the American Philosophical Association* 56 (1982): 68. This paper was Plantinga's presidential address to the Western Division of the American Philosophical Association (1982).

[23] Ibid.

[24] Thomas Aquinas, *The Disputed Questions on Truth*, trans. Robert W. Mulligan, S. J. (Chicago: Regnery, 1952), 1:11. The source is Aquinas's Reply in Question I, Article 2.

Truth is not independent of mind; it is necessary that for any proposition p, p is true only if it is believed, and if and only if it is believed by God. . . . every proposition has essentially the property of being true only if believed, and if and only if believed by God. In the same way propositions themselves, the things that are true or false, are not independent of mind. It is necessary that a proposition p exists only if it is conceived or thought of or the object of some other propositional attitude, for it is necessary that every proposition is conceived of by God; furthermore, every proposition has essentially the property of being conceived or thought of, for every proposition has essentially the property of being conceived by God.[25]

Obviously, this line of argument is not coercive in the sense that everyone will find all its premises acceptable (or possibly intelligible). But as I've pointed out repeatedly, this situation obtains with regard to a lot of arguments. For those fortunate enough and/or wise enough to recognize the truth of the claim made in the premises, they face a problem, namely, what is the ground of these eternal and unchanging true propositions? As Plantinga concluded his presidential address to the American Philosophical Association's Western Division in 1982, the claim that "truth is not independent of mind—is indeed correct. This intuition is best accommodated by the theistic claim that necessarily, propositions have two properties essentially; *being conceived by God* and *being true if and only if believed by God*. So how can we sensibly be anti-realists [that is, solve the problem raised in Plantinga's address]? Easily enough: by being theists."[26]

There is, then, a way of arguing for God's existence on the basis of truth. Those who find its premises plausible should find that this line of thinking provides significant support for belief in God.

THE ARGUMENT FROM THE IDEA OF GOD

One of the things many major philosophers ask is where certain ideas in the human mind come from. For example, Plato did this frequently in his effort to get people to recognize the existence of an eternal, immaterial world which contains the unchanging essences he called forms. Where, Plato asked, do our ideas of the Good, the True, and the Beautiful come from?[27] For thinkers like Plato, human sense-perception is never a sufficient explanation. While our senses may bring us into contact with particular things that we judge to be instances of the standard or concept, our knowledge of the standard must come about in some other way.[28]

---

[25]Plantinga, "How to be an Anti-Realist," pp. 68–69. Those readers who like are welcome to turn back a few pages and read Gordon Clark's less technical version of the argument.

[26]Ibid., p. 70.

[27]Students of Plato's philosophy will know that Plato was not asking for an account of our awareness of particular things in this world to which we ascribe the properties of goodness, truth, and beauty. He was asking for the source of our ideas of the concepts of Goodness, Truth, and Beauty themselves. If any reader needs help on this, see Ronald Nash, *Christianity and the Hellenistic World* (Grand Rapids: Zondervan, 1984), pp. 32ff.

[28]For more on this, see Ronald Nash, *The Word of God and the Mind of Man* (Grand

The French philosopher René Descartes (1596–1650) raises a similar question (with similar results) about our idea of God. As Descartes sees it, the idea of God can be present in the mind of any mature, rational human being. All that's necessary for the idea of God to be present in any person's mind is for that person to think about a being who is perfect. Of course, it takes some people longer than others to get their thinking about God and perfection clear. Perhaps the following discussion may help.

One of the more important tracks in the history of Christian thinking about God is what we might call *Perfect Being Theology*. Once we recognize everything involved in the notion of perfection and then recognize that God is the perfect being,[29] the logical entailments of divine perfection lead straight to many important Christian convictions. Some of the major representatives of Perfect Being Theology are the medieval Christian thinkers Augustine (A.D. 354–430), Anselm (1033–1109), and Aquinas (1225–1274).

Anselm made an important contribution to thinking about God in this way when he defined God's perfection as follows: God is that being than which no greater being can be conceived. Consider any candidate for the title God that you like, Anselm taught; suppose we call that candidate A. Now if you can conceive of a being greater than A, it follows that A cannot be God. Suppose A (your first candidate for God) is lacking in power or knowledge or holiness or some other great-making property. Suppose further that some other possible (that is, conceivable) being (B) possesses one or more great-making properties lacking in A's nature. It then follows that A cannot be God. Even though humans can never fully comprehend the perfect essence of God, one thing is certain: if it is possible for us to think of a being greater than the being we call God, then the lesser of the two beings cannot be God. Once again, God is that being than which no greater being can be conceived.[30]

Rapids: Zondervan, 1982), chaps. 7 and 8, and Ronald Nash, *The Light of the Mind: St. Augustine's Theory of Knowledge* (Lexington: University Press of Kentucky, 1969).

[29] A little reflection should show that there can be only one perfect being. If we had two different candidates for the title of perfect being, they would have to differ in at least one respect. If they didn't differ at all, they would not be two beings; they'd be the same being. So given the fact that the two candidates for the perfect being have to differ with respect to at least one property, the presence or absence of that one property (depending on what it is) would be enough to disqualify one of the candidates.

[30] Many readers will know that it is at this point that Anselm introduces his famous ontological argument for God's existence. I believe I owe such readers an explanation why my discussion of the theistic arguments does not include the ontological argument. The question is made even more relevant by the fact that I appear to be one of a relatively small number of people who believes there is a sound version of the ontological argument. The answer is simple. Every version of the ontological argument I know about that relative newcomers to philosophy can understand is probably unsound. The sound versions I know about require a strong background in philosophy before they can be understood. So I have decided—with regret—to pass over one of my favorite arguments. But all is not lost. If I have perchance generated some interest in this subject in some readers, they can see for themselves by checking out just three sources. However, all three sources must be read to get the total picture. They are Alvin Plantinga, *God, Freedom and Evil* (Grand Rapids: Eerdmans, 1974), pp. 84–112; Ronald Nash, *The Concept of God* (Grand Rapids: Zondervan, 1983),

Let's return to Descartes and his argument. Descartes invites us to think about the question, Where do we get our idea of God from?[31] And since God is the perfect being, the question can be worded, Whence comes our idea of a perfect being? Clearly, Descartes thinks, anyone able to read this book can have the idea of a perfect being in his or her mind. All that is necessary for that to happen is for the person *to think about* a perfect being, i.e., that being than which no greater being can be conceived. In other words, humans can have the idea of a perfect being in our minds. Given this fact, then, it makes sense to ask for an explanation or cause or sufficient reason for our idea of God.[32]

We should not be surprised to discover that Descartes's argument includes a step or two (or three) that some may find difficult to take, at least at first. But this should hardly be news for anyone who has read the preceding chapters of this book. First of all, some have difficulty with the claim that they actually have (or can have) an idea of God. How, someone might ask, can I have an idea of God if I'm an atheist? Or how can any human have an idea of a being so perfect and so unsurpassable that he must be incomprehensible? Since my idea of God will necessarily fall short of comprehending the full extent of God's perfection, how can I say that such an inadequate idea is really of *God*? These are good questions that require several different answers.

It is helpful at this point to remember that the Christian world-view includes the belief that God created humans with what theologians call the *sensus divinitatis*. Though it would be unfair at this point to treat this claim as a premise, it does remind us that if the doctrine is true, humans are not creatures whose minds are empty of all knowledge of God. Our minds are not blank tablets. Since we approach the search for God already equipped with some implicit knowledge of God (even though that knowledge has been affected by sin), we have some idea what we're looking for. As for how we can comprehend the incomprehensible, we can't—at least comprehensively. Humans seem to differ greatly in the capacity to comprehend certain concepts; we should hardly be surprised to find that this situation obtains

---

chap. 9; and Alvin Plantinga, "Self-Profile" in *Alvin Plantinga*, ed. James E. Tomberlin and Peter Van Inwagen (Boston: D. Reidel, 1985), pp. 64–71.

[31]The argument appears in Meditation 3 of Descartes's *Mediations on First Philosophy*.

[32]Before going any further, I should indicate that I am aware of the objections that have been raised to Descartes's argument, and I want to make clear that I agree, given the argument's role in Descartes's system, that the argument cannot carry the weight Descartes assigns to it. That is, Descartes backs himself into a corner from which only one apparent escape is possible; the escape requires that Descartes prove the existence of a perfect being. Unfortunately, Descartes's proof has to appeal to presuppositions in a way that makes his procedure circular. In other words, Descartes attempts to use the argument to get from point A to point B; and unless the argument works as a bridge or link between critically important points in his scheme, his system collapses. But just because the argument failed to do the required job in Descartes's system, there is no reason to think it has no value as part of an inductive approach to God's existence. At least, we can check it out. For readers wanting a fuller account of this, see Frederick Copleston, *History of Philosophy* vol. 4 (Westminster, Md.: Newman Press, 1961), chap. 3.

with regard to the concept of God. One of the nice things about Anselm's definition of God is that when it is understood, it helps us grasp something of what it means to be a perfect being at the same time that we see that we can never approach the limits of God's being. While God *is* that being than which a greater being cannot be conceived—while we will never be able to conceive of a being more perfect than God—our concept of God will never include all that he is. And when we move from Anselm to more traditional definitions of God, there seems to be an abundance of predicates that we can understand well enough to say truthfully that we have an idea of God in our minds. Whatever problems scholars might have with some of the details,[33] we know what it means to say that God is an eternal, all-powerful, all-knowing, perfectly good, perfectly just, perfectly loving personal Spirit.

For anyone professing difficulty comprehending the moral traits of God (goodness, justice, love, and so on), Christians can give additional content to these words by directing people to Jesus Christ who is the living Word of God. All that is necessary to have the idea of God is to think of God. And as that thinking becomes increasingly adequate for the task, the idea of God will become sharper. The important point, though, is that having the idea of God in our minds does not mean understanding absolutely everything about God. Right now, I have an idea of a perfect being who created me and the world. Right now, any atheist who happens to be reading the book can have the same idea, even though he may happen to believe that there is no existing thing that corresponds to his idea.

The next step in Descartes's argument has him ask, What is the sufficient reason for our idea of God? What is the ultimate ground for our idea? To ask this question is not simply to ask for the persons who may have been instrumental in helping us become conscious of this idea of God. In many cases, our parents or teachers played an important role in this. But as we'll see, other human beings can never be the final answer to Descartes's question. Even more obvious is Descartes's recognition that *he* could not be the source of his idea of God. Here is how Descartes states this point:

> By the name God I understand a substance that is infinite [eternal, immutable], independent, all-knowing, all-powerful, and by which I myself and everything else, if anything else does exist, have been created. Now all these characteristics are such that the more diligently I attend to them, the less do they appear capable of proceeding from me alone; hence from what has been already said, we must conclude that God necessarily exists.[34]

One reason why Descartes finds himself incapable of believing that he himself is the author of his idea of a perfect being is his awareness that he is anything but perfect. Like every other human, Descartes is finite, imperfect, and—in short—lacking in all the properties of God mentioned above. How can a finite, imperfect being possibly give rise to the idea of such perfection? There is, of course, an important assumption behind what Descartes is

---

[33]For examples of some of the problems the attributes of God can raise, see Nash, *Concept of God.*

[34]René Descartes, "Meditation 3," in *The Philosophical Works of Descartes,* trans. Elizabeth S. Haldane and G. R. T. Ross (Cambridge: Cambridge University Press, 1931), 1:165.

saying here. He believes that the cause of any effect must have as much reality as the effect. While it can be rather difficult explaining what this assumption means, its major application occurs in the case of our idea of a perfect being. How, Descartes wonders, can imperfection give rise to that which is perfect? How can the finite produce the infinite? Of course, some will say, we're only dealing with an *idea* of perfection; it's not as though some finite, imperfect human being were actually producing something that really was perfect.

In an effort to overcome the misunderstanding that rests at the root of this objection, it may be helpful to refer to an analogous argument in one of Plato's writings.[35] Plato asks, What must be the case before any person can judge that one thing is equal to another? Consider a case where we judge that two sticks or two line segments are equal to each other. What must be the case before we can make the judgment that *a* is equal to *b*? We must have perceptual awareness of the two line segments. That is obvious. But, Plato insists, we must also have knowledge of something else—"The Equal" itself. That is, in addition to particular things like sticks or lines on a paper that we apprehend with our senses, there is something else (the standard or idea or concept of Equality) that must exist and be known (in some way) before we can judge that the sticks or lines are equal. A person who did not know the essential nature of The Equal itself would be incapable of making true judgments about Equality, would never be able to judge that two line segments are equal in length or that two stones are equal in size.

But this raises the obvious question, Where does our knowledge of the standard or form of Equality come from?[36] How is our knowledge of the concept of Equality acquired? As Plato sees it, there is one answer to this question that *cannot* be correct. According to this incorrect view, human beings first perceive through their senses several things that are similar in a certain way. In this case, the things are equal (for example, in size or length). From these several particulars, the people then abstract an idea of the property or relation they share in common, namely, Equality. Only then does the mind through abstraction or some other means grasp the universal essence of Equality.

Plato offers two objections to this theory. First, it is absurd to believe that one first knows that *a* is equal to *b*, that *c* is equal to *d*, and then, from these judgments about equal things, derives the more general knowledge of what Equality is. One could not know that *a* and *b* were equal to begin with unless he already knew the standard, The Equal itself. Knowledge of the concept is logically prior to knowledge of that which exemplifies the concept. But since the awareness that *a* and *b* are equal is impossible without a logically prior knowledge of the concept (Equality), the theory that our knowledge of Equality arises from sense experience is false.

In his second objection, Plato argues that no particular thing or group of particular things is ever sufficient to provide a notion of the universal concept. Universals like Equality, Truth, and Goodness (and, Descartes would add, Perfection) always have properties that can never be found in the earthly particulars that exemplify them. It is impossible, for example, to

---

[35] See Plato's *Phaedo* 72e–77a.
[36] Compare this to, Where does our knowledge of Perfection come from?

obtain an idea of the perfect circle by contemplating examples of imperfect circles. The concept of Equality could not possibly be derived from the senses. Our knowledge of the perfect standard is logically prior to our first set of judgments about particular things that exemplify that standard or concept, and the perfect standard is superior to the imperfect copies of it that we contact through our bodily senses.

How is this brief detour in Plato's thought relevant to our discussion of Descartes? We noted the possible objection that Descartes, after all, is only talking about the *idea* of perfection, as though the idea of perfection raised less of a problem than actual perfection. One thing Plato can teach us is that when we deal with the ideas of the concepts or standards (like Equality, Goodness, Truth, and Perfection) that function as necessary conditions for human knowledge, their status as ideas does not make them less important or less real than physical objects. For thinkers like Plato and Descartes, these ideas are not simply thoughts in some individual mind. They exist in some way independent of human minds.[37] Because the idea of perfection possesses the same kind of objective reality as the concept of Equality, no being with any less reality (i.e., no being that is imperfect) can possibly be the cause of the idea of a perfect being. Just as unequal particular things cannot be a sufficient reason for our concept of The Equal itself, so no imperfect being can be the sufficient reason for our idea of a perfect being.

So where are we? Every reader of this book can have an idea of a perfect being. What is the sufficient reason for our idea of a perfect being? is a reasonable question. Given the impressive features of the being intended by this idea and given the abundant evidence of our own finitude and imperfection, there are certainly good prima facie reasons to believe that the source of our idea of a perfect being must lie in some being other than ourselves. Suppose we discover good reasons to believe that neither we nor other members of the human race can possibly be the sufficient reason for our idea of a perfect being. Then only one other conclusion would make sense. *The only adequate cause of our idea of God must be God.* As the earlier quotation from Descartes said, if this line of reasoning is correct, "we must conclude that God necessarily exists."

One of the more interesting features of the rest of Descartes's account of his argument is the way in which he considers the more plausible alternatives to his conclusion and answers them. For example, what is wrong with the claim that I arrive at my idea of a perfect being by simply negating my idea of imperfection? After all, we can form our idea of darkness by negating the idea of light. But this won't work in the case of ideas like perfection, Descartes replies.

> I see that there is manifestly more reality in infinite substance than in finite, and therefore that in some way I have in me the notion of the infinite earlier than the finite—to wit, the notion of God before that of myself. For how would it be possible that I should know that I doubt and desire, that is to say, that something is lacking in me, and that I am not quite perfect, unless I had within me some idea of a Being more perfect

---

[37] This might be a good time to review my discussion of properties, universals, and propositions earlier in this chapter.

than myself, in comparison with which I should recognize the deficiencies of my nature?[38]

To see Descartes's point here, we must think back to Plato's discussion of Equality. Which is logically prior, our knowledge of The Equal itself or our knowledge that two particular things are equal? As we saw, knowledge of the standard must come first logically. And so, in a similar vein, Descartes declares it impossible to form an idea of the perfect or the infinite by negating some prior idea of imperfection or finiteness. After all, Descartes adds, he is quite aware of his own imperfections. Since the knowledge of the perfect standard is always logically prior to judgments made on the basis of that concept, how could Descartes possibly know that he was finite and imperfect unless he already had an idea of infinity and perfection? Therefore, I cannot form my idea of perfection by negating my knowledge of imperfect things.

Nor will it do to claim that my idea of God is simply false, thus ruling out the need for any sufficient reason. As Descartes words his reply, "As this idea [of a perfect being] is very clear and distinct and contains within it more objective reality than any other, there can be none which is of itself more true, nor any in which there can be less suspicion of falsehood. The idea, I say, of this Being who is absolutely perfect and infinite, is entirely true."[39]

To use a now familiar example, consider two things I know. Consider first my examination of two separated line segments that appear to be equal. Then consider my knowledge of the standard or concept of Equality that is logically basic to my judgment that *a* and *b* are equal. Which object of knowledge is *more* real (in Descartes's and Plato's sense)? Is it not possible to see how my knowledge of the concept of Equality is more clear and more objectively real than my belief about the relative lengths of the two line segments? As we noticed in our discussion of foundationalism, some propositions are so self-evident or incorrigible that it is impossible to doubt them. Descartes believes that our idea of perfection has this same kind of privileged status and that anyone who doubts the truth of the idea (and the reality to which that idea points) is suffering from some kind of noetic malfunction. We would certainly think this the case of any person who, while making judgments that this or that is equal, declares his uncertainty about the concept of Equality.

Well then, perhaps we simply get our idea of God from our parents or some other source less than God. But if we've been paying attention, this suggestion won't impress us any more than the others. Even though the instruction of our parents and other human teachers may have been the immediate occasion of our becoming conscious of our idea of God—in the same way that the instruction of a human teacher brought us to consciousness that two plus two equals four—this kind of learning can never be the sufficient condition for either our knowledge of mathematical truth or our knowledge of God.[40] Clearly, two plus two equals four is not true simply because our parents or teachers *said* it was true. Their teaching helped us recognize the truth of a proposition that is eternally and necessarily true.

---

[38] Descartes, *Philosophical Works*, 1:166.

[39] Ibid.

[40] For more on this, see Augustine's work *On The Teacher* or my account of Augustine's position in *The Light of Mind*, pp. 84–92.

Similarly, the most that human religious instruction can do vis-à-vis God is provide an occasion by which we come to recognize what is objectively the case. Any attempt to postulate parents or earlier members of the human race as the sufficient reason for the idea of the perfect being stumbles over one obvious problem, namely, where did they get *their* idea of the perfect being from? Every reason noted earlier that precludes Descartes's being the cause of his idea of God also rules out every other member of the human race.

Descartes believes that when we comprehend what is included in the idea of a perfect being and when we recognize why all attempts to provide an alternative source for the idea fail, we are forced to one conclusion. God created me with an idea of God as part of my nature; my idea of God is innate. In other words,

> it is not possible that my nature should be what it is, and indeed that I should have in myself the idea of a God, if God did not veritably exist—a God, I say, whose idea is in me, i.e., who possesses all those supreme perfections of which our mind may indeed have some ideas but without understanding them all, who is liable to no errors or defect [and who has none of all those marks which denote imperfection].[41]

Obviously, I believe that Descartes was on to something. There are lots of things we have a right to seek sufficient reasons for: the existence of the contingent universe, the presence of order and design within that universe, apparently veridical experiences of God, the moral law, and the existence of truth. Is it an illusion or coincidence that Christian theism is able to explain each of these and *all* of these so well? But as Descartes reminds us, there is something else in our inner world that requires an explanation, namely, our idea of God. If something like the argument we've examined in this section has merit, it will do more than provide another reason for believing that God exists. Since the being this argument points to is the perfect being, it also provides us with a possible basis for attaining important knowledge about God's nature.

CONCLUSION

While I must bring Part 3 and its discussion of theistic arguments to a close, the question of God's existence will continue to occupy us through the rest of the book. Part 4 will look at the most plausible contemporary objection to God's existence. The weaknesses of this argument will, I believe, enhance the credibility of belief in God. Part 5 will take note of still further phenomena for which the best explanation appears to be the God of Christian theism.

For Further Exploration—Chapter Twelve

1. Summarize and evaluate the moral argument for God's existence.
2. Summarize and evaluate the argument from truth.
3. Summarize and evaluate the argument from the idea of God.
4. Based on your study of Part 3, how would you answer someone who asked why *you* believe God exists?

---

[41]Descartes, *Philosophical Works*, p. 171.

Part 4

THE PROBLEM
OF EVIL

Chapter 13

THE DEDUCTIVE PROBLEM OF EVIL

Objections to theism come and go. Arguments many philosophers thought cogent twenty-five years ago have disappeared from view.[1] A few other problems continue to get a sympathetic hearing from one constituency or another.[2] But every philosopher I know believes that the most serious challenge to theism was, is, and will continue to be the problem of evil. I share the view that the most serious intellectual obstacle that stands between many people and faith is uncertainty about the existence of evil. For this reason, I have decided to devote all of Part 4 to this question.

---

[1] For a glimpse of some objections that were fashionable twenty-five years ago, see Part 2 of Alvin Plantinga's *God and Other Minds* (Ithaca, N.Y.: Cornell University Press, 1967). The criticism of Plantinga and others is the major reason why one does not hear much about these arguments any more.

[2] Most of these other problems seem to arise because of misunderstandings about the supposed conflict between science and religion. One good place to go for a discussion of challenges from the direction of natural science is Richard Bube's *The Human Quest* (Waco, Tex.: Word, 1971). Two older sources that are still worth consulting are Bernard Ramm's *The Christian View of Science and Scripture* (Grand Rapids: Eerdmans, 1954) and Carl F. H. Henry's chapter, "Science and Religion," in *Contemporary Evangelical Thought*, ed. Carl F. H. Henry (New York: Harper, 1957), pp. 247–82. A good introduction to questions in the philosophy of science may be found in Del Ratzsch, *Philosophy of Science* (Downers Grove, Ill.: InterVarsity Press, 1986). As for challenges from the social sciences, see J. P. Moreland, *Scaling The Secular City* (Grand Rapids: Baker, 1987), pp. 228–31; William J. Abraham, *An Introduction to the Philosophy of Religion* (Englewood Cliffs, N.J.: Prentice-Hall, 1985), pp. 58–61; and C. Stephen Evans, *Philosophy of Religion* (Downers Grove, Ill.: InterVarsity Press, 1985), pp. 127–30. Also worth a look is Carl F. H. Henry, ed., *Horizons of Science* (San Francisco: Harper and Row, 1978).

WHAT IS THE PROBLEM OF EVIL?

A number of related and essential Christian beliefs about God appear to be incompatible with the evil we find in the world. Christians believe that God is totally good (omnibenevolent), all-knowing (omniscient), and all-powerful (omnipotent). We also believe that God created the world. The difficulties that these beliefs engender with respect to evil are obvious.

1. If God is good and loves all human beings, it is reasonable to believe that he wants to deliver the creatures he loves from evil and suffering.
2. If God is all-knowing, it is reasonable to believe that he knows how to deliver his creatures from evil and suffering.
3. If God is all-powerful, it is reasonable to believe that he is able to deliver his creatures from evil and suffering.

Given what Christians believe about God's omnibenevolence, omniscience, and omnipotence, it seems to follow that God wants to eliminate evil, that God knows how to eliminate evil, and that God has the power to eliminate evil. But evil exists. In fact, great amounts of evil exist. Indeed, great amounts of apparently senseless and purposeless evil seem to exist. Since evil and suffering exist, it seems to follow that it is reasonable to believe that God doesn't want to eliminate evil (thus casting doubt on his goodness) or doesn't know how to eliminate evil (raising questions about his knowledge) or lacks the power. In short, the existence of evil seems inconsistent with our belief in God's goodness or omniscience or power. Troubled by their reflection on these difficulties, many have found it easy to take the additional step and conclude that the existence of evil in the world makes it unlikely that God exists.

Thinking Christians appear to be stuck between a rock and a hard place. They cannot deny any of the factors that make up the problem of evil. They can hardly deny that the world God created contains large amounts of evil, much of it apparently gratuitous or meaningless. But as theists, these Christians must affirm their belief that this world with all its evil was created by a good, loving, omnipotent, and omniscient God. The challenge for theists is to show that the existence of the evils we find in this world fit or are consistent with the Christian view of God and the world. In other words, we must explain how the conceptual scheme that is the Christian world-view is consistent with the amount and kinds of evil we find in creation.

Two Kinds of Evil

Two kinds of evil are distinguished: moral evil and natural evil. Moral evil results from the choices and actions of human beings.[3] When the question *why* is asked about some moral evil, the answer will include a reference to something that a human or humans did or did not do. Moral evil sometimes results when human beings act, for example, by pointing a loaded gun at a person and pulling the trigger. But moral evil may also occur

---

[3]It is difficult to explain moral evil in a way that is entirely satisfactory to some philosophers. For one thing, the phrase *results from* is ambiguous. Nonetheless, our formulation is close enough for the reader to get the idea.

as a result of human inaction, the failure to do something. Perhaps someone could have prevented the person from getting the gun and didn't.

So moral evil is evil brought about by human choices and actions; any other kind of evil is what we call natural evil. The class of natural evils includes such things as earthquakes, tornadoes, and diseases not resulting from human choices.[4]

While the question of whether a particular evil is moral or natural may appear academic to the person encountering that evil, the distinction is important for the philosopher of religion and apologist. The two kinds of evil require, many think, different kinds of answers.[5]

Different Forms of the Problem

The problem of evil usually appears in one of two basic forms: the deductive problem of evil and the inductive problem of evil. Deductive versions of the problem attempt to show that the existence of evil is logically inconsistent with one or more major tenets of Christian theism. Proponents of the deductive version claim that Christian theism contains a logical contradiction at its very core. If this should turn out to be true, Christian theism would not simply be false; it would be logically or necessarily false. As the rest of this chapter will show, however, even many former proponents of the deductive problem of evil now admit that this version has been answered successfully. On the surface, the advocates of the inductive problem of evil seem satisfied to make a more modest claim. Instead of stating that the existence of evil shows that Christian theism is necessarily false, the inductive version simply suggests that the existence of evil shows that Christianity is probably false. The problem of evil is serious business in any of its forms, and it would be unwise for any theist to think the probabilistic version is somehow less of a threat because it only claims to show that it is improbable that God exists. The inductive problem of evil will be examined in chapter 14.

The problem of evil assumes different forms in another way that has led some to distinguish between evil as a theoretical problem and evil as a personal or pastoral problem. It is one thing to deal with evil on a purely theoretical or philosophical level. It is something quite different to encounter evil in a personal way. Sitting in a philosophy classroom and thinking about the problem of evil are different from struggling with the news that a loved one has just died in an automobile accident. At the time when one is being hammered existentially by some particular instance of evil, pain, or

---

[4]Perhaps this reference to disease underscores the need for a third kind of evil, namely, mixed evils. The diseases of cancer, emphysema, and heart disease are natural evils in a sense. But it is also clear that human choice and actions play a role in some people getting the disease. If someone knows that smoking, for example, is a contributing cause to these diseases but smokes anyway, would his getting lung cancer be an example of natural evil or moral evil? Perhaps it makes sense to view it as a little of both.

[5]The first line of defense with regard to moral evil usually involves an appeal to the importance of God's creating humans with free will. Since it is difficult to see how human free will is relevant to hurricanes, floods, and other natural evils, many have sought to deal with natural evil in terms of what are called the natural law and soul-making defenses. I discuss this later.

suffering, it is easy to forget that some philosophical argument once seemed to suggest answers as to why evil exists. When someone is troubled by aspects of the philosophical problem of evil, the assistance of a good philosopher or apologist may help. But when one is confronted by the personal problem of evil, what that person may need is a wise and caring friend, pastor, or counselor.

WHAT IS THE DEDUCTIVE PROBLEM OF EVIL?

The deductive version of the problem of evil claims that the existence of evil is logically incompatible with one or more essential Christian beliefs. When a Christian affirms that a good, omnipotent, and omniscient God created the world and also believes that God's creation contains evil, the Christian is allegedly assenting to a contradiction. Since a contradictory set of beliefs is necessarily false, the deductive version of the problem of evil would—if sound—pose the most serious threat possible to Christian theism. It would mean that Christianity was not simply possibly false, but necessarily false. Things can't get much worse than that.

Evil in the world—or so the argument goes—points to a logical contradiction at the very center of Christian theism. Christians, it is said, believe a set of propositions that are internally self-contradictory. This is precisely how philosopher J. L. Mackie saw things in 1955 when he wrote:

> I think, however, that a more telling criticism can be made by way of the traditional problem of evil. Here it can be shown, not that religious beliefs lack rational support, but that they are positively irrational, that the several parts of the essential theological doctrine are *inconsistent* with one another.[6]

As late as 1969, H. J. McCloskey made a similar claim when he wrote: "Evil is a problem for the theist in that a *contradiction* is involved in the fact of evil, on the one hand, and the belief in the omnipotence and perfection of God on the other."[7] To quote Mackie once more,

> In its simplest form the problem is this: God is omnipotent; God is wholly good; yet evil exists. There seems to be some contradiction between these three propositions so that if any two of them were true the third would be false. But at the same time all three are essential parts of most theological positions; the theologian, it seems at once, *must* adhere and *cannot* consistently adhere to all three.[8]

The definitive reply to the deductive problem of evil has been given by Alvin Plantinga.[9] Because of the importance of Plantinga's work on the

[6]J. L. Mackie, "Evil and Omnipotence," in *The Philosophy of Religion*, ed. Basil Mitchell (London: Oxford University Press, 1971), p. 92. Mackie's article appeared originally in 1955 in the journal *Mind* (vol. 64).

[7]H. J. McCloskey, "God and Evil," *The Philosophical Quarterly* 10 (1969): 97. For still another statement of the same view, see H. D. Aiken, "God and Evil," *Ethics* 68 (1957–58): 79.

[8]Mackie, "Evil and Omnipotence," pp. 92–93.

[9]One convenient place to see Plantinga's reply laid out is in his book, *God, Freedom*

subject, this chapter will examine the various steps of his argument in some detail. Though this procedure can sometimes tax the patience of readers, the importance of the subject and the significance of Plantinga's position make the extra effort required to follow the argument worthwhile.

Clarifying the Problem

Plantinga's first step in responding to the charge that Christian theism is inherently contradictory because of what it believes about God and evil is to help his reader better understand what the atheologian like Mackie is claiming. Plantinga does this by introducing the notion of what has become known as *the theistic set*. The theistic set is nothing more than the following set of propositions, each one of which is an essential belief of Christian theism:

1. God exists.
2. God is omnipotent.
3. God is omniscient.
4. God is omnibenevolent.
5. God created the world.
   and
6. The world contains evil.[10]

Atheologians like J. L. Mackie and H. J. McCloskey were claiming that the person who believes all the propositions in the theistic set is guilty in some way of believing a contradiction. Somehow, the atheologian thinks, if the world really were created by the kind of God in whom theists believe, no evil would exist. The existence of evil is somehow logically inconsistent with the other claims made in the theistic set. And of course, if this were true, it would then follow that theism (which owns each member of the theistic set as an essential belief) is logically false in much the same way that the proposition "Some bachelors are married men" is logically false. If news of this were to become common knowledge, it could have a detrimental effect on Christian evangelism.

At this point, Plantinga asks for some clarification. Where, he asks, *is* the alleged contradiction? What we normally mean by a contradiction is a proposition that conjoins two contradictory claims, for example, "It is true that Marie is a spinster and it is false that Marie is a spinster." Now *this* is a contradiction! But where precisely is the contradiction within the theistic set? None of the identified propositions belonging to the set contradicts any of the others. Plantinga suggests that perhaps the atheologian means to say that while the theistic set is not *explicitly* contradictory,[11] it is *implicitly* contradictory.

---

and Evil (Grand Rapids: Eerdmans, 1974), Part 1. An earlier statement of the position he develops more fully in the 1974 book can be found in his *God and Other Minds*.

[10]My treatment simplifies many details of Plantinga's discussion.

[11]Once again, a set of propositions is explicitly contradictory if and only if one proposition is the denial of another member of the set. If the theistic set included the two propositions "Evil exists" and "It is false that evil exists," then the theistic set would be explicitly contradictory.

Consider the following set of propositions as an example of an implicitly contradictory set:

1. Pittsburgh is east of Cleveland.
2. Cleveland is east of Chicago.
3. Chicago is east of Pittsburgh.

Even if we ignore momentarily the obvious falsity of 3 ("Chicago is east of Pittsburgh"),[12] we should be able to sense that something is wrong with our set. Because none of the propositions is a denial of any other member of the set, the set is not explicitly contradictory. But perhaps it is implicitly contradictory. If it is, there is a very easy way of showing that. All we have to do is add one or more additional propositions to the set that, in conjunction with propositions already in the set, will entail a proposition that is the denial of one of the original propositions. Suppose we add an extra proposition to our Pittsburgh-Cleveland-Chicago set and see what happens.

1. Pittsburgh is east of Cleveland.
2. Cleveland is east of Chicago.
3. Chicago is east of Pittsburgh.
4. If Pittsburgh is east of Cleveland and if Cleveland is east of Chicago, then it is false that Chicago is east of Pittsburgh.

Using elementary logical principles known to every freshman logic student, our new premise 4 conjoined with 1 and 2 entails:

5. It is false that Chicago is east of Pittsburgh.

But 5 is the denial of 3. Therefore, we have succeeded in showing that the original set of propositions that we suspected of being contradictory really is; and we accomplished this by deducing a new proposition that is the denial of one of the original members of the set.

There seems to be good reason to believe that when atheologians like J. L. Mackie claimed that the theistic set was contradictory, they meant that it was implicitly contradictory. Mackie himself says as much when he writes:

> According to traditional theism, there is a god who is both omnipotent (and omniscient) and wholly good, and yet there is evil in the world. How can this be? It is true that there is no explicit contradiction between the statements that there is an omnipotent and wholly good god and that there is evil. But if we add the at least initially plausible premisses that good is opposed to evil in such a way that a being who is wholly good eliminates evil as far as he can, and that there are no limits to what an omnipotent being can do, then we do have a contradiction. A wholly good omnipotent being would eliminate evil completely; if there really are evils, then there cannot be any such being.[13]

In this paragraph Mackie suggests some additional premises that, in conjunction with other members of the original theistic set, would entail that

---

[12]Because even a semiconscious reader might stir when seeing the claim that Chicago is east of Pittsburgh, my example might be improved if I used three unfamiliar names or simply said: (1) A is east of B; (2) B is east of C; and (3) C is east of A. Obviously, other relations could also be used, e.g., A is taller than B.

[13]J. L. Mackie, *The Miracle of Theism* (Oxford: Clarendon Press, 1982), p. 150.

evil does not exist. If the atheologian is successful in this attempt, he will show that the theistic set not only includes the proposition "Evil exists"; it must also include (because entailed by other members of the set) "It is false that evil exists." Once the atheologian has turned the implicitly contradictory set of Christian beliefs into an explicitly contradictory set, he will have uncovered for all the world to see the essentially contradictory nature of Christian belief.

Let me summarize the ground covered so far. Atheologians like J. L. Mackie used to claim that Christian theism contained a contradiction at its core. This contradiction lay somewhere in what we've called the theistic set, the collection of essential Christian beliefs that included God's existing, God's being omnipotent (and so on), God's creating the world, plus the acknowledgment that evil exists. But as we've seen, this set is not explicitly contradictory. So, to make his charge of inconsistency stick, the atheologian must produce one or more additional propositions that, when added to the original set, will entail (necessarily imply) the contradiction of one member of the original set. More specifically, the atheologian needs to demonstrate that the theist's beliefs about the nature of God entail the proposition "It is false that evil exists." Two questions therefore become relevant. Has any atheologian actually produced acceptable propositions that prove that the theistic set is explicitly contradictory? And is it even possible for the atheologian to do this?

THE SEARCH FOR THE MISSING PREMISE

As we've noted, in order to make good on his claim that the theist contradicts himself, the atheologian has to come up with one or more additional premises that will turn what he thinks is an implicitly contradictory set into what everyone can see is an explicitly contradictory set. The first thing we need to notice is that any proposed new premises must meet one or two conditions. After all, if the additional premise (or premises) is untrue or not believed by Christians or not essential to Christian theism, the alleged demonstration of theism's inconsistency will fail. If one of these conditions is left unmet, the Christian can avoid the charge of inconsistency by simply pointing out that since the new proposition is false or can be rejected by Christians, the alleged demonstration fails. We'll need to keep these conditions in mind as we consider candidates for the missing premise.

Can an Omnipotent Being Do Absolutely Anything?

One candidate for our missing premise that has been thought to do the trick for the atheologian is "God can do absolutely anything." If it were implicit in the notion of divine omnipotence that God can do absolutely anything, then it would certainly follow that God could create a world containing no evil. If we also understand that God's goodness entails that God wants to eliminate evil and that God's omniscience includes his knowing how to do this,[14] it would then follow that the omnipotent God who *could* create a world without evil *would* create a world without evil.

---

[14]I myself have no interest in challenging these entailments of God's goodness and knowledge.

Putting aside for the moment my assessment of their theological literacy, I have met a number of Christians who seem to believe that divine omnipotence includes the ability to do anything.

But is this belief correct? Unfortunately for our atheologian, it is not. For one thing, the claim that an omnipotent being can do anything is not an essential Christian belief; for another thing, the claim is not true. Christians have long held that there are many things even an omnipotent God cannot do; divine omnipotence has always been understood by Christian thinkers to be compatible with certain limitations upon God's power. This is clearly evident in the thought of Thomas Aquinas who wrote: "Everything that does not imply a contradiction is numbered among those possibles in respect of which God is called omnipotent; whereas whatever implies contradiction does not come within the scope of divine omnipotence, because it cannot have the aspect of possibility."[15]

According to Christian thinkers like Aquinas, something may be said to be possible or impossible in two distinct ways: physical possibility or logical possibility. Most Christian thinkers have followed Aquinas in holding that logical consistency–not merely physical possibility—is a necessary condition for divine omnipotence. In the first sense, physical possibility, something is possible for any being if he possesses the power to do it. If someone has the power to lift three hundred pounds, for example, then obviously the act of lifting three hundred pounds is physically possible for that person. Some acts (like running a mile in thirty seconds or swimming across the Atlantic) do not appear to be physically possible for any human being. Aquinas realized that nothing can be gained from analyzing divine omnipotence in terms of physical possibility. In his words, if "we were to say that God is omnipotent because He can do all things that are possible to His power, there would be a vicious circle in explaining the nature of His power. For this would be saying nothing else but that God is omnipotent because He can do all that He is able to do."[16]

The more promising approach to an explanation of divine omnipotence, Aquinas thought, lay in the second type of possibility, logical possibility. Something is possible in the logical sense if it does not violate the law of noncontradiction. Any act that is logically impossible must also be physically impossible. Squaring the circle is logically and physically impossible. Aquinas denied that the exclusion of logically impossible acts from the sphere of divine power constituted any limitation on God's power. He regarded logically impossible tasks, such as creating two mountains without a valley between them, as pseudotasks. A being's inability to perform a pseudotask (for example, creating a square circle) cannot count against its power. Thus logical possibility, as Aquinas saw it, is a necessary though not a sufficient condition for any exercise of God's power.

Richard Swinburne argues that those who think a truly omnipotent being ought to be able to do the logically impossible err because they regard

> a logically impossible action as an action of one kind on a par with an action of another kind, the physically impossible. But it is not. A logically impossible action is not an action. It is what is described by a form of

---

[15]Thomas Aquinas, *Summa Theologica* 1. 25. 3.
[16]Ibid.

words which purport to describe an action, but do not describe anything which it is coherent to suppose could be done. It is no objection to A's omnipotence that he cannot make a square circle. This is because "making a square circle" does not describe anything which it is coherent to suppose could be done.[17]

A logical contradiction can at most describe a pseudotask. And God's inability to perform a pseudotask cannot count against his omnipotence. As Aquinas noted, it is better to state that such pseudotasks cannot be done, period, than to say that God cannot do them.

This discussion about the relationship between omnipotence and logic makes it clear that omnipotence does not include the ability to do everything. There are limits even to what an omnipotent being can do. As we have seen, an omnipotent being cannot do what is *logically* impossible. But the Christian Scriptures identify other things that God cannot do: God cannot lie, for example, or swear by a being greater than himself (Heb. 6:18, 13).[18]

Any attempt to establish an inconsistency within the theistic set that depends on the claim that an omnipotent being can do absolutely anything must be judged a failure. The claim is neither a necessary truth nor an essential Christian belief.

Nor would it be advisable for the atheologian to attempt to push this matter further by suggesting, for example, that Christians ought to believe that God *can* do the logically impossible. Any Christian who believed *that* would scarcely be troubled by the news that the theistic set contained a contradiction. After all, he would say, if God can do the logically impossible, then God can bring it about that a logically contradictory set of propositions is true, thus eliminating the supposed objection to theism. It makes sense, then, to drop any talk about God's being able to do absolutely anything and look elsewhere for our missing proposition.

Is It True that a Good Being Always Eliminates Evil as Far as It Can?

Earlier we noticed J. L. Mackie suggesting two additional premises that he thought would help bring out the inconsistency in the theistic set. To quote the key sentence again: "But if we add the at least initially plausible premisses that good is opposed to evil in such a way that a being who is wholly good eliminates evil as far as he can, and that there are no limits to what an omnipotent being can do, then we do have a contradiction."[19] We have already observed the problems with his second suggestion, namely, "there are no limits to what an omnipotent being can do." What about his first claim, namely, "that a being who is wholly good eliminates evil as far as

---

[17]Richard Swinburne, *The Coherence of Theism* (Oxford: Clarendon Press, 1977), p. 149.

[18]In my book, *The Concept of God*, I explore the possibility that these other limitations upon the divine power are really extensions of the more basic claim that God cannot do the logically impossible. While it is physically possible for humans to sin, it may be that it is logically impossible for a perfect being like God to sin. For a discussion of this and other points related to divine omnipotence, see Ronald Nash, *The Concept of God* (Grand Rapids: Zondervan, 1983), chap. 3.

[19]Mackie, *Miracle of Theism*, p. 150.

he can"? Is there any reason to believe this is true? Or will a little reflection provide us with reasons to think it false?

Suppose that it is logically possible for God to eliminate some evil, but the elimination of that evil would result either in the existence of a greater evil or in the nonexistence of a greater good. If I hit my thumb with a hammer, the resulting pain is an evil. Suppose a doctor tells me he can eliminate the throbbing in my thumb by amputating my hand at the wrist. While the doctor would have eliminated one evil, he would have done so at the cost of a much greater evil. There seem to be many evils in the world that can be eliminated only by producing situations containing more evil or costing us some greater good. Suppose that many evils result from human free will or from the fact that our universe operates under natural laws or from the fact that humans exist in a setting that fosters soul-making.[20] And suppose further that a world containing free will and natural law that fosters soul-making contains more good than a world that does not. If it makes no sense for God to eliminate an evil that would bring about a state of affairs in which there would be less good or more evil, our newest candidate for the missing proposition—that a good being always eliminates evil as far as it can—may safely be dismissed as neither true nor an essential Christian belief. As we progress through Part 4, we will have to consider the possibility that God allows certain evils to exist because their elimination would result in the existence of greater evils or the loss of greater goods.

A Final Candidate

But, someone might think, why can we not rescue the central idea in our last candidate-proposition by coming up with a suitable qualification? This would give us the following proposition: "A good God will eliminate evil as far as he can without either losing a greater good or bringing about a greater evil."[21] This proposition is faithful to our intuition that a good God will want to eliminate evil and also take care of those troubling counterinstances where the elimination of some evils results in a situation containing more evil or less good.

As it turns out, our new proposition looks pretty good; it is hard to see why any theist would object to it. Unfortunately for the atheologian, the new proposition won't do the job he wants it for. This will become clear as soon as we realize that our new proposition does not entail the falsity of "Evil exists"; our new proposition is totally consistent with the existence of evil in God's creation. Hence, our final candidate seems true enough, but it turns out to be useless for the atheologian's purpose, namely, to demonstrate that the theistic set really entails the nonexistence of evil.

What conclusion can we draw from our brief consideration of attempts to produce a proposition that, in conjunction with other members of the theistic set, will demonstrate the inconsistency of that set? Even though atheologians have been claiming for decades that the theistic set is self-contradictory, none of them has yet produced the required missing

---

[20]I'll have more to say about soul-making later on. For now, let us say that soul-making is a process in which God allows human persons to grow and develop in response to challenges.

[21]See Plantinga's discussion in *God, Freedom, and Evil*, pp. 19ff.

proposition that will prove the claim. All propositions produced thus far are false or not essential Christian beliefs or irrelevant. Though the atheologian claims that the theistic set is self-contradictory, we are still waiting for him to show that his claim is true. If there really is a deductive problem of evil, it still remains for some atheologian to prove it.

CAN THEISTS SHOW THAT THE THEISTIC SET *IS* CONSISTENT?

Although no atheologian has successfully demonstrated that the theistic set contains a contradiction, the possibility remains that someone in the future could yet discover a proposition that would, when added to the theistic set, uncover the contradiction atheologians believe it contains implicitly. There is considerable importance, then, in removing this possibility—however remote—once and for all. If that can be done, there will no longer be any possibility that someone could yet discover a way of establishing that a contradiction exists.

There is a well-known way of demonstrating that a set of propositions is logically consistent with some other proposition. In our case, there is a way of demonstrating that the proposition (1) ("An omnipotent, omniscient, omnibenevolent God created the world") is consistent with (3) ("The world contains evil").[22] This procedure requires us to add a premise or premises—in this case a proposition I'll number (2)—that, when combined with (1) entails that the world contains evil.

This new proposition must meet the following criteria: (a) it must be logically consistent with (1); (b) it must describe a logically possible state of affairs, that is, it must be possibly true in the sense of logical possibility; and (c) the new proposition should, when joined with (1), entail (3) ("The world contains evil"). But it is also important to note that the new proposition need not meet two other conditions. First, it is not necessary that we know the new proposition (2) is true, only that it is possibly true; it is not even necessary that the new proposition *be* true. And second, it is not necessary that anyone actually believe (2) or even think that (2) is plausible. What is necessary is that (2) describe a logically possible state of affairs; in other words, it must be logically possible that (2) is true, whether in fact it is or is not true.

Theodicy and Defense

We have reached a point where it is very easy for people to get confused and lose their way. A distinction that Plantinga makes between a theodicy and a defense[23] will be helpful in staying on course.

Throughout most of the history of the Christian church, Christian thinkers have sought to counter the problem of evil by offering examples of what can be called a *theodicy*.[24] Alvin Plantinga has distinguished his own

---

[22]It will be helpful in this section to reduce the original six propositions of the theistic set to just two. As should be clear, the first five are lumped together into our new (1) and the proposition "Evil exists" is our new (3).

[23]Plantinga explains the difference in *God, Freedom and Evil*, pp. 26–29.

[24]The book most often associated with the word is Gottfried Leibniz's *Theodicy*, trans. E. M. Huggard (New Haven: Yale University Press, 1952). The book was first

approach to the problem of evil from the theodicies of such earlier Christian thinkers as Augustine and Leibniz by referring to it as a *defense*.

When a theist offers a defense (as opposed to a theodicy), all he is attempting to do is show that his belief in God is plausible, rational, or consistent in the face of difficulties raised by the presence of evil in the creation. A defense attempts to show the coherence of theism by offering logically possible reasons why God permits evil. When engaged in a defense, the philosopher or apologist does not have to prove that his reasons are actually true;[25] all he has to show is that they are *possibly* true. Alvin Plantinga has become rather well-known among his philosophical peers for what he calls the Free Will *Defense*. Plantinga uses the theist's rather traditional appeal to human free will as one logically possible reason why God permits evil. As Plantinga explains, it is not necessary for him or anyone else to show that his appeals to free will are true; only that they are possibly true (in the sense of logical possibility).

A defense, then seeks to show that the atheologian's argument does not succeed in proving the falsity of essential theistic claims. A defense shows at most that the critic of theism has failed to make his case. A theodicy, on the other hand, attempts to show that God *is* justified in permitting evil; the Christian thinker attempts to show that his reasons as to why evil exists are true, not just possibly true.

A number of criticisms of Plantinga's Free Will Defense are irrelevant because they are inattentive to his distinction between a theodicy and a defense.[26] Such critics complain because of what they take to be the implausibility of some of Plantinga's reasons for the existence of evil. But, I repeat, it is not necessary that the reasons offered in a defense be either true or plausible. All that matters is that they be possibly true (in the sense of logical possibility).

A defense is especially relevant with regard to the deductive problem of evil where the atheologian thinks he can demonstrate a logical inconsistency within the set of theistic beliefs. All that is required of a theist in such a situation is that he offer a logically possible reason[27] explaining why evil exists in a world created by an all-powerful, all-knowing, all-benevolent God.[28]

published in 1710. The word *theodicy* is based on two Greek words and means, literally, a justification of the ways of God.

[25]Indeed, as stated earlier, he does not even have to *believe* that his reasons are true. If this is puzzling, read on.

[26]For one example of this, see Mackie, *Miracle of Theism*, pp. 162–63.

[27]All that is required for a reason to be logically possible is that the proposition expressing the reason not be contradictory.

[28]As the following chapters will show, recent movement from the deductive to the inductive problem of evil has left many thinkers dissatisfied with a mere defense. When we are dealing with probabilities and the plausibility of the Christian faith in the presence of evil, it is not enough—they say—to believe that God has logically possible reasons for permitting evil. We want to know that the reasons are plausible, make sense, and have a certain fit with what we know about God and the world.

Demonstrating the Consistency of the Theistic Set

After our brief detour into the differences between a theodicy and a defense, a short summary may help us get back on track. We have seen that the atheologian's claim that the theistic set is self-contradictory remains nothing more than wishful thinking because of the atheologian's failure to produce the missing premise required to show that the set is explicitly contradictory. Rather than rest on our laurels and live with the possibility that some atheologian might discover the missing proposition some time in the future, we have decided to see if we cannot beat the atheologian to the punch and actually demonstrate that the theistic set is consistent. Once done, this will eliminate any possibility of theism's being shown to be logically inconsistent because of the existence of evil in the world. The method of demonstrating consistency requires that we add a premise (or premises) to the original set that logically entails the other proposition, which, in our case, is "The world contains evil." In order to do the job, it is not necessary that our new premise be true or even that it be believed to be true. All that is necessary is that it be logically possible.

Consider, then, the following argument:

1. An omnipotent, omniscient, omnibenevolent God created the world.
2. God creates a world containing evil and has a good reason for doing so.[29]
3. Therefore, the world contains evil.

Numbers 1 and 2 taken together do, of course, entail 3. Therefore, the propositions from our original theistic set that now make up 1 are logically consistent with the existence of evil. The only relevant question regarding 2 is whether it is possibly true. Obviously it is since it is not logically false. Therefore, the theistic set is logically consistent from which follows the impossibility of anyone's ever demonstrating that it is not.

THE FREE WILL DEFENSE

However, a critic might reply, the theist still has some work to do. Perhaps we cannot really judge that 1 and 2 are consistent until we have an example of a possible reason why God might create a world containing evil. One way to meet this problem is the so-called Free Will Defense. According to this argument, God has good reasons for creating a world containing creatures that are significantly free, that is, free with regard to actions that have moral significance. To say that they are significantly free means that these creatures are free either to do *A* or not to do *A*, where *A* is a morally significant action. A world containing significantly free creatures will include a greater balance of good over evil than a world that did not contain significantly free creatures. But such creatures cannot be significantly free unless their freedom includes the ability to do evil. As William J. Abraham summarizes the view before us, moral evil

---

[29]The wording of (2) is Plantinga's. See his *God, Freedom, and Evil*, p. 26.

results from God's creating human agents who are significantly free. God himself does not cause such evils. The evils are brought about by persons acting contrary to God's will, having chosen to act as they do. God could, of course, have prevented such evils either by restricting human choice or refusing to create human beings at all. But God cannot create genuinely free human beings and then not permit them to bring about moral evils. As the creation of persons with genuine choices is a good thing, then the existence of moral evil is both logically and rationally consistent with belief in God.[30]

In order for humans to be significantly free, there must be the possiblity that they perform morally evil actions. As Plantinga states,

Now God can create free creatures, but He can't *cause* or *determine* them to do only what is right. For if He does so, then they aren't significantly free after all; they do not do what is right *freely*. To create creatures capable of *moral good*, therefore, He must create creatures capable of moral evil; and He can't give these creatures the freedom to perform evil and at the same time prevent them from doing so. As it turned out, sadly enough, some of the free creatures God created went wrong in the exercise of their freedom; this is the source of moral evil. The fact that free creatures sometimes go wrong, however, counts neither against God's omnipotence nor against His goodness for He could have forestalled the occurrence of moral evil only by removing the possibility of moral good.[31]

Eliminating completely the possibility of moral evil would require eliminating the possibility of God's creating significantly free moral agents. But this would diminish the amount of good in the world. After all, Plantinga states, "a world containing creatures who are significantly free (and freely perform more good than evil actions) is more valuable, all else being equal, than a world containing no free creatures at all."[32]

THE ATHEOLOGIAN'S COUNTERATTACK

The most formidable objection to the Free Will Defense has been stated by J. L. Mackie:

If God has made men such that in their free choices they sometimes prefer what is good and sometimes what is evil, why could he not have made men such that they always freely choose the good? If there is no logical impossibility in a man's freely choosing the good on one, or on several occasions, there cannot be a logical impossibility in his freely choosing the good on every occasion. God was not, then, faced with a choice between making innocent automata and making beings who, in acting freely, would sometimes go wrong; there was open to him the obviously better possibility of making beings who would act freely but always go right. Clearly, his failure to avail himself of this possibility is inconsistent with his being both omnipotent and wholly good.[33]

---

[30]William J. Abraham, *An Introduction to the Philosophy of Religion* (Englewood Cliffs, N.J.: Prentice-Hall, 1985), p. 65.

[31]Plantinga, *God, Freedom and Evil*, p. 30.

[32]Ibid.

[33]Mackie, "Evil and Omnipotence," p. 100.

Mackie's point is that it is logically possible for God to have created free moral creatures who always do what is right. *Since God can do whatever is logically possible,* it follows that God could have created a world without moral evil by simply following up on this possibility and creating free creatures who always do what is good. The italicized words in the last sentence merit special attention because they constitute the key assumption in Mackie's new argument that Plantinga must counter.

Earlier we noted that an omnipotent being cannot do anything that is logically impossible, a fact that hardly counts against that being's power. Now, in response to Mackie's challenge, the theist must point out that there are also some logically possible things that an omnipotent being cannot do, a fact that also will not count against his power. One of the logically possible things God might not be able to do is to satisfy Mackie's demand.

To clarify the issues, let me state Mackie's point in a more formal way. Mackie's objection to the Free Will Defense hinges on the following argument:

1. If x is a logically possible state of affairs, then God can bring about x.
2. A state of affairs in which humans are free and always do what is right is logically possible.
3. Therefore, God can bring it about that humans are free and always do what is right.

When the conclusion of this argument is coupled with the recognition that a totally good God would want to eliminate moral evil and that an omniscient God would know how to bring it about that humans are free and always do what is right, the theist seems to be stuck once more with a serious challenge. *Since God clearly could have created free creatures without the possibility of moral evil, why didn't he?*

In his answer to Mackie, Plantinga admits that premise 2 is true. There is no apparent logical impossibility involved in a state of affairs in which significantly free human beings always do what is right. Mackie's mistake comes in step 1, the claim that it is necessarily the case that God can bring about any logically possible state of affairs. The first premise tells us two things about Mackie's position. First, it tells us that he accepts the point made earlier that the power of an omnipotent being extends only to logically possible actions. But once he accepts this claim, Mackie goes on to insist that the power of an omnipotent being must extend to *all* logically possible actions. And since a world in which free humans always do what is right is logically possible, it follows—for Mackie—that God can create such a world. So why didn't he?

Plantinga challenges Mackie's first premise by arguing that there are logically possible states of affairs that God cannot bring about; and among these states of affairs is one in which humans are free and always do what is right. Stephen Davis provides an example that can help us see Plantinga's point:

> Let us imagine a certain free human being Jones and a set of circumstances (e.g., involving temptation) in which Jones will freely decide to do what is wrong rather than what is right. It follows, then, that it is not in

God's power to actualize a world in which Jones, in those same circumstances, will do what is right. That is a possible world which, despite God's omnipotence, God cannot actualize.[34]

Since God is omniscient, God knows that given the set of circumstances leading up to Jones's action at a particular time (we'll call that time *t*), Jones will freely choose to do wrong. Let us suppose that at *t*, Jones chooses to steal some candy. Given God's knowledge of what Jones will freely choose to do at *t*, God cannot bring it about that Jones *freely* chooses not to steal the candy. As long as humans really are significantly free creatures, there are logically possible states of affairs regarding those free creatures that God cannot bring about. This is because what actually happens with regard to these free creatures is up to them. God's options are limited by what God knows Jones will freely do at *t*, under the conditions existing prior to his action. God has other options, of course. He might decide not to create Jones in the first place or decide to alter the conditions under which Jones chooses or decide to override Jones' freedom with regard to stealing the candy. But so long as Jones really is free with regard to his action, there are logically possible states of affairs that the omnipotent God cannot bring about.

Once God creates significantly free creatures, Plantinga argues, it is no longer true that God can bring about any logically possible state of affairs. Because we are significantly free,[35] it is now partly up to us which possible states of affairs will be realized. This is what it means to be significantly free! To be sure, God could have brought about different states of affairs by *forcing us to choose* in some different way; but then we would not have been free with regard to that action.

This means that Mackie's first premise is false. In order for Mackie's argument to work, he must maintain that divine omnipotence necessarily includes the power to perform all logically possible actions, one of which is bringing about a state of affairs in which free humans always do what is right. But Plantinga has shown that there are some logically possible states of affairs that God cannot bring about, namely, those guaranteeing that *free* creatures will act only in certain prescribed ways. It is logically possible that among the states of affairs that God cannot bring about are any containing only moral good and no moral evil. This is so because it is logically possible that all human beings suffer from a moral defect that Plantinga calls transworld depravity, which is to say that in any possible world, there is at least one action with respect to which the person would do wrong. "What is important about the idea of transworld depravity," Plantinga explains, "is that if a person suffers from it, then it wasn't within God's power to actualize any world in which that person is significantly free but does no wrong—that is, a world in which he produces moral good but no moral evil."[36]

In other words, God cannot guarantee that significantly free creatures will always do what is good without depriving them of their freedom. Moreover, it is logically possible that every human being suffers from a moral

---

[34]Stephen Davis, "The Problem of Evil in Recent Philosophy," *Review and Expositor* 82 (1985): 544.

[35]Unless we are significantly free, we cannot perform actions that are morally good.

[36]Plantinga, *God, Freedom, and Evil*, p. 48.

defect such that in any possible set of circumstances, there is some action with respect to which he would do wrong, and do so freely.

> Obviously it is possible that there be persons who suffer from transworld depravity. More generally, it is possible that *everybody* suffers from it. And if this possibility were actual, then God, though omnipotent, could not have created any of the possible worlds containing just the persons who do in fact exist, and containing moral good but no moral evil. For to do so He'd have to create persons who were significantly free (otherwise there would be no moral good) but suffered from transworld depravity. Such persons go wrong with respect to at least one action in any world God could have actualized and in which they are free with respect to morally significant actions; so the price for creating a world in which they produce moral good is creating one in which they also produce moral evil.[37]

The whole purpose to the Free Will Defense is to show that the Christian's belief (1) "God is omniscient, omnipotent, and wholly good" is logically consistent with "Evil exists." The way to demonstrate this consistency is to come up with one or more propositions that in conjunction with (1) will entail that evil exists. Utilizing Plantinga's reply to Mackie, we may formulate the Free Will Defense as follows:[38]

1. God is omnipotent, omniscient, and wholly good.
2. It was not without God's power to create a world containing moral good without creating one containing moral evil.[39]
3. God created a world containing moral good.
4. Therefore, God created a world containing moral evil.
5. Therefore, evil exists.

Plantinga reminds his reader that "to serve in this argument 2 and 3 need not be known to be true, or likely on our evidence, or anything of the sort; they need only be consistent with 1. Since they are, there is no contradiction in [the theistic set]; so the Free Will Defense appears to be successful."[40]

Plantinga is not alone in his belief that the Free Will Defense has successfully blunted the force of the deductive problem of evil. Shortly before he died, J. L. Mackie conceded that the deductive "problem of evil does not, after all, show that the central doctrines of theism are logically inconsistent with one another."[41] Mackie also conceded Plantinga's central

---

[37]Ibid., pp. 48–49. Plantinga goes on to consider other possible objections. For example, to counter the objection that God could have created other people who were not afflicted with transworld depravity, Plantinga replies that it is logically possible that every creaturely essence suffers from transworld depravity. It is possible that every free being suffers from transworld depravity. It is beyond the scope of this book to pursue these additional and technical features of Plantinga's position. But every reader is certainly encouraged to do so.

[38]My account here uses Plantinga's language but alters the numbers he assigns to the propositions. See *God, Freedom, and Evil*, pp. 54–55.

[39]Once again, all that Plantinga needs for his argument to succeed is that premise 2 be possibly true. The arguments supporting its describing a logically possible state of affairs have already been given.

[40]Plantinga, *God, Freedom, and Evil*, pp. 54–55.

[41]Mackie, *Miracle of Theism*, p. 154.

point that a wholly good God "might not eliminate evils, even though it was logically possible to do so and though he was able to do whatever is logically possible, and was limited only by the logical impossibility of having the second-order good without the first-order evil."[42] Another atheologian, William Rowe, concurs:

> Some philosophers have contended that the existence of evil is *logically inconsistent* with the existence of the theist God. No one, I think, has succeeded in establishing such an extravagant claim. Indeed, granted incompatibilism, there is a fairly compelling argument for the view that the existence of evil is logically consistent of the theistic God.[43]

These interesting concessions from Mackie and Rowe should not be taken to mean that they thought the entire problem of evil had been answered. At most, their remarks meant that the deductive problem of evil—the attempt to uncover a logical contradiction at the heart of theism—must be judged a failure. What we see happening—now that there is growing recognition of the difficulties of the deductive problem of evil—is a wholesale turning on the part of critics of theism to a different form of the problem of evil, the inductive or evidential problem of evil. This second version of the problem of evil will be the subject of my next chapter.

For Further Exploration—Chapter Thirteen

1. Distinguish between moral evil and natural evil.
2. Distinguish between the deductive and inductive forms of the problem of evil.
3. Is the theistic set explicitly contradictory? Why or why not?
4. What must atheologians do before they can show that the theistic set contains a contradiction?
5. What is wrong with the propositions atheologians might use to make their case?
6. Why is it important to show that the theistic set *is* consistent?
7. How can that be done?
8. Explain the difference between a defense and a theodicy.
9. How does the Free Will Defense show the consistency of the theistic set?
10. Do you understand why many contemporary atheologians have abandoned the deductive problem of evil? Try to explain this in a few sentences.

---

[42] Ibid.

[43] William L. Rowe, "The Problem of Evil and Some Varieties of Atheism," *American Philosophical Quarterly* 16 (1979): 335. The incompatibilism Rowe mentions corresponds to the view of freedom utilized in Plantinga's Free Will Defense, namely, that if I am free with respect to some action (A), I can either do A or not do A. But if what I do is determined in some way, then I am not free.

Chapter 14

THE INDUCTIVE PROBLEM OF EVIL

$\mathbf{A}$t the end of the last chapter, we noticed the concession of two prominent atheologians that the deductive problem of evil should be judged a failure. Given the work of philosophers like Alvin Plantinga, the existence of evil in the world cannot be shown to be logically incompatible with other essential Christian beliefs about the nature and actions of God. It is simply not true that, because of evil, Christian theism is self-contradictory and hence necessarily false.

But the shortcomings of the deductive problem of evil do not mean that atheologians have given up on the problem of evil. It simply means that they have turned their attention to a different way of formulating the problem. As William Rowe explains, "There remains, however, what we may call the *evidential* form—as opposed to the *logical* form—of the problem of evil: the view that the variety and profusion of evil in our world, although perhaps not logically inconsistent with the existence of the theistic God, provides, nevertheless, *rational support* for atheism."[1] As Rowe sees it, this evidential or inductive version of the problem of evil "presents a rather severe difficulty for theism."[2]

The move from the deductive to the inductive form of the problem of evil is a shift from the strong claim that theism is logically false to the more modest assertion that it is probable (or even highly probable) that theism is false. According to advocates of the inductive problem of evil, evil tips the scales of probability against theism; the existence of evil makes theistic belief

---

[1] William L. Rowe, "The Problem of Evil and Some Varieties of Atheism," *American Philosophical Quarterly* 16 (1979):335.
[2] Ibid.

improbable or implausible. It would be a mistake to think that the somewhat weaker claim that theism is probably false makes the inductive problem of evil any less potent a challenge to theistic belief. Inductive versions may be just as forceful or persuasive in convincing people that theism is unworthy of belief. While the existence of evil may not prove that God does not exist, atheologians maintain, it shows that God's existence is so improbable as to make belief in him appear less rational than atheism.

William Rowe summarizes the inductive form of the problem of evil in two sentences:

> It seems quite unlikely that all the instances of intense human and animal suffering occurring daily in our world lead to greater goods, and even more unlikely that if they all do, an omnipotent, omniscient being could not have achieved at least some of those goods without permitting the instances of suffering that lead to them. In the light of our experience and knowledge of the variety and scale of human and animal suffering in our world, the idea that none of these instances of suffering could have been prevented by an omnipotent being without the loss of a greater good seems an extraordinary, absurd idea, quite beyond our belief.[3]

James Cornman and Keith Lehrer set up the problem in this way:

> If you were all-good, all-knowing, and all-powerful and you were going to create a universe in which there were sentient beings—beings that are happy and sad; enjoy pleasure, feel pain, express love, anger, pity, hatred—what kind of world would you create? . . . Try to imagine what such a world would be like. Would it be like the one which actually does exist, this world we live in? Would you create a world such as this one if you had the power and know-how to create any logically possible world? If your answer is "no," as it seems to be, then you should begin to understand why the evil of suffering and pain in this world is such a problem for anyone who thinks God created this world. . . . Given this world, then, it seems, we should conclude that it is *improbable* that it was created or sustained by anything we would call God. Thus, given this particular world, it seems that we should conclude that it is *improbable* that God—who, if he exists, created the world—exists. Consequently, the belief that God does not exist, rather than the belief that he exists, would seem to be *justified by the evidence* we find in this world.[4]

Given the amount of evil we find in the world—to say nothing of the apparent senselessness of much of this evil—it seems improbable or unlikely that the world was created by or is supported in its existence by a good, omnipotent, and omniscient God. The existence of evil, including large amounts of apparently senseless evil, tends to disconfirm belief in the existence of God.

Inductive versions of the problem of evil sometimes differ by the amount or kind of evil they regard as counting against God's existence. For some people, the mere fact that evil exists counts against belief in God. For others, it is the quantity of evil they see in the world that makes the existence

---

[3] William L. Rowe, *Philosophy of Religion: An Introduction* (Encino, Calif.: Dickenson, 1978), p. 89.

[4] James W. Cornman and Keith Lehrer, *Philosophical Problems and Arguments: An Introduction* (New York: Macmillan, 1970), pp. 340–41

of God unlikely. And for still others, the disturbing presence within the world of apparently purposeless or gratuitous evil serves to disconfirm the proposition that God exists.

The inductive problem of evil raises too many issues for one chapter of reasonable length. Therefore, my treatment has been divided into two chapters. In the rest of this chapter, I will do two things. First, I will attempt to dispose of any problem that might be thought to arise because of the *quantity* of evil in the world. The sheer amount of evil in the world, it seems to me, is something from which very little, if anything, seems to follow. Second, I will spend a fair amount of time explaining three lines of defense that theists have taken in an attempt to develop a proper response to the challenge before us. Chapter 15 will explore the serious difficulties that arise from reflection about the *quality* of evil in the world. The most troubling dimension of evil for morally sensitive and reflective people is the utter senselessness, meaninglessness, and purposelessness of so much of it. What should trouble any sensitive theist is not merely the existence of evil or even the existence of so much evil in the world; it is existence of gratuitous evil — evil for which there is apparently no reason or meaning.

THE QUANTITY OF EVIL IN THE WORLD

Many people can see how the existence of evil is logically consistent with the existence of God. But in spite of this, many of these same people find themselves wondering why there is so much evil. Could not God have created a world that contains far less evil than our world contains? Some people's faith in God has wavered because of their concern about the sheer quantity of evil in the world. What should a theist say to someone troubled about the amount of evil in the world?

According to Michael Peterson, "The proper theistic response seems to be to refuse to fix a limit on what evils God might allow. The theist can argue that it is entirely possible that God could countenance very extreme evils for a number of different reasons; for example, to preserve free will or to allow the regular operation of nature."[5] Peterson is trying to help us see how difficult as well as how possibly absurd it is to think that there is some kind of line or limit that might separate a "reasonable" quantity of evil from an unreasonable amount. Peterson continues by stating:

> Essentially, the troublesome assumption in the atheistic attack now is that a loving and just God would allow only a certain amount of evil and no more. But this is hard to justify. In principle, how much evil is *too much* for God to allow? Further, how could we ever ascertain that the present amount of evil in the world far exceeds the divinely set limit? These and other perplexing questions make it difficult to imagine how the atheist could ever establish such claims. There does not seem to be any clear limit placed upon evil by Christian theology. Neither is there any accepted method by which one could ascertain whether such a limit has been surpassed.[6]

---

[5] Michael L. Peterson, *Evil and the Christian God* (Grand Rapids: Baker, 1982), p. 108.
[6] Ibid., p. 72.

In other words, before we begin to worry that there might be too much evil in the world, we need to answer a number of preliminary questions: Is there a limit to the amount of evil we might reasonably expect to find in a world created by God? What precisely is that limit? How might anyone arrive at a knowledge of that limit? Of course, there are no answers to these questions. And since there aren't, there is no objective means by which anyone could determine that a reasonable quantity of evil in the world had been exceeded. Claims that the existence of God is somehow made less plausible because of the quantity of evil in the world rest on the quicksand of subjective opinion. As the next chapter will reveal, the *quality* of the evil encountered in our world is a much more serious problem for the theist than anything that might be thought to follow from subjective opinions about the *quantity* of evil.

THREE LINES OF REPLY

Most attempts to answer the problem of evil are variations of one basic theme, namely, that God permits evil either to make possible some greater good or to avoid some greater evil. God, it is claimed, always has some reason for allowing evil.[7] Even though we may not know what that reason is,[8] we can be sure that the evil occurs because it is necessary to bring about some greater good or to prevent some greater evil. This basic approach to the existence of evil takes three subsidiary forms that appeal respectively to the value and importance of (1) human free will, (2) humans living in an orderly universe governed by law, and (3) humans growing and developing in the face of challenge. These three lines of response are often called the free will theodicy, the natural law theodicy, and the soul-making theodicy.[9]

---

[7]This is a good time to introduce a distinction between evil in general and specific instances of evil. Many of the considerations theists set forth in an attempt to deal with the problem of evil may explain the existence of evil in general. Why does God allow moral evil (in general)? Why does he allow natural evil (in general)? While the answers offered to such questions may be valuable as far as they go, the really difficult questions arise when one is trying to find a reason for some *specific instance of evil* such as the slow, painful death of a child. It is one thing to claim to understand why natural or moral evil in general exists; it is something else to try to understand why some specific instance of moral or natural evil exists. Some theists suggest that perhaps no human can really know God's reasons for permitting moral and natural evil in general. In this chapter and the next, I part company with theists in this group and side with those who believe we can detect at least the broad outlines of an answer. But when we turn to specific instances of evil, I think the wise theist will admit his ignorance.

[8]What might follow from a theist's admission that he doesn't know God's reason for permitting evil? According to Alvin Plantinga, "Very little of interest. Why suppose that if God *does* have a good reason for permitting evil, the theist would be the first to know? Perhaps God has a good reason, but that reason is too complicated for us to understand. Or perhaps He has not revealed it for some other reason. The fact that the theist doesn't know why God permits evil is, perhaps, an interesting fact about the theist, but by itself it shows little or nothing relevant to the rationality of belief in God" (*God, Freedom and Evil,* [Grand Rapids: Eerdmans, 1974], p. 10).

[9]I will continue to use Plantinga's distinction between a theodicy and a defense. In the context of the inductive problem of evil, I believe, the theist has a responsibility to

We often find that theists writing on this subject limit their reply to the problem of evil to one of these approaches. As we've seen, Alvin Plantinga has written exclusively about the role of free will in his dealings with the problem of evil.[10] British philosopher and theologian John Hick attempts to counter the force of evil through an appeal to the soul-making theodicy.[11] An even stronger theodicy would combine elements of all three approaches. I will show that the three types of theodicy are consistent; indeed, each seems to involve elements of the others. Moreover, each line of argument deals with aspects of evil more adequately than the others. For example, while the appeal to free will eases some issues raised by moral evil, it hardly seems relevant to natural evil.[12] For this, it seems, one needs the additional help afforded by the natural law theodicy. A more adequate approach to the problem of evil, therefore, will utilize insights from the free will, natural law, *and* soul-making theodicies. On this more comprehensive approach, some instances of evil have their ground in human free will while others have theirs in natural law and/or God's purpose for the human race, namely, that God is engaged in a process of soul-making.

The Free Will Theodicy

A free will theodicy would build on the outline of the Free Will Defense described in chapter 13. According to this approach, much of the evil (most notably the *moral* evil) that exists in the world is a consequence of God's endowing humans with significant moral freedom. God allows moral evil in order to bring about the greater good of allowing his creation to include significantly free moral agents, without whom there could be no moral good.

Of course, as developed by Alvin Plantinga, it is only required that this reason for evil be logically possible. Anyone involved in presenting and defending a free will *theodicy* must be prepared to undertake the more strenuous task of showing that the appeal to free will is true. Since doing that adequately would require a separate book fully as long as this work, the task is best left to another occasion.[13] The discussion in chapter 13 certainly presents some reasons that support the plausibility of an appeal to free will. It also offers suggestions as to how some of the more common objections to

---

do more than simply show that his suggested reasons for evil are possibly true in the logical sense of the term. He should be prepared to show why he believes his reasons are actually true; his reasons should have a certain fit with what he believes about God and the world. Therefore, we have to talk about these lines of reply as theodicies.

[10]But as we also saw, Plantinga uses free will in the peculiar kind of logical argument he has developed, making his effort a defense instead of a theodicy.

[11]See John Hick, *Evil and the God of Love*, rev. ed. (New York: Harper, 1978).

[12]Students of Plantinga's thought are aware of the way he utilizes the Free Will Defense to deal with natural evil. But once again he develops that argument in the context of the deductive problem of evil. See Plantinga, *God, Freedom and Evil*, pp. 57–59.

[13]Since any position on this issue will be a metaphysical theory, the procedure for examining the truth of competing claims about human free will, will resemble the process (described in chapter 4) by which we test world-views and other metaphysical theories. One of these tests is reason or the principle of noncontradiction; the other is experience, namely, testing the theory against what we know about the inner and outer worlds.

that appeal can be answered. Subsequent discussions of the natural law and soul-making theodicies will have a bearing on the plausibility of the appeal to free will. Since this book adopts the view that the most adequate theodicy is one that combines elements of the appeal to free will, natural law, and soul-making, I suggest that any reader having reservations about a free will theodicy put them aside temporarily until I have a chance to show how all three approaches can be merged. There will be plenty of time then to decide if this comprehensive approach makes sense by way of being internally self-consistent (the test of reason) and also fitting what we know about the inner and outer worlds (the test of experience).

The Natural Law Theodicy

The natural law theodicy states that the existence of a lawlike and orderly creation is a necessary condition for a number of divine objectives. Just as it makes sense to believe that God endowed humans with significant moral freedom, it is also reasonable to believe that God placed these free moral agents in a universe exhibiting order. One can hardly act intentionally and responsibly in an unpredictable environment. F. R. Tennant drew attention to this point when he wrote:

> It cannot be too strongly insisted that a world which is to be a moral order must be a physical order characterized by law or regularity. The theist is only concerned to invoke the fact that law-abidingness . . . is an essential condition of the world being a theatre of moral life. Without such regularity in physical phenomena there could be no probability to guide us: no prediction, no prudence, no accumulation of ordered experience, no pursuit of premeditated ends, no formation of habit, no possibility of character or of culture. Our intellectual faculties could not have developed. . . . And without rationality, morality is impossible.[14]

According to Michael Peterson, "there must be some kind of natural order within which free creatures can operate. Free rational action requires a world of natural objects governed by natural laws. Such an order is essentially independent from the rational agent in that it consists of relatively enduring things behaving in regular ways."[15] What this natural order does, Peterson goes on to say,

> is to provide a range of objects and actions as a field of deliberation and choice, a condition which is necessary to free will. Parts of this natural order can be manipulated to some extent by the free agent as a means of expressing his choice, another necessary condition of free will. If the objects in the world acted in sporadic and unpredictable ways, deliberation and action would be severely impaired if not eliminated. Further, if the external objects of the world failed to respond, at least to some degree, to the internal commands of the will, meaningful choice and action would be precluded.[16]

---

[14]F. R. Tennant, *Philosophical Theology* (New York: Cambridge University Press, 1928), 2:199–200. A careful reading of Tennant's comments will show that he also hints at the importance of a regular natural order as a precondition for soul-making.
[15]Peterson, *Evil and the Christian God*, p. 108.
[16]Ibid.

Clearly we live in a universe that exhibits order, an order expressed in the laws of nature described by the appropriate science. Moral freedom could not exist apart from such an orderly environment. If the world were totally unpredictable, if we could never know from one moment to the next, what to expect from nature, both science and meaningful moral conduct would be impossible. While we often take the natural order for granted, this order and the predictability that accompanies it function as a necessary condition for free human action. But if nature sets the stage for moral good, it does the same for moral evil. "The very same framework which allows free will to be exercised in acts of respect, courtesy, modesty, charity, and love also allows free will to be expressed in acts of hostility, greed, cruelty, and hate."[17] One reason people can be held accountable when they pull the trigger of a loaded gun is the predictability of what will follow such an action. As Swinburne says:

> If we are to know the effects of our actions, things must behave in regular ways. Only if my action is going to have an effect similar to that of similar actions done by others on other occasions, can I know what effect that action is going to have. Only if I know what effects my actions will have can I set about making a difference to things. It follows that if agents are to mould the world and themselves, the world has to be on the whole a pretty deterministic sort of place; deterministic laws of nature have to operate fairly universally . . . basically the world has to be governed by laws of nature if agents are to be able to control it.[18]

A regular natural order is a necessary condition for moral evil, and it also quite obviously functions in any account of natural evil. As Peterson notes, "The same water which sustains and refreshes can also drown; the same drug which relieves suffering can cause crippling psychological addiction; the same sun which gives light and life can parch fields and bring famine; the same neural arrangements which transmit intense pleasure and ecstasy can also bring extreme pain and agony."[19] Many human complaints about the occurrence of specific natural evils such as a flood, earthquake, or tornado seem to be expressions of a desire that—at least in that instance—the natural order of things had been suspended or different somehow. If it makes sense to believe that God created the universe with the kind of regularity and order that makes the formulation of scientific laws possible, if it makes sense to think that this kind of orderly universe would be better overall than a chaotic and unpredictable universe, we might be wise to think twice before cursing some particular outcome of that order.

Two basic objections have been raised against the natural law theodicy I've described. First, one can ask, *Why doesn't God intervene miraculously every time the natural order is about to produce some evil?* After all, theists believe that miracles occur. Why doesn't God simply intervene in the natural order to make certain that evils resulting from the laws of nature do not take place?

David Basinger explains that "God could not significantly lessen the amount of natural evil we experience unless he either directly intervened in our present natural system in a continuous and widespread manner or

---

[17]Ibid., p. 110.
[18]Richard Swinburne, "Natural Evil," *American Philosophical Quarterly* 15 (1978): 298.
[19]Peterson, *Evil and the Christian God*, p. 111.

modified our present natural system in some significant fashion."[20] Basinger is drawing attention to the fact that the person who asks our first question— Why doesn't God intervene?—apparently has little idea of the scope of his demand. Such a person is not simply asking that God intervene whenever something is about to go wrong because of the natural order. He is not simply recommending that God step in and suspend whatever law is about to serve as the condition for some evil. He is really demanding suspension of the natural order as we know it.

Let's consider some of the more obvious consequences of continuous divine intervention with the natural order. For one thing, systematic divine intervention in the world would, Peterson points out, tend "to destabilize the world in a way which jeopardizes rational planning and free, responsible action. A world which is to be a moral order must be a relatively stable and predictable natural order. All things considered, then, it is absurd for God to intervene miraculously to eliminate natural evil. It appears, therefore, that God must create a world which is characterized by natural laws."[21] Or as Basinger puts the point, "Continuous, widespread divine intervention into our present natural system would make meaningful human choice impossible (or at least greatly lessen its meaningfulness)."[22]

Suppose God did intervene every time a natural evil was about to take place. Why wouldn't such intervention become predictable? If God's intervention took place before every natural evil became apparent, humans might never know that they were in any jeopardy; because no one would even know that a natural evil had been averted in such cases, humans would never have reason to thank God for his acts of deliverance. But if God's intervention were to occur after the event—thus taking the form of negating any possible harm from the event—humans would soon realize that they are fortunate enough to live in a universe in which nothing (or nothing serious) can ever go wrong. Should a weatherman warn that a tornado is heading for a trailer park, the residents need hardly worry since past experience has taught them that God (or something) will intervene to prevent any harm. On the first scenario, there would never be natural evils as earthquakes or tornadoes; on the second scenario, there would never be anything to worry about since God would continuously intervene to negate any possible harmful effects from the event. Any request, then, for continuing divine intervention with the natural order in order to prevent every possible instance of natural evil appears to exceed the bounds of rationality.

A second possible objection to a natural law theodicy asks, Why didn't God create a different natural order with different laws that would have precluded the natural evils presently plaguing humanity? After all, could not an omnipotent

[20]David Basinger, "Evil as Evidence Against God's Existence: Some Clarifications," Modern Schoolman 58 (1980–81): 180.

[21]Michael Peterson, "Recent Work on the Problem of Evil," American Philosophical Quarterly 20 (1983): 330.

[22]Basinger, "Evil as Evidence," p. 181. A correct understanding of miracles is consistent with what Peterson and Basinger argue. Unlike the kind of total and systematic intervention implicit in our question, miracles occur infrequently and thus are not a threat to the natural order. For more on this aspect of miracles, see Part 5 of this book.

God have created a different world order sufficiently like the present one that would include all the good without any of the natural evil?

Once again, it seems unlikely that people asking such a question understand fully all that they want. It is hard to see how different natural laws could result in the same kinds of good we've come to appreciate without also producing natural evils of some kind. As David Basinger states, "The atheologian has yet to demonstrate that God could create a significantly modified natural system which, when considered in terms of the entire world system of which it would be a part, would produce significantly less natural evil and yet preserve the integrity of human freedom and retain as much good as we have in our present world."[23] A natural order is a *system;* even an apparently minor change in one part of the order would have to have repercussions throughout the system. Basinger continues,

> Moreover in order to demonstrate that some modification of our present natural system would greatly reduce the amount of physical evil we experience, the atheologian must do more than cite isolated contexts in which such modifications would greatly help. He or she must demonstrate that, in the context of the entire world system of which it would be a part, such modification would actually result in a significant increase in the net amount of good in comparison to the actual world.[24]

No atheologian has given us any reason to suppose that a different world order might result in as much good and less natural evil than the present system.

Michael Peterson amplifies this point:

> It is not obvious that God could have created a significantly better world than this one with different natural laws, laws whose regular operation produces the good and approvable effects of the present system without the ostensibly evil consequences. . . . natural laws are simply descriptive statements about how natural objects act and react under certain conditions, which means that a change in our present natural laws entails a change in the natures of the relevant natural objects. Since almost all natural objects are capable of producing harmful as well as beneficial results, virtually all of them would have to be modified to suit the critic. And even a small change in the objects in the present system may bring about manifold and intricate differences in the effects they produce. Such changes end up being so vast and complicated that it becomes unclear what the new system would be.[25]

A possible example of what Peterson has in mind is fire. To make sense of the atheologian's alternative world order, we have to try to imagine something in this other world that would do the job of fire (e.g., provide heat, cook food, consume waste) without also burning when coming in contact with human flesh. Or we have to imagine neural arrangements that would make pleasant sensations possible without also serving as a condition of pain.

---

[23] Ibid.
[24] Ibid.
[25] Peterson, "Recent Work on the Problem of Evil," p. 330.

When the critic requires "only a small change" in the present set of natural laws in order to avoid their gratuitous evil consequences, we might not realize how great a change is involved. Since almost all natural objects are capable of producing harmful as well as beneficial results, virtually all natural laws would have to be modified, with the correlative modification of virtually all natural objects. Even the slightest modification may produce manifold and intricate differences between this present natural order and the envisioned one. The whole matter becomes so complex that no finite mind can conceive of precisely what modifications the envisioned natural world would have to incorporate in order both to preserve the good natural effects and to avoid the . . . evil ones. And if the desired modifications cannot be detailed, then the further task of conceiving how the proposed natural world is better than this present one seems patently impossible.[26]

Nothing that has been said implies that the natural law theodicist regards the present world as the best possible world or the only possible world. The point is simply that unless there is some natural order, there cannot exist important goods like moral freedom. And there seems to be good reason to believe that without a world order like our present one, we could not have the good things so familiar to us. Moreover, no matter what the laws of nature might have been, there would have been unpleasant side effects as long as they operated as *laws*.

It appears, then, that the objections to a natural law theodicy raise more problems than they solve.

The Soul-Making Theodicy

The soul-making theodicy states that in order for God to produce the virtuous beings with whom he wants fellowship, these individuals must face challenges that teach them the intrinsic worth of the virtues he possesses perfectly. Virtues cannot be created instantaneously; the process by which they are acquired is part of the nature of having them. Each of us is given an opportunity to develop into a better or worse person. But we cannot grow in an environment that is free of risk and danger and disappointment. Just as God had good reasons for creating us with free will and for placing us in a lawlike environment, God also had good reasons for placing us in an environment that is challenging, that tests us.

When we fully understand the kinds of character God wants us to exemplify, it becomes clear that God could not have created us with those characters. We can only become that kind of being by engaging in struggle, conflict, and challenge. We cannot develop virtuous dispositions without living in a world in which there are real challenges and the threat of real loss. The process through which we pass in life is designed to surround us with a challenging environment in which we can grow and develop toward being the mature persons God expects us to be. As John Hick puts it,

The world is not intended to be a paradise, but rather the scene of a history in which human personality may be formed towards the pattern of Christ. Men are not to be thought of on the analogy of animal pets, whose life is to be made as agreeable as possible, but rather on the

---

[26]Peterson, *Evil and the Christian God*, pp. 115–16.

analogy of human children, who are to grow to adulthood in an environment whose primary and overriding purpose is not immediate pleasure but the realizing of the most valuable potentialities of human personality.[27]

Once we see the analogy between the purposes of God for humans and the purposes of wise, loving parents for their children, Hick continues, "we have to recognize that the presence of pleasure and the absence of pain cannot be the supreme and overriding end for which the world exists. Rather, this world must be a place of soul-making. And its value is to be judged, not primarily, by the quantity of pleasure and pain occurring in it at any particular moment, but by its fitness for its primary purpose, the purpose of soul-making."[28]

Most of what we consider significant with regard to human spiritual and moral development arises as a result of interaction with challenge. An athlete cannot accomplish his best without sacrifice, effort, training, and struggle. Human spiritual and moral growth also arises out of a struggle against various kinds of challenge. Imagine a person who wishes to accomplish something significant, such as reaching the top of Mount Rainier. But then suppose this person decides to get to the top in a painless, easy way, for example, by having a helicopter carry him to the top. Having reached the top without any real sacrifice would preclude any sense of real accomplishment from the fact that he reached the mountaintop. As Richard Purtill explains, "To be able to play like Heifetz, or philosophize like Wittgenstein, is not really separable from the long years of practice and playing, or the long years of wrestling with philosophical problems. But even if the end result could be achieved without pain, it would thereby be less valuable."[29]

As Hick sees it, God's love for humans

presupposes a "real life" in which there are obstacles to be overcome, tasks to be performed, goals to be achieved, setbacks to be endured, problems to be solved, dangers to be met; and if the world did not contain the particular obstacles, difficulties, problems, and dangers that it does contain, then it would have to contain others instead. The same is true in relation to the virtues of compassion, unselfishness, courage, and determination—these all presuppose for their emergence and for their development something like the world in which we live. They are values

---

[27]Hick, *Evil and the God of Love*, p. 258. While Hick's important work on the soul-making theodicy makes it necessary to quote him several times, I have at least three major objections to his particular formulation of this position. (1) In treating the church father Irenaeus as the original Christian source of the soul-making theodicy, Hick exaggerates the differences between his Irenaean theodicy and the Augustinian approach to evil. Hick does this by exaggerating Augustine's stress on the privative nature of evil. The real value of Augustine's theodicy was its stress on free will. (2) Hick goes too far in his use of the modern theory of evolution; he combines Irenaean insights with evolutionism and, in the process, places too much blame for human shortcomings on our animal ancestry rather than on sin. (3) Hick combines his soul-making theodicy with a universalism that holds that no soul can ultimately be lost. I object to this universalism in more detail later in this chapter.
[28]Ibid., p. 259.
[29]Richard L. Purtill, *Reason to Believe* (Grand Rapids: Eerdmans, 1974), p. 57.

of personal existence that would have no point, and therefore no place, in a ready-made Utopia. And therefore, if the purpose for which this world exits (so far as that purpose concerns mankind) is to be a sphere within which such personal qualities are born, to purge it of all suffering would be a sterile reform.[30]

We cannot live, then, in a plastic environment that bends to our every desire, in which we get everything we want. That environment would stifle growth and development.

One of the more puzzling aspects of the human situation is what John Hick calls our "epistemic distance" from God.[31] This epistemic distance explains why it is sometimes so difficult to be morally certain that God exists or why it is often so easy to doubt God. God placed us in a world in which doubt, unbelief, and faithlessness are possible. Why did God create us with this epistemic distance between himself and us? Why do we exist in a setting in which it sometimes seems as though God does not exist?

If God had made himself so readily available that we could never doubt his existence, an important element of soul-making would have been missing. In the words of C. Stephen Evans, if God's reality

> were too obvious, then even the most selfish, meanspirited person would believe in him and even (for selfish reasons) try to serve him. Even we humans believe that true love must be freely given and we wouldn't value very highly someone who only "loved" us to get our money or avoid punishment. God, if he is real, must feel the same way. There is good reason to think, then, that God would give people "room" to reject him, because he only wants people to believe in him who are willing to believe in him.[32]

God's creation of humans at an epistemic distance from himself is a reflection of his loving desire that men and women choose to worship and love him freely. If things were such that we could not help being conscious of him, we would have little or no independence within which to make our religious choices.

Three major objections to a soul-making theodicy have been raised. First, some claim, *the soul-making theodicy deals inadequately with the fact that much evil seems to overpower its victims and thus fails to result in any compensating virtue or development.* Even if we grant some point to the basic soul-making thesis, must the world still contain all of the more serious errors we find in it? Are not the challenges of life often greater than they need to be? Such evils as insanity appear to make no contribution to soul-making. Indeed, such evils often seem to destroy the soul. Evil often injures character so badly as to preclude any possibility of further growth.

A proper response to this serious objection notes that any world that is to serve as the arena for the kind of soul-making engaged in by God must include the real possibility of defeat and loss. As Hick states,

---

[30]Hick, *Evil and the God of Love*, p. 326.
[31]Ibid:, p. 373.
[32]C. Stephen Evans, *The Quest for Faith* (Downers Grove, Ill.: InterVarsity Press, 1986), p. 21.

It therefore does not seem to me that there is a viable possibility of a "soul-making" world from which we exclude all risk of severe hardship and injury, with desperate and even suicidal misery as the extreme point of the one continuum, and death as the extreme point of the other. The world, as a person-making environment, does not have to include the particular perils that it contains, but it does have to contain some particular perils and challenges which are real and which inevitably have, to us, an arbitrary and sometimes threatening character which is beyond our control.[33]

Hick admits that the presence of "excessive and undeserved suffering" in our world "is a real mystery, impenetrable to the rationalizing human mind. It challenges Christian faith with its utterly baffling, alien, destructive meaninglessness."[34] But its very meaninglessness means that our world can function as an arena in which genuine goodness can develop. "What was necessary," Hick concludes, "was a world which contains real contingencies, real dangers, real problems and tasks and real possibilities of failure and tragedy as well as of triumph and success, because only in a world having this general character could human animals begin their free development into 'children of God.' "[35]

The second objection draws attention to the fact that *many humans fail to come through the soul-making process victoriously.* The answer here must note again that the possibility of real loss must be present. For example, the virtue of courage can be achieved only as we endure struggles with various kinds of challenges; but the challenges must be real. How can one acquire courage when he deals with situations that only appear to be dangerous or where the challenge is only an illusion? As noted earlier in a footnote, even Hick wavers on the point and takes refuge in a universalism where the process of soul-making continues even past death to the stage where eventually all humanity is saved. Hick needs to take his own soul-making theodicy seriously. Unlike Hick, I suggest that human existence includes the possibility of *total* failure and *total* loss found in the biblical teaching of the second death and ultimate, irremediable separation from God. The soul-making process is not a game. The soul-making theodicy is negated when adherents like Hick tell us that when the game is finally over, we will discover that everyone has won and no one has lost.

The third objection to the soul-making theodicy concerns *the existence of gratuitous evils, that is, evils so senseless and/or so out of proportion to any good they might produce as to leave us with feelings of utter hopelessness, despair, or outrage.* This is what Jane Mary Trau had in mind when she wrote:

> The world seems to be for the most part populated by reasonably good people who try hard and sometimes fail. These well intentioned people hardly seem to merit the many bad things which befall them. There are also those who ardently strive to be virtuous and still are not immune to hard times. Most of all, there are the real innocents who appear to be wholly undeserving of any suffering at all.[36]

---

[33] Hick, *Evil and the God of Love*, pp. 378–79.
[34] Ibid., p. 336.
[35] Ibid., p. 375.
[36] Jane Mary Trau, "Fallacies in the Argument from Gratuitous Suffering," *The New Scholasticism* 60 (1986): 485.

I happen to take this third objection so seriously that I am going to devote almost all of the next chapter to it. Nothing can undermine one's confidence in any theodicy more quickly than the growing conviction that the world contains evil for which there is no possible reason—in short, gratuitous evil. Until we have an opportunity to see what can be said about evil for which there is no apparent reason, we can close this chapter by summarizing its main contention. In reply to the proponent of the inductive problem of evil who maintains that the existence of evil provides evidence that disconfirms belief in God, the theist appears justified in arguing that God has good reasons for creating morally free creatures and for placing them in an orderly universe (a necessary condition for the exercise of significant freedom) and for placing them in a challenging environment that provides an opportunity for soul-making.

For Further Exploration—Chapter Fourteen

1. Suppose a theist admits that he doesn't know why some particular evil has occurred. Discuss what might follow from this.
2. Explain the natural law theodicy. Is it relevant only to natural evil?
3. Why doesn't God intervene miraculously every time some natural evil is about to occur?
4. Why didn't God create a different natural order that would have precluded the natural evils presently plaguing humanity?
5. Explain the soul-making theodicy.
6. Evaluate the answers given in this chapter to the major objections to a soul-making theodicy.

Chapter 15

THE PROBLEM OF GRATUITOUS EVIL

The responses to the problem of evil taken in the previous chapter are all versions of an appeal to greater good; they involve the claim that God permits evil because it is a necessary condition for the attainment of some greater good or the avoidance of some greater evil. But what if the world contains gratuitous evil, that is, truly senseless, mindless, irrational, and meaningless evil? If this were true, the appeal to greater good would collapse and with it, apparently, would also fall the theist's responses to the inductive problem of evil. After all, the theistic defenses against evil noted thus far consist of claims that God has a reason for allowing evil to exist. But how can such a defense possibly succeed when the theist stands in the presence of gratuitous evil?

Jane Mary Trau explains how the theist's problem at this point is created by cases of "unmerited suffering that pose a seemingly unsurmountable wall to belief. For even the atheist could reconcile the existence of merited suffering with the existence of God. However, it seems clear to the atheist that if God exists, there should not be any cases of unmerited suffering. Thus, the case of unmerited suffering seems to argue against the existence of God."[1] As Trau uses the term, *gratuitous suffering* means "any suffering the purpose of which seems to exceed necessity, and any suffering which seems to serve no purpose at all."[2]

---

[1] Jane Mary Trau, "Fallacies in the Argument from Gratuitous Suffering," *The New Scholasticism* 60 (1986): pp. 485–86.
[2] Ibid., p. 486.

THREE FORMS OF THE PROBLEM OF GRATUITOUS EVIL

To help us work our way into the problem of gratuitous evil, I will briefly consider three formulations of the argument. Before I do that, however, there is merit in allowing William Rowe to show us the general nature of the difficulty:

> We must then ask whether it is reasonable to believe that all the instances of profound, seemingly pointless human and animal suffering lead to greater goods. And, if they should somehow all lead to greater goods, is it reasonable to believe that an omnipotent, omniscient being could not have brought about any of those goods without permitting the instances of suffering which supposedly lead to them? When we consider these more general questions in the light of our experience and knowledge of the variety and profusion of human and animal suffering occurring daily in our world, it seems that the answer must be no. It seems quite unlikely that all the instances of intense human and animal suffering occurring daily in our world lead to greater goods, and even more unlikely that if they all do, an omnipotent, omniscient being could not have achieved at least some of those goods without permitting the instances of suffering that lead to them. In the light of our experience and knowledge of the variety and scale of human and animal suffering in our world, the idea that none of these instances of suffering could have been prevented by an omnipotent being without the loss of a greater good seems an extraordinary, absurd idea, quite beyond our belief.[3]

A Deductive Formulation

A deductive formulation of the argument from gratuitous evil can be set up as follows:

1. If God exists, then all evil has a justifying reason.
2. But it is not the case that all evil has a justifying reason.[4]
3. Therefore, God does not exist.

What can we say about this argument? To begin with, it is certainly valid. If the premises are true, then the conclusion must be true. But are the premises true? Later in this chapter, I'll explore the possibility that the first premise may be false; that is, I'll consider the claim of some theists that even if God exists, there may still be gratuitous evil. For now, the more obvious problem with our argument is the second premise, i.e., the claim that it is not the case that all evil has a justifying reason or, to put it more directly, there is gratuitous evil. Several questions must be asked about this claim. For one thing, how does the atheologian know that premise 2 is true? And to get right to the heart of the matter, how could any human being know that there is gratuitous evil? Any sensitive and observant person must admit that the world contains many evils that appear to be gratuitous: accidents that strike people down in the prime of life, diseases that result in long periods of horrible suffering, birth defects, natural disasters that can suddenly kill

---

[3]William L. Rowe, *Philosophy of Religion: An Introduction* (Encino, Calif.: Dickenson, 1978), p. 89.

[4]This premise is simply another way of saying that the world contains gratuitous evil.

hundreds of people and destroy the lives of survivors. But given the limitations of human knowledge, it is hard to see how any human being could actually *know* that a specific instance of evil really is gratuitous. In fact, it looks as though a person would have to be omniscient before he would be warranted in claiming that he *knows* that some particular evil is totally senseless and purposeless.

It seems, then, that the most any human can claim to know is that the world contains evil that *appears* gratuitous. But of course such a claim in the place of premise 2 would not entail the conclusion. Therefore, we would do well to pass over this first argument and look for something better.

One Inductive Formulation

Jane Mary Trau has provided an inductive formulation of the argument:

> It seems that unless it can be shown that all cases of apparently gratuitous suffering are in fact not purposeless, it is most reasonable to believe that they are as they appear to be; and since it cannot be shown that they are in fact not purposeless, it is reasonable to believe that they are as they appear to be; since there appear to be such cases it is more reasonable to believe that God does not exist.[5]

While this is an interesting argument, it raises at least two questions. The first and less serious question concerns the placement of the burden of proof in this matter. How did the theist suddenly get stuck with the burden of proof? After all, he was simply minding his own business as he went about the task of believing in God and living in the world. Suddenly, he is told that unless he (the theist) can show that none of the evils in the world are gratuitous, belief in the existence of God must be judged to be unreasonable. But, we should remember, it is the atheologian who is attempting to prove that God does not exist; in this case, the atheologian is attempting to make his case for the nonexistence of God by pointing to the existence of gratuitous evil. Since the atheologian is issuing the challenge, should not the burden of proof be on his shoulders? Should not the atheologian be the one required to show that there *is* gratuitous evil in the world? My point, of course, is that the atheologian knows fully well that no human being can show that there is or that there is not really gratuitous evil in the world. So he simply adopts an attitude of philosphical imperialism, throws down the gauntlet, and adds in passing, "By the way, I thought you should know that you also have the burden of proof in this matter."

I am not trying to defend theism by default in the last paragraph. I am simply pointing out that it is not at all clear that the theist has the burden of proof in this matter. And unless the theist has that burden, the argument before us cannot succeed. Moreover, when dealing with a problem where no human being can know what is the case, how can we say fairly that *anyone* has the burden of proof.

But Trau's argument, as stated, suffers from still another problem as she herself points out. The second premise of the argument involves an appeal to ignorance, a common logical fallacy that all freshman logic students

---

[5] Trau, "Fallacies in the Argument," pp. 487–88. As we will see shortly, Trau only presents the argument; she does not accept it.

are warned to avoid. Simply because the theist cannot prove that all evils in the world are not gratuitous, it hardly follows that some of them are. Indeed, Trau goes on to say,

> the most reasonable position to hold appears to be this: we cannot explain cases of apparently gratuitous suffering until we know whether or not they are indeed gratuitous. And this we can never claim unless we are sure as to the ontological status of God. Since we cannot prove or disprove His non-existence [via the argument from gratuitous evil], we must first prove or disprove His existence. Until that is accomplished we cannot know whether there are such cases.[6]

According to Trau, the one sure way of showing that the world does contain gratuitous evils is to prove that God does not exist. But it would then seem to follow that one cannot appeal to gratuitous evils while arguing against the existence of God—unless, that is, one is unconcerned about begging the question.

William Rowe's Formulation

In a 1979 article, William Rowe presented a formulation of the inductive problem of evil that succeeds admirably as a teaching tool in the study of the problem. Rowe sets up the argument as follows:[7]

> (1) There exist instances of intense suffering which an omnipotent, omniscient being could have prevented without thereby losing some greater good or permitting some evil equally bad or worse.

> (2) An omniscient, wholly good being would prevent the occurrence of any intense suffering it could, unless it could not do so without thereby losing some greater good or permitting some evil equally bad or worse.

> (3) Therefore, there does not exist an omnipotent, omniscient, wholly good being.

I begin by conceding that Rowe's argument is formally valid. If the premises are true, then the conclusion is true. I will also allow premise (2) to pass for now.[8] After all, as Rowe explains, premise (2) "claims only that *if* an omniscient, wholly good being permits intense suffering *then* either there is some greater good that would have been lost, or some equally bad or worse evil that would have occurred, had the intense suffering been prevented."[9] This seems to summarize what the theist has in mind in the three theodicies explained in the last chapter. It would appear, then, that if the theist wishes to counter Rowe's argument, the debate will have to revolve around the truth or falsity of the first premise ("There exist instances of intense suffering which an omnipotent, omniscient being could have prevented without

---

　　[6]Ibid., p. 489.

　　[7]William L. Rowe, "The Problem of Evil and Some Varieties of Atheism," *American Philosophical Quarterly* 16 (1979): 335–41. The wording of the argument above comes (with the exception of my adding "Therefore" to the conclusion) from page 335 of Rowe's article.

　　[8]In other words, even if later in this chapter I appear to express reservations about the content of (2), I will not now raise any objection to it. In fact, nothing I say later in this chapter constitutes a disagreement with (2) when (2) is understood properly.

　　[9]Rowe, "Problem of Evil," pp. 336–37.

thereby losing some greater good or permitting some evil equally bad or worse").

But Rowe himself admits that no human can prove that (1) is true.[10] However, Rowe goes on to insist, we may still have *rational grounds* that support the belief that (1) is true. It is possible, Rowe states, to be in a position to *believe* some proposition without *knowing* it is true or ever being able to prove its truth. Though it may be reasonable for me to believe that Jerry Falwell will never be elected president of the United States, I cannot be said to know this with complete certainty. So Rowe turns his attention to presenting the grounds that rationally support *his* belief that (1) is true. He writes:

> It seems quite unlikely that *all* the instances of intense suffering occurring daily in our world are intimately related to the occurrences of greater goods or the prevention of evils at least as bad; and even more unlikely, should they somehow all be so related, that an omnipotent, omniscient being could not have achieved at least some of those goods (or prevented some of those evils) without permitting the instances of intense suffering that are supposedly related to them.[11]

In Rowe's view of things, it is reasonable to believe (1), even though it seems impossible to prove that (1) is true. This is so because "our experience and knowledge of the variety and profusion of suffering in our world provides *rational support* for the first premise."[12] And this means, for Rowe, that we have rational support for our conclusion: "It is reasonable for us to believe that the theistic God does not exist."[13]

While Rowe recognizes that the theist who wishes to counter his argument will have to attack premise (1), he advises the theist against trying a *direct* attack.

> By a direct attack, I mean an attempt to reject (1) by pointing out goods, for example, to which suffering may well be connected, goods which an omnipotent, omniscient being could not achieve without permitting suffering. It is doubtful, however, that the direct attack can succeed. The theist may point out that some suffering leads to moral and spiritual development impossible without suffering. But it's reasonably clear that suffering often occurs in a degree far beyond what is required for character development.[14]

Rowe points out two difficulties with a direct attack on premise (1):

> First, it cannot succeed, for the theist does not know what greater goods might be served, or evils prevented, by each instance of intense human or animal suffering. Second, the theist's own religious tradition usually maintains that in this life it is not given to us to know God's purpose in allowing particular instances of suffering. Hence, the direct attack against

---

[10] Ibid., p. 337.
[11] Ibid., pp. 337–38.
[12] Ibid., p. 338.
[13] Ibid.
[14] Ibid.

premise (1) cannot succeed and violates basic beliefs associated with theism.[15]

According to Rowe, the theist's best hope of countering (1) rests with an *indirect* attack, somewhat similar to what an earlier chapter in this book called The *G. E. Moore Shift*.[16] In other words, Rowe's argument looks like this:

(1)
(2)
Therefore, (3)

The theist can attack Rowe's argument indirectly by retaining premise (2), rejecting the conclusion (3), thus justifying his rejection of premise (1). In other words, the theist's counterargument looks like this:

not (3)
(2)
Therefore, not (1)

Or to put the theist's counterargument into words:

not-(3)   There exists an omnipotent, omniscient, wholly good being.[17]

(2) An omniscient, wholly good being would prevent the occurrence of any intense suffering it could, unless it could not do so without thereby losing some greater good or permitting some evil equally bad or worse.[18]

not-(1)   Therefore, it is not the case that there exist instances of intense suffering which an omnipotent, omniscient being could have prevented without thereby losing some greater good or permitting some evil equally bad or worse.[19]

Rowe admits that this new counter argument is valid. But, being an atheist, Rowe obviously prefers *his* argument to the theist's counterargument because of what he takes to be the greater rational support for his first premise (1) than for the theist's new first premise.

But now something quite interesting emerges. Rowe describes himself as a "friendly atheist." Though he rejects the existence of God, he can easily understand why a reasonable person could believe in God and be rational in holding that belief.[20] In other words, Rowe sees nothing irrational in a theist's accepting not-(3) as his first premise, which results in the theist's rejecting Rowe's first premise, the key to his inductive argument against God's existence. But where does this leave Rowe's argument against theism? We have two opposing arguments that turn on what different people believe about the rationality of competing claims. And Rowe admits that a person can be rational in believing the theist's first premise.

---

[15]Ibid., pp. 338–39.

[16]See chapter 8 of this book.

[17]This, of course, is the denial of the conclusion to Rowe's original argument.

[18]This is the same as Rowe's original premise (2).

[19]And this new conclusion is the denial of Rowe's original premise (1). While I've used different numbers, the wording for each premise is Rowe's. See his article, already cited, p. 339.

[20]See p. 340f. of Rowe's article or p. 94 of his book, *Philosophy of Religion.*

Where does all this leave us? While theists can admire Rowe's tolerance in admitting the rationality of their beliefs, it is difficult to see how this admission on Rowe's part can possibly enhance the persuasive force of his argument. Has the debate between the theist and nontheist over evil not reached a point of stalemate?

VICTORY OR STALEMATE?

The particular formulations of the inductive problem of evil already noted in this chapter are hardly overpowering. Even Rowe, whose version seems the strongest, admits that theists who reject his key premise can do so without sacrificing the rationality of their position. Is it possible that the debate must be judged a draw?

David Basinger points out all that the atheologian still must do before theists need to begin sweating over efforts to disconfirm the existence of God. First, the atheologian must provide "acceptable definitional criteria for 'rationality,' 'evidence' and 'good reasons' as these terms apply to inductive, inter-world view discussions concerning God's existence."[21] Then the atheologian must "demonstrate that the amount of evil we experience counts strongly against God's existence by demonstrating that an omnipotent, omniscient, wholly good God could, in fact, have created an entire world system containing not just significantly less evil but on the whole a much better balance of good over evil than that which exists in the actual world."[22] And finally, the atheologian must "demonstrate that no recent formulation of the traditional arguments and no other form of argumentation furnish positive evidence for God's existence or demonstrate that such evidence, if it exists, cannot outweigh the evidence against God's existence."[23]

Basinger then continues his argument by claiming that theists and atheists

> may well agree that in a comparison of two possible worlds the one containing the greatest net balance of good over evil is superior. But how are we to assess the quantity of good and evil in each? Let us suppose, for example, that in the mind of a given atheologian the undeserved suffering of a single individual outweighs any amount of good which might be generated in such a world, while in the mind of a given theist the intrinsic value of "human freedom" outweighs any amount of evil such freedom might entail. How would we determine who is correct? I, for one, have no idea how an objective, nonquestion-begging determination of this sort could be made.[24]

William Hasker verbalizes the kind of thinking that might lead someone to conclude that we have reached a stalemate. "The atheist can point to many examples of apparently pointless evil but cannot conclusively demonstrate that these evils serve no good purpose. The theist stoutly maintains

---

[21] David Basinger, "Evil as Evidence Against God's Existence: Some Clarifications," *Modern Schoolman* 58 (1980–81): 184.

[22] Ibid.

[23] Ibid.

[24] Ibid.

that God permits evil only as it serves the purposes of a greater good, but is quite unable to show how this is so in many individual cases."[25]

However, Hasker warns, this would be a bad time for any theist to congratulate himself since such a draw would end up favoring the atheologian. Here's why.

> The general run of human experience strongly favors the view that gratuitous evil not only exists but is abundant, and if the theist holds that gratuitous evil is inconsistent with theism this experience cannot fail to reduce the reasonableness of theistic belief below what it would otherwise be. And so the theist's venture into the arena of theodicy ends rather unhappily. He began by boldly maintaining strong principles concerning God's providential governance of the world, but he is quickly reduced to a stone-walling mode of defense in which he maintains on *a priori* grounds a view which runs against the grain of universal human experience.[26]

For the rest of this chapter, I am going to take the position that the theist should seek more than a draw in this disagreement over evil. He should attempt to show that further considerations definitely tip the probabilities in his favor. I propose to do this by arguing that even *if* the world contains instances of gratuitous evil, the existence of such evils would not disconfirm the existence of God. I do not know, of course, that gratuitous evils exist; I have already given my reason for thinking it impossible for any human to attain such knowledge. But even should gratuitous evils exist, theists would be justified in believing in the existence of God. Indeed, I will even go beyond this view and show why some theists think it is important to admit that gratuitous evils do exist, even though no one can know this for sure. If this line of argument is successful, it will have the effect of removing the last bit of support from under the atheologian's belief that the problem of evil tips the scales of probability in the direction of atheism.

GRATUITOUS EVIL AND THE DOCTRINE
OF METICULOUS PROVIDENCE

Many Christian thinkers—perhaps most of them—deny the existence of *any* gratuitous evils. This seems to be Richard Purtill's position when he writes: "Now the whole Christian answer to the problem of apparently useless suffering is that no suffering is really useless."[27] Even when it is not apparent—as is usually the case—Christians should believe that all suffering is a means to a greater good. The view that God's creation does not and indeed cannot contain any instances of gratuitous evil is often linked with what has been called the *doctrine of meticulous providence*. As William Hasker explains, those who hold this doctrine believe that

> God exercises . . . a *meticulous providence*—that is, a providence in which all events are carefully controlled and manipulated in such a way that no evils are permitted to occur except as they are necessary for the production of a greater good. The only gratuitous evils that could be

---

[25]William Hasker, "Must God Do His Best?" *International Journal for Philosophy of Religion* 16 (1984): 216–17.

[26]Ibid., p. 217.

[27]Richard L. Purtill, *Reason to Believe* (Grand Rapids: Eerdmans, 1974), p. 57.

allowed would be those already mentioned, consisting of the morally wrong choices of free beings and of the immediate consequences of those choices—and even these only insofar as God determines in each particular case that the good involved in allowing the creature to make that particular choice outweighs the evil that results from the choice that is made.[28]

For those who hold to the doctrine of meticulous providence, there has to be a good reason for every evil, regardless of its severity; therefore, no evil is really meaningless. This doctrine, then, is the belief that God would *never* allow *any* instance of meaningless, pointless, purposeless, gratuitous evil.

According to some theists, Hasker included, it is not necessary to affirm the doctrine of meticulous providence. As they see it, theists can admit that the God of Christian theism could, in ways consistent with his nature and intentions, create a world in which gratuitous evils are possible. Such thinking brings these theists into disagreement with the much larger company of theists who seem to regard meticulous providence as a vital tenet of their faith. To a large degree, the debate over meticulous providence centers on different interpretations of perhaps the key biblical text: "And we know that in all things God works for the good of those who love him, who have been called according to his purpose" (Rom. 8:28).

Those who accept meticulous providence interpret Romans 8:28 to mean that God would never allow gratuitous evils to afflict those who love him.[29] On this interpretation, God works for the good of those who love him in every detail *of this earthly life*. Those who reject meticulous providence understand Romans 8:28 differently. They read it as teaching that all things work together for good *when viewed from the perspective of eternity*. In this life, senseless and irrational evils may occur. But when redeemed believers are able to look back upon those evils from their glorified standing in heaven, they will know what the apostle Paul meant when he wrote: "I consider that our present sufferings are not worth comparing with the glory that will be revealed in us" (Rom. 8:18). This comment does not mean that believers will then realize that particular evils were not really gratuitous; it means that God will have overcome those gratuitous evils.

One Christian philosopher who has explored the consequences of a theodicy based on a rejection of meticulous providence is Michael Peterson. According to Peterson, there are several reasons why the doctrine should be abandoned. "First, accepting the existence of some gratuitous evil is more consonant with our common experience than is the position which denies gratuitous evil *a priori*. Second, rejecting the principle of meticulous providence opens the way for a deeper and more profound apprehension of God than that widely accepted principle allows."[30] In Peterson's opinion, Christians should explore a view of God's relationship with the world and humankind in which God's plan is consistent with his permitting significant

---

[28]Hasker, "Must God Do His Best?" p. 216.

[29]Of course, even this interpretation leaves open the possibility of gratuitous evils affecting everyone else. The view that faithful believers are protected from gratuitous evil while other people are not seems inconsistent with other passages of Scripture, e.g., Matthew 5:45.

[30]Michael L. Peterson, *Evil and the Christian God* (Grand Rapids: Baker, 1982), p. 89.

amounts of gratuitous evil. In fact, Peterson argues, if Christians take seriously their convictions about the importance of free will, natural law, and soul-making, they may see how a good, all-powerful God could have reasons for permitting large amounts of gratuitous evil. It is instructive to see how theists like Peterson amplify this claim.

Free Will and Gratuitous Evil

As we have seen, the existence of significantly free moral agents entails the possibility of moral evil. Given what we learned about the necessary role that natural law plays in providing an environment in which freedom is possible, there is also a link between free will and natural evil. It is now time to see how free will is related to gratuitous evil. Michael Peterson sets the stage:

> If God is to bestow upon man a kind of freedom which is not just artificial but really significant, He must allow man a wide scope of choices and actions. Indeed, the kind of freedom which is basic to the accomplishment of great and noble actions is the kind of freedom which also allows the most atrocious deeds. In creating man and giving him free will, God thereby created an astonishing range of possibilities for both the creation and the destruction of value. Although some freely chosen evils sometimes have more disastrous consequences than intended, others seem to be motivated by the very desire to do irreparable damage. Perhaps this second kind of free choice is the true love of evil.[31]

When proponents of meticulous providence suggest that God prevents or eliminates all gratuitous evil, they (perhaps unwittingly) place constraints on the type of human freedom that makes possible the most praiseworthy human actions. How can humans have the freedom to maximize goodness without also possessing the frightening power to maximize evil? According to the free will theodicy, a God who wills to create free moral agents cannot also eliminate the possibility of those creatures producing moral evil. But it then follows as well that God cannot eliminate the possibility of their producing gratuitous moral evils unless he significantly reduces their free will. Among the options open to free moral agents are not merely great moral goods but also the most depraved kinds of gratuitous evil. God's program for humanity includes this risk.

Peterson adds an important qualification to his claim that a free will theodicy entails the possibility of gratuitous evil:

> None of this is meant to imply that God always allows men to carry out their most destructive intentions, since God overrides some human choices in order to accomplish His own general purposes. But God cannot always meticulously override human choices in order to prevent or eliminate their gratuitous effects and still protect a significant range of free will. . . . Those authors who agree that God should allow man significant free will and who also insist that God must not allow any gratuitous evil . . . are unwittingly asking for the impossible.[32]

---

[31]Ibid., p. 103.
[32]Ibid., pp. 104–5.

Peterson ends his discussion of the relationship between free will and gratuitous evil by stressing "the utter seriousness of what it is for mankind to possess significant freedom and with it the awesome possibility of creating gratuitous evil."[33] To demand that God eliminate or reduce the possibility of great evil is also to ask that God eliminate or reduce the possibility of great good.

Natural Law and Gratuitous Evil

We have already examined the reasonableness of a natural law theodicy. Unless humans exist in a regular and predictable environment, they cannot act freely and responsibly. In such a universe, natural evils will occur. Even advocates of meticulous providence concede this. But in the view of theists who reject meticulous providence, such a universe will also include instances of gratuitous natural evil. In order to argue for the impossibility of gratuitous natural evils in a universe governed by divinely created natural laws, advocates of meticulous providence must take refuge in one or both of the mistaken beliefs raised against a natural law theodicy. That is, they must believe either that a different set of natural laws might have been possible (which would have had the effect of producing different kinds of gratuitous natural evil) or that God eliminates gratuitous natural evils through constant intervention in the natural order. The serious difficulties raised by both views have already been discussed in the last chapter. If it makes sense for a theist to explain natural evil in the terms of a natural law theodicy, it is difficult to see why the same laws of nature will not also produce instances of gratuitous natural evil.

Soul-Making and Gratuitous Evil

We should hardly be surprised to find gratuitous evil in a world that serves as the arena for soul-making. We live in a world in which there are genuine risks and the threat of real loss; it is a world in which we face real, not imaginary, dangers and challenges. Without gratuitous evils, Peterson explains, "the operation of the world would verge on becoming a sham, a trivialization of the environment in which outstanding achievement as well as real disaster can occur."[34] God could not prevent gratuitous moral evils without seriously impairing moral freedom; he could not eliminate gratuitous natural evils that are a natural outcome of the world order without imperiling other significant values.

At this point, it might seem to a prospective critic that the theists who affirm the possible existence of genuinely gratuitous evils are guilty of an inconsistency. If evils that these theists are willing to regard as gratuitous end up serving a higher purpose such as free will, natural law, or soul-making, how can they be gratuitous? After all, a gratuitous evil is one for which there is no purpose or meaning. The proper answer to the question requires reflection about a distinction made in passing earlier, namely, the distinction between evil in general and specific instances of evil. When a theist says that he believes God's creation contains gratuitous evil, he means that it includes *specific instances* of moral and/or natural evil for which there is

---

[33] Ibid., p. 106.
[34] Ibid., p. 113.

no specific reason or purpose in God's plan. The event or action happened because the natural outworking of the world order or the decisions of human beings resulted in unfortunate things happening to whatever people happened to be in the path of those occurrences. Such specific evils might well be gratuitous even though God has good reasons for permitting moral and natural evil in general. In other words, the importance of free will, natural law, and soul-making means that God has good reasons for permitting moral evil in general and natural evil in general. But as evil human beings make choices and as an ongoing world order works out its successive stages, there may occur specific instances of moral and natural evil for which God has no direct purpose. Or so say theists who reject the doctrine of meticulous providence.

Michael Peterson extends the consequences of his doubts about meticulous providence to the ultimate evil when he writes:

> It is reasonable to believe that the terrifying human potential for evil includes the possibility of some person's willing and loving evil to the extent that hell becomes the emergent, dominant choice of his whole life. Hell is simply the natural culmination of things which he has voluntarily set in motion. Just as God cannot override a person's every evil choice, He cannot contravene the larger, cumulative evil orientation of one's life. If God is going to allow us to exist as significantly free beings, capable of the highest achievements, then He must allow us the most depraved and senseless errors—even if they lead to hell. Hell is the logical extension of the idea that man has the radical power to create gratuitous evil.[35]

In chapter 14, I suggested a three-pronged theodicy as the best approach to the inductive problem of evil; it takes account of how human free will, natural law, and the process of soul-making require conditions that provide the occasion for moral and natural evils. This chapter has shown how some theists go on to suggest that when we take free will, natural law, and soul-making seriously, we'll come to see how the world in which God has placed humans can also include instances of gratuitous evil. Each of us will lose certain goods and be confronted by certain gratuitous evils as a result of other humans using their free will, as a consequence of the natural order of the universe, and as a result of the fact that God has placed us in a challenging environment in which there is the danger of real loss, which includes the ultimate loss, the loss of one's soul. While free will, natural law, and soul-making serve as justifying grounds for evil in general, it is possible that some, perhaps many, of the specific evils that afflict us have no direct or immediate purpose.

Conclusion

Each theist must decide for himself whether his understanding of God and the world should include or exclude the doctrine of meticulous providence; each will have to decide whether his particular response to the inductive problem of evil will result in his arguing that there are no gratuitous evils in God's creation or in his arguing that even the presence of gratuitous evils in God's creation fails to disconfirm God's existence.

Theism isn't worth much if it doesn't help people make sense of the

---

[35] Ibid., pp. 124–25.

world in which they live. This world is obviously a place in which large amounts of evil that often appears senseless and irrational exists. For many, the arguments of this chapter help make sense of all this. The three-pronged theodicy offered can handle the most difficult kind of evil, gratuitous evil. A universe created by God can contain particular instances of evil that are just as senseless and irrational as they appear.

Several pages back, we were left with the possibility that the debate over evil might have to end in a stalemate. This is a good time to reflect on a claim by Michael Peterson: "Not only are real and potential gratuitous evils not a devastating problem for a theistic perspective, but, properly understood, they are a part of a world order which seems to be precisely the kind God *would* create to provide for certain goods."[36] We have already noted enough reasons to conclude that the existence of natural and moral evils—even gratuitous evils—is not enough to tip the scales of probability in favor of the atheologian. If Peterson's observation is correct and if the arguments concerning gratuitous evil in the last few pages are sound, there would seem to be good reason to believe that the stalemate is over and that the probabilities favor theism. The presence of gratuitous evils in God's creation is consistent with God's purposes for creation; moreover, it is what we might expect to find in a natural order designed to serve as an arena in which free human beings are given an opportunity to respond to real dangers and challenges in the process known as soul-making.

For Further Exploration—Chapter Fifteen

1. Define *gratuitous evil*; give several examples.
2. Take a careful look at the first premise of Rowe's version of the argument for gratuitous evil. Can this premise be proven? What's the reason for your answer? What follows?
3. What is the doctrine of meticulous providence? What is your evaluation of it?
4. In your view, can a theist consistently allow for the existence of gratuitous evil in a world created by God?

---

[36]Ibid., p. 117.

Part 5

MIRACLES

Chapter 16

DAVID HUME'S ATTACK ON MIRACLES

In the next few chapters, I plan to examine several questions related to the crucially important notion of miracle. It is impossible to think seriously and responsibly about the *historic* Christian faith[1] without bumping into claims that some pretty remarkable events occurred in the early history of the church and that the historicity of those miracles is a necessary condition for the truth of Christianity. This is certainly the position of the apostle Paul who declared that if the miracle of Christ's resurrection had not actually happened in history, Christianity would be false and anyone believing in it would be a fool (1 Cor. 15:1–19). Another miracle essential to Christianity's truth is the Incarnation, the fact that Jesus Christ was God incarnate (John 1:1–14).[2]

It is clear, then, that reflection about the various problems raised by the issue of miracles is anything but idle speculation. The conclusions people reach with regard to these questions will likely affect their final verdict about the truth or falsity of the Christian world-view.

---

[1] I have chosen the words in this sentence carefully. It requires little effort to discover writings that assert that the alleged miracles of early Christianity can be disposed of without altering or harming the nature of the faith. I provide examples of such attempts and offer my objections to them in several books. See Ronald Nash, *Christian Faith and Historical Understanding* (Grand Rapids: Zondervan, 1984), and Ronald Nash, *Christianity and the Hellenistic World* (Grand Rapids: Zondervan, 1984). The end result of all such efforts must be a totally different religion from historic Christianity. The honorable thing for all who make such claims to do is to find some new name for their new religion.

[2] In my *Christianity and the Hellenistic World*, I discuss and criticize various attempts to explain away the New Testament's emphasis on the Incarnation and the Resurrection.

My investigation of the topic begins with an analysis of David Hume's essay on miracles, unarguably the most influential writing on the subject. My examination of Hume's work will give me an opportunity to introduce several preliminary questions, e.g., should miracles be regarded as violations of the laws of nature? It will also give me a chance to dispose of several of the most frequently encountered objections to miracles.

HUME'S ESSAY ON MIRACLES

The writings of David Hume (1711–76) are a watershed in the history of philosophy and theology.[3] The most frequently discussed study of miracles continues to be Hume's essay on the subject that appears as Section 10 of his *Enquiry Concerning Human Understanding*.[4] Hume's essay still merits attention for a number of reasons. (1) The essay continues to be widely read in philosophy, religion, and even literature courses. It is easy for uninformed college students to think, after reading the essay and hearing some professors' comments about it, that believing in miracles is rationally suspect. (2) Hume's essay on miracles is often treated as the necessary starting point for any serious study of the subject. (3) Many later attacks on miracles are often just variations or elaborations of Hume's points. And finally, (4) one often hears the claims—frequently made by professors who make the essay a required reading in their courses—that Hume's arguments have never been answered. Anyone who wants to be considered informed on the subject of miracles *should* read Hume's essay, should try to understand what he said, and should then assess the strengths and weaknesses of his argument. In this chapter, I want to help the reader achieve the last two objectives. He or she can attain the first goal by simply reading the essay.

Like many philosophical classics, Hume's essay on miracles contains some obstacles that make the author's meaning difficult to discern at times. In Hume's case, it seems that he often wrote with a twinkle in his eye and utilized irony to have some fun at the expense of those orthodox Christians of his time who scanned his works looking for signs of heresy.[5] Irony, of course, is the use of language to convey a meaning quite different from what the author appears to say. Consider, for example, the last sentences of Hume's essay on miracles:

> So that, upon the whole, we may conclude, that the *Christian Religion* not
> only was at first attended with miracles, but even at this day cannot be

---

[3] For more on this point, see Ronald Nash, *The Word of God and the Mind of Man* (Grand Rapids: Zondervan, 1982), chaps. 1 and 2.

[4] Hume first published this work in 1748 under the title *Philosophical Essays Concerning Human Understanding*. He changed the title to *An Enquiry Concerning Human Understanding* when the second edition was published in 1751.

[5] Of course, it also appears that Hume sometimes attempted to camouflage some of his more radical religious views. Students of Hume's philosophy are often frustrated by their inability to determine whether a particular passage is an example of his use of irony or a significant change in his thought. For a good example of such a passage, see the last part of Hume's *Dialogues Concerning Natural Religion* where he brings his study of arguments for God's existence to a close by suggesting that God does exist.

believed by any reasonable person without one. Mere reason is insufficient to convince us of its veracity: And whoever is moved by *Faith* to
assent to it, is conscious of a continued miracle in his own person, which
subverts all the principles of his understanding, and gives him a
determination to believe what is most contrary to custom and experience.[6]

It is not difficult to imagine many rather naive readers in Hume's
Scotland who read these words and concluded that Hume believed in
miracles after all when, in fact, he was indirectly poking fun at believers.
What he says in this paragraph is that since it requires a miracle (in which
people allow an irrational faith to subvert reason and common sense) to
believe in miracles, it is possible to say that at least one kind of miracle
exists![7]

Because Hume's essay is so easily misunderstood, there is at least one
point where it is important to explain what Hume did *not* say. The
importance of this clarification is linked to the frequency with which one can
still hear some of Hume's interpreters attributing the position to him.

DOES HUME'S ESSAY CLAIM THAT MIRACLES ARE IMPOSSIBLE?

A large number of people who ought to know better believe that one
reason—perhaps the major reason—why Hume wrote his essay was to
argue that miracles are *impossible*. Such people base this opinion on a
superficial reading of the following words: "A miracle is a violation of the
laws of nature; and as a firm and unalterable experience has established
these laws, the proof against a miracle, from the very nature of the fact, is as
entire as any argument from experience can possibly be imagined."[8]
In the view of those who hold this interpretation, the laws of nature tell
us what can and cannot happen. A violation of the laws of nature cannot
happen. But a miracle is supposed to be a violation of the laws of nature.
Therefore, a miracle cannot happen. This thinking is mistaken on two
counts. First, the laws of nature do not and, indeed, cannot function as a
kind of metaphysical straightjacket; they do not prescribe what can or cannot
happen. And anyone who thinks this only reveals his need for a course in
the philosophy of science. But attributing this view to Hume is also mistaken
because it contradicts Hume's own clear teaching about the laws of nature. If
Hume really had held the view before us, it would have directly contradicted
other essential elements of his philosophical system. To see how all this is so,
we need a little background in what Hume taught about the laws of nature.
According to Hume, careful thinking about the laws of nature will lead
us to distinguish two things.[9] The first thing is what the law says about the
past, i.e., what human experience testifies has happened up to the present
moment. Up to the present, the world has exhibited a certain pattern or

---

[6]David Hume, *An Enquiry Concerning Human Understanding* in *Hume's Enquiries*, ed.
L. A. Selby-Bigge, 2d ed. (Oxford: Clarendon Press, 1902), p. 131.
[7]J. L. Mackie had this in mind when he titled his last book *The Miracle of Theism*.
[8]Hume, *Enquiry*, p. 114.
[9]Hume's account can be found in earlier sections of his *Enquiry* or in Book 1, Part 3
of his *A Treatise of Human Nature*, available in many editions.

order. Perhaps human experience about the kind of phenomena covered by the law has been uniform in the sense that there are no records (or at least believable records) of anything occurring that was an exception to this pattern. A scientific law, then, tells us what humans have observed about this part of the natural order up to the present. The law is a *description* of what has uniformly been the case up to now—or at least what available information suggests has been uniformly true.

But a law of science also purports to go beyond its description of what has uniformly been the case in the *past* and projects that pattern into the *future*. Basic to every law of nature is an *assumption* that the future will be like the past. Perhaps we can know enough about what has happened in the past to capture this in what we believe is a true description. But when we project our "law" into the future, we leave our evidence and observations behind. Perhaps we do know what has happened in the past. But what can possibly ground our expectation that the universe will continue to exhibit the same patterns and regularities *in the future*?

According to Hume, all that human experience can tell us is what has happened in the past and what is happening in our present. But a law of science requires that we make a huge leap from what we believe has always happened in the *past* to what we *believe* must also happen in the *future*. But can we really be said to *know* that something must happen in the future just because we believe it has always happened in the past? Even Hume admitted that we cannot have this kind of *knowledge*. There is no way that knowledge about the past can serve as a ground for knowledge-claims about the future.

Hume taught, then, that what we call the laws of nature are simply an account of what has happened up to the present *plus* a belief that the future will continue to be like the past. Because something has always happened in the past—for example, the sun has always risen in the East or unsupported objects have always fallen to the ground—we take it as a matter of faith (induced by custom or habit) that the future will be like the past. But in the strictest sense of the word *know*, we do not really know that the sun will rise in the East tomorrow or that some object I'm holding will fall when I release it. There is always the possibility that the next time I release this object, it will remain suspended in space.

For Hume, the laws of science express the faith that humans have that the future will continue to be like the past. But Hume saw that we can never know this for certain. According to Hume's position, then, the laws of science contain an element of expectation about the future that goes beyond all available evidence. The laws of science always say more than the available evidence warrants because our evidence reports only what has happened in the past; our evidence cannot tell us what *must* happen in the future.

The obvious question is this: How could anyone holding Hume's view of natural law also believe—without contradicting himself—that *any* event that might be a violation of or an exception to such a law is impossible? The answer, of course, is that he couldn't—at least he couldn't without introducing a major inconsistency into his philosophical system. As Keith Ward explains, "A law of nature, for Hume, is an observed regularity, postulated by habit or custom. Since, according to him, there are no necessities in nature, it is always possible that a law of nature may be violated. A violation may be improbable; but it will never be maximally so (so unlikely as to be virtually out of the question)."[10]

If a miracle is thought to be a violation of a law of nature that is nothing more than a descriptive generalization of what humans take to be the regular pattern of nature, how could it possibly follow that miracles are impossible? Obviously, it cannot. If such laws are simply descriptive generalizations of what has normally (or even uniformly) happened in the past, it is certainly possible that something might happen in the future that would appear to conflict with the experience of the human race to this point. This is so because there is nothing about these descriptive laws that prescribes what can or cannot happen in the future. Hence, even if miracles are defined as violations of the laws of nature, this fact alone does not prove that they are impossible. Since Hume was a pioneer in developing this view of the laws of nature, we must conclude—assuming that his system does not contain the grandest example of a contradiction in the history of philosophy—that Hume was not attempting to prove that miracles are impossible. Indeed, to be consistent, he must maintain that miracles (in his sense of violations of the laws of nature) are possible.

Since Hume could not have been arguing that miracles are impossible, we must seek the thrust to his attack on miracles in another direction. Instead of attacking miracles metaphysically (by arguing that they are impossible), Hume's challenge turns out to be epistemological in nature. That is, he argues that even though miracles could occur, it is never rational to believe that any alleged miracle took place. Hume develops this epistemological attack on miracles in two stages. In Part I of his essay, he argues on philosophical grounds that the evidence that might be thought to support belief in a miracle will normally, by the nature of the case, be less than the evidence against belief in the miracle. The evidence against the alleged miracle will typically outweigh the supporting evidence. Most of his interpreters treat this argument in Part I as Hume's major argument. In Part II, Hume presents several subsidiary arguments that are more evidential than philosophical; he attempts to show why in practice the evidence against any alleged miracle will always outweigh the putative supporting evidence.

Having shown what Hume did not intend to argue, I can now begin my exposition of his major argument against miracles as it appears in Part I of his essay.

HUME'S MAJOR ARGUMENT

The best way to begin is to let Hume speak for himself. He writes:

A miracle is a violation of the laws of nature; and as a firm and unalterable experience has established these laws, the proof against a miracle, from the very nature of the fact, is as entire as any argument from experience can possibly be imagined. . . . Nothing is esteemed a miracle, if it ever happens in the common course of nature. It is no miracle that a man, seemingly in good health, should die of a sudden; because such a kind of death, though more unusual than any other, has yet been frequently observed to happen. But it is a miracle that a dead man should come to

---

[10]Keith Ward, "Miracles and Testimony," *Religious Studies* 21 (1985): 134.

life; because that has never been observed in any age or country.[11] There must, therefore, be a uniform experience against every miraculous event, otherwise the event would not merit the appellation. And as a uniform experience amounts to a proof, there is here a direct and full proof, from the nature of the fact, against the existence of any miracle; nor can such a proof be destroyed, or the miracle rendered credible, but by an opposite proof, which is superior.[12]

As we've already learned, Hume could not be saying that violations of the laws of nature are impossible; such a claim would have contradicted his view of such laws. Hence, he is not saying that miracles are impossible. What then is his point?

To begin with, Hume's declaration that miracles are violations of the laws of nature should be understood as a hypothetical statement. If a person believes in miracles, then he must also believe in natural laws that those miracles violate. If someone believes that x is a miracle, he must regard x as an exception to or a violation of the natural order of things. Richard Purtill summarizes Hume's point here nicely:

> If anyone holds that there is no natural order, that the universe is chaotic, that the apparent order and understandability of the universe is an illusion, then that person can give no meaning to the idea of miracle, for that idea depends on contrast. Before there can be exceptions there must be rules or patterns for them to be exceptions of.[13]

On this interpretation, it is not Hume who is presuming the existence of natural laws for which there may or may not be exceptions. The theist himself must make this assumption as a precondition of his claim that miracles occur. Natural laws function as a necessary condition for miracles. But once we assume the existence of this natural order—as the theist must do—we discover that the probability of any supposed exception to that natural order will always be lower than the probability that the law has not been violated.

First, Hume cleverly manipulates the theist into admitting that he (the theist) must believe in a natural order since without such an order, there cannot be any way of recognizing exceptions to the order. Then, Hume hammers the theist with the obvious fact that the probability for the theist's alleged violations of natural laws must always be much less than the probability that the exception has not occurred. In Hume's words,

> The plain consequence is (and it is a general maxim worthy of our attention),"That no testimony is sufficient to establish a miracle, unless the testimony be of such a kind, that its falsehood would be more miraculous than the fact, which it endeavours to establish; and even in that case there is a mutual destruction of arguments, and the superior only gives us an assurance suitable to that degree of force, which remains, after deducting the inferior." When anyone tells me, that he saw a dead man restored to life, I immediately consider with myself, whether it be

---

[11]Christian readers may feel justified in thinking that, in this sentence at least, Hume begs a question or two.

[12]Hume, *An Enquiry*, pp. 114–15.

[13]Richard Purtill, *Thinking About Religion* (Englewood Cliffs, N.J.: Prentice-Hall, 1978), pp. 68–69.

more probable, that this person should either deceive or be deceived, or that the fact, which he relates, should really have happened. I weigh the one miracle against the other; and according to the superiority, which I discover, I pronounce my decision, and always reject the greater miracle. If the falsehood of his testimony would be more miraculous, than the event which he relates; then, and not till then, can he pretend to command my belief or opinion.[14]

Suppose you and I had been part of the small group present in the room where the wounded Abraham Lincoln had been taken after being shot in Ford's Theater. Imagine that we watch the unconscious president's condition gradually worsen until he stops breathing. You may even have been the person who checked for a pulse or heart beat. There was no question about it: Lincoln was dead. But then suppose that a few days later, you and I meet on a Washington street and you hear me excitedly report that Lincoln is alive! "What makes you say that?" you ask. And I respond by saying that I and others who knew him personally have seen him and have heard him talk and have even touched his body to be sure we were not hallucinating. The natural reaction to such a testimony would be to find some explanation other than the claim that a dead man had returned to life. Perhaps this is some kind of macabre joke that suggests disturbing possibilities about the state of my mental health; possibly I hallucinated under the influence of some chemical; or perhaps my total devotion to Lincoln made it impossible for me to face reality.

Disbelief, skepticism, and the search for alternative answers are natural human responses to testimony on behalf of any event such as the one described above. Now, I take it, this is Hume's point. It is always easier to believe that those who testify on behalf of such an event are mistaken than it is to believe that the event really took place. Over the history of the human species, a great deal of evidence has accumulated to the effect that dead people stay dead. The effect of this accumulated testimony from the past is so strong as to override claims to the contrary.

Instead of arguing that miracles are impossible, Hume's position, then, is that it is unreasonable ever to believe that a miracle has occurred. Since the laws of nature are established by such strong testimony, the evidence against any alleged exception to that natural order is also very strong. After all, no principle would be regarded as a law of nature unless humans had repeatedly observed things happening in accordance with the law. Therefore, it seems that one could never be reasonable in believing that a violation of such a law had taken place. As C. Stephen Evans puts it,

What is the intrinsic probability of a miracle? According to Hume, it is extremely low, as low as one could imagine. The probability of an event, he says, is determined by the frequency with which it has been observed to occur. A miracle, as an exception to the laws of nature, must then be the least likely event possible. . . . Hume is in effect claiming that miracles are by definition so improbable that even the most impressive testimony would merely balance the counterevidence provided by the improbability of the miracle. Only testimony so strong that its falsehood

---

[14]Hume, *Enquiry*, pp., 115–16.

would itself be more miraculous than the alleged miracle would convince Hume of a miracle.[15]

All this means that

the probability that a violation of a natural law has occurred depends on the evidence for and against it. The evidence for miracles takes the form of testimony. But this testimony, by the nature of the case, as testimony that there has been a violation of a natural law, must be far less than the "uniform experience" of men that established the natural law in the first place. Otherwise there would be no natural law and no occasion to speak of a violation. Consequently, no evidence can be sufficient to establish or even make probable the occurrence of a violation of a natural law.[16]

Hume's first argument against miracles can be summarized in the following claims. (1) The probability of any testimony in support of the occurrence of an alleged miracle must, by the nature of things, always be lower than the probability that attaches to the relevant law of nature. (2) In fact, the relative probability of the alleged miracle is so low in comparison to the probability of the relevant law as to approach zero. (3) Given these relative probabilities plus the fact that the wise man or woman will always proportion his or her faith to the relative probabilities, the wise person will reject the testimony on behalf of the alleged miracle on the grounds that it is more probable that the witnesses were mistaken or lying than that the event occurred.

At this stage, we are forced to admit that Hume appears to have mounted a powerful assault against belief in miracles. But of course we have heard only one side of the argument. It is now time to see what objections can be raised to Hume's analysis.

A RESPONSE TO HUME'S MAJOR ARGUMENT

Replies to Hume's first argument have drawn attention to at least four weaknesses in his presentation. I present them in what I regard as an order of increasing significance.

1. Hume's argument assumes that any person who comes to believe in a miracle does so on the basis of testimony. It is unfortunate that he slights the possibility that someone might observe a miracle directly. Were this to happen, of course, it would avoid whatever problems might arise in connection with our believing the testimony of other people. Of course, were such direct experience of a miracle to be claimed, it would always be possible for Hume to challenge the veridicality of the experience.

2. Hume's argument also ignores the many times when direct testimony against what has been the uniform experience of a people turns out to have been correct. British philosopher C. D. Broad made this point more than seventy years ago:

---

[15]C. Stephen Evans, *Philosophy of Religion* (Downers Grove, Ill.: InterVarsity Press, 1985), pp. 111–12.

[16]J. Kellenberger, "Miracles," *International Journal for Philosophy of Religion* 10 (1979): 147.

Clearly many propositions have been accounted laws of nature because of an invariable experience in their favor, then exceptions have been observed, and finally these propositions have ceased to be regarded as laws of nature. But the first reported exception was, to anyone who had not personally observed it, in precisely the same position as a story of a miracle, if Hume be right. Those, then, to whom the first exception was reported ought to have rejected it, and gone on believing in the alleged law of nature. Yet, if the report of the first exception makes *no* difference to their belief in the law, their state of belief will be precisely the same when a second exception is reported as it was on the first occasion. Hence, if the first report ought to make no difference to their belief in the law, neither ought the second. So that it would seem on Hume's theory that if, up to a certain time, I and everyone else have always observed A to be followed by B, then no amount of testimony from the most trustworthy persons that they have observed A not followed by B ought to have the least effect on my belief in the law. . . . If scientists had actually proceeded in this way, some of the most important natural laws would never have been discovered.[17]

Clearly, Broad is saying, the advancement of science itself would be hindered by a universal skepticism toward alleged counterinstances of what are regarded as laws of nature. If it is important that scientists exhibit some degree of openmindedness toward such claims, perhaps the rest of us should resist the tendency to toss all such claims aside.

3. Hume was wrong when he suggested that miracles are supported only by *direct* evidence cited in the testimony of people who claim to have witnessed them. There can also be important *indirect* evidence for miracles. Even if some person (Jones, let us say) did not observe some alleged miracle (thus making him dependent on the testimony of others who did), Jones may still be able to see abiding effects of the miracle. Suppose the miracle in question concerns the healing of a person who has been blind for years. Jones may be dependent on the testimony of others that they saw the healing occur, but perhaps Jones is now able to discern for himself that the formerly blind person can now see. The situation here is analogous to that of someone who hears testimony that a tornado has ravaged his city. Since he was not an eyewitness to the storm, he is dependent on the testimony of eyewitnesses who were there. But when this person arrives on the scene and sees the incredible devastation—cars on top of houses, other houses blown apart, trees uprooted—all this functions as indirect evidence to confirm the eyewitness testimony of others. In this way, certain effects of a miracle that exist after the event can serve as indirect evidence that the event happened.

C. D. Broad appealed to such indirect evidence in some comments he once made about the resurrection of Christ:

We have testimony to the effect that the disciples were exceedingly depressed at the time of the Crucifixion; that they had extremely little faith in the future; and that, after a certain time, this depression disappeared, and they believed that they had evidence that their Master

---

[17]C. D. Broad, "Hume's Theory of the Credibility of Miracles," *Proceedings of the Aristotelian Society* 17 (1916–17): 77–94. I quote from the reprint of Broad's essay in *Human Understanding: Studies in the Philosophy of David Hume,* ed. Alexander Sesonske and Noel Fleming (Belmont, Calif.: Wadsworth, 1965), p. 91.

had risen from the dead. Now none of these alleged facts is in the least odd or improbable, and we have therefore little ground for not accepting them on the testimony offered us. But having done this, we are faced with the problem of accounting for the facts which we have accepted. What caused the disciples to believe, contrary to their previous conviction, and in spite of their feeling of depression, that Christ had risen from the dead? Clearly, one explanation is that he actually had arisen. And this explanation accounts for the facts so well that we may at least say that the indirect evidence for the miracle is far and away stronger than the direct evidence.[18]

And so it appears that one's belief in some alleged miracle need not be totally dependent on the testimony of others. One can find traces of the event that can confirm such testimony.

4. Finally, critics of Hume have complained that his argument is based on a defective view of probability. For one thing, Hume treats the probability of events in history like miracles in the same way he treats the probability of the recurring events that give rise to the formulation of scientific laws. In the case of scientific laws, probability is tied to the frequency of occurrence; the more times scientists observe similar occurrences under similar conditions, the greater the probability that their formulation of a law is correct. But historical events including miracles are different; the events of history are unique and nonrepeatable. Therefore, treating historical events including miracles with the same notion of probability the scientist uses in formulating his laws ignores a fundamental difference between the two subject matters.[19]

For another thing, as everyone knows, events that are highly improbable can still occur. For example, hitting five consecutive home runs in one major league game is a highly improbable event as is getting two consecutive holes in one in golf. But improbable though they may be, they can still happen.

Moreover, as John King-Farlow and William Niels Christensen point out, "an irregularity relative to the limited sample of our experiences might really be a regularity relative to a vastly larger sample."[20] Imagine a rather small opening (just large enough for a hand and an arm to enter) of what appears to be a container where everything about that container except the opening is hidden from view. We cannot tell if the container is large or small. Suppose, then, that I am asked to make a judgment about the contents of the container by reaching in and withdrawing samples of its contents. Suppose I do this for a while and find that every thing I withdraw from the container is a red marble. Based on the frequency of red marbles relative to my limited sampling, I might appear justified in concluding that it is highly improbable that anything other than red marbles will come out of the container.

But imagine that the container is so large that no matter how many marbles (even red marbles) I pull out of it, the number of marbles (or whatever else may be in the hidden container) remaining is many times the

18Broad, "Hume's Theory," pp. 91–92.

19For more on the logic of historical explanations, see Ronald Nash, *Christian Faith and Historical Understanding* (Grand Rapids: Zondervan, 1984), and Ronald Nash, ed., *Ideas of History* (New York: Dutton, 1969), vol. 2.

20John King-Farlow and William Niels Christensen, *Faith and the Life of Reason* (Dordrecht-Holland: D. Reidel, 1972), p. 50.

number withdrawn. If continued withdrawals begin to produce a large sampling of blue marbles, it is possible that more complete information might lead me to reverse an earlier judgment about the contents of the jar. King-Farlow and Christensen are simply saying that while a particular kind of event might indeed appear irregular and out of the ordinary when compared to a limited sample, the same event might well appear rather normal in the light of a larger sampling. In this way, events that seem miraculous to us might prove—should we ever achieve a more complete and comprehensive understanding of the cosmos—to be quite unexceptional. This argument is not based on an appeal to ignorance. It simply draws attention to one of the perils of reaching hasty conclusions about important matters based on a limited sampling that can be overruled by a larger sampling. Hume's reasoning is inconclusive.

Finally, C. Stephen Evans gives wise counsel when he writes:

> The defender of miracles may claim that whether miracles occur depends largely on whether God exists, what kind of God he is, and what purposes he has. Given enough knowledge of God and his purposes in relation to human history, occurrence of a miracle might be in some situations highly probable, or at least not nearly so improbable as Hume suggests. . . . In the absence of any firm knowledge about God and his purposes, it would still be rash to claim with Hume that the probability of a miracle is vanishingly small. Rather it would appear more reasonable to conclude that it is hard, if not impossible, to estimate the a priori probability of a miracle; and therefore one should try to look at the evidence for miracles with a somewhat open, though cautiously skeptical, mind.[21]

Of course, even Hume recognizes that his major argument against miracles still leaves open the possibility—however slight Hume thought it might be—of a miracle's occurring. This is why he goes on in Part II of his essay to argue against the possibility of evidence or testimony for a miracle ever being sufficient to justify belief that such an event has occurred. But before we look at Hume's four subsidiary arguments, the record should show that his major argument must be judged a failure.

HUME'S FOUR SUBSIDIARY ARGUMENTS

Hume's line of argument in Part I is consistent with the possibility that violations of natural laws occur. "More than this," J. Kellenberger notes, "it allows that evidence could count for such a violation having occurred, and under certain circumstances, establish that one had occurred. Nothing in the argument rules out the in-principle possibility of testimony from so many reliable witnesses that it would overbalance the heretofore 'uniform experience' in support of some natural law."[22] Since Hume recognized this, he saw the need for several additional arguments—evidential or historical in nature—that would slam shut the door on any possible evidence for an alleged violation of a law of nature.

[21]Evans, *Philosophy of Religion*, p. 113.
[22]Kellenberger, "Miracles," p. 147.

The First Argument

Hume begins by showing that we would always have reason to question the competence of any who would seek to serve as witnesses for some alleged miracle. As Hume put it,

> There is not to be found, in all history, any miracle attested by a sufficient number of men, of such unquestioned good-sense, education, and learning, as to secure us against all delusion in themselves; of such undoubted integrity, as to place them beyond all suspicion of any design to deceive others; of such credit and reputation in the eyes of mankind, as to have a great deal to lose in case of their being detected in any falsehood; and at the same time, attesting facts performed in such a public manner and in so celebrated a part of the world, as to render the detection unavoidable: All which circumstances are requisite to give us a full assurance in the testimony of men.[23]

In short, Hume says, whenever people begin to offer testimony on behalf of an alleged miracle, we will find plenty to question in their education, common sense, integrity, or reputation. But read carefully. Hume has not given us an *argument*; he has simply offered a dogmatic assertion that turns out to be a sweeping generalization for which no proof could ever be found.[24] Colin Brown makes the proper response to Hume's first argument when he writes:

> Hume's first argument complained of the lack of discerning, competent witnesses. But the qualifications that he demands of such witnesses are such as would preclude the testimony of anyone without a Western university education, who lived outside a major cultural center in Western Europe prior to the sixteenth century, and who was not a public figure. A hostile critic of Hume might be tempted to think that Hume had formulated his qualifications not so much with the need to define qualities desirable in a witness but with the preconceived aim of deliberately excluding any testimony issuing from the ancient world.[25]

Of course, Brown, adds, "it is questionable whether Hume would ever have accepted any testimony to the miraculous that met his stringent conditions."[26]

Hume's first criterion would do more than rule out testimonies to miracles; it would also—if applied rigorously—make doubtful most of what we believe about the history of the world prior, say, to the sixteenth century. Hume seems to be engaged in drawing the boundaries to fit his prejudices.

The Second Argument

Hume refers next to the human tendency to gossip and exaggerate the truth. He writes:

---

[23] Hume, *Enquiry*, pp. 116–17.

[24] If the reader doubts my claim, think a bit about the people in the entire history of the human race who have testified to the existence of miracles and then figure out how one could come up with sufficient evidence to show that every one of those people suffered from the failings Hume attributes to them.

[25] Colin Brown, *Miracles and the Critical Mind* (Grand Rapids: Eerdmans, 1984), p. 97.

[26] Ibid.

The many instances of forged miracles, and prophecies, and supernatural events, which, in all ages, have either been detected by contrary evidence, or which detect themselves by their absurdity, prove sufficiently the strong propensity of mankind to the extraordinary and the marvellous, and ought reasonably to beget a suspicion against all relations of this kind. . . . The pleasure of telling a piece of news so interesting, of propagating it, and of being the first reporters of it, spreads the intelligence. And this is so well known, that no man of sense gives attention to these reports, till he find them confirmed by some greater evidence. Do not the same passions, and others still stronger, include the generality of mankind to believe and report, with the greatest vehemence and assurance, all religious miracles?[27]

In other words, Hume claims, people are often fascinated by wondrous stories, even to the point of accepting fantastic claims that, in more sober moments, they would quickly dismiss. This is especially true, Hume thinks, of religious believers who often show themselves to be victims of vanity and fanaticism.

There is little point in denying that religious believers may be as prone to exaggerate the truth in the pursuit of a good cause as some secular humanists. But Hume's claim simply cannot stand as a general test. As Colin Brown points out, "Not all people are credulous and gullible with a natural penchant for embroidering the truth. There are plenty of others who are natural sceptics. As a general criterion for assessing testimony to the unusual and miraculous, Hume's argument will not do, as it stands. In assessing any given testimony, we have to assess the character and motivation of the testifier."[28]

From the fact that some people are susceptible to exaggeration and untrue claims, absolutely nothing follows as to the occurrence or nonoccurrence of miracles. The most that Hume's claim does is point out the importance of giving every claim about an alleged miracle careful examination. Few contemporary believers in miracles would have it any other way. But, as Brown objects, "it is irresponsible to brand all religious believers as naturally prone to disseminate untruth whether wittingly or unwittingly."[29]

One final point needs to be made. Though Hume is correct in noting the extent to which our nonrational nature can lead us to accept miracle-claims uncritically, he fails to mention what should also be obvious, namely, that the nonrational nature of unbelievers can produce an uncritical attitude that rejects miracles.

The Third Argument

In this third argument, Hume notes that most reports of miracles originate among people who are uneducated and uncivilized. According to Hume, miracles "are observed chiefly to abound among ignorant and barbarous nations," and whenever civilized people affirm belief in the miraculous, those beliefs have come "from ignorant and barbarous ances-

---

[27] Hume, *Enquiry*, pp. 118–19.
[28] Colin Brown, "History, Criticism and Faith," in *History and the Believer*, ed. Colin Brown (Downers Grove, Ill.: InterVarsity Press, 1976), p. 160.
[29] Brown, *Miracles and the Critical Mind*, p. 97.

tors, who transmitted them with the inviolable sanction and authority, which always attend received opinions."[30]

Once again, we find, Hume offers a sweeping generalization unsupported by evidence. Even worse, his argument is a non sequitur, as David Cook so ably points out. "The mere fact," Cook writes, "that stupid people easily believe what is false does not mean that they never believe anything that is true, or that more sensible people do not believe truly and properly in miracles. Merely because people are barbarous does not mean that they do not believe true things. Perhaps Hume makes too much of the supposed ignorance and barbarity of these nations."[31] After all, even though the people who lived in biblical times lacked knowledge of modern science, they knew enough to question anyone who might claim that a dead man had been resurrected or that a virgin had given birth to a child. Unbelievers in first-century Jerusalem rejected claims about the resurrection of Christ as intensely as twentieth-century unbelievers.

The Fourth Argument

Finally, Hume points to the fact that competing religions attempt to support the truth of their faith by appealing to their own miracles. More attention needs to be paid to the fact that such rival claims cancel each other out. If two or more competing religions offer miracles in support of their claims, it should be obvious that miracles become worthless as a possible basis of support for the truth of any religion. Christians claim that certain miracles prove the truth of their religion. But other religions have their own miracles that supposedly prove the truth of these other faiths. But two contradictory religions cannot both be true. Hence the miracles of religion A, if actual, would count against the actuality of the other religion's miracles and against the truth of the other religion (B). But religion B's miracles would likewise discredit the miracles of religion A. Therefore, Hume says, "in destroying a rival system, it likewise destroys the credit of those miracles, on which that system was established; so that all the prodigies of different religions are to be regarded as contrary facts, and the evidence of these prodigies, whether weak or strong, as opposite to each other."[32]

This is probably the strongest of Hume's four subsidiary arguments. A proper response will begin by pointing out that Hume's conclusion would follow only in cases where alleged miracles in two competing religions provide support for beliefs in those religions that are both incompatible and essential to those faiths. Richard Purtill explains:

> What would threaten the argument from miracles for the truth of Christianity would be genuine miracles worked in opposition to Christian claims or in support of incompatible claims. If, for instance, a Moslem holy man raised a man from the dead in order to persuade Christians that Mohammed's revelation had superseded that of Christ, this would be a case of genuine incompatibility. However, so far from any case of this

---

[30]Hume, *Enquiry*, p. 119.
[31]David Cook, *Thinking About Faith* (Grand Rapids: Zondervan, 1986), p. 110.
[32]Hume, *Enquiry*, pp. 121–22.

kind being established, it is hard to show that any case of this kind has even been claimed.[33]

Richard Swinburne has offered a similar counterargument:

In fact evidence for a miracle "wrought in one religion" is only evidence against the occurrence of a miracle "wrought in another religion" if the two miracles, if they occurred, would be evidence for propositions of the two religious systems incompatible with each other. It is hard to think of pairs of alleged miracles of this type. If there were evidence for a Roman Catholic miracle which was evidence for the doctrine of transubstantiation and evidence for a Protestant miracle which was evidence against it, here we would have a case of the conflict of evidence which Hume claims occurs generally with alleged miracles. . . . Most alleged miracles, if they occurred as reported, would show at most the power of a god or gods and their concern for the needs of men, and little more specific in the way of doctrine. A miracle wrought in the context of the Hindu religion and one wrought in the context of the Christian religion will not in general tend to show that specific details of their systems are true, but, at most, that there is a god concerned with the needs of those who worship, which is a proposition accepted in both systems.[34]

The New Testament does not teach that God's goodness is restricted only to believers.[35] There is no reason for a Christian to suppose that God might not reveal his glory and power in some miraculous way to non-Christians.

CONCLUSION

Upon careful analysis, then, there is good reason to conclude that neither Hume's major argument nor his subsidiary arguments constitute grounds for taking miracles any less seriously than informed believers have since the beginning of the Christian church. What I mean here is that informed religious believers will always recognize the difference between faith and credulity. The apostle Paul recognized the right of people to evidence that would support his claim and the claims of others that Christ had indeed risen from the dead. That is why Paul provided evidence in the fifteenth chapter of 1 Corinthians. No doubt this is why writers of the Gospel accounts of the Resurrection provided their own little details that serve as evidence.[36] Few informed Christians accept miracle-claims without taking a careful look at the supporting evidence. Responsible believers like this *and* the careful New Testament witnesses to such miracles as the resurrection of Christ bear no resemblance to the ignorant, uncivilized, untruthful, and fanatical miracle-mongers ridiculed in Hume's "arguments." If there is an overpowering case against belief in miracles, it is not to be found in Hume's famous essay.

---

[33] Purtill, *Thinking About Religion*, p. 74. The rest of Purtill's discussion is worth careful study. See pages 74ff.

[34] Richard Swinburne, *The Concept of Miracle* (London: Macmillan, 1970), pp. 60–61.

[35] See such passages as Matthew 5:43ff.; Acts 14:16ff.; Romans 13:1ff.; and 1 Peter 2:13ff.

[36] I go over some of this evidence in a later chapter.

For Further Exploration—Chapter Sixteen

1. Discuss why it makes sense *not* to interpret Hume's essay in a way that has him arguing that miracles are impossible.
2. Consider the question, Will the future be like the past? Discuss its relevance for scientific laws.
3. Evaluate attempts to define a miracle as a violation of a law of nature.
4. Explain what the chapter means by describing Hume's attack on miracles as *epistemological* in nature.
5. Summarize Hume's major argument against miracles.
6. Outline the major objections to this argument.
7. Evaluate the first three of Hume's subsidiary arguments.
8. Summarize Swinburne's answer to Hume's fourth subsidiary argument.

Chapter 17

OTHER QUESTIONS ABOUT MIRACLES

With Hume's essay out of the way, I can turn my attention to other basic questions about miracles. Several of these questions concern the relationship between miracles and the laws of nature. As we saw, Hume defined a miracle as a violation of the laws of nature. Is it wise for theists to begin with Hume's definition and go on from there? Or should theists look for a more adequate definition of the term?

A PRELIMINARY POINT

I want to begin by drawing attention to an important point often overlooked when philosophers and theologians start arguing over miracles. Jerry Gill reminds us

> that the concept of miracles is not derived from the Judeo-Christian Scriptures. The Bible does not speak of miracles or laws of nature, but rather of God as the one who orders nature and is active in all events. The most common biblical terms are "mighty acts" (extraordinary as distinguished from ordinary events) and "signs" (vehicles of divine significance). The notion of miracles as violations of the laws of nature is a modern, intellectual one, developed by religious thinkers influenced by Greek philosophers and scientific investigations. This is not to say that it is a useless or false notion, but it is to say that perhaps the whole question of the possibility of miracles needs to be restructured.[1]

I agree. The modern notion of a miracle does not appear in the Bible; nor does Scripture contain a theory about the nature of scientific law.

---

[1]Jerry H. Gill, *Faith in Dialogue* (Waco, Tex.: Word, 1985), pp. 33–34.

According to Gill, it is entirely possible for some person to believe that Jesus Christ rose from the dead and for this same person to be puzzled by what he hears philosophers saying in their technical debates about miracles. Such a person might well say to the philosophers, "I have no idea what you're talking about; all I know is that I believe that the Resurrection really happened in history!" It is far more important for our nonphilosopher to believe *that* than for him to recognize that the Resurrection is a member of the class of things philosophers call miracles. The important thing is that these remarkable events occurred; less important is what we happen to call them (miracles) and how we understand the relation between miracles and the laws of nature.

Having said all this, I am still a philosopher writing a book about the philosophy of religion. For anyone in my situation, it's a little late in the game to pretend that the philosophical concept of miracle doesn't exist or that the long debate over the issues I'll be considering never happened. But it helps nonetheless to realize how distant the modern debate is from the original and biblical context.

GOD AND THE LAWS OF NATURE

In the last chapter, I explained Hume's contribution to our modern understanding of the laws of nature. There is a distinctly theistic slant on the laws of nature that is perfectly respectable. Once theists recognize this point, it throws new light on the relationship between God and the laws of nature.

Theists believe (or should believe) that God created the laws of nature.[2] Scientist Richard Bube rules out all such phrases as "God intervenes in the natural order," "God violates the laws of nature," or even "God works through natural law." For Bube,

> The natural order exists only because God is constantly active in upholding it. God does not use natural processes as if they existed without him. God does not take advantage of natural laws to accomplish his will as if the laws existed without him. We see immediately why the question "Can God intervene in a world ruled by orderly laws?" is meaningless. There *is* no world ruled by orderly laws except that one constantly maintained in existence by the activity of God.[3]

According to Bube, it is wrong to think of miracles as results of divine intervention in the natural order. Both as a scientist and as a Christian, Bube is uncomfortable with the view that the laws of nature can be interfered with. As far as God is concerned, there are no miracles. Miracles are a result of the way in which humans interpret things that God does naturally. For God to raise a human from the dead does not require any more extraordinary effort

---

[2] A point of clarification: the phrase *law of nature* may mean either the scientist's formulation of what he regards as the order of nature or the natural order itself. In this chapter, for the most part, I mean the latter.

[3] Richard H. Bube, *The Human Quest* (Waco, Tex.: Word, 1971), p. 28. Malcolm Jeeves compares the world to a television set. The images we see are those of a lawlike, orderly universe; but when the plug is pulled, everything disappears, that is, stops existing. See Malcolm A. Jeeves, *The Scientific Enterprise and Christian Faith* (London: Tyndale Press, 1969), pp. 23–24.

or power than anything else God does. Bube admits that miracles will appear to violate the laws of nature as we currently understand them or will appear as extremely improbable coincidences of diverse elements. But informed theists will understand that the extraordinary event does not really violate the divinely ordained order of things.

Philosopher Edward John Carnell made a similar point in a book published in 1948. Carnell wrote:

> The Christian defines nature as what God does with His creation, and a natural law as but a mathematically exact description upon the part of man of how God has elected to order His creation. For the Christian there are no "absolute natural laws," but only the mind of God. From man's point of view, the regularity of the universe is called "law," but from God's point of view it is "will."[4]

When we grasp the point made by Carnell and Bube, when we realize

> that the very existence of the world from moment to moment depends upon the creative and sustaining power of God, that no natural law has any power of its own to continue, that no "expected" circumstance has any ability to bring itself into being, we come to the conclusion that God's activity in a miracle is not qualitatively different from God's activity in natural phenomena. In bringing to pass the law of gravity or the law of electromagnetic radiation, God acts freely and continuously. He is not constrained by these laws, as if he had to meddle with them to produce a different result. At rare times and in accordance with his specific purpose, he acts freely to produce what the world interprets as a miracle.[5]

For reasons like these, Bube concludes,

> miracles pose no problem in the modern encounter between science and Christian faith when it is realized that God is always acting freely in both the natural occurrences of everyday life and in those special and unique occurrences of particular religious significance that we recognize as miracles. Thus, miracles are not some kind of interference by God in the normal course of events, as though events would go on in their own way without him if he didn't intervene, but a particular way in which God's unlimited free activity manifests itself.[6]

Clearly, Christians believe, God can act in ways that appear out of the ordinary, as we see things. But such an extraordinary action should not be regarded as a violation of any law of nature. As we've seen, the laws of nature are not rules that prescribe how God must act; they are simply expressions of how God has willed to act. When exceptional events occur, it means only that God has willed something different; but to compare this to what happens when a human being breaks a law is to set up a false analogy.

---

[4] Edward John Carnell, *An Introduction to Christian Apologetics* (Grand Rapids: Eerdmans, 1948), p. 251.

[5] Bube, *Human Quest*, pp. 115–16.

[6] Ibid., p. 130.

ANOTHER FEATURE OF MIRACLES

As we've seen, a miracle will appear to humans either as an exception to the laws of nature or as an extremely improbable coincidence of more ordinary elements. But this is hardly all there is to a miracle. As Bube says, in order to qualify as a miracle, an event must also "have a deeper significance than simply being a rare and unusual event for the persons involved, usually related to their religious perspective."[7]

First, a miracle must be the sort of occurrence that catches our attention. This is accomplished by its extraordinary nature. While God can undoubtedly bring about miracles that are unobserved, such events will hardly function as miracles until they get someone's attention. Now, we begin to see that events that qualify as miracles must also have religious significance. God does not bring about miracles to entertain people. A miraculous event must have the potential of inducing faith or trust or fear or awe or worship. Genuine miracles always fulfill some legitimate religious function.

All this leads Carnell to define a miracle as follows: "A miracle is an extraordinary visible act of divine power, wrought by the effective agency of the will of God, through secondary means accompanied by valid, covenantal revelation, and having as its final cause the vindication of the righteousness of the triune God."[8]

What this means can be summarized in three points:

> First, *God* is the author of the miracle. This sets our definition squarely in the center of the Christian world-view. Secondly, the means used are the same type He uses to order any phenomenon. This sets our definition squarely in the realm of science, and relieves the scientist of his false notion that miracles are inexplicable, mysterious, and beyond rational explanation. Thirdly, the end of a miracle is to seal and sign the whole counsel of God as found in Holy Writ. This sets our definition squarely in the picture of our need for personal happiness and immortality.[9]

The fact that any alleged miracle must have the kind of religious significance described above makes it possible for informed and responsible theists to ignore a large number of supposed miracles that appear frivolous or spiritually insignificant. Perhaps this point also suggests a way in which alleged miracles can be ranked in order of importance. If so, this would clearly give priority to a small group of miracles mentioned in the Old and New Testaments, e.g., the Exodus, the Incarnation, the Resurrection, and so on.

THE NOTION OF COINCIDENCE-MIRACLE

Earlier in this chapter, I said that a miracle will be an event that either appears to violate the laws of nature as we currently understand them[10] or

---

[7] Ibid., p. 115.

[8] Carnell, *Christian Apologetics*, p. 249.

[9] Ibid., pp. 249–50.

[10] In case the reader was not paying attention earlier, the key word in this clause is *appears*. I have already stated repeatedly that it is a mistake to regard a miracle as a genuine violation of or an exception to the laws of nature that are only laws of God.

appears as an extremely improbable coincidence of other conditions and events. While I have said much about the first disjunct, it is time that I explain the second.

In the view of a number of recent writers, an event may be regarded as a miracle if it exhibits no features that appear to violate the natural order. A widely discussed example of this second kind of miracle appears in an article by philosopher R. F. Holland. Holland wrote:

> A child riding his toy motor-car strays on to an unguarded railway crossing near his house and a wheel of his car gets stuck down the side of one of the rails. An express train is due to pass with the signals in its favor and a curve in the track makes it impossible for the driver to stop the train in time to avoid any obstruction he might encounter on the crossing. The mother coming out of the house to look for her child sees him on the crossing and hears the train approaching. She runs forward shouting and waving. The little boy remains seated in his car, looking downward, engrossed in the task of pedaling it free. The brakes of the train are applied and it comes to rest a few feet from the child. The mother thanks God for the miracle; which she never ceases to think of as such, although as she in due course learns, there was nothing supernatural about the manner in which the brakes of the train came to be applied. The driver had fainted, for a reason which had nothing to do with the presence of the child on the line, and the brakes were applied automatically as his hand ceased to exert pressure on the control lever. He fainted on this particular afternoon because his blood pressure had risen after an exceptionally heavy lunch during which he had quarrelled with a colleague, and the change in blood pressure caused a clot of blood to be dislodged and circulate. He fainted at the time when he did on the afternoon in question because this was the time at which the coagulation in his blood stream reached the brain.[11]

I suggest that under the circumstances described in Holland's example, not even the most eloquent secular humanist would have luck persuading the relieved and thankful mother that she had been witness to anything less than a miracle, even though the entire event is explicable without any necessary reference to divine intervention or anything remotely resembling a violation of the natural order. Holland's article helped to draw attention to the fact that an event need not appear to violate the natural order to be considered a miracle. These so-called coincidence-miracles are manifestations of God's causal intervention in human affairs in ways that do not involve any apparent disruption of the natural order. As Kellenberger describes them, coincidence-miracles "are rare coincidences that, when seen against a religious background, have religious significance. As coincidences they are natural events and wholly answerable to natural explanation. Yet they retain the nature of the miraculous."[12] Such events are candidates for the class of miracles because of the way disparate happenings come together in a fortuitous manner at a time of crisis. What is crucial to the notion of a

---

[11] R. F. Holland, "The Miraculous," in *Readings in the Philosophy of Religion: An Analytic Approach*, ed. Baruch A. Brody (Englewood Cliffs, N.J.: Prentice-Hall, 1974), p. 451.

[12] J. Kellenberger, "Miracles," *International Journal for Philosophy of Religion* 10 (1979): 155.

coincidence-miracle is the *timing* or coming together of several events, each of which by itself is quite unexceptional.

Coincidence-miracles are consistent with the point made earlier that all of the natural order is under God's direct and ongoing control. God can be responsible for a religiously significant event even though its occurrence was not a result of anything that appears to be a direct intervention with the natural order. Devout and perceptive believers may be correct in their belief that a remarkable instance of healing from a deadly disease following surgery and medication was a work of God.

One of the negative things about so-called coincidence-miracles is the fact that they are often apologetically inconclusive. At least this is David Basinger's claim when he writes:

> Whether an event is awe-producing is a relative issue—relative to the psychological perspective of each individual or group of individuals making the judgment. In other words, once the awe-producing timing or sequencing of a direct act of God becomes the criterion for determining whether it is miraculous, the identification of a miracle becomes a very subjective matter—i.e., it seems to follow that a theist can only affirm that a given occurrence is miraculous to him.[13]

Though it is hard to disagree with Basinger's verdict, we would be wise not to take it too far. As we will see, there is a subjective side to the judgments people make about most miracles. Even the New Testament says as much. In Jesus' parable of Lazarus and the rich man in Luke 16, both the rich man and Lazarus the beggar die. But the rich man, finding himself in hell and wishing to warn his five brothers of the similar fate awaiting them, begs Abraham to return Lazarus to life so that he might deliver the warning in a way likely to produce results. Jesus' parable ends with the following words (vv. 27–31):

> He [the rich man] answered, "Then I beg you, father, send Lazarus to my father's house, for I have five brothers. Let him warn them, so that they will not also come to this place of torment." Abraham replied, "They have Moses and the Prophets; let them listen to them." "No, father Abraham," he said, "but if someone from the dead goes to them, they will repent." He [Abraham] said to him, "If they do not listen to Moses and the Prophets, they will not be convinced even if someone rises from the dead."

Human nature being what it is, the various noetic and psychological factors that affect belief mean that some will persist in a state of unbelief, regardless of how extraordinary some experience may be.

Some have wondered if we might someday discover that all miracles, even those that appear to be exceptions to the natural order, were really coincidence-miracles. This appears possible since our knowledge of the *real* order of nature is fallible and incomplete. But Colin Brown offers a negative answer to this question. He admits that some biblical miracles do show the presence of natural factors coming together at just the right time. The plagues in Egypt might be one example. Also, he notes, "the parting of the

---

[13]David Basinger, "Christian Theism and the Concept of Miracles: Some Epistemological Perplexities," *Southern Journal of Philosophy* 18 (1980): 148–49.

Red Sea was caused by 'a strong east wind' blowing all night (Exodus 14:21). The providential provision of manna and quails likewise has a natural side to it." However, Brown points out, other miracles in the Bible involve no such natural factors. One example stands out. Clearly, Brown writes, "an event like the resurrection of Jesus involves more than a series of naturally explicable circumstances."[14]

We must conclude this brief look at coincidence-miracles by admitting the need for caution or some degree of tentativeness. It would be rash to see the hand of God in every set of fortuitous circumstances. But for anyone holding to a Christian view of God and the world, it would appear foolish to suppose that truly remarkable events in which otherwise normal occurrences come together at a time of crisis in a way that has deep religious significance, especially following a prayer or cry for divine aid, are not acts of God. Perhaps coincidence-miracles point out the extent to which our identification of miracles is person-relative. But news like this should hardly be surprising to anyone who has read the rest of this book.

SOME CONTEMPORARY OBJECTIONS TO MIRACLES

Contempory objections to miracles are often just restatements of Hume's arguments noted in the last chapter. Once in a while, one does encounter arguments novel enough and worthy enough to merit attention. In this section of the chapter, I'll examine three such objections.

Does a Belief in Miracles Entail Chaos in Nature?

Jerry Gill provides a nice summary of this line of thought. He writes:

> It is argued that if the notion of miracles is allowed there can be no such thing as science, since the latter depends upon the assumption of the uniformity of nature. In other words, if it is possible for nature's basic patterns to be interrupted, then it becomes impossible to establish any causal inferences and general laws, since one would never know when a miracle would be in operation. Besides, how would we tell the difference between a supernatural event and a simple freak of nature? In short, the notion of miracle opens the door to scientific chaos, which means no science at all.[15]

It is also possible to extend this line of thinking and use it to allege an inconsistency in the position of any theist who believes both in miracles and in the kind of natural law theodicy described in Part 4 of this book. In my explanation of the natural law theodicy, I pointed out the importance of God's allowing humans to grow and exercise their free will in a lawlike, orderly universe. Is not the existence of miracles inconsistent with the kind of lawlike universe required by a natural law theodicy? And, as Gill's account brings out, does not the existence of miracles entail so much chaos and uncertainty in nature that science becomes impossible?

The first steps toward providing an answer to this question were taken earlier in this chapter in my discussion of God's relation to the laws of

---

[14]Colin Brown, *That You May Believe* (Grand Rapids: Eerdmans, 1985), p. 72.

[15]Gill, *Faith in Dialogue*, p. 33. For the record, Gill does not accept the argument he describes.

nature. Because the laws of nature are divine laws, it is a mistake to regard miracles as violations of God's laws. Even though a miracle may *appear* to be an exception to the natural order,[16] "God's activity in a miracle," Richard Bube reminds us, "is not qualitatively different from God's activity in natural phenomena."[17] On rare occasions when it suits some specific divine purpose, God is free to bring about what human beings understand as miracles.

It is important at this point for Christians to reject any suggestion that miracles are random events. According to Colin Brown,

> God is not a God of chaos. Miracles are not necessarily unrepeatable events that science cannot explain. The reason why science cannot explain them is not that they do not belong to any order at all, but that they do not belong to the *natural* order. . . . [Miracles like the resurrection of Jesus represent] the incursion of the new order into our present order. Such events defy our human understanding. They do not belong to our present range of experience. From our standpoint they clearly violate what we *know* of nature. But from God's standpoint, according to the New Testament, they have their place as part of God's new creation.[18]

Scientists are constantly seeking theories and laws that have greater applicability and that tie more and more of the natural order into increasingly more comprehensive laws. What humans regard as the laws of nature at different stages in the development of science are a reflection of our best efforts at understanding the ultimate nature of that order. Perhaps those remarkable events we see as miracles are really expressions of the more ultimate natural order that scientists have yet to comprehend.

To make a similar point without referring to something like the ultimate or "deep structure of the universe," I can use the example of a flying airplane. If all we knew were the law of gravity, we'd be justified in thinking that a modern jetliner could never leave the ground. But when that plane passes a certain speed so that the airflow around its wings produces sufficient lift, something that people living centuries ago would have regarded as a miracle occurs. When such a plane leaves the ground and flies, the law of gravity has not been suspended; that is made clear whenever such planes lose sufficient air speed. There are times when the presence of new conditions brings about a situation in which a new law supersedes another law. Those rare and extraordinary events that humans understand as miracles may well be occasions when a new order or the ultimate order becomes manifest in human experience. I believe Colin Brown was trying to say something along these lines when he wrote:

> From the standpoint of our understanding of nature [a miracle] violates our scientific understanding of the world, which is founded on generalizations based on observed, repeated experience. Whereas miracles may be repeated, they have not been repeated in such numbers as to enable scientists to formulate "laws" concerning them. On the other hand, from the standpoint of faith such miracles appear to have their own "laws."

---

[16]One exception to this claim, of course, concerns the so-called coincidence-miracles discussed earlier.

[17]Bube, *Human Quest*, p. 116.

[18]Colin Brown, *That You May Believe*, p. 72.

They represent not the abandonment of all order but the breaking into our present world order of the order of the world to come. The resurrection of Jesus is the prime example of this type of miracle. It presents the greatest instance of God's interfering with nature by introducing the order of the new creation into our present order.[19]

There is no contradiction in assuming, on the one hand, that nature is regular and that the laws of nature are reliable, and arguing, on the other hand, that an irregularity within nature has occurred. The regularities that we attribute to nature could always fall slightly short of total uniformity; that is, we could hold that nature nearly always acts in a regular way. All that prevents us from making correct predictions is the incompleteness of our knowledge. Because we see certain regularities elsewhere in nature, we can easily recognize an irregularity when it appears. Nothing in this position is destructive of science in the sense that it throws open the door to any kind of explanation whatever in cases thought to be miracles. As Stephen Davis explains,

> The only control we either have or need have over proposed explanations of events, once miracles are allowed, is the same control we have, quite apart from miracles, over proposed explanations in science and history in general. We simply accept the most plausible explanations we can find and reject the others. In my view at least, it is far more plausible to hold that God raised Jesus from the dead than to say, for example, that his body inexplicably disappeared or that the Jewish leaders forgot they had removed it.[20]

All of this means that a belief in miracles is compatible with a belief in regularities in the natural order that make science possible or that make a natural law theodicy plausible.

The Improbability of Miracles

At this point, a critic of miracles could concede that while miracles are not impossible, they must certainly be viewed as highly improbable. After all, scientific claims do not achieve the status of law without confirmation from enormous amounts of evidence. Each piece of supporting evidence increases the probability that the law is true and decreases the probability of any counterinstances being observed. Given the extremely low probability that any supposed exception to a scientific law must have, doesn't it make sense to judge the probability of a miracle as so low as to cast doubt on the rationality of persons who believe some miracle has occurred? In such a case, Jerry Gill replies,

> it must be noted that the degree of probability of an event does not, in the final analysis, settle its actuality. Many highly improbable events do actually occur, and it will hardly do for people to object that they *could not* have occurred *because* they were improbable. Whether or not a given event has occurred must be established on the basis of evidence including but going beyond antecedent probabilities.[21]

---

[19]Ibid., p. 73.

[20]Stephen T. Davis, "Is It Possible to Know That Jesus Was Raised From the Dead?" *Faith and Philosophy* 1 (1984): 150.

[21]Gill, *Faith in Dialogue*, p. 33.

It is clear, then, that this particular argument proves nothing.

Can We Know that an Event Was Caused By God?

Even if we encounter an event that is astounding, appears to violate the laws of nature, and has deep religious significance, how could we be sure that such an event was *caused by God*? After all, the causal activity of God is a *sine qua non* of any miracle. If we cannot know God caused the event, how can we know it was a miracle? Humans cannot "see" God actually causing events today. Moreover, theists admit that God's ways are unfathomable; how can they be sure what God would do in this particular instance?

A good answer to this question has been given by William Rowe who, as we remember, describes himself as a friendly atheist. Rowe writes:

> If we already have good reason to believe that God exists and that he exercises providential care over his creation, then we might have good reasons for thinking that a particular [apparent] violation of a law of nature is due to God. For the event itself and the circumstances in which it occurs might be just what one would expect given that God exists and exercises providential care over his creation. Indeed, insofar as we have reasons to believe that God exists and exercises providential care over his creation, the occurrence of miracles now and then might be what one would reasonably expect.[22]

Suppose one is an eyewitness to an extraordinary event that occurs in a religious context,[23] has deep religious significance,[24] is supported by other evidence and/or testimony, and has no plausible natural explanation. When this eyewitness already holds such essential theistic beliefs as that God exists and cares for humans, his confidence that the event was caused by God seems justified. Richard Swinburne draws attention to a well-known distinction between two kinds of explanation.[25] *Scientific explanations* make events intelligible by subsuming the events under general laws. But *personal explanations* account for events in terms of the purposes of some rational being. Suppose we let the letter E stand for any event remarkable enough to be viewed as a possible miracle, Swinburne states. Because God does not have a body,[26] humans cannot see God cause E in the way we might see a baseball player hit four home runs in a row. But, Swinburne continues,

> suppose that E occurs in ways and circumstances otherwise strongly analogous to those in which occur events brought about intentionally by human agents, and that other violations occur in such circumstances. We would then be justified in claiming that E and other such [apparent] violations are, like effects of human actions, brought about by agents, but agents unlike men in not being material objects. This inference would be justified because, if an analogy between effects is strong enough, we are

---

[22]William L. Rowe, *Philosophy of Religion: An Introduction* (Encino, Calif.: Dickenson, 1978), p. 136.

[23]We can suppose, for example, that people are praying for God to act.

[24]We can assume that the event induces faith, reverence, and thanksgiving to God.

[25]See Richard Swinburne, *The Concept of Miracle* (London: Macmillan, 1970), pp. 53ff.

[26]Because Swinburne is thinking generally, his remarks should not be applied to the Incarnation.

always justified in postulating slight difference in causes to account for slight difference in effects.[27]

Obviously, reasoning like this does not produce logical certainty. But that should not be a problem since we are dealing with a subject matter that does not allow logical certainty. This kind of subject matter does permit moral certainty that results from careful reflection about the plausibility of one explanation relative to alternative explanations. The reasoning here is similar to that used by every historian when seeking an explanation for some historical event.[28] Just as no historian can ever prove for certain that his explanation for a particular event is true, no theist can prove that God is the cause for some event thought to be a miracle. But, Stephen Davis argues,

> if a certain event that occurs is scientifically inexplicable and fits well with a given view of God and his aims, it surely is rational for people who hold that view of God and his aims to believe that the event was brought about by God. If there is good reason ahead of time to believe that a miracle-working God exists who is likely in certain circumstances (say after prayers or as aspects of epiphanies or incarnations) to cause events like this one, it seems reasonable to hold (though we cannot prove) that this event was caused by God.[29]

CONCLUSIONS

Conclusions about whether a particular event should be identified as a miracle or not always occur within the context of the world-view held by the people making the judgment. But this is hardly new information. This feature of miracles may drive us back to a closer examination of our own world-views and the competing conceptual systems of nontheists. But this is precisely the point I argued for in Part 1 of this book; and this is precisely what we discovered in our examination of arguments for God's existence and the major argument (from evil) against God's existence. And this is the reason why, in the next chapter, I explore more fully the relationship between world-views and what the holders of those conceptual systems take to be the plausibility of belief in miracles.

For Further Exploration—Chapter Seventeen

1. Explain why Richard Bube thinks it is wrong to define a miracle as a violation of scientific law.
2. Discuss the importance of including religious significance in one's definition of miracle. Can you think of any alleged miracles that this test would preclude?
3. Explain the notion of a coincidence-miracle. What are your thoughts on the subject?
4. Summarize and evaluate the answer of this chapter to the question of how we can know that a supposedly miraculous event is caused by God.

---

[27]Swinburne, *Concept of Miracle*, p. 57.
[28]See chapters 4 and 8 of this book.
[29]Davis, "Is It Possible to Know?" p. 150.

Chapter 18

WORLD-VIEWS AND MIRACLES

One major claim of this book is that every issue investigated in this study needs to be seen in the context of competing world-views. The dispute over miracles is no exception to this rule. Many people find it impossible to believe in miracles because such a belief would be logically incompatible with their world-view, the system by which they approach and interpret all of reality. As David and Randall Basinger explain,

> Miracles do not exist in a vacuum. They function theoretically as a part of the broader theistic conceptual scheme and practically as events in the lives of individual believers. Therefore, any examination of the miraculous cannot be complete until we explore that extent to which miracles can be coherently related to other theistic concepts, beliefs and practices.[1]

John M. Frame is correct when he observes that "the cogency of miracle requires, not a barely theistic, but a full-blown Christian world-view." Moreover, he adds, "miracles are of no evidential value without a theistic presupposition."[2] In the final analysis, the battle over miracles must be fought at the level of competing world-views and the basic presuppositions of those world-views. One's final assessment of the possibility of miracles will be a function of that person's world-view. On the question of miracles, the critical world-view distinction is between Naturalism and *Super*naturalism. In the next section of this chapter, I will explain what Naturalism is and show why a commitment to Naturalism is logically incompatible with a belief

---

[1]David and Randall Basinger, *Philosophy and Miracle, The Contemporary Debate* (Lewiston, N.Y.: Edwin Mellen, 1986), p. 107.

[2]John M. Frame, "Van Til and the Ligonier Apologetic," *Westminster Theological Journal* 47 (1985): 297.

in miracles. I will then suggest some reasons why rational people ought to reject Naturalism.

NATURALISM

As we saw earlier in the book, Naturalism is the belief that the universe is a closed, self-explanatory system. For a naturalist, the universe is analogous to a box. Everything that happens inside the box is caused by or is explicable in terms of other things that exist within the box. *Nothing* (including God) exists outside the box; therefore, nothing outside the box we call the universe or nature can have any causal effect within the box.[3]

As S. D. Gaede explains Naturalism,

> The naturalistic world view rests upon the belief that the material universe is the sum total of reality. To put it negatively, naturalism holds to the proposition that the supernatural, in any form, does not exist. . . .
> The naturalistic world view assumes that the matter or stuff which makes up the universe has never been created but has always existed. This is because an act of creation presupposes the existence of some reality outside of, or larger than, the world order—incompatible with the tenet that the material universe is the sum total of reality. Naturalism normally assumes that always-existing matter has developed into the ordered universe which we see by a blind, timeless process of chance. The human being, as one part of the natural universe, is also the result of matter, time, and chance. Within the context of the naturalistic world view, miracles, as such, do not exist; they are natural events which have yet to be explained.[4]

---

[3]I must devote a rather long footnote to a strange but influential type of *religious* Naturalism that has become prominent in some theological circles. While a religious naturalist may believe that something (God perhaps) exists outside nature (the box), he rejects any possibility that God can exercise any causal influence within the box. The two leading representatives of this religious naturalism in recent years have been Paul Tillich (1885–1965) and Rudolf Bultmann (1884–1976). Both men taught that God is essentially unknowable to the human intellect, a point made clear when one realizes that for them the human intellect cannot comprehend anything beyond the limits of the box. (See Ronald Nash, *The Word of God and the Mind of Man* [Grand Rapids: Zondervan, 1982].) While Tillich used the word *miracle*, he gave the term a meaning consistent with his basically naturalistic approach to reality. Bultmann, of course, claimed that modern men and women simply cannot (or at least should not) believe in the miraculous. (See Ronald Nash, *Christian Faith and Historical Understanding* [Grand Rapids: Zondervan, 1984], chap. 4.) The basic presuppositions of both men's systems are essentially anti-Christian. One further note of clarification is necessary. It is seldom easy to figure out Tillich's position on many issues. While the "god" of Bultmann's Naturalism may be described as existing "outside" the box, Tillich's "god" seems to have been inseparable from the box. That is, Tillich seems to have been something of a panentheist. (See Ronald Nash, ed., *Process Theology* [Grand Rapids: Baker, 1987].) What this meant, for Tillich, is that God and the world are coeternal and interdependent. A panentheistic God needs the world as much as the world needs God. Few panentheists have made much sense on the rare occasions when they attempted to explain the causal interrelationship between God and the world. Tillich was no exception in this regard.

[4]S. D. Gaede, *Where Gods May Dwell* (Grand Rapids: Zondervan, 1985), p. 35. Or as one religious naturalist puts it: "Since the scientific revolution in the seventeenth

One of the better books relating the dispute over miracles to competing world-views is C. S. Lewis's *Miracles*. In that book, Lewis provides his own account of Naturalism:

> What the Naturalist believes is that the ultimate Fact, the thing you can't go behind, is a vast process in space and time which is *going on of its own accord*. Inside that total system every particular event (such as your sitting reading this book) happens because some other event has happened; in the long run, because the Total Event is happening. Each particular thing (such as this page) is what it is because other things are what they are; and so, eventually, because the whole system is what it is. All the things and events are so completely interlocked that no one of them can claim the slightest independence from "the whole show." None of them exists "on its own" or "goes on of its own accord" except in the sense that it exhibits at some particular place and time, that general "existence on its own" or "behaviour of its own accord" which belongs to "Nature" (the great total interlocked event) as a whole. Thus no thoroughgoing Naturalist believes in free will: for free will would mean that human beings have the power of independent action, the power of doing something more or other than what was involved by the total series of events. And any such separate power of originating events is what the Naturalist denies. Spontaneity, originality, action "on its own," is a privilege reserved for "the whole show," which he calls *Nature*.[5]

A naturalist, then, is someone who believes (or who would believe if he or she were consistent) the following propositions:

1. Only nature exists. By *nature*, I mean (following Stephen Davis) "the sum total of what could in principle be observed by human beings or be studied by methods analogous to those used in the natural sciences."[6] It follows, then, on such a view that the kind of God theists believe in does not exist.[7]

2. Nature has always existed. Naturalists have no room for anything like a doctrine of creation. There never was a time when nature did not exist. Nature does not depend upon anything else for its existence.[8]

3. Nature is characterized by total uniformity. The regularity of nature precludes the occurrence of anything like a miracle. Miracles are impossible because there is nothing outside the box that could bring about any occurrence within nature. But they are also impossible because the regularity and uniformity of the natural order precludes the occurrence of any irregular event.

4. Nature is a deterministic system. The belief in free will presupposes a theory of human agency whereby human beings acting apart from any

---

century the conviction has grown that all events have natural causes, and that the natural sequence of cause and effects is never interrupted" (David Ray Griffin, *A Process Christology* [Philadelphia: Westminster, 1973], p. 22).

[5] C. S. Lewis, *Miracles* (New York: Macmillan, 1960), pp. 6–7.

[6] Stephen T. Davis, "Is It Possible to Know That Jesus Was Raised From the Dead?" *Faith and Philosophy* 1 (1984): 154.

[7] For a necessary qualification to this, see footnote 3 about religious Naturalism.

[8] Compare this to my discussion of the cosmological argument in Part 3. No self-respecting naturalist can tolerate the suggestion that nature (the sum total of all existing things) is contingent.

totally determining causes can themselves function as causes in the natural order. That belief is incompatible with the presuppositions of Naturalism.

5. Nature is a self-explanatory system. Any and every thing that happens within nature must, at least in principle, be explainable in terms of other elements of the natural order. It is never necessary to seek the explanation for any event within nature in something beyond the natural order.

It should be clear by now that any person under the control of naturalistic presuppositions could not consistently believe in the miraculous. For such a person, evidence of putative miracles can never be persuasive. Miracles are impossible *a priori*, that is, before the fact. No arguments on behalf of the miraculous can possibly succeed with such a person. The only proper way to address the unbelief of such a person is to *begin* by challenging his or her Naturalism.

Supernaturalism disagrees with the five identified features of Naturalism.

1. Supernaturalism affirms the existence of a God who transcends nature, who exists "outside the box."

2. Supernaturalism denies the eternity of nature. God created the world freely and *ex nihilo*. The universe is contingent in the sense that it could not have begun to exist without God's creative act and it could not continue to exist without God's sustaining activity.

3. With regard to the uniformity of nature, the position of Supernaturalism is a bit more complex. As I explained in an earlier chapter, theists believe that nature exhibits patterns of order and regularity. But theists also believe that this uniformity results from God's free decision to create the universe in a particular way. Supernaturalism recognizes the same cause-and-effect order within the natural order as the naturalist. But the supernaturalist believes that the natural order depends on God for both its existence and its order. The supernaturalist also believes that God is capable of exerting causal influence within the natural order; but this does not mean necessarily that such divine action entails a suspension or violation of the natural order. The world is not closed to divine causal activity.

4. Supernaturalism may permit or be consistent with some forms of determinism. But even when a theist opts for a form of determinism, it will differ significantly from the mechanical, nonpurposeful determinism of Naturalism. That is, even should a theist be a determinist, he will recognize that God—a free rational agent—can act causally upon nature and within the natural order. In other words, even for a deterministic theist, there is a point at which the series of determining causes and effects ends in the free choices of at least one free agent—God. Of course, many supernaturalists believe that human beings sometimes exhibit a similar kind of agency.

5. Finally, Supernaturalism denies that nature is a self-explanatory system. The very existence of the contingent universe requires that we seek the cause of its being in a necessary being. The laws operating within the natural order owe their existence to God's creative activity. And many things that happen within the natural order are affected by or influenced by or brought about by free acts of the personal God.

THE CHOICE BETWEEN NATURALISM AND SUPERNATURALISM

The debate over miracles requires that one first settle the question of the relative merits of Naturalism and Supernaturalism as world-views. What kinds of considerations are relevant to making a choice between these two systems? It is obvious why any naturalist thinks the issue of miracles must be decided in a way that is damaging to theism. But what if a careful investigation of Naturalism reveals that the system is beset by serious difficulties? What if Supernaturalism turns out to be a more rational option? Clearly, in such a situation, the case for miracles will be greatly strengthened.

THE CASE AGAINST NATURALISM

A careful analysis of Naturalism will reveal a problem so serious that it fails one of the major tests that rational men and women will expect any world-view to pass. In order to see how this is so, it is necessary first to recall that Naturalism regards the universe as a self-contained and self-explanatory system. There is nothing outside the box we call nature that can explain or that is necessary to explain anything inside the box. Naturalism claims that *everything* can be explained in terms of something else within the natural order. This dogma is not an accidental or nonessential feature of the naturalistic position. All that is required for Naturalism to be false is the discovery of one thing[9] that cannot be explained in the naturalistic way. As C. S. Lewis set up this line of argument,

> If necessities of thought force us to allow to any one thing any degree of independence from the Total System—if any one thing makes good a claim to be on its own, to be something more than an expression of the character of Nature as a whole—then we have abandoned Naturalism. For by Naturalism we mean the doctrine that only Nature—the whole interlocked system—exists. And if that were true, every thing and event would, if we knew enough, be explicable without remainder . . . as a necessary product of the system.[10]

With a little effort, we should be able to see rather quickly that there is at least one such thing that no thoughtful naturalist can ignore. C. S. Lewis explains:

> All possible knowledge . . . depends on the validity of reasoning. If the feeling of certainty which we express by words like *must be* and *therefore* and *since* is a real perception of how things outside our own minds really "must" be, well and good. But if this certainty is merely a feeling *in* our minds and not a genuine insight into realities beyond them–if it merely

---

[9] The word *thing* is a perfectly good word to use in this context. It is a general term that can apply to physical objects, objects of thought, properties, principles, and scientific laws, as well as the laws that govern human conduct and reasoning.

[10] Lewis, *Miracles*, p. 12. For any experts on C. S. Lewis reading these words, I am following Lewis's argument in the second edition of his book. As students of Lewis's thought know, the first edition contained an argument against Naturalism that Lewis came to see was fallacious.

represents the way our minds happen to work—then we can have no knowledge. Unless human reasoning is valid no science can be true.[11]

The human mind, as we know, has the power to grasp contingent truths, that is, whatever *is* the case. But the human mind also has the power to grasp *necessary* connections, that is, what *must* be the case. This latter power, the ability to grasp *necessary* connections, is the essential feature of human *reasoning*. If it is true that all men are mortal and if it is true that Socrates is a man, then it *must* be true that Socrates is mortal.

Every naturalist must appeal to this kind of necessary connection in his or her own arguments for Naturalism; indeed, in his or her own reasoning about *everything*. But can naturalists account for this essential element of the reasoning process that they utilize in their own arguments for their own position? Lewis thinks not. As Lewis sees it, Naturalism "discredits our processes of reasoning or at least reduces their credit to such a humble level that it can no longer support Naturalism itself."[12] Here is Lewis's argument for this claim:

> It follows that no account of the universe [including Naturalism] can be true unless that account leaves it possible for our thinking to be a real insight. A theory which explained everything else in the whole universe but which made it impossible to believe that our thinking was valid, would be utterly out of court. For that theory would itself have been reached by thinking, and if thinking is not valid that theory would, of course, be itself demolished. It would have destroyed its own credentials. It would be an argument which proved that no argument was sound—a proof that there are no such things as proofs—which is nonsense.[13]

Lewis is careful to point out that his argument is *not* grounded on the claim that Naturalism affirms that every human judgment (like every event in the universe) has a cause. Lewis knows that even though my belief about some matter may be caused by nonrational factors, my belief may still be true.[14] In the argument before us, Lewis is talking about something else, namely, the logical connection between a belief and the logical ground of that belief. It is one thing for a belief to have a nonrational cause; it is something else for a belief to have a reason or ground. The ravings of a madman may have a cause but lack any justifying ground. The reasoning of a philosopher may also have a cause but possess a justifying ground.[15] What Naturalism does, according to Lewis, is sever what should be unseverable, the link between conclusions and the grounds or reasons for those conclusions. As Lewis says, "Unless our conclusion is the logical consequent from a ground it

---

[11]Ibid., p. 14.

[12]Ibid., p. 15.

[13]Ibid., pp. 14–15.

[14]The kind of argument Lewis rejects here is similar to the fallacious argument he himself had advanced in the first edition of *Miracles*.

[15]For example, a person suffering from a particular form of mental illness might believe something because he "hears" an inner voice. We tend to judge such people as mad when their conclusions lack any justifying ground. The beliefs of the philosopher I describe may also have a cause, e.g., something that happened in the philosopher's childhood perhaps. Hopefully, anyone aspiring to the title of philosopher can also produce grounds for his beliefs.

will be worthless [as an example of a *reasoned* conclusion] and could be true only by a fluke."[16] Therefore, Naturalism "offers what professes to be a full account of our mental behaviour; but this account, on inspection, leaves no room for the acts of knowing or insight on which the whole value of our thinking, as a means to truth, depends."[17] In Naturalism, Lewis continues,

> acts of reasoning are not interlocked with the total interlocking system of Nature as all its other items are interlocked with one another. They are connected with it in a different way; as the understanding of a machine is certainly connected with the machine but not in the way the parts of the machine are connected with each other. The knowledge of a thing is not one of the thing's parts. In this sense something beyond Nature operates whenever we reason.[18]

In this last paragraph, the thrust of Lewis's argument against Naturalism becomes clear. By definition, Naturalism excludes the possible existence of anything beyond nature, outside the box. But the process of reasoning *requires* something that exceeds the bounds of nature.

The American philosopher Richard Purtill has developed a similar argument against Naturalism. Purtill understands Naturalism in a way that allows naturalists the option of explaining occurrences as the result of either pure chance or determinism. But on either ground, Naturalism

> gives us no reason at all to suppose that our reasoning *is* valid. Only conscious minds can have plans or purposes, so there is no plan or purpose that will ensure that our reasoning will attain truth. Forces that are without our mind *might* happen to give us powers of valid reasoning, but they equally *might* happen to give us defective or invalid reasoning powers. And there is no reason to suppose that they would give us powers of valid reasoning rather than defective powers. Thus the views we have been considering are self-defeating in the sense that even if they were true we could never have any good reason to think that they were true.[19]

Whether the naturalist explains some event as the result of chance or of deterministic causes, he leaves us (and himself) without grounds to believe that our reasoning is valid or that our thinking puts us in touch with truth.

> If I pose a mathematical problem and throw some dice, the dice may *happen* to fall into a pattern which gives the answer to my problem. But there is no reason to suppose that they will. Now in the Chance view, all our thoughts are the result of processes as random as a throw of dice. In the Determinist view, all our thoughts result from processes that have as little relation to our minds as the growth of a tree.[20]

The result of all this is the destruction of "our confidence in the validity of *any* reasoning—including the reasoning that may have led us to adopt these theories! Thus they [the naturalistic theories] are self-destructive, rather like the man who saws off the branch he is sitting on. The only cold

---

[16]Lewis, *Miracles*, p. 16.
[17]Ibid., p. 18.
[18]Ibid., p. 25.
[19]Richard L. Purtill, *Reason to Believe* (Grand Rapids: Eerdmans, 1974), p. 44.
[20]Ibid.

comfort they hold out is that some of our thought might happen to agree with reality."[21] Naturalism's major problem, then, is explaining how mindless forces give rise to minds, knowledge, and sound reasoning. But every naturalist wants others to think that his Naturalism is a consequence of *his* sound reasoning.

All things considered, it's hard to see why Naturalism is not self-referentially absurd. Before any person can justify his or her acceptance of Naturalism on rational grounds, it is first necessary for that person to reject a cardinal tenet of the naturalist position. In other words, the only way a person can provide rational grounds for believing in Naturalism is first to cease being a naturalist.

I am not suggesting that this self-defeating feature of Naturalism proves by itself that theism is true. There are enough other alternatives so that the falsity of Naturalism would not entail the truth of theism. Nevertheless, the incoherence of Naturalism holds an important implication for our study of miracles. As we've seen, most of the opposition to the possibility of miracles in the West comes from people controlled by the presuppositions of Naturalism. Most such people refuse even to consider evidence that appears to support the actuality of miracles such as the Incarnation or the Resurrection because—consciously or unconsciously—their minds are closed on that subject. Miracles are judged to be impossible *before the fact*.

Two things need to be done in cases like this. First, every attempt should be made to help such people recognize the extent to which their conclusions about miracles are dictated by their naturalistic presuppositions. Their opposition to miracles is not a function of their education or greater degree of enlightenment; it is a function of their world-view. Any theist who can bring an opponent of the miraculous to recognize how his conclusion is determined by his naturalistic premises will have helped that person achieve a better understanding of himself and of his reasons for opposing the miraculous. Second, the attempt should then be made to help such people recognize the self-defeating nature of Naturalism. Would this dual discovery result in a changed attitude—in a more open mind–toward the possibility of miracles? That depends, of course, on a lot of other factors; a proper study of those other factors might make it necessary to reread this book from the beginning. Any truly open-minded person, assuming he or she exists, will admit that if the God of theism exists, then miracles are possible. Whether they have actually occurred will depend on how one assesses the historical evidence. In the next chapter, I will present some evidence that many find sufficient to justify belief in the actuality of two essential Christian miracles.

For Further Exploration—Chapter Eighteen

1. Explain the five major tenets of Naturalism.
2. With regard to those five points, explain how Supernaturalism differs.
3. Explain and evaluate C. S. Lewis's argument against Naturalism.
4. How does Lewis's argument differ from any claim about the supposed causes of the naturalist's belief in his system?

---

[21] Ibid.

Chapter 19

TWO INDISPENSABLE MIRACLES

In the earlier chapters of Part 5, I argued that miracles are possible. As we saw, the debate over this issue is clearly philosophical in nature. In this chapter, I want to consider whether any miracle essential to the truth of Christianity really happened. This second issue is historical in nature inasmuch as it involves the discovery and evaluation of historical evidence. Once we eliminate—as we should—the *a priori* rejection of miracles,[1] the question of whether any alleged miracle really happened should be answered on the basis of an honest evaluation of the evidence, regardless of how incredible the event may appear to people of a particular mind-set such as Naturalism.[2]

I will limit my investigation to just two miracles: the Incarnation and the Resurrection. As every student of Christianity knows, the historicity of these miracles is a necessary condition for the truth of Christianity.[3] If Christ had

---

[1] That is, the rejection of the possibility of miracles before any consideration of the evidence.

[2] To keep the above paragraph simple, I am not repeating some additional points made in earlier chapters. For example, I am on record as holding that any credible miracle must be an event that has religious significance. In the last chapter, I argued that our assessment of the relative probability of a belief will to a large extent be a function of our world-view. If I believe that the God described in the Old and New Testament exists, then I should believe that miracles of a certain kind are possible. But the world-view that flows from Scripture will often justify different attitudes toward various miracle-claims outside the canon of Scripture depending on their particular "fit" with that world-view.

[3] Or as *liberal* students of Christianity know, historic Christianity has regarded these miracles as such a necessary condition.

not risen from the dead, his claims to have been the Son of God would have been proven false (Rom. 1:4). If Jesus Christ was not in truth the incarnate Son of God, Christians would be left without a ground for their salvation. Hence, my use of these two miracles as test cases results from neither arbitrariness nor dogmatism.

THE INCARNATION

Christians use the word *incarnation* to express their belief that the birth of Jesus Christ marked the entrance of the eternal and divine Son of God into the human race. Jesus was not simply a human being. Nor is it correct to say that Jesus was Godlike. The historic Christian position is that Jesus Christ is fully God and fully man.[4] As British theologian John Stott explains: "Jesus was the Son of God. We shall not be satisfied with a verdict declaring his vague divinity; it is his deity which we mean to establish. We believe him to possess an eternal and essential relation to God possessed by no other person. We regard him neither as God in human disguise, nor as a man with divine qualities, but as the God-man."[5]

The doctrine of the Incarnation is one of those beliefs that makes Christianity unique among the religions of the world. The doctrine expresses the Christian conviction that "God has made himself known fully, specifically and personally, by taking our human nature unto himself, by coming amongst us as a particular man, without in any way ceasing to be the eternal and infinite God."[6] Christians believe that the sovereign triune God who can be known only as he chooses to reveal himself has, because of his love for humankind, "made himself known to us, in the most direct and

---

[4] The Nicene Creed, Christianity's oldest theological statement, settled the question of the relationship between Jesus Christ, who is God the Son, and God the Father. But it left unanswered the relation between Jesus' human nature and his divine nature. If we say, with the Nicene Creed, that Jesus was fully God, what should Christians believe about Jesus' humanity? Was he fully human? Was he simply God masquerading as a human being? These questions were answered in the Chalcedon Creed (A.D. 451). The essence of the Chalcedonian doctrine is that Jesus possessed two natures in one person. While the person of Jesus was undivided, this one person possessed, as a result of the Incarnation, two natures: one divine and one human. Jesus was fully God *and* fully human. He was the God-man. When dealing with the person of Jesus and his divine and human natures, we must not divide the person of Jesus nor confuse the two natures.

[5] John Stott, *Basic Christianity* (Grand Rapids: Eerdmans, 1957), p. 22.

[6] Brian Hebblethwaite, "Jesus, God Incarnate," in *The Truth of God Incarnate*, ed. Michael Green (Grand Rapids: Eerdmans, 1977), p. 101. Hebblethwaite goes on to add an important comment about the Christian doctrine of the trinity and its relation to the Incarnation. He writes, "It was because the early Christians, in the light of the resurrection of Jesus from the dead, came to recognize his divinity and to experience him as the self-revelation of God, that they perceived the necessity of believing that God himself, in his own being, exists in an eternal relationship of love given and love received. That love, they saw, exists in an internal relationship of Jesus to the Father. That same love they experienced in their own lives: not only was it poured out upon them but it was a relationship in which they too were caught up and came to share. But they also came to realize that the very notion of a God who is Love requires us to think in terms of an internally differentiated and relational deity" (Ibid., pp. 101–2).

comprehensible way possible, by coming amongst us as one of us, and sharing our life, its heights and depths, its joys and sorrows."[7]

Without question, then, the Christian claim that Jesus Christ was fully God and fully human is difficult for many to accept. But unless we cheat a bit and rule it out *a priori*, it is a claim that deserves our most careful scrutiny.[8] If it should turn out to be true and we be part of the company of people who rejected it, some very important values will have been lost. But how can we assess the rationality of the belief that Jesus Christ was God incarnate?

One perfectly sensible approach to this issue involves several steps. The first step requires that one identify all the reasonable (or at least initially reasonable) alternatives to the traditional Christian understanding of Jesus. In the second step, one carefully analyzes those alternatives. Such an analysis will bring one to an evaluation of the relative probability of each alternative vis-à-vis the Christian belief that Jesus was God incarnate. Suppose we refer to the belief in the Incarnation as *A* and use the letters *B*, *C*, *D*, and so on to refer to alternative hypotheses. I am suggesting that we set up a series of disjunctive syllogisms where the major premise of the first argument is *A* (the Christian hypothesis) or *B*, the major premise of the second argument is *A* or *C*, then *A* or *D*, and so on. In a valid disjunctive syllogism, the denial of one of the disjuncts necessarily implies the truth of the other disjunct. So if we have, let us say, four alternatives to *A* and find that in each case we have good reason to believe that the other disjunct is false, we are justified in concluding in each case that *A* is true. In other words, our four arguments would look like the following:

A or *B*	*A* or *C*	*A* or *D*	*A* or *E*
not *B*	not *C*	not *D*	not *E*
Therefore, *A*	Therefore, *A*	Therefore, *A*	Therefore, *A*

Each individual argument-form shows that in any choice between *A* and the other disjunct of that argument, the falsity or likely falsity of the other disjunct entails the truth of *A*, the Christian hypothesis. Of course, no single argument of itself proves that *A* is true. But when, after all these arguments are taken together, *A* emerges as the clear victor, it would seem that we've provided all the confirmation for *A* that any reasonable person could expect. Should someone raise the possibility of additional hypotheses, all he has to do is to produce them in a form that permits us to evaluate their plausibility. The theist will be happy to evaluate them in a new disjunctive syllogism.

Now the major alternative to the Christian hypothesis (*A*) is well-known. It is the claim (let us treat this as our *B*) that instead of being God incarnate, Jesus Christ was simply a human being. Of course, as it turns out, even the strongest opponents of the Christian hypothesis are forced to admit that it hardly does justice to Jesus to say that he was just another human being. Most opponents of the Incarnation are willing to acknowledge that

---

[7]Ibid., p. 102.

[8]Some thinkers have alleged that the Incarnation entails a contradiction in the sense that the union of a divine nature and a human nature in one person is somehow *logically* impossible. For an answer to this challenge, see Thomas V. Morris, *The Logic of God Incarnate* (Ithaca, N.Y.: Cornell University Press, 1986).

Jesus was still a pretty remarkable human being; he is up there with Moses, Gautama, St. Francis of Assisi, Gandhi, and perhaps Mother Teresa. In other words, Jesus was—it seems fair to say—a good man. So let us set up the disjunction for our first argument as follows:

(A) Either Jesus was God incarnate or (B) Jesus was merely a good human being.

Following many other writers, I am going to argue that (B) makes absolutely no sense. Therefore, the falsity of (B) will entail the truth of (A). While we will then have to go on to consider other alternatives, we'll discover that none of the other alternatives is any more promising.

The falsity of (B) becomes evident when we become familiar with the kinds of things Jesus said and did. A great many of Jesus' statements and actions are totally inconsistent with the hypothesis that he was simply a good human being. In assessing these claims and deeds of Jesus, we must remember that Jesus did these things in the context of a strict Jewish monotheism, a context in which people who understood his meaning sought to kill him for blasphemy. John Stott provides an account of the many times when Jesus claimed to be God. According to these claims, Stott explains, Jesus taught that

> to know him was to know God;
> to see him was to see God;
> to believe in him was to believe in God;
> to receive him was to receive God;
> to hate him was to hate God;
> to honour him was to honour God.[9]

What should be obvious at this point is that someone who is just a good human being does not say things like this. Imagine that you're the parent of two or three children who have become fascinated with a new neighbor down the street. Even though he's a carpenter, let's say, he seems remarkably literate. Even more, he is clearly a special human being. You and your spouse admire his character. His love for other human beings is manifested in everything he does. You and your spouse often express the wish that nothing would please you more than that your children grow up to be just like this neighbor. But then suppose one day your children come home after spending an hour or two with the carpenter and tell you some of the things he told them that day. Suppose they tell you that the carpenter said that he existed before Abraham,[10] that he and God are equal,[11] and that at the end of the world he would come on the clouds of the sky, with power and great glory, to judge the nations for their sins.[12] Under such circumstances, I wonder if you would continue to want your children to grow up

---

[9]Stott, *Basic Christianity*, p. 27. Stott supports his statements with the following verses in the New Testament: Mark 9:37; John 5:23; John 8:19; 12:44–45; 14:1, 7, 9; 15:23. This list could be expanded by including Matthew 11:27; John 5:17; 10:30; 14:10–11; 19:7; and many more.

[10]John 8:58.

[11]John 10:30. Jews who heard Jesus say this sought immediately to kill him for blasphemy.

[12]Matthew 24:30 and other verses.

and be just like this neighbor. Jesus' very words prevent us from regarding him as a good man. While we might continue to view him as a man, we could hardly continue to think of him as good.

But Jesus' *actions* were also inconsistent with the theory that he was simply a good man. For example, he allowed people to worship him with a reverence that is appropriate only to God.[13] But in an especially subtle kind of example—subtle in the sense that its significance often escapes people until it's pointed out to them—Jesus claimed to have the power to forgive sins. When Jesus forgave people, he went beyond what any of us are able to do. Any of us can forgive people for things they do to *us*. Jesus did that, of course; but he also went around forgiving people for the sins they had committed against other people! In all these cases, Jesus actually acted as though the sins against other human beings were violations of *his* law and sins against him as well. Consider the following words of C. S. Lewis:

> Now unless the speaker is God, [the claim to forgive sins] is really so preposterous as to be comic. We can all understand how a man forgives offenses against himself. You tread on my toe and I forgive you, you steal my money and I forgive you. But what should we make of a man, himself unrobbed and untrodden on, who announced that he forgave you for treading on other men's toes and stealing other men's money? Asinine fatuity is the kindest description we should give of his conduct. Yet this is what Jesus did. He told people that their sins were forgiven, and never waited to consult all the other people whom their sins had undoubtedly injured. He unhesitatingly behaved as if He was the party chiefly concerned, the person chiefly offended in all offences. This makes sense only if He really was the God whose laws are broken and whose love is wounded in every sin. In the mouth of any speaker who is not God, these words would imply what I can only regard as a silliness and conceit unrivalled by any other character in history.[14]

The view that Jesus was nothing more than a good man is in deep trouble! At this point, adherents of the view begin to make some strained moves to ease their difficulties. Some attempt to argue that Jesus, the good man, never made the claims that are the source of such embarrassment to unitarians. But I'm afraid that won't fly. We now know that the Gospels were written within the lifetime of people who were eyewitnesses to the things Jesus said and did. In some instances like his forgiving sins, the very subtlety of the point gives it the ring of authenticity. As John Stott explains, "It is not possible to eliminate these claims from the teaching of the carpenter of Nazareth. It cannot be said that they were invented by the evangelists, nor even that they were unconsciously exaggerated. They are widely and evenly distributed in the different Gospels and sources of the Gospels, and the portrait is too consistent and too balanced to have been imagined."[15]

But what about some of the other alternatives? If it doesn't make sense to say that Jesus was just a good man, surely there are other options open to us. Unfortunately, the other alternatives appear to face even more insur-

---

[13]Matthew 16:16 and, for those willing to consider a verse describing a post-resurrection event, John 20:28.

[14]C. S. Lewis, *Mere Christianity* (New York: Macmillan, 1960), p. 55.

[15]Stott, *Basic Christianity*, p. 33.

mountable obstacles. One might say that if Jesus wasn't a good man, then perhaps he was an evil man. After all, who but an evil man would attempt to mislead people into worshiping him as God? But of course there is no way to square such an understanding of Jesus with the information we have about him. Perhaps then, others might say, he was insane, a move that allows us to take a more benign attitude toward his character while denying his sanity. Or maybe he was Satan incarnate, hardly a move that would commend itself to skeptics who reject the supernatural.

C. S. Lewis has disposed of all these alternatives in a paragraph that has become a classic.

> I am trying here to prevent anyone from saying the really foolish thing that people often say about Him: "I'm ready to accept Jesus as a great moral teacher, but I don't accept His claim to be God." That is the one thing we must not say. A man who was merely a man and said the sort of things Jesus said would not be a great moral teacher. He would either be a lunatic—on a level with the man who says he is a poached egg—or else he would be the Devil of Hell. You must make your choice. Either this man was, and is, the Son of God: or else a madman or something worse. You can shut Him up for a fool, you can spit at Him and kill Him as a demon; or you can fall at His feet and call Him Lord and God. But let us not come with any patronizing nonsense about His being a great human teacher. He has not left that open to us. He did not intend to.[16]

Whenever I have presented Lewis's argument to audiences of college students, I have always had one or two in the group offer still another alternative. Perhaps, they suggest, Jesus was simply mistaken. Such people agree that the Jesus of the Bible could not have been merely a good man; and they see quite clearly the unacceptability of theories that treat him as evil or insane. But, their argument goes, surely there are degrees of error this side of lunacy that permit us to retain some respect for Jesus without buying into the Christian view. The obvious reply that must be made to such a suggestion goes like this: there are little mistakes and then there are big— really *big*—mistakes. Beliefs like "Ron Nash is Cleveland's greatest philosopher" might represent the class of little mistakes.[17] Beliefs like "Ron Nash is America's greatest philosopher" would clearly represent a big mistake. But a claim like "Ron Nash (or pick the name of any human being) believes he is God" is a *really big* mistake. Surely those people who intend to pass off Jesus' judgment that he was God as an error so insignificant as to leave our admiration of him untouched make it difficult for others to admire their reasoning powers—at least on this issue.

It is hardly surprising, then, that so many people who have looked at

---

[16]Lewis, *Mere Christianity*, pp. 55–56. Lewis's argument has been caricatured by many who oppose his conclusion; as we know, it's always easier to attack straw men. Lewis's argument is not reducible to the "God or lunatic" disjunction claimed by his critics. Lewis argued essentially what I have argued: bring out your alternatives to the Christian hypothesis and we'll consider them one by one. That Jesus was merely a good man is one hypothesis; that he was mad is another. None of the alternatives make as much sense as the shocking alternative, namely, that Jesus Christ really was God incarnate.

[17]There really is not much competition for this title.

this argument have concluded that the most sensible choice to make, given the alternatives, is to believe that Jesus Christ is God. Such a decision is not a blind leap of irrational faith—an act made possible only by a suspension of their critical faculties. It is a decision that makes perfectly good and rational sense to anyone whose own critical faculties are not under the control of naturalistic presuppositions.

If and when a person sees that Jesus Christ is God, some pretty important implications begin to follow. For one thing, if Jesus Christ is God, then it follows that God exists. In other words, it is possible that the line of reasoning we've been considering in this section may function for some people as an argument for God's existence. Second, if Jesus Christ is God, his teachings are not guesses or mere human speculation; Jesus' words are the Word of God. This means that there really is divine special revelation in which God reveals truth to human beings.[18] Moreover, if Jesus Christ is God, we have more than a revelation from God in human language. God has revealed *himself*—his person, his nature, his character—in a living way.[19] To know Jesus' teaching is to know God's teaching; to know Jesus' character is to know God's character; to believe in Jesus is to believe in God; to know Jesus is to know God!

Furthermore, consider all the other things we can settle once we know that Jesus is God and that his words are God's words. We then have an authoritative answer to all our most important questions: Is there a personal God who loves us? What is our duty in life? How do we become children of God? Why did Jesus die? Is there life after death?

Our decision regarding the Incarnation and the deity of Christ turns out therefore to take place at the most important fork in our personal and intellectual quest for the truth. As I have tried to show, a decision *for* the Christian hypothesis is one in which we have reason on our side.[20]

THE RESURRECTION

The New Testament presents the resurrection of Jesus Christ as a historical event that is supported by the strongest possible eyewitness

---

[18]Obviously, this sentence is not claiming that the teachings of Jesus are the only examples of special revelation we have. But they constitute a start. Of course, Jesus taught his disciples to regard the Old Testament as the revealed Word of God. And he also promised that God would reveal the truth that would become what we today know as the New Testament. See John 16:13.

[19]See John 1:1–14 and Hebrews 1:1–2.

[20]Because of its importance, the subject of the Incarnation touches on numerous other topics that deserve careful study. I can certainly recommend *The Truth of God Incarnate*, ed. Michael Green (Grand Rapids: Eerdmans, 1977), as a competent, nontechnical place to begin. In my book, *Christianity and the Hellenistic World* (Grand Rapids: Zondervan, 1984), I discuss and criticize numerous attempts to explain away the early Christian belief in the Incarnation that allege, for example, that the formation of the doctrine was influenced by pagan mystery religions. In my book, *Christian Faith and Historical Understanding* (Grand Rapids: Zondervan, 1984), I provide a brief introduction to attempts to undermine confidence in the biblical picture of Jesus through the use of various types of biblical criticism. The literature on these and related subjects is endless.

testimony (1 Cor. 15:5–8). For the apostle Paul, the historicity of the Resurrection is a necessary condition for the truth of Christianity and for the validity of Christian belief (1 Cor. 15:12–19). Paul writes, "And if Christ has not been raised, your faith is futile; you are still in your sins. Then those also who have fallen asleep in Christ are lost. If only for this life we have hope in Christ, we are to be pitied more than all men" (1 Cor. 15:17–19).

The Resurrection is the central event of the New Testament. The culmination of each Gospel is the Resurrection; it was not just something tacked on at the end of a story about the life of Jesus. Rather, the life of Jesus was presented as a preparation for his death and the Resurrection that followed. Peter's sermon on Pentecost, the birthday of the Christian church, emphasized several times that the Jesus who had died on the cross had been raised from the dead by the power of God. Paul repeatedly explained his otherwise unaccountable conversion to Christianity as a result of his encounter with the risen Christ. For the first disciples, A. M. Ramsey writes, "the Gospel without the Resurrection was not merely a Gospel without its final chapter; it was not a Gospel at all. . . . Christian theism is Resurrection theism."[21] According to Alan Richardson,

> The pervading truth which can be learnt from every part of the Gospels, and not merely from their concluding sections, is that the central conviction of the communities in which and for which they were written was faith in Jesus as the Risen Lord; without this faith the Gospels would not have been written. Faith in the resurrection is not one aspect of the New Testament teaching, but the essence of it.[22]

In some parts of Christendom, it has become fashionable to attempt to explain away the miracle of Christ's resurrection. In one such view, Jesus simply continued to live in the hearts of his followers. Such a theory, however, is totally out of step with the New Testament evidence and with historic Christianity, which insists that Christ rose from the dead. The tomb was empty; the risen Christ appeared to his disciples on numerous occasions. These appearances were not hallucinations; the body had not been stolen; Jesus had not simply lost consciousness on the cross and then revived in the tomb. He was dead but now he was alive! Without this fact, it is impossible to explain the existence of the Christian church.

So long as we are not controlled by naturalistic presuppositions, miracles are possible; indeed, the miracle of the Resurrection is possible. But when our attention turns to the issue of its actuality, we need to look at the evidence and what that evidence says with regard to the plausibility of alternative explanations. In other words, it makes sense to approach the historicity of the Resurrection using the same method utilized in connection with the Incarnation. Each alternative to the Resurrection can be combined with the belief that Christ rose in a disjunctive syllogism. As we discover how each successive alternative is unacceptable for one reason or another, we find that belief in the Resurrection makes more sense—does more justice to the evidence—than the belief that Christ did not rise from the dead.

---

[21] A. M. Ramsey, *The Resurrection of Christ* (London: Press, 1945), pp. 7–8.
[22] Alan Richardson, *History, Sacred and Profane* (Philadelphia: Westminster, 1964), p. 198.

The approach being recommended here is similar to that taken by George Eldon Ladd in his book, *I Believe in the Resurrection of Jesus*. In Ladd's view of things,

> The *hypothesis* that Jesus actually rose from the dead is the best hypothesis to account for the known historical facts. . . . It is our purpose to establish the thesis that the bodily resurrection of Christ is the only adequate explanation to account for the resurrection faith and the admitted "historical" facts. Thus we hope to show that, for one who believes in the God who has revealed himself in Christ, the resurrection is entirely rational and utterly consistent with the evidence.[23]

Any theory about what happened following the crucifixion of Jesus that wishes to be taken seriously must be consistent with the following points.[24]

1. Jesus was dead. One frequently encountered alternative to the Christian belief in the Resurrection holds that Jesus only fainted or lost consciousness on the cross. One can only regard this as an example of wishful thinking on the part of skeptics. There was no way the Romans would have allowed a still-living Jesus to be taken off the cross. The so-called swoon theory assumes that the Romans were so incompetent that they would have allowed a living Jesus to be turned over to his friends. In addition to the excruciating effects of crucifixion, which included not only the spike wounds but also the dislocation of joints and finally the inability to draw breath, Jesus suffered the spear wound to his side. While this wound did not kill him, it provided evidence that he was already dead.[25]

2. Following the crucifixion, the disciples were in a state of fear, confusion, and bewilderment. Some opponents of the Resurrection have suggested that the disciples stole the body of Jesus and then made up the story of the Resurrection. This theory requires a group of strong-willed men who began hatching a plot even while Jesus' body was being prepared for burial. The truth is that the disciples were too frightened and confused to

---

[23]George Eldon Ladd, *I Believe in the Resurrection of Jesus* (Grand Rapids: Eerdmans, 1975), p. 27.

[24]It would take an entire book to deal with all the related issues, some of which I must relegate to footnotes that direct the reader to more complete discussions. Some opponents of the Resurrection point to apparent inconsistencies in the Gospel accounts as though these alleged discrepancies are sufficient to cast doubt on the essential point that Jesus was alive. Two excellent discussions of this issue are John Wenham, *The Easter Enigma* (Grand Rapids: Zondervan, 1985), and chapter 8 of Ladd's *I Believe in the Resurrection of Jesus*.

[25]John Stott notes other absurdities of the swoon theory. Are we to believe, he asks, "that after the rigours and pains of trial, mockery, flogging and crucifixion he could survive thirty-six hours in a stone sepulchre with neither warmth nor food nor medical care? That he could then rally sufficiently to perform the superhuman feat of shifting the boulder which secured the mouth of the tomb, and this without disturbing the Roman guard? That then, weak and sickly and hungry, he could appear to the disciples in such a way as to give them the impression that he had vanquished death? That he could go on to claim that he had died and risen, could send them into all the world and promise to be with them unto the end of time? That he could live somewhere in hiding for forty days, making occasional surprise appearances, and then finally disappear without any explanation? Such credulity is more incredible than Thomas' unbelief" (*Basic Christianity*, p. 49).

think about much more than their own survival as they hid from their enemies. Jesus' death plunged them into deep despair.

3. Jesus was buried in a new tomb that had been cut into solid rock. The tomb was then closed by rolling a large stone in front of it. Concerned that the disciples might steal the body of Jesus, Pontius Pilate ordered that a guard be posted to keep the tomb undisturbed and secure.[26] In this way, the enemies of Jesus helped ensure the credibility of the Resurrection by guarding the grave so that no one could steal the body. Of course, some skeptics suggest that even though the friends of Jesus could not have stolen the body of Jesus (because of the guards), the body might have been stolen by the enemies of Jesus. But this is the last thing either the Romans or the Jews would have done. They wanted no further trouble in this matter, something that an empty tomb would have produced. Moreover, even if the enemies of Jesus had stolen the body, they would gladly have produced it as soon as the Christians began preaching about the Resurrection.

4. Then suddenly Jesus was alive, and the tomb was empty. Many different people in different circumstances saw, heard, and touched the living Jesus. The empty tomb is something that many alternatives to the actual resurrection of Jesus cannot explain. For example, many have tried to account for the experiences of those who saw, heard, and touched Jesus as hallucinations. But if all these encounters were hallucinations, we still have to account for the fact that the body of Jesus that had been placed in a closed, sealed, and guarded tomb was gone. Moreover, these alleged hallucinations don't fit the pattern. Hallucinations are not contagious. Had only one or two people claimed to "see" Jesus, it might be possible to dismiss their "experiences" as hallucinations. William Lane Craig points out some of the many things wrong with the hallucination theory:

> First, not just one person but many saw Christ appear. Second, they saw Him not individually, but together. Third, they saw Him appear not just once, but several times. Fourth, they not only saw Him but touched Him, conversed with Him, and ate with Him. Fifth and decisively, the religious enthusiasm hypothesis fails to explain the nonproduction of the body. It would have been impossible for Jesus' disciples to have believed in their master's resurrection if His corpse still lay in the tomb. But it is equally incredible to suppose that the disciples could have stolen the body and perpetrated a hoax. Furthermore, it would have been impossible for Christianity to come into being in Jerusalem if Jesus' body were still in the grave. The Jewish authorities would certainly have produced it as the shortest and completest answer to the whole affair. But all they could do was claim that the disciples had stolen the body. Thus, the hypothesis of religious enthusiasm [the hallucination theory], in failing to explain the absence of Jesus' corpse, ultimately collapses back into the hypothesis of conspiracy and deceit, which . . . has pretty much been given up in view of the evident sincerity of the apostles, as well as their character and the dangers they underwent in proclaiming the truth of Jesus' resurrection.[27]

---

[26]See Matthew 27:57–66. While Matthew does not report it, it is hard to believe that a company of soldiers ordered to guard such a tomb would have failed to check first to make certain that the body was in the tomb. It is surely what I would have done.

[27]William Lane Craig, *Apologetics, An Introduction* (Chicago: Moody, 1984), p. 174.

Hallucinations typically require a prepared receiver, someone who wants to see something or who expects to see something. The disciples were not psychologically prepared for such a hallucination. The last thing any of them expected to see was a living Jesus.

The eyewitness testimony for the Resurrection is exceptionally strong. For one thing, the people who claimed to see Jesus were individuals of unimpeachable character. Records of this eyewitness testimony come very early in the history of the Christian movement.[28] Accounts of the Resurrection are not a legend that began circulating years later. It is testimony based on eyewitness accounts that can be located in the years immediately following the event and publicly proclaimed during the lifetime of people who were alive when the events occurred.

5. The eyewitnesses of the Resurrection suddenly became changed, indeed transformed, people. Immediately following the death of Jesus, the terrified disciples hid behind locked doors, fearful that they would be the next to die. But on Pentecost, just a few weeks later, these same people boldly and publicly preached the resurrection of Jesus. No longer afraid to die, most of them were martyred for their faith, especially for their conviction that Christ had risen. One of the major pieces of evidence that alternatives to the Resurrection must explain is the origin of the Christian church. If the Resurrection never happened, what transformed that small band of terrified disciples into men and women who were willing to suffer torture and horrible deaths because of their refusal to renounce the Resurrection? What changed them into bold men and women whose evangelistic efforts carried the gospel to every corner of the Roman world and beyond?

There is a considerable body of additional evidence—both direct and circumstantial—that I do not have time to discuss.[29] But the thing to which we keep returning is the fact that good, honorable, trustworthy people who had nothing to gain and everything earthly to lose honestly believed that Jesus had risen bodily from the dead. As George Eldon Ladd says, "Here we are on bedrock. It is impossible to question the facticity of the disciples's belief in Jesus' resurrection." But then we must ask, "What is the *historical* cause of this faith? What historical event caused them to believe that Jesus

---

[28]Even though Paul's conversion, based as it was on his own encounter with the living Christ, came very early in the history of the Christian movement, Paul made it clear that the Resurrection message that was central in his preaching had been received from others (1 Cor. 15:3). As far as raw numbers go, the number of eyewitnesses exceeded five hundred (1 Cor. 15:6).

[29]This other evidence includes the undisturbed grave clothes and possibly the widely discussed Shroud of Turin. Of course, there are also other alternatives to the Resurrection that I have not had time to mention. For more complete discussions, I commend the reader to such books as the following: George Eldon Ladd, *I Believe in the Resurrection of Jesus;* Ronald Nash, *Christian Faith and Historical Understanding;* William Lane Craig, *Apologetics, An Introduction;* Arlie Hoover, *Dear Agnos: A Defense of Christianity* (Grand Rapids: Baker, 1976); Terry Miethe, ed., *Did Jesus Rise From the Dead?* (San Francisco: Harper and Row, 1987); J. N. D. Anderson, *The Evidence for the Resurrection* (Downers Grove, Ill.: InterVarsity, 1966); Gary Habermas, *The Resurrection of Jesus: An Apologetic* (Grand Rapids: Baker, 1980); James Orr, *The Resurrection of Jesus* (Grand Rapids: Zondervan, 1965); and scores of other good sources.

had risen from the dead?"[30] What hypothesis best explains the belief of the early church that the Resurrection had really happened? "All of the evidence," Alan Richardson argues, "points to the judgment that the Church did not create the belief in the resurrection of Christ; the resurrection of Christ, historically speaking, created the Church by calling faith into being."[31] In other words, only the *actual Resurrection* is sufficient to explain the faith of the early disciples and the subsequent origin of the Christian church. William Lane Craig sums things up well when he writes:

> Numerous lines of historical evidence prove that the tomb of Jesus was found empty by a group of His women followers. Furthermore, no natural explanation has been offered that can plausibly account for this fact. Second . . . several lines of historical evidence [establish] that on numerous occasions and in different places Jesus appeared physically and bodily alive from the dead to various witnesses. Again, no natural explanation in terms of hallucinations can plausibly account for these appearances. And finally . . . the very origin of the Christian faith depends on belief in the resurrection. Moreover, this belief cannot be accounted for as the result of any natural influences. These three great, independently established facts—the empty tomb, the resurrection appearances, and the origin of the Christian faith—all point to the same unavoidable conclusion: that Jesus rose from the dead.[32]

This is not a claim that modern men and women find easy to accept; it was not—for that matter—a claim that the citizens of Jerusalem found easy to accept when they first heard it from the lips of the disciples. But it is the claim that best explains all we know about what happened following the death of Jesus.

CONCLUSION

My brief examination of the problem of miracles is now finished. It is impossible to reach a conclusion about the truth of the Christian world-view without also finding answers to the questions I have asked regarding miracles. We have found that David Hume's famous attack on miracles fails, as do the efforts of his many modern imitators. Philosophically and scientifically, there is no good reason to suppose that miracles are impossible. The possibility of miracles does not pose a threat either to science or to the laws science must postulate in its explanation of natural phenomena. Miracles, therefore, are possible.

As my analysis of the evidence for the Incarnation and Resurrection reveals, I believe it is all too clear that miracles—important miracles—are also actual. As it turns out, these miracles for which there is substantial evidence provide important confirmation for the Christian world-view. To be sure, the recognition of this requires placing oneself within that world-view. Since a deeply committed naturalist will not accept any miracle, he or she will certainly not accept the miracles of the Incarnation and the Resurrection. But when one sets aside the presuppositions of the naturalistic world-view,

---

[30]Ladd, *I Believe in the Resurrection*, pp. 24–25.
[31]Richardson, *History, Sacred and Profane*, p. 200.
[32]Craig, *Apologetics*, p. 205.

places oneself within a world-view in which the universe is open to the causal influence of the sovereign, personal God, and then honestly examines the alternatives in the light of the evidence, he or she may well discover that this system demonstrates all that is required for it to be consistent with reason and with what we know about the outer world.

In the next chapter—the concluding chapter of the book—I will examine what this world-view has to offer us with regard to the important demands of our inner world.

For Further Exploration—Chapter Nineteen

1. Show that you understand the method used in this chapter to defend the Incarnation.
2. Evaluate the claim that Jesus was just a good man.
3. What is your position with regard to the Incarnation? What reasons support your view?
4. List the major pieces of evidence that any adequate theory of the Resurrection must explain.
5. Evaluate the following alternatives to the Resurrection:
   a) Jesus didn't really die.
   b) The disciples stole the body.
   c) The Romans or the Jews stole the body.
   d) The appearances of Jesus were hallucinations.
6. Discuss the relevance of the empty tomb in all this.
7. Look up Romans 10:9–10 in the Bible. How are the two miracles discussed in this chapter relevant to these verses?

Part 6

CONCLUSION

Chapter 20

UNFINISHED BUSINESS

Before I bring this book to a close, several pieces of unfinished business require attention. The first is the important matter of survival after death.

PERSONAL SURVIVAL AFTER DEATH

Human beings do not want to admit that death means the termination of our existence as conscious persons. Human beings want an answer to the problem of death. If there is no answer to the question posed by death, if there is no hope beyond this life, then of course we must attempt to make peace with that fact. Since a naturalistic world-view closes the door on any possibility of survival after death, anyone who is a naturalist must approach life with the conviction that someday everyone he or she loves and everything he or she values will cease to exist for him or her. However much they may long to survive death, consistent naturalists must treat the appearance of this desire as a superstitious relic of a preenlightened period in their lives or in the life of the species.

And so naturalistic presuppositions do rule out any hope of personal survival after death. But a more basic question comes to the surface at this point. Why would anyone choose to be a naturalist? As we've seen, there are plenty of reasons to look elsewhere for an adequate and rational world-view. We have found good reasons to consider favorably an alternative world-view that happens to teach that we live in a universe in which personal survival after death is possible.

As it turns out, a properly informed Christian view of the self and the survival of that self after death is more complicated than many friends—and many enemies—of theism recognize. Because of some of these subtleties, the Christian position is often misunderstood or misrepresented; and because of this, many attempts to defend it and attack it miss the mark.

To begin with, Christian theism clearly affirms that human beings are not simply physical creatures. As C. Stephen Evans explains,

> The identity of a human being is not found merely by looking at the body as a physical object. I am who I am because of my thoughts, feelings, actions, memories and other rich elements of consciousness, which form my personal history. Even in this life I am not simply a physical object; the atoms which compose my body are constantly changing, yet my "person" remains. Christians have traditionally affirmed this truth that we are more than physical objects by speaking of people as *souls* and *spirits* as well as *bodies*.[1]

Claims like this are greeted with objections from several directions. One line of attack incorrectly equates "the Christian position" with the kinds of radical mind-body dualism philosophers associate with thinkers like Plato and Descartes. It has become fashionable to claim that for such thinkers, the human soul is a ghost in a machine. Christian theists have a stake in avoiding any view of the human person that might appear to support this metaphor. C. Stephen Evans points them in the right direction when he writes that to speak of a person's soul

> is not to speak of a ghost residing in a person. It is to speak of the person himself (or herself)—that essential core which makes us persons. Christians are very clear that we are meant to be embodied. In this life and in our ultimate intended state after death, personhood is expressed in bodily form; it is incarnated. But our personhood can survive the death of our present bodies. The power of God, which gives us life now, can continue our conscious, personal history in a new body.[2]

So an informed Christian theist will avoid thinking of mind and body as radically different substances that somehow link up to make a human being. The human soul is *not* an invisible ghost that inhabits the machine we call the human body.

But this gives rise to a different kind of objection that William Rowe summarizes in these words:

> The evidence we have indicates that our mental life is *dependent* on certain bodily processes, particularly those associated with the brain. We know, for example, that damage to various parts of the brain results in the cessation of certain kinds of conscious states—memories, thought processes, and the like. It seems eminently reasonable to infer from this that consciousness is dependent for its existence on the existence and proper function of the human brain. When at death the brain ceases to function, the reasonable inference is that our mental life ceases as well.[3]

---

[1] C. Stephen Evans, *The Quest for Faith* (Downers Grove, Ill.: InterVarsity Press, 1986), p. 122. Incidentally, Evans is the author of another book that serves as an excellent introduction to a number of other issues related to human personhood. See C. Stephen Evans, *Preserving the Person* (Downers Grove, Ill.: InterVarsity Press, 1977).

[2] Ibid., p. 123.

[3] William L. Rowe, *Philosophy of Religion: An Introduction* (Encino, Calif.: Dickenson, 1978), p. 141.

There is no point in pretending that this is not a serious problem for anyone who believes that human consciousness can continue after physical death. However, at least two lines of reply are available.

First, as Rowe himself indicates, the theist may be able to ease this problem by pointing out how the objection

> depends on a *false analogy* of the relation of the mind to the body. If we think of the mind as a person enclosed in a room with only one window, we can readily understand the dependence of mental functions on the body without having to suppose that with the death of the body the life of the mind must cease. For while a person is enclosed in the room, experience of the outside world will *depend* on the condition of the window. Board up the window partly or completely and you will affect tremendously the sorts of experiences the person in the room can have. So too, when the human person is alive in a body, changes to that body (particularly the brain) will have considerable effect on the sorts of mental experiences the person is capable of having. But perhaps bodily death is *analogous* to the person gaining freedom from the enclosed room so that she or he is no longer dependent on the window for experience of the outside world. At death perhaps . . . the mind loses its dependency on the bodily organs such as the brain. The mere fact that the mind is dependent on the functioning of the brain *while it (the mind) is associated with a living body* is no more proof that the mind will cease functioning at bodily death than is the fact that the person is dependent on the window *while she or he is in the room* proof that when the room and window are no more the person will cease having experiences of the outside world.[4]

This alternative analogy helps us see how the human mind can exhibit the kinds of dependence on the body with which we are so familiar while leaving open the possibility that familiar forms of consciousness may continue after the body, including the brain, has died. Rowe is not sure he wants to recommend this other analogy, however. For one thing, "the evidence seems to show that the relation between our bodies and our mental life is enormously more intimate and complex than that between a human being and a room in which he or she happens to be enclosed."[5] I agree with Rowe's comment. The analogy does not explain everything we'd like it to; but few analogies do when the subject before us is something as complex as the nature of the human self. In this case, the analogy is not supposed to solve our problem, only make it a little easier for us to understand how the human mind can often exhibit dependence upon the body without being reducible either to the body or to its functions.[6]

What the wise theist will do next is point out how important the body is in the New Testament view of a human being. The doctrine of the inherent immortality of the human soul and the claim that the ultimate destiny of that immortal soul lies in its being freed from dependence upon a despised, corruptible body belong not to the New Testament but to the philosophy of Plato. When the New Testament describes the final destiny of the believer, it

---

[4]Ibid., p. 151.

[5]Ibid.

[6]A good, albeit somewhat technical, discussion of the contemporary debate over some of these issues can be found in J. P. Moreland, *Scaling the Secular City* (Grand Rapids: Baker, 1987), chap. 3.

speaks not of a disembodied soul but of *resurrection*! The relevant New Testament passage here states: "When the perishable has been clothed with the imperishable, and the mortal with immortality, then the saying that is written will come true: 'Death has been swallowed up in victory.' . . . The sting of death is sin, and the power of sin is the law. But thanks be to God! He gives us the victory through our Lord Jesus Christ" (1 Cor. 15:54, 56–57). This passage is the only place in the Bible where "immortality" is applied to human beings.[7] It is important to note that humans *become* immortal only after the resurrection of the body.[8]

Even Rowe wants to dissociate the biblical position from Platonism. As Rowe explains, the Christian view teaches that

> the body is not simply the prison house of the real person, the soul. Instead the person is generally viewed as some sort of *unity* of soul and body, so that the continued existence of the soul after the destruction of the body would mean the survival of something less than the full person. On this view, a belief in a future life of the full person requires the reuniting of the soul with a resurrected body.[9]

This New Testament emphasis upon the resurrection of the body carries an important implication that is often overlooked by people who believe—for whatever reason—that human beings must be understood in materialistic or physicalist terms. Even were such a materialistic view of the human person justified, it would not provide grounds for dismissing the New Testament view of survival after death. Because our ultimate destiny is linked to the resurrection of the body, no one can use his or her commitment to a materialistic or physicalist view of the human being as an excuse for rejecting the biblical position. Such a materialism would be incompatible with the theories of Plato and Descartes; but that's an entirely different matter.[10]

The informed Christian, then, is not interested in defending the immortality of the *soul*; he'll let the Platonist worry about that! The task for the Christian is showing people that the Christian doctrine of survival after death is linked essentially to resurrection. As it turns out, I have already said a thing or two about the topic of resurrection. In Part 5, I defended the possibility of miracles and then presented some of the evidence that suggests that at least one resurrection—albeit the resurrection that turns out to have been the most important one—actually happened. The New Testament leaves no doubt about the fact that *this* resurrection—the resurrection of Christ—holds important implications for our survival after death. If the

---

[7] See 1 Timothy 6:16, which states that only God is essentially immortal. Human immortality is contingent upon God's making possible the continued existence of the human person.

[8] Students of Christian theology know about the so-called intermediate state between death and the resurrection where Scripture implies that believers continue to survive in a conscious state while they await the resurrection. It is in connection with this intermediate state where the analogy of the window and the room seems most relevant.

[9] Rowe, *Philosophy of Religion*, p. 141.

[10] I am arguing hypothetically here. I do not believe there is any reason to accept a materialistic or physicalist view of the human being. Once again, to see the problems such views have, see Moreland, *Scaling the Secular City*, chap. 3.

Resurrection never happened, the apostle Paul makes plain, Christians are in big trouble.[11] But, Paul continues, "Christ has indeed been raised from the dead" (1 Cor. 15:20), and his resurrection is only the beginning. Paul describes Christ's resurrection in terms of an agricultural metaphor: he is the firstfruits or the first gleaning of what will be a more complete harvest later on. His resurrection guarantees the resurrection of all believers. The certainty of our future resurrection rests upon his resurrection.

But now, it appears, we're almost back to where we were at the beginning of this book—back to the subject of competing world-views and the effect they have on our thinking about such matters. It is interesting to see, therefore, that William Rowe recognizes quite clearly that the strongest argument for survival after death "rests on the belief that the theistic God exists. If we begin with this belief as a foundation, a quite formidible argument for human survival can be built. For according to theism, God has created finite persons to exist in fellowship with himself. . . . Consequently, if it is reasonable to believe that the theistic God exists it is certainly reasonable to believe in life after death."[12] If belief in the God of the Bible can be placed legitimately in the foundation of one's noetic structure, it is reasonable to believe in survival after death. If it is reasonable to believe in the Christian world-view, it is reasonable to believe in one of the major tenets of that world-view, namely, that God will keep his promises to believers regarding eternal life.

Christian theism does more, therefore, than simply provide a conceptual framework in which survival after death is possible. It goes even further and promises eternal life to humans who meet certain conditions. On one occasion, Jesus said: "For God so loved the world that he gave his one and only Son, that whoever believes in him should not perish but have *eternal life*" (John 3:16, emphasis added). Some time later, Jesus spoke these words: "I am the resurrection and the life. He who believes in me will live, even though he dies; and whoever lives and believes in me will never die" (John 11:25–26). Needless to say, if Christian theism is true, the person who spoke these words was God incarnate and conquered death in his own resurrection from the dead.

PEACE, ETERNAL LIFE, AND THE HIGHEST GOOD

Suppose, for the sake of argument, that what the Christian world-view teaches about God and his creation of human beings is true. It makes sense, then, to believe that a personal, loving God who desires that humans freely choose to love and worship him would provide humans with any number of clues that might lead us to seek him in the first place and that might also help to point us in the right direction. Throughout this book, I've examined a number of possible clues. We encountered some of them in our study of the theistic arguments in Part 3. One such clue might be the impressive signs of design and order in the universe; another might be our moral consciousness; a third might be our remarkable capacity to reason and to become aware of

[11] By all means, read all that Paul says on the subject in the fifteenth chapter of 1 Corinthians. In connection with the point just made, see 1 Corinthians 15:12–19.
[12] Rowe, *Philosophy of Religion*, p. 150.

eternal and unchanging truths; a fourth might be experiences in which we become aware of God's personal presence; a fifth might be the very idea of God; a sixth might be our desire for eternal life.

In this section of the chapter, I want to examine another possible clue or divine calling card that many especially sensitive religious people have found as part of their inner world. As I explained in chapter 3, Søren Kierkegaard tried to help others become aware of this. One of the best discussions of this subject can be found in Book 19 of St. Augustine's work, *The City of God*.

Augustine begins by asking, What is a human being's highest good (*summum bonum*)? What is the ultimate end of a human being? Is there any one thing that stands above all other goods? Is there any one thing toward which all humans should strive? What is our highest good, the purpose for which we exist?

Augustine answers these questions with two terms that he regarded as synonyms. First, he writes that "eternal life is the supreme good and eternal death the supreme evil. . . . we should live rightly in order to obtain the one and avoid the other."[13] Several chapters later, Augustine explains that what he calls "eternal life" can also be studied under the term "peace." The interchangeability of "eternal life" and "peace" makes it clear that Augustine has more than the quantity of life in view; "eternal life" has more to do with the quality of existence than with unending existence.

Augustine describes the peace or eternal life that he regards as humankind's highest good in the following words:

> But, in that final peace which is the end and purpose of all virtue here on earth, our nature, made whole by immortality and incorruption, will have no vices and experience no rebellion from within or without. There will be no need for reason to govern non-existent evil inclinations. God will hold sway over man, the soul over the body; and the happiness in eternal life and law will make obedience sweet and easy. And in each and all of us this condition will be everlasting, and we shall know it to be so. This is why the peace of such blessedness or the blessedness of such peace is to be our supreme good.[14]

Of course, many who read such words may not find such a state very appealing. To some extent, their disinterest may reflect an inability to understand and appreciate all that is promised in the words. Others may find the described state distasteful because of the grip that human sin has on them.

Augustine is describing a state in which there is no pain—physical, mental, or emotional. More important than the absence of pain is the presence of positive joy, fulfillment, blessedness—in short, *peace*. Is it possible that there are humans who could understand what is being said here and not really want what Augustine describes?

Augustine not only states that eternal peace is our highest good; he also believes that God has implanted within each human being a desire or longing for this quality of existence. No matter how hard we may try to

[13]Saint Augustine, *City of God*, ed. Vernon J. Bourke (Garden City, N.Y.: Doubleday Image Books, 1958), bk. 19, chap. 4, p. 437.
[14]Ibid., bk. 19, chap. 27, p. 481.

ignore this longing,[15] there are times when it still rises to the level of consciousness. Even when it remains below the threshold of consciousness, it is evident in such moods as boredom, despair, and dread.

God made us for fellowship with himself. God made us for eternal peace and life. But not every human being will achieve that blessed state. In fact, no human being *can* achieve it in this earthly life. Throughout our earthly existence, the eternal peace that we all desire eludes us.

We can never possess it through our bodies, a fact made clear when we consider what can happen to the human body:

> There is no pain of body, driving out pleasure, that may not befall the wise man; no anxiety that may not banish calm. A man's physical integrity is ended by the amputation or crippling of any of his limbs; his beauty is spoiled by deformity, his health by sickness, his vigor by weariness, his agility by torpor and sluggishness. There is not one of these that may not afflict the flesh even of a philosopher.[16]

Nor do things look any more promising when we turn to the human mind. Here we often find frustration, disappointment, unhappiness, to say nothing of depression and other forms of mental illness. Even if we manage to avoid most of these during our good years, old age may find us afflicted with senility or illnesses like Alzheimer's disease. Few things are more sad than the sight of an elderly man or woman whose entire adult life was spent in intellectual pursuits but whose present mental condition makes rational reflection impossible.

And so our mental powers fail; and our bodies grow old and feeble; and eventually we die. Just as our eternal happiness cannot be found in our body or mind, Augustine continues, it also eludes us in our relations with other humans. "All human relationships are fraught with . . . misunderstandings."[17] Friendships and marriages are often destroyed; families break up. "If, then, the home, every man's haven in the storms of life, affords no solid security, what shall one say of the civic community? The bigger a city is, the fuller it is of legal battles, civil and criminal, and the more frequent are wild and bloody seditions or civil wars. Even when the frays are over, there is never any freedom from fear."[18] Anyone who thinks he can find his eternal peace in this life is chasing an impossible dream, Augustine teaches.

In contrast to the lack of peace that plagues our earthly existence, Augustine describes the heavenly peace that awaits all who satisfy God's conditions:

> Where, all of our natural endowments—all that the Creator of all natures has given to our nature—will be both good and everlasting, where every wound in the soul is to be healed by wisdom and every weakness of body to be removed by resurrection; where our virtues will be no longer at war with passion or opposition of any kind, but are to have, as the prize of victory, an eternally imperturbable peace. This is what is meant by that

---

[15] I described some of the ways we do this in the anthropological section of chapter 3. Some of the best accounts of this can be found in Søren Kierkegaard's work, *Either/Or*.

[16] *City of God*, bk. 19, chap. 4, p. 437.

[17] Ibid., bk. 19, chap. 5, p. 443.

[18] Ibid., bk. 19, chap. 5, p. 444.

consummate beatitude, that limitless perfection, that end that never ends.[19]

This state, Augustine says, is a "peace so good that no peace could be better, a peace so great that a greater would be impossible."[20]

Augustine's observation of others and of himself convinces him that what he has described is something that every human being really wants. "Any man who has examined history and human nature will agree with me that there is no such thing as a human heart that does not crave for joy and peace."[21] One way to see this is to consider why men wage war. "What they want," Augustine says, "is to win, that is to say, their battles are but bridges to glory and to peace."[22] In other words, the reason men wage war is to attain *peace*. Even criminals reveal their ultimate desire for peace:

> Take even the case of a robber so powerful that he dispenses with partnership, plans alone and single-handed robs and kills his victims. Even he maintains some kind of peace, however shadowy, with those he cannot kill and whom he wants to keep in the dark with respect to his crimes. Certainly in his own home he wants to be at peace with his wife and children and any other members of his household.[23]

One of the essentials of peace is order. Before there can be peace, everything must be in its right place. Augustine defines peace as the tranquillity that results from order—everything being in its right place. Eternal life is the paradigm of peace because when it is achieved, for the first time everything will finally be in its proper place.

The peace of the body and soul consists, he writes,

> in the well-ordered life and health of the living whole. Peace between a mortal man and his Maker consists in ordered obedience, guided by faith, under God's eternal law; peace between man and man consists in regulated fellowship. The peace of a home lies in the ordered harmony of authority and obedience between the members of a family living together. . . . The peace of the heavenly City lies in a perfectly ordered and harmonious communion of those who find their joy in God and in one another in God. Peace, in its final sense, is the calm that comes of order. Order is an arrangement of like and unlike things whereby each of them is disposed in its proper place. . . . those who are unhappy, in so far as they are unhappy, are not in peace, since they lack the calm of that order which is beyond every storm; nevertheless, even in their misery they cannot escape from order, since their very misery is related to responsibility and to justice. They do not share with the blessed in their tranquility, but this very separation is the result of the law of order.[24]

The opposite of peace, of course, is war. It should not surprise us, then, to discover that the New Testament uses the imagery of war to describe what stands between human beings and the peace we all want. Because all sorts of

---

[19]Ibid., bk. 19, chap. 10, p. 450.
[20]Ibid.
[21]Ibid., bk. 19, chap. 10, pp. 451–52.
[22]Ibid., bk. 19, chap. 10, p. 452.
[23]Ibid.
[24]Ibid., bk. 19, chap. 13, p. 456.

things are out of place within us, there is war within.[25] Because all sorts of things related to our relationship with God are out of place, we are at war with God—the only one who can give us the peace we want.[26] It is interesting, then, to consider a number of New Testament passages that describe how these wars can be ended. This theme is especially prominent in the writings of Paul who, among other things, writes that Christ "came and preached peace."[27] Not only that, Paul writes in another passage, Christ *made* peace "through his blood, shed on the cross."[28] Because of Christ's sacrifice, Paul says in still another place, "we have peace with God through our Lord Jesus Christ, through whom we have gained access by faith into this grace in which we now stand."[29]

All I am doing here is showing the connection between Augustine's important teaching about peace and the obvious source of his insight, the New Testament. Whether we get the teaching from Augustine or from the New Testament, the notion of peace we've been considering is an important part of Christian belief.

As I've said, it is easy for humans to ignore or deny this divine calling card. Ironically, Augustine himself ignored it for the first thirty years of his life. As his book, *The Confessions*, reveals, he spent those thirty years trying to satisfy that inner longing with things other than God. But then Augustine discovered that the eternal factor that God has implanted within us leaves all of us ultimately frustrated, unhappy, and restless until we finally enter into his rest and peace. As Augustine put it, God has made us for himself, and our hearts are restless until they rest in him.[30]

THE END OF OUR SEARCH

Throughout this book, I've been defending a world-view, a conceptual system, a way of looking at God, self, and the world. In this defense, I have stressed the importance of evaluating world-views on the basis of several tests. One of those tests is logic; logical inconsistency is a sure sign of error. Though some of its critics have accused Christian theism of being internally inconsistent in one way or another, the charges don't hold up.[31] Naturalism, on the other hand, appears to have more than it can handle on this score.

Another important test for any world-view is experience. Here, we found, world-views should fit what we know about the world outside us and the world we find within us. Christian theism passes this test. As C. Stephen

---

[25]A worthwhile exercise at this point would be a careful reading of the New Testament passages that speak of the war going on within each human being. See Romans 7:21–25; Galatians 5:16–17; James 4:1; and 1 Peter 2:11.
[26]See, for example, Romans 5:10.
[27]Ephesians 2:17.
[28]Colossians 1:20.
[29]Romans 5:1–2.
[30]See Augustine's *Confessions*, bk. 1, chap. 1.
[31]By way of reminder, one of these alleged inconsistencies served as the basis of the deductive problem of evil that we answered back in chapter 13. A different set of charges that allege that the theistic concept of God is internally incoherent are considered and answered in my book, *The Concept of God* (Grand Rapids: Zondervan, 1983).

Evans expresses the result of his own investigation, "Belief in God is genuinely coherent with all we know about ourselves and our universe. It contradicts no known facts and it makes sense of many things that would otherwise be inexplicable."[32] The Christian does not have to pretend that there are no objective moral laws or that one does not sometimes feel like thanking God or calling on God for help. The Christian does not have to borrow important beliefs from some other system. The Christian's noetic structure explains why he or she and other humans often feel a sense of duty, a sense of guilt, a longing for eternal life, and a desire for forgiveness.

Christian theism also passes the important practical test. It is a system of beliefs that one can live and live consistently.

In short, Christian theism is a system that commends itself to the whole person. But all this is only part of the story. Christian theism is a system, but it is also more than that. Therefore, it requires more of human beings than mere intellectual assent to a set of propositions. Most people recognize that there is a difference between *belief that* and *belief in*. It is one thing to *believe that* some proposition is true; it is another thing to *believe in* a person.[33]

In this connection, Christian theism announces that it is a system with a Person at its center. As John Stott explains,

> Christianity is Christ. The person and work of Christ are the rock upon which the Christian religion is built. If he is not who he said he was, and if he did not do what he said he had come to do, the foundation is undermined and the whole superstructure will collapse. Take Christ from Christianity, and you disembowel it; there is practically nothing left. Christ is the centre of Christianity; all else is circumference.[34]

C. Stephen Evans points out what must come next:

> There is a gap between an intellectual recognition of who Jesus is and a commitment to him. Logically, it would seem that anyone who admits that Jesus is the Son of God should be willing to follow him and obey him. It is a truth which ought to transform their lives. But in fact there are many people who will give at least verbal assent to the proposition "Jesus is God," but who do not seem to care very much about Jesus, or even pay him much attention. It is clear then that what is necessary to become a Christian is not merely acceptance of a proposition on the basis of evidence, but *a change in a person's whole orientation to life*.[35]

Evans is right. The world contains a lot of people who *believe that* the essential claims of Christian theism are true but who have never taken the additional step of coming to *believe in* the divine Person whose incarnation, death, and resurrection are the point to the whole thing. In this connection, it is interesting to remember what the apostle Paul wrote in his Epistle to the Romans: "That if you confess with your mouth, 'Jesus is Lord,' and believe in your heart that God raised him from the dead, you will be saved" (Rom.

---

[32]Evans, *Quest for Faith*, p. 131.

[33]In other writings, I argue that *belief in* requires *belief that;* the subjective act of commitment requires an objective ground of information. See Ronald Nash, *Christian Faith and Historical Understanding* (Grand Rapids: Zondervan, 1984), chap. 8.

[34]John Stott, *Basic Christianity* (Grand Rapids: Eerdmans, 1958), p. 21.

[35]Evans, *Quest for Faith*, p. 74.

10:9). In these words, Paul ties the solution to the basic human problem—our alienation from God because of sin and its consequences—to the two indispensable miracles discussed in chapter 19. The reference to the Resurrection is impossible to miss. What may be less clear is what Paul means by *confessing Jesus as Lord:* acknowledging that Jesus is God. When we confess Jesus as Lord and God, we are acknowledging that nothing else, including ourselves, will function as God in our lives. And when we believe *in our heart* that God raised Jesus from the dead, we cross the line from a purely intellectual assent to a proposition to a commitment of the entire self to the Person who is both risen Savior and Lord.

Throughout two thousand years of human history, many have found that their personal search for a faith has brought them to this precise point. The argument of this book, is that such a faith is a *rational* faith.

For Further Exploration—Chapter Twenty

1. Explain the difference between the Platonic belief in the inherent immortality of the soul and the New Testament doctrine of resurrection.
2. Summarize and evaluate this chapter's argument in support of survival after death.
3. Give your personal reaction to Augustine's teaching about peace and eternal life.
4. Give your personal reaction to the last section of the book.

FOR FURTHER READING

Readers interested in further exploring the topics of this book will find the following books to be helpful places to begin. Additional sources are identified in the notes to this book and in the bibliographies of many of the books listed below. Books identified as "advanced" presuppose a considerable background in philosophy.

Abraham, William J. *An Introduction to the Philosophy of Religion.* Englewood Cliffs, N.J.: Prentice-Hall, 1985.

Basinger, David, and Randall Basinger. *Philosophy and Miracle, The Contemporary Debate.* Lewiston, N.Y.: Edwin Mellen, 1986. Advanced.

Brody, Baruch A., ed. *Readings in the Philosophy of Religion: An Analytic Approach.* Englewood Cliffs, N.J.: Prentice-Hall, 1974.

Brown, Colin. *Miracles and the Critical Mind.* Grand Rapids: Eerdmans, 1984.

Bube, Richard H. *The Human Quest.* Waco, Tex.: Word, 1971.

Carnell, Edward John. *The Case for Biblical Christianity.* edited by Ronald Nash. Grand Rapids: Eerdmans, 1969.

————. *An Introduction to Christian Apologetics.* Grand Rapids: Eerdmans, 1948.

Clark, Gordon H. *A Christian View of Men and Things.* Grand Rapids: Eerdmans, 1952.

————. *Religion, Reason and Revelation.* Philadelphia: Presbyterian and Reformed, 1961.

Evans, C. Stephen. *Philosophy of Religion.* Downers Grove, Ill.: InterVarsity Press, 1985.

————. *The Quest for Faith.* Downers Grove, Ill.: InterVarsity Press, 1986.

Green, Michael, ed. *The Truth of God Incarnate.* Grand Rapids: Eerdmans, 1977.

Ladd, George Eldon. *I Believe in the Resurrection of Jesus.* Grand Rapids: Eerdmans, 1975.

Lewis, C. S. *Mere Christianity.* New York: Macmillan, 1960.

————. *Miracles.* New York: Macmillan, 1960.

————. *The Problem of Pain.* New York: Macmillan, 1962.

Mavrodes, George. *Belief in God.* New York: Random House, 1970.

Miller, Ed L. *God and Reason.* New York: Macmillan, 1972.

Mitchell, Basil. *The Justification of Religious Belief*. New York: Seabury, 1973.

Moreland, J. P. *Scaling the Secular City*. Grand Rapids: Baker, 1987.

Morris, Thomas V. *Francis Schaeffer's Apologetics*. Grand Rapids: Baker, 1987.

_____. *The Logic of God Incarnate*. Ithaca, N.Y.: Cornell University Press, 1986. Advanced.

Nash, Ronald. *Christian Faith and Historical Understanding*. Grand Rapids: Zondervan, 1984.

_____. *Christianity and the Hellenistic World*. Grand Rapids: Zondervan, 1984.

_____. *The Concept of God*. Grand Rapids: Zondervan, 1983.

_____. *Dooyeweerd and the Amsterdam Philosophy*. Grand Rapids: Zondervan, 1962.

_____. *The Light of the Mind: St. Augustine's Theory of Knowledge*. Lexington: University Press of Kentucky, 1969.

_____. *The Word of God and the Mind of Man*. Grand Rapids: Zondervan, 1982.

_____. "The Life of the Mind and the Way of Life." in *Francis A. Schaeffer: Portraits of the Man and His Work*, edited by Lane T. Dennis. Westchester, Ill.: Crossway, 1986.

_____, ed. *Ideas of History*. 2 vol. New York: Dutton, 1969.

_____, ed. *The Philosophy of Gordon H. Clark*. Philadelphia: Presbyterian and Reformed, 1968.

_____, ed. *Process Theology*. Grand Rapids: Baker, 1987.

Peterson, Michael L. *Evil and the Christian God*. Grand Rapids: Baker, 1982.

Plantinga, Alvin. *God, Freedom and Evil*. Grand Rapids: Eerdmans, 1974.

Plantinga, Alvin, and Nicholas Wolterstorff, eds. *Faith and Rationality: Reason and Belief in God*. Notre Dame, Ind.: University of Notre Dame Press, 1983. Advanced.

Pojman, Louis J., ed. *Philosophy of Religion: An Anthology*. Belmont, Calif.: Wadsworth, 1987.

Rowe, William L. *Philosophy of Religion: An Introduction*. Encino, Calif.: Dickenson, 1978.

Swinburne, Richard. *The Coherence of Theism*. Oxford: Clarendon Press, 1977. Advanced.

_____. *The Concept of Miracle*. London: Macmillan, 1970.

_____. *The Existence of God*. Oxford: Clarendon Press, 1979. Advanced.

_____. *Faith and Reason*. Oxford: Clarendon Press, 1981. Advanced.

Wenham, John. *The Easter Enigma*. Grand Rapids: Zondervan, 1985.

INDEX OF PERSONS

INDEX OF SUBJECTS

We want to hear from you. Please send your comments about this book to us in care of the address below. Thank you.

ZONDERVAN™

GRAND RAPIDS, MICHIGAN 49530

www.zondervan.com